Hasidism, Suffering, and Renewal

SUNY series in Contemporary Jewish Thought

Richard A. Cohen, editor

Hasidism, Suffering, and Renewal

The Prewar and Holocaust Legacy of
Rabbi Kalonymus Kalman Shapira

Edited by
DON SEEMAN, DANIEL REISER,
and ARIEL EVAN MAYSE

Cover: Passport photograph of Rabbi Kalonymus Shapira superimposed on manuscript of *Derekh Ha-Melekh*, courtesy of Rabbi Avraham Hammer. Photographed by Shalom (Matan) Shalom.

Published by State University of New York Press, Albany

For information, contact State University of New York Press, Albany, NY
www.sunypress.edu

Library of Congress Cataloging-in-Publication Data

Title: Hasidism, suffering, and renewal : the prewar and Holocaust legacy
    of Rabbi Kalonymus Kalman Shapira / edited by Don Seeman, Daniel Reiser,
    Ariel Evan Mayse.
Description: Albany : State University of New York Press, [2021] | Series:
    SUNY series in contemporary Jewish thought | Includes bibliographical
    references and index.
Identifiers: LCCN 2020056931 (print) | LCCN 2020056932 (ebook) | ISBN
    9781438484013 (hardcover : alk. paper) | ISBN 9781438484006 (pbk. : alk.
    paper) | ISBN 9781438484020 (ebook)
Subjects: LCSH: Ḳalonimus Ḳalmish ben Elimelekh, 1889–1943—Influence. |
    Rabbis—Poland—Piaseczno (Piaseczno)—Biography. | Hasidim—Poland—
    Piaseczno (Piaseczno)—Biography. | Hasidism—Influence. | Holocaust, Jewish
    (1939–1945)—Poland—Sources. | Suffering—Religious aspects—Judaism. |
    Piaseczno (Piaseczno, Poland)—Religious life and customs.
Classification: LCC BM755.K2834 H37 2021 (print) | LCC BM755.K2834
    (ebook) | DDC 296.8/332092 [B]—dc23
LC record available at https://lccn.loc.gov/2020056931
LC ebook record available at https://lccn.loc.gov/2020056932

10 9 8 7 6 5 4 3 2 1

For our children

And for all the children whose childhood was taken from them

עַל זֹאת בָּאנוּ אֵלֶיךָ בֶּן יַקִּיר...

חֵן הַשְּׁכִינָה עַל פָּנֶיךָ יָאִיר

מֹחֲךָ, לִבְּךָ וְכָל אֲבָרֶיךָ לַתּוֹרָה וַעֲבוֹדַת ה׳ יִפָּתְחוּ

לִבְּךָ וְנַפְשְׁךָ בְּקִרְבַת אֱלֹהִים אֲשֶׁר עַל יָדְךָ יַרְגִּישׁוּ

וְאֶת כָּל בַּקָּשׁוֹתֶיךָ לְפָנָיו יִתְבָּרַךְ כִּלְפְנֵי אָב אוֹהֵב תִּשְׁפֹּךְ

וְהוּא כְּאָב לְבֵן אָהוּב לַעֲנוֹתְךָ וּלְרַצּוֹתְךָ יָחִישׁ.

חוֹבַת הַתַּלְמִידִים, פֶּרֶק א.

Contents

Acknowledgments   ix

Introduction   1

Part I: Hasidism and Renewal

1 The Place of Piety: Piaseczno in the Landscape of
  Polish Hasidism   29
  Marcin Wodziński

2 The Rebbe of Piaseczno: Between Two Trends in Hasidism   53
  Moshe Idel

3 The Devotional Talmud: Study as a Sacred Quest   79
  Ariel Evan Mayse

4 Mystical Fraternities: Jerusalem, Tiberius, and Warsaw:
  A Comparative Study of Goals, Structures, and Methods   107
  Zvi Leshem

5 Self-Creation through Texts: Kalonymus Kalman Shapira's
  Incarnational Theology   131
  David Maayan

6 Hasidism in Dialogue with Modernity: Rabbi Kalonymus
  Shapira's *Derekh ha-Melekh*   153
  Ora Wiskind

Part II: Text, Theodicy, and Suffering

7   A New Reading of the Rebbe of Piaseczno's Holocaust-Era
    Sermons: A Review of Daniel Reiser's Critical Edition   179
        Moria Herman

8   Creative Writing in the Shadow of Death: Psychological and
    Phenomenological Aspects of Rabbi Shapira's Manuscript   191
    "Sermons from the Years of Rage"
        Daniel Reiser

9   Miriam, Moses, and the Divinity of Children: Human
    Individuation at the Cusp of Persistence and Perishability   213
        Nehemia Polen

10 Raging against Reason: Overcoming *Sekhel* in R. Shapira's
    Thought   235
        James A. Diamond

11 At the Edge of Explanation: Rethinking "Afflictions of Love"
    in *Sermons from the Years of Rage*   259
        Erin Leib Smokler

12 "Living with the Times": Historical Context in the Wartime
    Writings of Rabbi Kalonymus Kalman Shapira   281
        Henry Abramson

13 Covenantal Rupture and Broken Faith in *Esh Kodesh*   305
        Shaul Magid

14 Pain and Words: On Suffering, Hasidic Modernism,
    and the Phenomenological Turn   333
        Don Seeman

Contributors   361

Index   365

Acknowledgments

The editors would like to express their appreciation to the Polin Museum in Warsaw for sponsoring a 2017 Research Workshop on "R. Kalonymos Shapira: New Directions in Scholarship." We also wish to acknowledge the generous support of the Judith London Evans Director's Fund of the Tam Institute for Jewish Studies at Emory University and of the Laney Graduate School.

Chapter 7, Moria Herman, "A New Reading of the Rebbe of Piaseczno's Holocaust-Era Sermons: A Review of Daniel Reiser's Critical Edition," was first published in *Yad Vashem Studies* 46: 1 (2018).

Chapter 13, Shaul Magid, "Covenantal Rupture and Broken Faith in *Esh Kodesh*," first appeared in Shaul Magid, *Piety and Rebellion: Essays on Hasidism* (Boston: Academic Studies Press, 2019).

Introduction

ATTENTION!!

> Blessed is God. I have the honor of requesting the esteemed
> individual or institution that finds my enclosed writings . . . to
> please exert themselves to send them to the Land of Israel to
> the following address. . . . When the Blessed One shows mercy
> so that the remaining Jews and I survive the war, please return
> all materials to me or to the Warsaw rabbinate for Kalonymus,
> and may God have mercy upon us, the remnant of Israel, in
> every place and rescue us, and sustain us, and save us in the
> blink of an eye.

On the first of December 1950, Warsaw construction workers unearthed
two aluminum milk canisters from an excavation site at 68 Nowolipki
Street. Like a message in a bottle from a destroyed world, they were
found to contain a treasure of previously unknown documents from the
clandestine "Ringelblum archives" documenting the lives, deaths, and mass
murder of Warsaw Jewry.[1] A similar cache of ten metal boxes (containing
some 25,540 pages of documentation) had been discovered in the same
location in 1946, and a third (that we know of), buried elsewhere, has
never been found.[2] The two canisters discovered in 1950, containing 9,829
pages of documentation, were better preserved than the previous cache.
It is our good fortune that the handwritten manuscripts of R. Kalonymus
Kalman Shapira (1889–1943), otherwise known as the Piaseczner Rebbe,
were among the documents preserved.

Rabbi Shapira was the scion of a relatively minor Hasidic dynasty, but
he founded one of the largest Hasidic academies in interbellum Warsaw.

He experimented with new literary forms, and his influence among a wide variety of readers has only continued to grow. Before the war, he had already published one innovative tract on Hasidic pedagogy (*Hovat ha-talmidim*, published in English as *A Student's Obligation*) and had distributed a handbook on mystical fraternities (*Benei mahshavah tovah*, published as *Conscious Community*) among his close disciples.[3] A volume of sermons from the 1920s and 1930s was published posthumously under the title *Derekh ha-melekh* (*The King's Way*).[4] His students also separately published his Yiddish-language sermon for the Sabbath before Yom Kippur in Piaseczno in 1936.[5] The buried Warsaw archive brought several additional manuscripts to light. These included mystical and pedagogical tracts devoted to students and devotees at different developmental levels: *Hakhsharat ha-avrekhim* (*The Young Men's Preparation*), *Mevo ha-she'arim* (*Entrance to the Gates*), and his personal journal, *Tsav ve-zeruz* (*Command and Urging*). It also included a one hundred page handwritten manuscript of wartime sermons, *Hiddushei torah mi-shnot ha-za'am 5700–5702*, originally published under the title *Esh kodesh* (translated as *Sacred Fire*) by Piaseczner Hasidim who survived the war.[6] The sermons were all composed in Warsaw between September 1939 (Hebrew year 5700) and July 1942 (5702). Reiser has shown that R. Shapira consigned his manuscripts to the underground archive for safekeeping in January 1943, coinciding with the beginning of armed Jewish resistance in the Warsaw Ghetto; they were buried at 68 Nowolipki that February. By the middle of May, the last of the Jews in Warsaw (estimated around four hundred thousand at the Ghetto's most populous phase) were dead or facing almost certain death under deportation to various camps. It is believed that R. Shapira was sent to the Trawniki work camp, whose surviving prisoners were marched into the forest and shot on or around November 3, 1943. He would have been just fifty-four years of age.

Since their discovery, R. Shapira's texts have been published, republished, and in several cases translated for a broad popular audience. They have engendered a dedicated readership across a wide range of religious communities, from ultra-Orthodox to New Age and Neo-Hasidic, and have contributed to a public renaissance in appreciation for Hasidic ideas and texts. They have also engendered a significant and growing body of scholarly research. Our own volume, *Hasidism, Suffering, and Renewal*, was made possible by the recognition that a critical mass of such scholarship now invites reflection across a wide variety of methods and disciplines. This interdisciplinary volume thus includes contributions from scholars whose interest in Hasidic studies has been inflected by social history, literature, anthropology, modern Jewish thought and theology, phenomenology of religion, and the history of ideas. This generates some degree of incommensurability among the approaches taken by our writers, but it also allows the volume as a whole to explore some of the more important tensions and controversies raised by the study of R. Shapira's legacy. What is his relationship to the different spiritual and intellectual genealogies of Hasidism and, later, Neo-Hasidism? How insistent must we be about locating his activity in the context, not just of Hasidism, but of interbellum Poland or modern Jewish thought? What literary techniques did he employ, and how are they related to the various registers in which these texts might be read—theological, literary-aesthetic, phenomenological? What light, if any, can the prewar and Holocaust writings shed upon one another? Or, to frame this in more existential terms, to what extent do the Warsaw Ghetto sermons bear witness to the resilience of faith in extremis or to the final rupture of meaning and human subjectivity? While academic scholarship must have its due, none of these are exclusively academic problems or concerns, nor are academics the only audience for these debates.

One reason for our decision to publish this volume at this time was our recognition that this field has been changed irrevocably by the publication of Daniel Reiser's groundbreaking critical edition of R. Shapira's wartime sermons. These were originally published in 1960 by survivors of the Piasezcno Hasidic community under the title *Esh kodesh* (*Sacred Fire*), but the title of Reiser's volume, *Derashot mi-shnot ha-za'am* (*Sermons from the Years of Rage*), is closer to the author's description of his own work (no consistent title appears in the original manuscript), and we use it throughout. For the first time, thanks to Reiser, we can now encounter the text as R. Shapira apparently intended it to appear, free of inadvertent distortion by editors who may have had difficulty deciphering his handwriting (written under almost unbelievable duress) or the numerous notes and symbols that he left as guidance for some future editor.

No less important, Reiser also demonstrates that R. Shapira continued to edit his work, including the *Sermons from the Years of Rage*, until the very end of his capacity to go on doing so. Reiser devotes an entire volume to clarification of the handwritten corrections, marginalia, and even additions or deletions of whole passages, which sometimes reflect the author's ongoing and emergent experience of the genocide unfolding all around him. This collection of sermons may well have been the last work of traditional Hasidic scholarship ever composed on Polish soil, and it remains one of the only surviving rabbinic works of any kind composed directly under Holocaust conditions (i.e., not composed by an author who had already escaped or had yet to suffer the full force of Nazi brutality). All of our authors used Reiser's new edition for their reflections upon *Sermons from the Years of Rage*, and this alone constitutes an advance over previous efforts to leverage these texts for our understanding of life in the context of almost unimaginable suffering.

Our decision to divide this volume into two sections, "Hasidism and Renewal" followed by "Text, Theodicy, and Suffering," reflects our conviction that while the prewar and Ghetto-era writings each deserve dedicated and detailed attention, the wartime sermons should no longer be read in a vacuum. While early scholarship on the Hasidism of Piasezcno understandably emphasized radical suffering and Holocaust experience, it has more recently become clear just how essential the prewar writings are for any honest appraisal of R. Shapira's contribution. These interbellum writings portray a Hasidic leader working hard to develop new literary strategies for communication with a diversifying and, in many cases, secularizing urban audience, focused particularly on youth.

After the terrible upheavals and dislocations of World War I, even faithful Hasidim were increasingly drawn to what Marcin Wodziński here calls "à la carte Hasidism," whose effect on the conditions of R. Shapira's work may have been decisive.[7] Newly urbanized interbellum Polish Hasidim had the option not just to secularize or leave the Hasidic community but also to draw, in eclectic and individualizing ways, upon a variety of Hasidic schools and masters simultaneously. This was the context in which R. Shapira developed some of his most interesting prewar teachings on pedagogy and new forms of visionary-contemplative technique. It was also the context for his distinctive interpretation of Jewish modernity through the lens of both prophetic renewal and the contemporary psychotherapeutic discourse of nervous disorder. Both of these were common themes in early-twentieth-century Jewish writing, but R. Shapira brings them together in exceptionally powerful and suggestive ways. It has already been noted that Abraham Joshua Heschel's later work on biblical prophecy may best be understood in light of Hasidic motifs very similar to those R. Shapira develops.[8]

We are gratified that *Hasidism, Suffering, and Renewal* will appear in a prominent series devoted to contemporary Jewish thought. This only serves to underscore a growing appreciation for the importance of

Hasidism—including "late" and not just allegedly pure or authentic "early" Hasidism—to the spiritual and intellectual contours of modern Jewish life.[9] Study of Piasezcno Hasidism should mediate against any claim that later Polish Hasidism as a whole had stagnated, was uninterested in the project of spiritual self-renewal, or had essentially given up on the potential for ecstasy and mystical experience.[10] Indeed, along with his unprecedented depiction of suffering, which pushes theological expression to its very limits, R. Shapira's emphasis on sociospiritual renewal, mystical technique, and literary outreach to a mobile and diversifying urban community all underline his potential relevance to contemporary spiritual life.

What Is Hasidism, and Who Is R. Shapira?

The movement of mystical renewal that came to be known as Hasidism grew out of the teachings of R. Israel ben Eliezer of Miedzhybozh (Ukr. Medzhibizh, d. 1760), popularly known as the Besht or Baal Shem Tov ("Master of the Good Name").[11] This enigmatic and creative mystic lived in Podolla (modern Ukraine) near the Carpathian Mountains.[12] There are few historical sources that shed light on the Baal Shem Tov's life, but Hasidic hagiography tells of humble beginnings followed by periods of solitude and mystical study. After "revealing" himself in the 1730s, he began to preach an approach to religious life that foregrounded the values of divine immanence, human joy, and ecstasy through prayer.[13] Hasidism has tended to reject the rigorous self-mortification of some earlier pietistic schools in favor of a more psychological and, in many cases, broadly pantheistic (or panentheistic) approach. Beshtian Hasidism typically emphasizes *devekut*, or cleaving to the divine, through the spiritual uprush of ecstatic prayer, performance of the commandments, and *avodah ba-gashmiyut*, or devotion through apparently mundane acts such as eating or drinking with proper intent.[14] Sometimes, Hasidism described the goal of devotional practice not just as personal *devekut* but also as "freeing the sparks" that had been trapped, according to Lurianic kabbalah, within the phenomenal world at the time of creation.[15] In some schools, this might even be described as a sort of divine ecology, with vitality "drawn down" through some activities (such as fasting, prayer, or even ritual weeping, identified with *tzimtzum*), then "raised up" again through others—especially acts of enjoyment or pleasure accompanied by correct intention.[16] These teachings frequently focused on the activity of the tsaddik, or rebbe, whose activities rendered him a veritable "axis mundi"[17] or channel for divine vitality and ritual efficacy, including what Moshe Idel has described as "magic."[18]

There is no evidence that the Baal Shem Tov sought to establish a new religious movement, though later Hasidic schools unanimously relate to him as a founder. It was only in the decades after his death that a social movement known as Hasidism began to crystallize, particularly under the leadership of "the Maggid," R. Dov Ber of Mezritsh, who was already a talmudic scholar and ascetic before he met the Baal Shem Tov.[19] The Maggid's own disciples included scholars from some of the most illustrious families in eastern Europe, who quickly began to develop their own distinctive devotional styles and to spread their diversifying schools, or "courts," through all the Jewish population centers in the region.[20] Among the Maggid's direct disciples was R. Shapira's paternal ancestor Elimelekh of Lizhensk, who did much to develop the centrality of the tsaddik to Hasidic devotion. Some of these developments were alarming to established rabbinic leadership, engendering more than a generation of bans and counterbans until the two sides attained some degree of rapprochement. Ultimately, Hasidism became the dominant form of Jewish traditionalism in the Jewish communities of the former Polish commonwealth (Galicia and Western Russia) before the Holocaust.

Some Hasidic leaders were clearly aware of the western European Haskalah (Jewish Enlightenment) by the early 1770s. Over the next four decades, however, those modernist ideals grew from a sporadic trickle to a steady stream of modernizing and, in many cases, secularizing influence, which also took new forms, such as socialism and various types of Jewish nationalism, as they traveled east. In this context, Hasidism had little choice but to join forces, to some degree, with its old opponents, the *mitnagdim,* who also opposed at least some forms of secularization.[21] Meanwhile, the position of Hasidic tsaddik developed into a hereditary office whose holders could not always match the charismatic force of their predecessors.[22] The deaths of the Maggid's immediate disciples by the first decade of the nineteenth century have been described as a turning point toward greater social and theological conservatism.[23] This century also saw the Hasidic movement reach the apogee of its demographic reach, its political influence, and its ability to selectively resist some unwelcome features of modernity.[24] Though possibly overemphasized by romanticizing scholars, there is evidence that some nineteenth-century Hasidim, such as R. Nahman of Bratslav, did seek to revitalize what they had come to perceive as an ossifying religious traditionalism.[25]

Anti-Jewish legislation and the pogroms that began during the 1880s helped to stimulate mass emigration from eastern Europe and brought any sense of a Hasidic golden age crashing down. Worsening conditions also increased the resonance of explicitly secularizing platforms such as socialism or Zionism, both of which tended to identify Hasidic piety with a kind of quietism that persecuted Jews could no longer afford. Soon enough, World War I and the fall of multiethnic empires would come to dislocate hundreds of thousands of Jews, forcing newly urbanized Hasidim now living in places like Warsaw and Vienna to find their way economically and politically within an unstable and frequently hostile constellation of European states.

This is the context within which R. Shapira's own life as a descendant of major figures in the Hasidic movement (on both his father's and his mother's side) begins to take shape.[26] Kalonymos Shapira was born on July 13, 1889,[27] to R. Elimelekh Shapira (known as the Grodzisker Rebbe, 1824–1892) and Hannah Berakhah, the daughter of R. Hayyim Shemuel Horowicz of Chęciny.[28] His father passed away before his third birthday, leaving him to be raised in the home of R. Yerahmiel Moshe Hopstein (the Kozhnitser Rebbe, 1860–1909), his father's grandson through a prior marriage. Hopstein later became Shapira's father-in-law when, at the age of sixteen, Shapira married the rebbe's daughter, Rahel Hayya Miriam, after an engagement that began when he was just thirteen.[29] Rahel Hayya Miriam was renowned for her erudition and took an active role in Kalonymus's writing before her untimely death in 1937. It is likely that she was memorialized in her husband's later sermons on the prophetess Miriam, but there is as yet no sustained study of her own possible stylistic or conceptual influence on her husband's teaching.[30]

Shapira was appointed rabbi of the city of Piaseczno in 1913, at the age of twenty-four. Following the Great War in 1917, he moved to nearby Warsaw but continued to visit Piaseczno frequently. In 1923, he founded a Warsaw yeshiva for boys, named Da'at Moshe in memory of his father-in-law, which became one of the largest Hasidic academies in the Polish capitol.[31] His Hasidim and students described R. Shapira as a person of elegant countenance, projecting an air of gravitas and nobility and evincing remarkable concern for the education of children.[32] His relationship to the world around him was complex and nuanced. In addition to his sacred studies in Hasidism, Jewish law, and Bible, he taught himself about medicine and other secular subjects.[33] He wrote Hasidic melodies and learned to play the violin like his wife's father but stopped playing when Rahel Hayya Miriam died at a young age.[34] R. Shapira served as a mohel (ritual circumciser)[35] and was an active member of the Orthodox Jewish political alliance Agudath Israel,[36] though he favored a section of the movement that was more positively disposed toward settlement in the land of Israel than most, and even purchased property there. His brother, Rabbi Yeshayahu Shapiro, "the Pioneer Rabbi," joined the religious Zionist movement Mizrachi and moved to an agricultural settlement in the Land of Israel before the war.[37] R. Shapira's only son, Elimelekh Ben-Zion, died a lingering death from shrapnel wounds during the festival of Sukkot on September 29, 1939. His daughter-in-law and sister-in-law—the latter a religious Zionist pioneer who had helped to build the Kfar Hasidim settlement—were also killed on September 26, when the hospital at which they were visiting Elimelekh came under German artillery fire. Not long after, his elderly mother passed away as well, and he recited Kaddish on her behalf.[38] Many of his own most intimate losses therefore occurred even before German troops had secured Warsaw.

The Warsaw Ghetto was established in October 1940 (its borders encompassed R. Shapira's home at 5 Dzielna) and sealed off from the rest of the city in November. Four hundred thousand Jews from Warsaw and surrounding towns were incarcerated there in an area of just 1.3 square miles. During the first two years of its existence alone, 83,000 people died of disease and starvation, and by late 1942, Ghetto governance had moved to an explicit policy of genocide through direct killing, starvation, and gradual deportation. Between late July and mid-September 1942, 265,000 Jews were sent to their deaths at Treblinka.[39] These realities, and the dawning realization of the annihilation of European Jewry, provide the background against which *Sermons from the Years of Rage* was composed.

R. Shapira apparently had a number of opportunities to leave the Ghetto before its liquidation in 1943 but "declared that it was unthinkable that he should save himself and leave his brothers to moan."[40] The American Joint Distribution Committee sought to procure him and some other Jewish leaders an exit visa from Poland but was rebuffed. A contemporary journalist cited him as saying, "I will not abandon my Hasidim at such a difficult time."[41] He continued to serve as a spiritual leader throughout his time in the Ghetto and even survived the Warsaw Ghetto Uprising, which led to its final "liquidation" after Passover 1943. Scholars are not sure about the place and circumstances of his death, but it is believed, as we have already mentioned, that he was among a group that was marched into the forest and shot in early November 1943.

Renewal, Vitality, and the Human Subject

The theme of renewal that dominates the first half of this book raises important questions about R. Shapira's relationship to the genealogy of Hasidism, past and present. Marcin Wodziński (chapter 1) sets the stage by locating R. Shapira within the context of newly urban "à la carte" Polish Hasidism between the wars. If the number of documented followers and *shtiblekh* (prayer houses) identified with Piaseczno Hasidim serves as any guide, Wodziński concludes, R. Shapira should be thought of as "a minor tsaddik but a major Hasidic innovator, who long after his death became one of the most prominent figures of Polish Hasidism." R. Shapira's innovations took several forms, including the development of extensive contemplative techniques grounded in earlier Hasidic and possibly even medieval kabbalistic practice but also taking on new "cinematic" qualities of sustained narrative visualization that go beyond earlier Jewish mystical writers.[42] Moshe Idel (chapter 2) identifies close parallels between certain passages in R. Shapira's pedagogic tracts and those in Abulafia's thirteenth-century ecstatic Kabbalah, though he notes that R. Shapira also wrote under the influence of more proximate Hasidic writers as well as modern psychological and therapeutic discourse related to mesmerism, hypnosis, and nervous disorder.[43]

Indeed, although the majority of his citations are to R. Shapira's immediate Hasidic forbears, Idel provocatively suggests that his phenomenological style—his emphasis on contemplative technique and mystical experience rather than the power of the tsaddik—betrays a kinship with other branches of Hasidism entirely, the diverse "spiritualizing" trends identified with the Maggid, Chabad, or Kotsk-Izhbits. More suggestive still is Idel's claim that these features of what Seeman (chapter 14) refers to as "Hasidic modernism" may have been influenced by growing familiarity with figures such as Swami Vivekananda, who had recently visited eastern Europe. At the same time, in his evaluation of R. Shapira's handbook for mystical fraternities, *Benei mahshavah tovah*, Zvi Leshem (chapter 4) offers an unprecedentedly detailed account of connections and parallels to the mystical fellowship of the Zohar and to nineteenth-century Hasidic fraternities established in the Galilean city of Tiberius. Collectively, the writers of this volume demonstrate the inadequacy of treating the search for intellectual genealogies in R. Shapira's oeuvre as if it were a simple taxonomic project. It should be viewed instead as a means of opening up the text in all of its potential keys and registers, including some that may not yet have been discovered. Rigorously establishing the contours of R. Shapira's own socioreligious context and taking his potential contemporary relevance as seriously as that of any other great author requires an openness to possibly unforeseen juxtapositions as well as resistance to any delimiting academic paradigms, including an overemphasis on historical "proximism."[44]

Hasidic renewal must be understood on a number of different levels simultaneously. On page after page of R. Shapira's text, it refers not only to the infusing of Hasidic life with a renewed sense of purpose or charisma in the Weberian sense but also to the literal repair of blocked or desiccated channels for the flow of divine vitality into human life and awareness. Kalonymus Shapira precedes Gershom Scholem in noting that Hasidism transformed the theosophy of medieval Kabbalah into a kind of mystical psychology that both describes and shapes the contours of human subjectivity—which is also, not insignificantly, where the locus of devotional activity has moved.[45] R. Shapira only sharpens this trend through his emotionally evocative sermons and pedagogic manuals as well as his handbook for mystical fraternities described by Leshem. Perhaps more surprising is that R. Shapira applied the same paradigm to the study of legal and talmudic texts, which were, after all, the strong backbone of the traditional rabbinic curriculum. A crucial hub of R. Shapira's teaching, made explicit by Ariel Evan Mayse in chapter 3, is that the flow of divine vitality—the "pulsing core of Torah"—is itself identified with the free flow of charged subjectivity, emotion, or feeling, "thus fusing the nomian with the emotive in order to generate a fully integrated religious experience."

Personalism is manifest everywhere in R. Shapira's work, deeply imbricated with his monistic appreciation for the sheer corporeality of human life, mediated and underwritten by sacred text and language through which, according to Beshtian Hasidism, the world is continually renewed. In slightly different ways, David Maayan (chapter 5) and Ora Wiskind (chapter 6) each analyze R. Shapira's striking focus on the religious legitimacy of the unique, embodied subjectivity of each individual (not just the tsaddik), that emerges from the prewar writings. Maayan claims that this "incarnational theology" mediates against the adoption of *bittul* or any other form of self-annihilation as a central motif in Piaseczno, as it is, for example, in Chabad.[46] Since all existence is underwritten by the vitality conveyed by the sacred letters, no aspect of corporeal life should be considered irredeemable. Wiskind, meanwhile, breaks new ground by attending to the nuanced and delicate literary strategies through which R. Shapira approaches these themes in order to promote particular forms of modern Hasidic "mindfulness" and emergent religious subjectivity in his still insufficiently studied prewar sermons. These themes would later be tested in the Warsaw Ghetto's crucible.

Rupture, Efficacy, and the End of Meaning?

Some of the most generative debates in this volume concern the problem of meaning in R. Shapira's oeuvre. There are at least two parts to this problem, the first of which is a general one (what sort of hermeneutic best reveals the significance of Hasidic texts?), while the second calls attention to the specific question of rupture and continuity in light of the Holocaust. With respect to the first problem, writers in this volume might be broadly divided between those who emphasize a theological-discursive paradigm seeking to clarify some area of R. Shapira's thought and a cluster of alternative readings that focus on textual practice through the prism of literary, psychological, or ritual efficacy: "how Hasidic authors do things with words."[47] The latter might include the literary-aesthetic evocation of existential drama and concern, the shaping of a distinctively Hasidic religious and ethical habitus, or the channeling of divine vitality and blessing. While any of these textual effects might also invoke particular Hasidic "doctrines" such as divine immanence or acosmism, scholars in this group emphasize the emergent properties of textual effects that are not easily abstracted from the particular literary and ritual contexts in which they appear. To take just one debate that resonates through this volume: Should "faith" be treated as belief in a set of propositional contents that can be stated abstractly or is it better understood as a kind of experience related to ritual efficacy and channeling of vitality? In the latter case, the medium really cannot be meaningfully separated from the message.[48]

Each of these two broad approaches offers certain advantages. One benefit of the intellectualist "Hasidic thought" paradigm (which remains dominant in contemporary Hasidic studies) is that it encourages readers to focus deeply on the specific theological content the texts avowedly convey, their intellectual genealogies and specialized terminologies. In the best cases, this approach makes the discursive content of Hasidic texts available for analytic comparison with other schools of Hasidism as well as other religious and intellectual traditions. Scholarship in Hasidic thought has rendered insupportable the views of earlier writers who once treated Hasidism as little more than an eruption of Dionysian irrationality and superstition, or who portrayed it as a shallow aberration from the sober rabbinic, philosophical, or emancipatory-secular forms of Jewish life to which scholars themselves may have been committed.[49]

A significant though not always realized concomitant of this intellectualist approach is that the translation of labyrinthine homiletic or exegetical literature into repositories of discursive content or doctrine might, under the right circumstances, accord to "Hasidic thought" the implied dignity of ideas that would allow it to be taken seriously in communities of readership outside of its native ritual or sectarian context. Daniel Reiser's painstaking archaeology of the *Sermons from the Years of Rage*, described in chapter 8 (and ably reviewed by Moria Herman in chapter 7), is therefore noteworthy for drawing R. Shapira's wartime sermons into conversation with recognized figures of Western thought, such as Franz Rosenzweig, Ernest Becker, even Socrates. Reiser nonetheless signals his own view that scholars should go beyond the philosophical "content" of the sermons by attending to the phenomenological contradictions that defined their composition in the face of genocide. Herman's and Reiser's accounts of the technical work involved in Reiser's critical edition are crucial here, because several of the subsequent chapters argue about the significance of textual features that would have been impossible to address without this painstaking research.

Nehemia Polen was one of the first scholars to treat *Sermons from the Years of Rage* (or *Esh Kodesh*, as it was popularly known) seriously on an intellectual level, so it is especially gratifying that he has taken the opportunity of his essay in chapter 9 of this volume to reexamine his own methodology in light of Reiser's critical edition. By analyzing a complete June 1942 sermon, available for the first time in its original layering and paragraphing, Polen demonstrates the emergent quality of themes such as gender and mortality, the desperate human "thirst" for God, and "the divinity of children" as bearers of human continuity in the face of death. These are not easily identifiable as "doctrines," inasmuch as they are said to depend upon an "architectural integrity" that emerges from the unfolding movement of the original sermon. Rather than mining the sermon for abstract ideas to be unearthed and carried away, in other words, Polen treats it like a musical score whose significance can only be appreciated through engagement with the context in which it unfolds.[50] Indeed, music, ritual, and homiletic writing are all arguably intractable to systematic formulation precisely because they have in common this temporal dimension of unfolding over time.[51] The tension (it probably should not be thought of as an outright contradiction) between these two paradigms runs throughout this volume, but become more explicit in the chapters dealing with R. Shapira's Holocaust-era sermons.

Even under duress, it is obvious that R. Shapira engaged broad dimensions of the Jewish literary and intellectual tradition. James A. Diamond (chapter 10) provocatively argues that *Sermons from the Years of Rage* invokes Maimonidean philosophical language precisely in order to establish a distinctively Hasidic, and determinedly nonphilosophical response to radical suffering, beyond all reason and intelligibility. In this reading, the Aristotelian unity of the knower and the known allows for the mystical identification of the divine with human suffering. Erin Leib Smokler (chapter 11), similarly, traces R. Shapira's daring use of a well-known talmudic concept, *yissurim shel ahavah* or "chastenings born of love," to engage and ultimately transcend any possible Jewish theodicy of justice and intelligibility under Ghetto conditions. Extraordinary in both chapters is the sense of a deep, possibly inevitable rupture in Jewish thought occasioned by the Holocaust yet conveyed in the language of the exegetical tradition.

Despite its considerable power, critics of the traditional academic emphasis on Hasidic "thought" argue that this focus threatens to overintellectualize religious life. Moshe Idel has critiqued the "theologization" of Hasidism and points in this volume (chapter 2) to the "conceptual fluidity" he associates with R. Shapira's approach, calling for a more phenomenological analysis of how Hasidic texts function. Several other authors also offer implicit or explicit critique of the intellectualist paradigm. Ora Wiskind (chapter 6) calls for a holistic literary analysis of the prewar and wartime sermons, attuned to the ways in which they consistently thematize "self-awareness, emotion, the need for inner psychic unity, empowerment, the urgency of communication, and an endless desire for divine presence." Don Seeman (chapter 14) endorses this formulation in the context of an expansive, anthropologically informed understanding of textual practice. Seeman focuses on the relationship between what he calls literary and ritual efficacy—the ways in which these texts are both written and read in attunement with urgent projects such as renewal, healing, and the defense of human subjectivity against collapse. These are contingent and quotidian goals that can only be appreciated against the backdrop of potential failure, to which R. Shapira was extraordinarily sensitive.

While these issues can be raised with respect to virutally any Hasidic text, they arise here with special force because of the extreme conditions under which R. Shapira labored. In his provocative essay (chapter 13), Shaul Magid argues that by the time R. Shapira consigned his manuscripts for burial, he had already been forced to acknowledge the apparent success of the Nazi genocide and with it the apparent collapse of Judaism's covenantal framework. While the sermons themselves may remain equivocal, Magid claims he can show on the basis of a late postscript that the author of *Sermons from the Years of Rage* suffered a crisis of faith profound enough to establish him as a "missing link" between traditional Judaism and radical post-Holocaust theology. This is a claim that has, not surprisingly, engendered some spirited public debate (mentioned in chapter 14), but on a scholarly level, Magid raises issues that must be addressed, and he does so with admirable clarity. Implicitly or explicitly, most of the authors in the second half of this book relate to the issue of rupture and faith that Magid raises.

With a few exceptions, R. Shapira typically makes only oblique reference to contemporary events in his Warsaw sermons. Henry Abramson (chapter 12) argues plausibly that historical research into the dates on which particular sermons were first composed can therefore shed significant new light on their meaning. He associates the intensifying urgency of sermons beginning in mid-February 1942, for example, with the eyewitness testimony of mass murders that a Jewish refugee from Chelmno had recently brought with him to Warsaw. Without such contextualization, we may fail to grasp the "original and primary purpose" of these sermons, which was ostensibly to address the fear, grief, and demoralization of Ghetto inhabitants. By the same token, Abramson insists that R. Shapira's own faith was never in question. "At no point does R. Shapira ever despair of God's existence and omnipotence, even up to his final will and testament. . . . He maintains an active, passionate relationship with God . . . sometimes raising his voice in anguish and fear but always confident in God's ability to save the Jewish people." While he may have come to despair of *history*, Abramson asserts, "even a cursory reading of the wartime writings demonstrates the absurdity of attributing a loss of faith to their author." Magid counters that he finds the proposed distinction between faith in God and faith in history untenable given the long Jewish commitment to covenantal/providential thinking.

Responding to Magid's challenge that his critics rarely define precisely what they mean by "faith" in these disputes, Seeman brings this volume to a close (chapter 14) by arguing that R. Shapira almost always refers to this term (Heb. *emunah*) in terms of ritual efficacy and unimpeded flow of divine vitality rather than "belief" in a propositional sense. Such efficacy is, to repeat, never a foregone conclusion; vital flow may be halting, susceptible to blockage, or to desiccating disconnection from its source. The identification between vital flow and the experience of affect in Hasidic thought therefore contributes to R. Shapira's phenomenological turn, inasmuch as the literary *description* of experience and its ritual *modulation* are deeply intertwined. With that, Seeman brings radical suffering and the problem of meaning that are emphasized in the second half of this volume back to the analysis of Hasidic renewal with which our volume began.

Hasidism, Neo-Hasidism, Hasidic Modernism

A few final words of context are in order. Very few Piaseczner Hasidim survived the second world war. The small group of followers who did survive were unable to reconstitute themselves in the manner of larger groups like Satmar, Ger, Belz, and Vizhnits, whose leaders all left Europe before the Holocaust, or Chabad, whose remarkable resurrection began with the escape of its leadership to the United States in 1940. Nevertheless, the last several decades have witnessed a surge in interest in the Hasidism of Piaseczno among a diverse group of scholars, seekers, and admirers.

Among the contemporary institutions laying claim to the Piaseczno legacy is a synagogue in Ramat Beit Shemesh, Israel, whose rabbi is the grandson of R. Shapira's younger brother Yeshayahu, who joined a religious agricultural settlement in Palestine before the war.[52] This synagogue and its associated study hall are located in a heavily Orthodox neighborhood, but its visitors are not necessarily Hasidim in any classical sense. The synagogue promotes the study of R. Shapira's writings, including his pedagogical tracts, and uses some of the *niggunim*, or melodies, that he wrote. Nevertheless, the fact that R. Shapira left no dynastic successor may have allowed his teachings to be perceived as the joint possession of the whole Hasidic, or even larger Jewish, community rather than being too closely identified with any contemporary "court." His books have been published and republished by a variety of Orthodox and Ultraorthodox publishing houses, have begun to engender commentaries of their own, and have been invoked in public reckoning with Jewish suffering and resilience in the twentieth and twenty-first centuries. Piaseczno has played a role for some time now in the "spiritual renaissance" of the Ashkenazi Haredi world (Yiddish-, Hebrew-, and English-speaking), as these communities grapple not only with the still-devastating losses of the Holocaust but also with a growing demand for broad access to spiritual resources.[53] This includes a return to the study of early Hasidic works that may have been underutilized in recent generations as well as the addition of a few important later works, including R. Shapira's own relatively accessible guides to contemplative practice and cultivation of inner life.

In recent years, R. Shapira's books have played an increasingly prominent role in both the "national religious" (*dati le'umi*) and "national Ultraorthodox" (*hardal*) wings of Religious Zionism in Israel.[54] His teachings are featured prominently in the libraries of many of the *yeshivot hesder*, which combine Israeli military service with Torah study for young men and where, together with select other works of Hasidism—such as those of Bratzlav, Izhbits-Radzin, and Chabad—they provide a counterbalance to the once nearly exclusive focus on Talmud and Bible in the Zionist yeshiva curriculum.[55] This has been less true of institutions with a close historical connection to the early-twentieth-century mystic and chief rabbi Abraham Isaac Kook, or whose "Lithuanian" focus on the absolute primacy of Talmudic study remain undisturbed, but these institutions are also not nearly as dominant in the broadly Zionist yeshiva world as was once the case. Smaller yeshivot with a variety of different intellectual and ideological agendas, including the diversication of the curriculum to include Hasidic studies, have multiplied. The late R. Shimon Gershon Rosenberg ("Shagar"), who was known for his attempts to bridge Hasidic and postmodern thought, became an important conduit for the study of Piaseczno and other Hasidic teachings in this world.[56]

Piaseczno has also figured prominently in North American Jewish Renewal and Neo-Hasidism in its Orthodox and liberal Jewish varieties. R. Shapira's works were, for example, an important resource for the charismatic teachers Shlomo Carlebach (1925–1994) and Zalman Schachter-Shalomi (1924–2014), both of whom had Hasidic roots.[57] Carlebach's adaptation, which emphasized R. Shapira's resilience in the face of tragedy, emphasized Jewish solidarity and offered a classically Orthodox portrait of the Piaseczner Rebbe. Carlebach's possibly apocryphal story "The Holy Hunchback" describes a chance encounter with a former student of the Piaseczner who

survived Auschwitz and had become a Tel Aviv street sweeper. He tells
Carlebach that the only thing keeping him from suicide is his childhood
memory of the Piaseczno Rebbe's voice. "Remember children, the greatest
thing in the world is to do somebody else a favor."[58] Schachter-Shalomi,
by contrast, emphasized the devotional aspects of R. Shapira's legacy,
focusing for his mostly non-Orthodox audience on the remarkable array
of contemplative techniques the Piasezcner Rebbe taught. We should also
note that Schachter-Shalomi was the first to suggest *Sermons from the
Years of Rage* as a dissertation topic for Nehemia Polen (author of chapter
9 of this volume), whose 1994 monograph, *Holy Fire*, ushered in a wave
of English-language scholarship whose distant reverberations include the
current volume.[59]

Several writers in this volume, including Marcin Wodziński, Moshe
Idel, Ariel Evan-Mayse, Ora Wiskind, and Don Seeman, have noted R.
Shapira's importance for contemporary Neo-Hasidism, a loosely defined
movement with both Orthodox and liberal Jewish manifestations. Though
he is not alone within American Orthodoxy, special mention should
be made of R. Moshe Weinberger, who was the founding rabbi of a
Piaseczno-inflected synagogue called Aish Kodesh in Woodmere, New
York, in 1992. Weinberger draws upon the teachings of many different
Hasidic masters along with those of Rav Kook (whose contribution to
Neo-Hasidism deserves special analysis, inasmuch as he was not, strictly
speaking, a Hasidic leader at all), but R. Shapira occupies a special place
in his spiritual library and lineage.[60] Weinberger's appointment in 2013 as
mashpia, or "spiritual guide," of Yeshiva College in New York was widely
understood as testimony to the growing influence of Neo-Hasidism among
modern or centrist Orthodox youth in America.[61] Perhaps predictably,
popular Neo-Hasidism tends to blur what we take to be important distinctions among different schools of classical Hasidic thought and practice.[62] A somewhat different but related blurring of historical boundaries
is also apparent in the non-Orthodox world, where the Neo-Hasidic turn
self-consciously blends Hasidic, Buddhist, and other contemplative forms.
An example might be the work of James Jacobson Maisels, a rabbi and
popular meditation teacher whose University of Chicago dissertation
focused on the Piasezcner and who acknowledges that his own Neo-Hasidic mindfulness practice has been shaped by various Buddhist teachings
as well as by R. Shapira.[63]

Proper ethnographic and sociology of knowledge analysis of R. Shapira's multifaceted "afterlife" remains an important desideratum.[64] During
the Second Palestinian Intifada, in October 2000, a child of American

immigrants named Esh Kodesh Gilmore, who was raised at Shlomo Carlebach's Moshav Modiin, was shot and killed while working as a security
guard at the Israeli National Insurance Institute in Jerusalem.[65] Within a
few months, an unofficial Israeli outpost or small settlement named Esh
Kodesh was erected in his name near the West Bank community of Shvut
Rachel, itself named for Rachel Drouk, the victim of a terror attack on a
civilian bus in 1991.[66] The temptation to omit these troubling nontextual
events from a scholarly account of R. Shapira's reception history is to be
resisted; one way or another, he would have been the first to acknowledge
that the fate of his teaching and the concrete, sometimes catastrophic
destiny of his people cannot be disentangled.

At the time of this writing, a group of more than nine hundred
people, including rabbis, academics, spiritual "tourists," Neo-Hasidim, and
spiritual fellow travelers meet in a "virtual *beis midrash*" on Facebook "to
share the teachings, inspiration, and anecdotes of the holy Piaseczno Rebbe
Kalonymus Kalmish Shapira."[67] There are very few Hasidic personalities (let
along twentieth-century Hasidic leaders) who can claim this kind of public
recognition and significance. While *Hasidism, Suffering, and Renewal* is
intended for academic scholars of religion, Hasidism, and Jewish thought
therefore, we also hope that this work will engage readers outside of the
academy among those who seek intelligent but accessible scholarship on
Hasidism in general or Piaseczno in particular. We are inspired not just
by the enormous growth in scholarly writing on R. Shapira's legacy, well
exceeding the scope of this volume, but also by the vitality and serious-
ness of readers (some of them also academics!) who look to Piaseczno
for wisdom and inspiration—for the emergence of what Buber might have
called a *teaching* that can "address the crisis of modern men and women."[68]

Readers outside the academy should be aware that the choice of individual authors to use or not use the honorific R. ("rabbi") for addressing
R. Shapira in this volume may reflect debates about the conventions of
academic writing that are not necessarily intended to convey any particular religious or spiritual sensibility (or lack thereof). All our authors
have shown R. Shapira the ultimate respect of devoting their time and
expertise to understanding his legacy.

Rather than claiming to have offered a final, authoritative account,
we are hopeful that this collection of essays will help to forestall prema-
ture closure on disquieting questions about the intellectual and existential
significance of Piaseczno, Hasidism, or suffering and the Holocaust. To
choose just one example from among many, authors in this volume have

described R. Shapira alternately as a precursor to radical Neo-Hasidism
(Idel, Mayse, Leshem, Wiskind) or post-Holocaust theology (Magid); as
the purveyor of an essentially conservative retrenchment (a kind of "Jewish counter-Reformation" [Wodzinski]);or as the initiator of a distinctive
"Hasidic Modernism" (Seeman) adopting strategies parallel to those of
modernizing Buddhist groups confronted by the crisis of colonialism, as
well as the challenges of modern science and psychotherapeutic models.
Piaseczno stands for the tenacity and resilience of faith (Reiser, Polen,
Abramson) as well as the rupture of faith and meaning (Diamond, Smokler);
for spiritual renewal (Mayse, Maayan) as well as catastrophic failure that
may never be repaired (Magid, Seeman). Do we need to choose decisively
among these views? Perhaps. Certainly, each author has made their best
case, and much is at stake. As editors though, we prefer to conclude with
the words of Rashi (the only medieval commentator mentioned by name
in *Sermons from the Years of Rage*) on the plenitude of scripture, which
also represents perforce the plenitude of life. Writing around the time that
Franco-German Jewry was convulsed and nearly destroyed by the First
Crusade, Rashi affirmed multiple—even apparently contradictory—readings
of the same scriptural texts, citing a midrash on the prophecy of Jeremiah:
"Is not my word like fire, says the Lord of hosts, or like a hammer that
splits a rock (Jer. 23:29)?" Just as the rock is split into many pieces, in one
version of the midrash that Rashi cites, so the word of God "is divisible
into many different understandings."[69]

Notes

R. Shapira's cover letter is reproduced in Kalonymus Kalman Shapira, *Sermons
from the Years of Rage* [in Hebrew], ed. Daniel Reiser, 2 vols. (Jerusalem: Herzog
Academic College, 2017), 1:328. Translation by Shaul Magid, this volume.

    1. Emmanuel Ringelblum, *Notes from the Warsaw Ghetto: The Journal of
Emmanuel Ringelblum* (New York: McGraw-Hill, 1958); and Samuel D. Kassow,
*Who Will Write our History?: Emanuel Ringelblum, the Warsaw Ghetto, and the
Oyneg Shabes Archive* (Bloomington: Indiana University Press, 2007).

    2. *Sermons from the Years of Rage*, 1:27.

    3. See Leshem, "Between Messianism and Prophecy," 5n15. One copy of
Benei mahshavah tovah is found in the New York Chabad Library, MS 1192:27,
and another, signed by Shapira (who notes that it is forbidden to copy the work
without his permission), is the property of R. Avraham Hamer in Bnei Brak.
This copy was given to his father, R. Eliyahu Hamer, who was one of Shapira's

main disciples and one of the first copiers of his sermons. R. Kalonymus Kalman Shapira, *Conscious Community*, trans. Andrea Cohen Kiener (Northvale, NJ: Jason Aaronson, 1977); idem., *A Student's Obligation: Advice from the Rebbe of the Warsaw Ghetto*, trans. Micha Odenheimer (Oxford: Roman and Littlefield, 1991).

4. Kalonymus Kalman Shapira, *Shalosh derashot* (Tel Aviv: Merkaz hasidei Koźnic, 1985); idem, *Derekh ha-melekh* (Jerusalem: Va'ad Hasidei Piaseczno, 1995); and, on the process of editing these sermons, *Sermons from the Years of Rage*, 1:26–53.

5. Kalonymus Kalman Shapira, *Derashah* (Warsaw: Hevrei ha-kehilah ha-Ivrit de-Pi'acetsna, 1936).

6. Kalonymus Kalman Shapira, *Esh Kodesh* (Va'ad hasidei Piaseczno, 1960); idem, *Sacred Fire: Torah from the Years of Fury 1939–1942*, trans. J. Hershey Worch (Jerusalem: Jason Aronson, 2000).

7. See also David Biale et al., *Hasidism: A New History* (Princeton: Princeton University Press, 2018), 587.

8. Don Seeman, "Ritual Efficacy, Hasidic Mysticism and 'Useless Suffering' in the Warsaw Ghetto," *Harvard Theological Review* 101 (2008): 465–505; see Idel, this volume.

9. See Moshe Idel, *Old World, New Mirrors: On Jewish Mysticism and Twentieth-Century Thought* (Philadelphia: University of Pennsylvania Press, 2010).

10. It is worth noting that Benjamin Brown, "Substitutes for Mysticism: A General Model for the Theological Development of Hasidism in the Nineteenth Century," *History of Religions* (2017): 248–88, specifically excludes R. Shapira from his consideration of mysticism's decline. See, however, Biale et al., *Hasidism*, 615.

11. The only single-volume history of this religious movement is Biale et al., *Hasidism*. For a recent anthology of Hasidic sources from the eighteenth century to the present, see Ariel Evan Mayse and Sam Berrin Shonkoff, eds., *Hasidism: Writings on Devotion, Community, and Life in the Modern World* (Waltham, MA: Brandeis University Press, 2020). The following summary of Hasidism draws on the introduction to that volume.

12. For two important biographies of the Besht, see Moshe Rosman, *Founder of Hasidism: A Quest for the Historical Ba'al Shem Tov* (Berkeley: University of California Press, 1996); and Immanuel Etkes, *The Besht: Magician, Mystic, and Leader*, trans. Saadya Sternberg (Waltham, MA: Brandeis University Press, 2005).

13. See Etkes, *The Besht*, 113–51. Scholars have noted the similarity between the Baal Shem Tov's emphasis on religious ecstasy and the devotional attitudes of some Christian mystics living in the same region. For a recent study, see Moshe Idel, "R. Israel Ba'al Shem Tov 'in the State of Walachia': Widening the Besht's Cultural Panorama," in *Holy Dissent: Jewish and Christian Mystics in Eastern Europe*, ed. Glenn Dynner (Detroit: Wayne State University Press, 2011), 69–103.

14. Gershom Scholem, "*Devekut*, or Communion with God," in *The Messianic Idea in Judaism and Other Essays on Jewish Spirituality* (New York: Schocken, 1971), 203–27.

15. Martin Buber and Gershom Scholem debated Hasidism's complicated relationship to the material world for many years. For a nuanced analysis of this controversy and an insightful new reading of the Hasidic sources, see Seth Brody, " 'Open to Me the Gates of Righteousness': The Pursuit of Holiness and Non-Duality in Early Hasidic Teaching," *The Jewish Quarterly Review* 89 (1998): 3–44.

16. See, for example, Gershon Hanokh Henikh Leiner of Radzin, *Sha'ar ha-emunah viysod ha-hasidut* (Bnei Brak, 1996), 154–55, where this is explicit.

17. Arthur Green, "The Zaddiq as *Axis Mundi* in Later Judaism," *Journal of the American Academy of Religion* 45 (1977): 327–47.

18. On ritual efficacy, see Seeman, "Ritual Efficacy"; Moshe Idel, "The *Tsadik* and His Soul's Sparks: From Kabbalah to Hasidism," *Jewish Quarterly Review* 103 (2013): 196–240; idem., *Hasidism between Ecstasy and Magic*; Jonathan Garb, *Manifestations of Power in Jewish Mysticism from Rabbinic Literature to Safedian Kabbalah* [in Hebrew] (Jerusalem: Magnes, 2004).

19. See Ariel Evan Mayse, *Speaking Infinites: God and Language in the Teachings of Rabbi Dov Ber of Mezritsh* (Philadelphia: University of Pennsylvania Press, 2020).

20. For a study of the debate in early Hasidism regarding the ideal form of spiritual leadership, see Arthur Green, "Around the Maggid's Table: *Tzaddik*, Leadership, and Popularization in the Circle of Dov Baer of Miedzyrzecz," in *The Heart of the Matter: Studies in Jewish Mysticism and Theology* (Philadelphia: Jewish Publication Society, 2015), 119–66; and Ariel Evan Mayse, "The Voices of Moses: Theologies of Revelation in an Early Hasidic Circle," *Harvard Theological Review* 112, no. 1 (2019): 101–25.

21. See Marcin Wodziński, *Haskalah and Hasidism in the Kingdom of Poland: A History of Conflict* (Oxford: Littman Library of Jewish Civilization, 2005).

22. On the emergence of these dynasties, see Nehemia Polen, "Rebbetzins, Wonder-Children, and the Emergence of the Dynastic Principle in Hasidism," in *The Shtetl: New Evaluations*, ed. S. Katz (New York: New York University Press, 2007), 53–84.

23. See Arthur Green, "Hasidism: Discovery and Retreat," in *The Other Side of God: A Polarity in World Religions*, ed. Peter L. Berger (Garden City, NY: Doubleday, 1981), 104–30.

24. This point is made with eloquence in Biale et al., *Hasidism*, esp. 257–90.

25. Ibid.

26. For additional biographical details, see Wodziński (this volume) as well as Nehemia Polen, *The Holy Fire: The Teachings of Rabbi Kalonymus Kalman Shapira, the Rebbe of the Warsaw Ghetto* (Northvale: Jason Aronson, 1994),

1–14; Esther Farbstein, *Hidden in Thunder: Perspectives on Faith, Halachah, and Leadership During the Holocaust*, trans. Deborah Stern (Jerusalem: Mossad Harav Kook, 2007), 479–88; Ron Wacks, *The Flame of the Holy Fire: Perspectives on the Teachings of Rabbi Kalonymous Kalmish Shapiro of Piaczena* (in Hebrew) (Alon Shevut: Tevunot, 2010), 21–33; *Sermons from the Years of Rage*, 1:13–24; Biale et al., *Hasidism*, 614–16, 660–62.

27. According to Grodzisk Mazowiecki birth registry book of 1889, registration no. 53.

28. Elimelekh Shapiro's marriage to Hannah Berakhah was his second, so Kalonymus Kalman Shapira had many siblings on both sides.

29. Shapira's father was also the great-grandfather of Hayyah Rahel Miriam.

30. See Polen, this volume; idem., *The Holy Fire*, 6; idem., "Miriam's Dance: Radical Egalitarianism in Hasidic Thought," *Modern Judaism* 12 (1992): 1–21; and Uziel Fuchs, "Miriam the Prophetess and the Rebbe's Wife: The Piaseczner Rebbe's Sermons on Miriam the Prophetess" [in Hebrew] *Masekhet* 3 (2005): 65–76.

31. *Sermons from the Years of Rage*, 1:14, 337.

32. Polen, *Holy Fire*, 6.

33. See Leibel Bein, *From the Notebook of a Hassidic Journalist* [in Hebrew] (Jerusalem, 1967), 31–32; Polen, *Holy Fire*, 160n17; and *Sermons from the Years of Rage*, 1:15–16.

34. See Malkah Shapiro, *The Rebbe's Daughter: Memoir of a Hasidic Childhood*, trans. Nehemia Polen (Philadelphia: Jewish Publication Society, 2002), xxii, 27, 51–52, 152. Regarding Shapira's violin playing, see Bein, *From the Notebook*, 30. Shapira remained in Hopstein's home until the age of twenty and witnessed him play every Saturday night, perhaps learning the craft from him. Also see Polen, *Holy Fire*, 6; Ya'el Levin, "Ha-Admor she-nigen be-kinor ve-hadal im histalkut ra'aiyato," *Daf le-tarbut Yehudit* 273 (2007): 39.

35. Ibid.; *Der Moment*, May 27, 1927, 10.

36. See *Ha-derekh*, Zurich, vol. 6–7 (February-March 1920): 1–3 (Shapira's signature on p. 3). He appeared again in *Kovets histadruti shel Agudat Yisra'el*, 5672–5683 (Vienna: Lishkat ha-merkaz shel Agudat Yisra'el ha-olamit, 1923), 24–32 (Shapira's signature on p. 29).

37. Hayyim Frankel and David Hayyim Zilbershlag, eds., *Zikharon Kodesh le-Ba'al Esh Kodesh* (Jerusalem: Va'ad Hasidei Pi'asechna-Grodzhisq, 1994), 15–20; *Sermons from the Years of Rage*, 1:25–26.

38. Polen, *Holy Fire*, 12. R. Shapira's sister-in-law, Hannah Hopstein, the daughter of Yerahmiel Moshe Hopstein, immigrated to Mandatory Palestine as a single woman in 1920. She was visiting R. Shapira at the time of the German invasion. This female pioneer, whose life came to a tragic end, has not yet received historical attention, and her fascinating journal and letters, which contain enough material for an excellent historical biography, currently reside in the Kfar Hasidim archive.

39. *Holocaust Encyclopedia of the United States Holocaust Memorial Museum*, s.v. "Warsaw," https://encyclopedia.ushmm.org/content/en/article/warsaw.

40. Bein, *From the Notebook*, 34.

41. Polen, *Holy Fire*, 7; According to the Yiddish newspaper *Forverts*, March 30, 1940.

42. Daniel Reiser, *Imagery Techniques in Modern Jewish Mysticism* (Berlin: De Gruyter, 2018).

43. Ibid.; Seeman, "Ritual Efficacy"; Reiser, *Imagery Techniques*.

44. See Idel, this volume and idem., *Hasidism between Ecstasy and Magic*, 6–9; *Old World, New Mirrors*, 215–16.

45. Gershom Scholem, *Major Trends in Jewish Mysticism* (New York: Schoken, 1941), 341; for sources in Piaseczno, see Seeman, "Ritual Efficacy."

46. See, for example, Rachel Elior, *The Theory of Divinity in Hasidut Habad* [in Hebrew] (Jerusalem, 1982), 178–243; Naftali Loewenthal, *Communicating the Infinite: The Emergence of the Habad School* (Chicago: University of Chicago Press, 1990), 180–86; Elliot R. Wolfson, *Open Secret: Postmessianic Messianism and the Mystical Revision of Menahem Mendel* (New York: Columbia University Press, 2009).

47. This is of course a play on the title of J. L. Austin's famous essay *How to Do Things with Words* (Cambridge: Harvard University Press, 1975).

48. Though almost all of the authors in this volume are dedicated to the study of a Hasidic textual tradition, this approach would also resonate with studies of visual culture and certain forms of media studies. See Maya Balakirsky Katz, *The Visual Culture of Chabad* (Cambridge: Cambridge University Press, 2014); Birgit Meyer, *Sensational Movies: Video, Vision, and Christianity in Ghana* (Berkeley: University of California Press, 2015).

49. See Jonathan M. Elukin, "A New Essenism: Heinrich Graetz and Mysticism," *Journal of the History of Ideas* 59 (1998): 135–48.

50. Not incidentally, see Nehemia Polen, "Niggun as Spiritual Practice, with Special Focus on the Writings of Rabbi Kalonymus Shapiro, the Rebbe of Piaseczna," in *The Contemporary Uses of Hasidism*, ed. Shlomo Zuckier (New York: Yeshiva University Press, 2020), 261–82.

51. Don Seeman, "Martyrdom, Emotion, and the Work of Ritual: R. Mordecai Joseph Leiner of Izbica's *Mei Ha-Shiloah*," *AJS Review* (27): 253–80.

52. See Beit Knesset and Beit Midrash Aish Kodesh, http://www.aishkodesh.org.il/newsite.

53. Jonathan Garb, "Towards the Study of the Spiritual-Mystical Renaissance in the Contemporary Ashkenazi Haredi World in Israel," in *Kabbalah and Contemporary Spiritual Revival*, ed. Boaz Huss (Beer Sheva: Ben Gurion University of the Negev Press, 2011), 117–40.

54. See Yair Sheleg, "The Extinguishing and Rekindling of the Holy Fire," *Haaretz*, April 19, 2004, available at https://www.haaretz.com/1.4782199.

55. See Nehemia Stern, *First Flowering of Redemption: An Ethnographic Account of Contemporary Religious Zionism* (PhD diss., Emory University, 2014).

56. See for example Shimon Gershon Rosenberg, *Kelim shevurim: Torah ve-tsiyonut-datit bi-svivah post-modernit: Derashot le-mo'ade zemanenu* (Efrat, 2003), 134–40.

57. For two examples of Schachter-Shalomi discussing R. Shapira's legacy and importance, see the following 1997 lectures found in the Zalman M. Schachter-Shalomi Collection at the University of Colorado Boulder: https://cudl. colorado.edu/luna/servlet, identifiers RRZ0001S0017 and JRRZ0001S0017N0019. Examples of Carlebach's use of R. Shapira's legacy appear in Magid's essay in the present volume.

58. See the discussion of this story in Arthur Green and Ariel Mayse, *A New Hasidism: Roots* (Philadelphia: Jewish Publication Society, 2019), 185–87.

59. See Polen, *Holy Fire*, x.

60. His lectures have been collected and revised as Moshe Weinberger, *Warmed by the Fire of Aish Kodesh: Torah from the Hilulas of Reb Kalonymus Kalman Shapira of Piaseczna*, ed. Binyomin Wolf (Nanuet, NY: Feldheim, 2015).

61. Barbara Bensoussan, "Rekindling the Flame: Neo-Chassidus Brings the Inner Light of Torah to Modern Orthodoxy," *Jewish Action*, 2014, available at https://jewishaction.com/religion/jewish-culture/rekindling-flame-neo-chassidus-brings-inner-light-torah-modern-orthodoxy/. The Yeshiva University affiliated *Torah U-Madda* book series will soon publish a volume on Neo-Hasidism primarily in the Modern Orthodox world.

62. Don Seeman, "The Anxiety of Ethics and the Presence of God," in *A New Hasidism: Branches*, ed. Arthur Green and Ariel Mayse (Philadelphia: Jewish Publication Society, 2019), 73–103.

63. See his reflections in James Jacobson-Maisels, "Neo-Hasidic Meditation: Mindfulness as a Neo-Hasidic Practice," in *A New Hasidism: Branches*, ed. Green and Mayse, 251–70.

64. For the term *afterlife* in this context, we draw on Samuel Heilman and Menachem Friedman, *The Life and Afterlife of Menachem Mendel Schneerson* (Princeton: Princeton University Press, 2012).

65. Charlotte Halle, "Disproportionate Number of Anglos Slain; Olmert Praises Families' Dignity," *Haaretz*, August 23, 2001, https://www.haaretz.com/ 1.5406131, accessed May 18, 2020. See Shaul Magid, "A New History of Holy Fire," *Tablet Magazine*, Feb. 3, 2019, https://www.tabletmag.com/sections/belief/articles/ a-new-history-of-holy-fire.

66. See Tamar El-Or and Gideon Aran, "Giving Birth to a Settlement: Maternal Thinking and Political Action of Jewish Women in the West Bank," in *Perspectives on Israeli Anthropology*, ed. Esther Hertzog et al. (Detroit: Wayne State University Press, 2009), 316–31.

67. See https://www.facebook.com/groups/481394495537008/permalink/763 210847355370/.

68. Martin Buber, *The Legend of the Baal-Shem* (1955), xii–xiii. See Wiskind, this volume.

69. Rashi on Exodus 8:9. *Perushei Rashi al-hatorah*, edited by Harav Hayyim Dov Chavel (Jerusalem: Mossad HaRav Kook, 1986), 191. Also see Rashi's glosses to Genesis 33:20 and Shabbat 88b s.v. *mah patish*.

Part I

Hasidism and Renewal

1

The Place of Piety

Piaseczno in the Landscape of Polish Hasidism

MARCIN WODZIŃSKI

Academic studies of Hasidism too often focus on the life, ideas, and doctrines of great personalities and assume a kind of natural correspondence between the intellectual achievements of Hasidic leaders (tsaddikim) and their social impact. This error is not unique to Jewish and Hasidic studies but may be exacerbated by the continuing influence of traditional yeshiva-style scholarship on academic research. At the same time, the rapid development of academic Jewish studies and its embrace of modern methodologies recapitulated the fascination with a privileged corpus of texts and their mostly elite male interpreters, at the expense of other concerns. The problem is especially egregious in Hasidic studies, which has not until recently paid much attention to the hundreds and thousands of rank-and-file Hasidic followers, focusing instead on the life and, especially, the ideas of the tsaddikim. Historians have all too often tended to forget about the vast majority of Hasidim, who lived outside of the Hasidic courts in countless townlets of eastern and east-central Europe.[1]

The case of the Piaseczner Rebbe, R. Kalonymus Kalman Shapira of Piaseczno, is no different in this regard. While there has been impressive progress in the study of the doctrine and teaching of the Piaseczner Rebbe, this very volume being the most impressive proof of this development, there has been no comparable progress in research on his social context and significance during his own lifetime. We know surprisingly little about the scale of this tsaddik's social influence or the demographic characteristics and geographical distribution of his followers. How many followers did he have? Where did they live? What was their socioeconomic profile? How was the Hasidism of Piaseczno positioned with respect to other contemporary Hasidic or non-Hasidic groups? To what degree was Piaseczno representative—or atypical—of interwar Hasidism in Poland?

In this introductory essay, I have neither the intention nor the ability to respond to all of these major questions. Instead, I will focus on outlining the essential contextual characteristics of the Hasidic presence in Piaseczno and how it might have influenced R. Shapira's activities, or, to put it another way, the extent to which R. Shapira's activities can be understood as representative of wider trends characterizing the Jewish community of interwar Poland. We will need to understand something about the size and influence of Piaseczno Hasidism (i.e., the followers of the Piaseczner Rebbe) and what these features can tell us about the rebbe and his teaching. My observations will of necessity be somewhat preliminary, as we are only at the beginning of this type of research into Piaseczno and other Hasidic groups.

Hasidism in Piaseczno

The town of Piaseczno was established in the thirteenth century as a rural settlement. It received municipal charter in 1429 and started to develop as a minor commercial center. The process was relatively slow, as Piaseczno was, like many such settlements, repeatedly destroyed by wars and fires, including the Polish-Swedish war of the mid-seventeenth century and then the series of wars and uprisings that took place at the end of the eighteenth century. At that time, about five hundred people lived in the town.

It was only at the end of the eighteenth century that Jews appeared in Piaseczno, since the town had previously enjoyed the right to exclude Jewish residents. Of a population of 565 people in 1808, only 26 (5 percent) were Jews. In the years following, the proportion of Jews in the town grew rapidly, reaching 515 people, or 42 percent of the total population, in 1857.[2] At that time, Piaseczno was not treated as an independent Jewish community but only as a filial branch of the kahal in nearby Nadarzyn. Despite its constant efforts to gain communal independence, the Jewish community of Piaseczno maintained its status as the filial extension of Nadarzyn until the end of the nineteenth century.[3]

By the middle of the nineteenth century, Hasidim had become an increasingly visible segment of the Jewish community and influenced the flavor of religious life in the town. When the Polish government introduced a ban on "Jewish attire" in the 1840s, the Hasidim in Piaseczno expressed strong opposition to the new law. Piaseczno had the third-highest number of people seeking legal exemptions to the ban in the whole province of Mazovia; it was surpassed only by the Hasidic strongholds of Amshinov (Mszczonów) and Vorke (Warka).[4] This is an indirect but suggestive indication of the relative strength of the town's traditionalist community, including Hasidim. In addition, the ten *kvitlekh* (petitionary notes) delivered by Piaseczno Jews to rabbi and semi-tsaddik R. Eliyahu Guttmacher of Graydits (Grodzisk Wielkopolski; 1795–1874) indicate a relatively high interest in Hasidic forms of religious life in Piaseczno.[5] Likewise, Jewish ethnological materials collected in Piaseczno at the beginning of the twentieth century testify to rich Hasidic traditions and bear witness to the strong cultural influence of popular Hasidic folk culture in the town.[6]

The growth of Hasidism was not, of course, uncontested. One non-Hasidic Jew complained that "in the good old times, Jews would gather in the synagogue for Rosh Hashanah (the Jewish New Year) early in the day and stay there until the afternoon. Now, on such holy days, the Hasidim smoke their pipes till eight or nine in the morning, and when they finally arrive [at the synagogue], they are done with their prayers in an hour."[7] A report by missionaries from the London Society for Promoting Christianity amongst the Jews, which was active in Poland, reported on significant conflicts over the rise of Hasidism in the town:

> In the town here, there exist two parties, the Hasidim and the so-called mitnagdim, that is, the opponents of the former, and they continually argue with each other. The former group has its own rabbi, and they want him to be recognized in his office by the rest of the Jews. Others brought a different rabbi, closer to their way of thinking, and they demanded that *he* be recognized as the town rabbi, while they persecute the other

one. The anger between these two sides supposedly reached
such a level of hostility that . . . the supporters of both parties
had a regular fistfight in the synagogue on Rosh Hashanah, for
when one party demanded that *their* rabbi deliver a sermon,
the others shouted that their rabbi should do it instead.[8]

This picture is fairly typical for a town in which, having already gained at
least relative institutional and financial autonomy, the Hasidim sought to
increase their social power by exercising decision-making authority over
communal institutions.[9]

It is true that Hasidim had been appointed to rabbinical positions
since the earliest stages of the movement, but in earlier periods these
appointments were more frequently made on the basis of other criteria,
such as Talmudic knowledge, ties with influential families in a town, or
willingness to accept a position in a small town with little remuneration.
Appointments to the rabbinate became a subject of political controversy
only when local Hasidic communities proposed their own candidates
despite doubts regarding those candidates' suitability for the post, or when
they opposed the non-Hasidic candidate only because of his views on
Hasidism. This only happened in situations in which the Hasidic group
felt strong enough to impose its views despite the lack of community
consensus, which was apparently the case in Piaseczno by the middle of
the nineteenth century.

Hasidim had many reasons for showing interest in the appointment of
communal rabbis, including, of course, the opportunity to spread Hasidic
values and thereby influence community norms. A second reason was
financial: rabbis received a salary from the communal budget, and even
if this remuneration was modest, it would typically be supplemented by
extra income for performing religious ceremonies. During the nineteenth
and early twentieth centuries, many tsaddikim found that their income
from donations by their immediate followers was insufficient, so they
had to seek other sources of income.[10] Several Hasidic leaders, such as R.
Henokh Lewin of Aleksandrów (Alexander), became rabbis only in the
wake of bankruptcy following a business failure.[11] Financial need, decreasing
numbers of followers due to secularization, and a sense of institutional
crisis may all have been reasons that someone like R. Kalonymus Shapira
would seek recognition as a communal rabbi during the first half of the
twentieth century.

Tsaddikim in and of Piaseczno

Despite the significant development of its Hasidic community, nine-teenth-century Piaseczno remained only a provincial center of the Hasidic movement. The strongest local group consisted of followers of the tsaddik of Grodzisk (father of the Piaseczner Rebbe),[12] but despite significant local influence, the town's Hasidic community never had the importance of those of neighboring towns such as Ger (Góra Kalwaria) and Amshinov (Mszczonów). It was only with the appearance of charismatic Hasidic leaders in the early twentieth century that this situation began to change.

It seems that the first Hasidic leader to settle in Piaseczno was R. Israel Yitzhak Kalisz, son of the tsaddik Simhah Bunim Kalisz of Otwock (Warka-Otwock dynasty). R. Kalisz came to Piaseczno around 1907 and became a local tsaddik there, combining this function with serving as tsaddik in Otwock. This was, however, only a short-lived leadership, as R. Kalisz does not seem to have spent World War I in Piaseczno, and he died in a typhus epidemic at the age of thirty-six, soon after the war.[13]

Another member of a prominent Polish Hasidic dynasty, R. Meir Israel Rabinowicz of the Przysucha dynasty, son of the tsaddik of Szydłowiec, Tsemah Rabinowicz, arrived in Piaseczno around 1909. After marrying a daughter of prominent Ger Hasid and communal Rabbi of Piaseczno Noah Sekewnik (1893–1913), R. Meir Israel also soon began to act as a tsaddik. While not much is known about his particular activities, we can assume that he acted like all other tsaddikim, leading a small group of followers, providing spiritual guidance, arranging festive gatherings, accepting petitions with requests for help, and so on. He continued in this vein until his death, in 1926, after which the dynasty was continued by his son, R. Ya'akov Rabinowicz. This brief dynasty was extinguished when R. Ya'akov was murdered, along with his whole family, during the Holocaust.[14]

This is the crowded field in which R. Kalonymus Kalman Shapira (1889–1943) emerged as one of three tsaddikim simultaneously active in Piaseczno. He was the son of tsaddik Elimelekh Shapira of Grodzisk, an offshoot of the Mogielnica-Kozienice dynasty. R. Shapira began his activities as a tsaddik in 1909 and became communal rabbi in 1913, after the death of the previous occupant of the position, R. Noah Sekewnik. This may not have been a very prestigious position. Yekhiel Yeshaia Trunk writes that Piaseczno replaced Chełm in Polish-Jewish folklore as the embodiment of *batlonut,* or idleness. The previous rabbi had even been made a popular laughingstock as the new incarnation of the well-known joke about the foolish "wise man of Chełm."[15] So it may not be entirely surprising that soon after rising to the position of communal rabbi, R. Shapira left Piaseczno. He moved to Warsaw toward the end of World War I and never returned to Piaseczno for permanent settlement, although he continued to own property there and to visit occasionally.[16] Though his writings, and especially his Holocaust sermons, made R. Shapira retrospectively the most important tsaddik associated with Piaseczno, he does not seem to have been considered the most important Hasidic figure to live there during his lifetime. Though sometimes referred to nostalgically as "the Rebbe of Piaseczno," it is probably more accurate to refer to him as *a* rebbe *in* Piaseczno.

R. Shapira's relocation to Warsaw during World War I should also be viewed in the context of a much wider "metropolitization" of Hasidic leadership around that time. It is significant, however, that even after his move to Warsaw, he continued to be identified with Piaseczno. Attachment to the name of an originary town in the branding of different Hasidic groups was a relatively new phenomenon. In nineteenth-century Poland, a tsaddik of Vorke (Warka), Simhah Bunim Kalisz of Vorke (1851–1907), who moved to Otwock, simply became the tsaddik of Otwock, and his followers were then the Otwock Hasidim rather than Hasidim of Vorke. As late as the beginning of the twentieth century, a tsaddik who settled in Boston could start a dynasty that came to be known by the name of that city. It was only around World War I that the dislocation of tsaddikim from small towns to large cities led to a certain tension or competition over the "branding" afforded by declarative connection to the seats of "traditional" dynasties. A tsaddik such as R. Shapira, who had once lived in Piaseczno but moved to Warsaw, could hardly become the "Warsawer Rebbe" alongside thirty other such tsaddikim in similar circumstances. Rabbi Shapira was one of those who heralded the change to a system wherein dislocated tsaddikim retained the authority and aura of tradition associated with their towns of origin. Today, some of the greatest conflicts in the Hasidic world revolve around who is entitled to retain the name of an ancestral dynasty.[17]

Piaseczno in Warsaw

The scale and consequence of Jewish and Hasidic resettlement during and after the war were incommensurate with anything that had come before. For example, while around fifteen thousand Jews had left Galicia every year before World War I, some four hundred thousand Jews, or half the Jewish population, left the province during the first year of the war alone. The effects of this relocation on all aspects of Hasidic life were considerable.[18] Increasing urbanization of both Hasidim and their leaders was one of the dramatic consequences of these mass dislocations, and R. Shapira's case is exemplary.[19] The Piaseczner Rebbe's life provides a clear expression of this pivotal phenomenon and is, in fact, the best example of the far-reaching consequences it had on the entire Hasidic movement in interwar Poland.

While many rank and file Hasidim were present in big cities by the nineteenth century, the tsaddikim by and large were not. Until the end of the nineteenth century, those tsaddikim who had settled in large towns, such as Czernowitz and Kraków, represented isolated and exceptional cases.[20] Until 1914, semi-urban small towns were clearly the settlements of choice for Hasidic leaders. The outbreak of World War I changed this situation drastically. First the panic-ridden escape from the battle zone and the atrocities of the war, then the burdens of military occupation, economic difficulties, and growing danger inclined an ever-growing number of tsaddikim to move to the urban centers of eastern and central Europe, especially Warsaw and Vienna. We do not have exact numbers, but it is quite clear that the phenomenon reached mass proportions. Twenty-six tsaddikim were living permanently in Warsaw alone during the interwar years, and most of them had settled there during the war, R. Shapira among them.[21]

Life in a large city was safer; it could also be more comfortable. As Ita Kalish, the daughter of the tsaddik of Otwock, recalled: "The war had lasted longer than had been expected. Jews began gradually to leave their old-established homes in towns and villages and to flock to the capital of Poland [Warsaw] in the hope of greater security and peace, and where they hoped to find shelter from the common enemy, i.e., hunger, and from the specifically Jewish fate, i.e., pogroms, expulsions, persecution."[22] For many tsaddikim, a move to the big city was an economic necessity.[23] As Pinhas Tsitron explained in his reminiscences of Kielce: "During the war, travel was restricted and the income of the tsaddikim suffered as a result; therefore, they moved to the large cities, which had major concentrations of Jews. In the large cities, there was greater personal security, as well as more readily available income."[24] However, economic success in a large city was not guaranteed, and metropolitan life brought problems of its own. For one thing, city life often meant a radical change in the status of Hasidic leaders. Before the Great War, Hasidim who lived in modern cities were able to look to the Rebbe's small-town court as a sinecure of the premodern world that they had left behind, suffused in their imagination with the moral values of tradition.[25] Indeed, at a time of dramatic modernizing, urbanizing, and industrial change, small-town courts provided ideological frames of reference for big-city Hasidim. As political struggles swept the Jewish world, these courts continued to function as bastions against modernity.[26] The flight to the big cities meant that Hasidim were deprived of an important moral touchstone, in which the tsaddik had often been a dominating personality and his court the most important social institution.

Tsaddikim in a large city had to adapt to the conditions of big-city life, which included openly and ostentatiously changing their relationship with the communities they led.[27] It suffices to recall that the visit of the tsaddik to a small town was always a great cultural/social event that attracted the attention not only of the Hasidim but of the whole town, including the mitnagdim (traditionalist opponents of Hasidism), the maskilim ("enlightened" Jews), and even Christians.[28] It was different in a large city: several different tsaddikim might live permanently within walking distance and be available to Hasidim on a daily basis. The status difference between a tsaddik and a Hasid was no longer so overt, for they lived in very similar conditions in the same environment, rubbing shoulders with one another.[29] One consequence of this new social arrangement was what might be called "à la carte Hasidism," namely, the sampling of different courts by young Hasidim who spent different festivals with different tsaddikim depending on individual taste or, indeed, on the way different tsaddikim enacted different elements of Hasidic ritual (see Seeman, this volume).[30]

One such "à la carte Hasid" who attended the Piaseczno *shtibl* (prayer house) in Radom in the 1930s recalled that on various occasions he would visit various tsaddikim and would not feel particularly attached to "his" tsaddik, R. Kalonymus Shapira. Why? Simply because R. Yosele of Wierzbnik would hold especially joyous Sabbaths, R. Arele of Kozienice had an attractive *tish* (table celebration), R. Shaul Yedidiah Taub of Modzhits was especially talented musically, and so on. At the same time, he would not go to R. Yitzhak Zelig of Sokołów, whom he considered too rationalistic, or R. Meir Shalom of Parysów, who was too young.[31] Equally unstable and inconsequential was his own identification with the *shtibl* of Piaseczno. He attended this prayer house, as he later recalled, without any particular emotional or ideological attachment to the Piaseczner Rebbe. In fact, his father (who was not a Hasid) moved from the communal *beit midrash* (study hall) to pray in the Piaseczno *shtibl* only because the *beit midrash* was too noisy, while the *shtibl* was quiet and supportive of intensive studies. Several other people attending the *shtibl* were equally non-Hasidic.[32]

Although such behavior, reflecting perhaps a hybrid religious identification, had already been present in earlier Hasidism,[33] urbanization during World War I meant that this phenomenon became more widespread and its effects deeper. The long-term consequence was an overall weakening of institutional bonds and, often, of identification with Hasidism. I have no doubt that many of the interwar activities of the Piaseczner Rebbe were in direct response to the sense of crisis brought on by this new reality. I will return to this issue in the closing section of this chapter.

Piaseczno in Hasidism

It is not easy to measure the size of Hasidic groups; we have no membership lists for different groups before the end of the twentieth century. Elsewhere, I suggested that an optimal substitute for such records would be the list of all the Hasidic prayer houses, or *shtiblekh* (sing. *shtibl*), in a given region.[34] *Shtiblekh* were usually associated with a particular tsaddik and were the basic institution through which tsaddikim could maintain links between their "court" and their followers in the provinces. Unlike spontaneous prayer groups, the *shtibl* was a relatively stable institution with a well-developed social structure and extensive membership requiring a material infrastructure and economic backing. This means that the *shtibl* is a reliable gauge of the relatively well-developed and enduring influence of Hasidism. At the same time, the *shtibl* was a small enough institution to reflect even minute divisions between Hasidic groups and is thus a relatively accurate instrument. For both these reasons, *shtiblekh* are the best basis for analysis of a great many phenomena, including the intra-Hasidic hierarchy of influence and the distinctive ethos of each leader and group.

My analysis here is based on a database of 2,854 *shtiblekh* in Eastern Europe from the end of the nineteenth century through the 1930s, most of them from the interwar period, which was the time of R. Shapira's activity. Although the list is far from complete, it appears to be representative enough, at least for some regions.[35] Most important, it is highly representative for central Poland (former Congress Poland, or Russian

Poland) and thus allows for a good estimation of the influence of the Piaseczner Rebbe, whose influence was extended throughout this area.

Out of 2,854 *shtiblekh* known to us, only seven claimed allegiance to R. Shapira, six of them in central Poland and one just outside, in Kraków (former Galicia). This means that the Hasidim of Piaseczno made up only 0.2 percent of all the east European *shtiblekh*. Even in central Poland, there were twenty-six groups larger than Piaseczno, which had only 0.5 percent of the *shtiblekh* in the province. By comparison, the largest group in the area, Ger (Góra Kalwaria), had 294 *shtiblekh*, or 24 percent of all the *shtiblekh* in central Poland; Aleksander (Aleksandrów) had 165 *shtiblekh* (13 percent); and Kock had seventy-four (6 percent).[36] Among the groups larger than Piaseczno, some were as small, unknown, and relatively insignificant as Kromołów (twelve *shtiblekh*), Parczew (nine), and Kołbiel (eight). Even within his family, R. Kalonymus Shapira did not hold any significant position. His brother, the tsaddik of Grodzisk, R. Israel Shapira, could boast as many as twenty-seven *shtiblekh*, or 2 percent of the *shtiblekh* in central Poland. Other family-related groups included Kozienice (sixteen) and Chęciny (twelve), also significantly larger than Piaseczno. Groups of the same size as Piaseczno included, among others, Rozprza, Pilov (Puławy), Kałuszyn, Pilica, Pińczów, Zwoleń, and Żarki.

Even if a few *shtiblekh* of Piaseczno Hasidim were not recorded, it is unlikely that this would change the picture in any significant way. Anecdotal evidence about *shtiblekh* of the Piaseczno Hasidim indicates that they were never numerous and were hardly among the most important Hasidic institutions of their towns. Interesting material can be found, for example, in memorial books, a collection of over seven hundred volumes produced after 1945. These volumes describe Jewish life in hundreds of towns and villages of eastern Europe before the Holocaust as recalled by their former Jewish inhabitants.[37] The memorial books of Gritsah (Grójec), Radom, and Żyrardów, for example, explicitly position the *shtiblekh* of Piaseczno among the minor Hasidic groups with no wider influence in their respective towns.[38] It is only in Kielce that the activities of the Piaseczno *shtibl* garnered some interest, but this was because of the surprising political activity of the group there.[39]

Other supplementary materials support this picture. Among 1,022 Hasidic groups mentioned in the collection of 611 in-depth interviews in the *Language and Culture Atlas of Ashkenazi Jewry*, part of which also deals with Hasidism and prayer rooms in 611 locations, Piaseczno Hasidim are mentioned only once, in Warka.[40] This emphatically confirms that in terms of social impact, the Hasidic group of the followers of the tsaddik of Piaseczno was relatively small and insignificant.

Small Is Beautiful

At the same time, it should be emphasized that the existence of only a small number of *shtiblekh* did not necessarily indicate failure. The differences between the small courts and the large ones should not necessarily be seen as a result of lesser or greater success but as an expression of different leadership models. Many "small" courts could and did compete successfully with more dominant groups but did not wish to extend the area of their influence beyond a small circle of one or two districts. The Galician court of Bluzev (Błażowa), for example, had in total just as many *shtiblekh* as well-known Bobowa (Bobov), but they were all concentrated in a very small area around Rzeszów, where the Bluzever Hasidim were the dominant group—perhaps surprisingly for those who never heard of the Bluzever Rebbe, Tsevi Elimelekh Shapira.[41] Similarly, among the twenty-three *shtiblekh* in the Garwolin district, the largest number belonged to the local court in Parysów, while in Będzin district (forty-eight *shtiblekh*), the regional Radomsko and Kromołów courts successfully competed with Ger for dominance. Why was this so?

The dominant courts, where the tsaddikim exerted mass leadership, attracted tens of thousands of followers, which gave the group power and was a source of pride and group identity. The inevitable cost, however, was that contact between these tsaddikim and the overwhelming majority of the Hasidim visiting them had to be minimal.[42] Among the thousands of followers of the tsaddikim of Ger or Bełz, a large majority never spent more than a few holy days at their courts (always in the company of thousands of other faithful), never studied with them, and rarely had any more meaningful personal contact. Such tsaddikim did not know most of their followers, or knew them only superficially.[43]

In smaller groups, by contrast, in which *shtiblekh* lay close to the court of the tsaddik, almost every Hasid was able to reach his rebbe's court many times a year, remaining in close, intimate contact with his spiritual leader. Numerous memoirs emphasize precisely this type of interpersonal relationship—radically different from that at more dominant courts—and point to the warm, intimate atmosphere of small Hasidic groups.[44] The tsaddik of Pińczów (six *shtiblekh*) made a point of knowing all his Hasidim well and of having an intimate atmosphere at his court, while the minor tsaddik of Sasów (seven *shtiblekh*) was renowned for "remembering [even] the names of his Hasidim who came to him only rarely."[45]

Piaseczno belonged, no doubt, to this latter category of small, intimate groups, and it seems that R. Shapira consciously aimed to create a small circle of intensive fellowship, as was expressed in his first book *Benei mahshavah tovah* (see Leshem, this volume), which was dedicated to the development of Hasidic confraternities. What is more, the Piaseczno *shtiblekh* were nearly all located in close proximity to the court in Piaseczno (and then in Warsaw), namely in Grójec, Kielce, Piaseczno, Radom, Warsaw, and Żyrardów. The median distance between the court and the *shtiblekh* was only forty-five kilometers, a typical distance for minor local courts, such as Kromołów, Kołbiel, or Chęciny. This is an important parameter, as there were also relatively small groups of Hasidim between the wars with high or extremely high median distances, which is characteristic of alternative models of territorial expansion. The tsaddik of Ostrowiec (median distance 165 kilometers), for example, applied an alternative leadership model in which his position was based not on an intimate relationship with the nearest Hasidim but rather on his fame as a scholar and mystic.[46] Similarly, the followers of a lesser tsaddik of Kapust (Kopyś; nine *shtiblekh*) were dispersed over hundreds of kilometers, with a median distance of 325 kilometers.

Given the extensive interest in R. Shapira and his teachings today (see Idel, Seeman, this volume), it is noteworthy that he seems not to have been particularly influential during his own lifetime as measured by the number of *shtiblekh* and followers. His network of *shtiblekh* was highly localized and his social influence, by this measure, surprisingly meager, especially when compared with the most powerful tsaddikim of his generation. To the extent that his writings or educational activities were significant (more on this below), this significance does not seem—according to the evidence we possess—to have translated into the social structures of traditional Hasidic institutions such as *shtiblekh*, Hasidic groups, and communal politics.

Limitations

There are some inherent limitations to the conclusions one can draw from the kinds of data I have presented here. R. Shapira would have had difficulty establishing new *shtiblekh* between the wars for demographic and circumstantial reasons unrelated to his relative skill or charisma. World War I was accompanied by mass destruction and dislocation of the Jewish community in Poland. Almost half of the Jewish population left Galicia in the first two years of the war. Thousands of Jews in central Poland were "evacuated" into the Russian interior, while many others were relocated within central Poland and lost their social and economic base. The social and spatial network of Hasidic communities was shattered in vast areas of eastern Europe. Countless synagogues, *batei midrash*, and prayer houses were destroyed. It was increasingly difficult under these conditions to find a coherent network of supporters located in one place for the creation of a *shtibl*.

According to contemporary testimonies, the proportion of Hasidim among Polish Jews seems to have decreased to as little as 20 percent during this period, an effect that was even more pronounced in large cities. According to one of the chroniclers, "The Hasidic movement was not very popular between the wars. Barely a trace of its former presence was left."[47] This decline was quite rapid; Hasidism had been the dominant social force in many areas of eastern Europe before the war.[48] This helps to explain the widespread sense of crisis in the Hasidic world at that time. No matter how skilled or charismatic their leaders, emerging groups such as Piaseczno would have had little chance to catch up with long-existing groups whose surviving *shtiblekh* dated from the nineteenth century.

Given these realities, interbellum communities necessarily lacked some of the homogeneity and coherence of their prewar predecessors, contributing to the rise of "à la carte Hasidism" even among the remaining faithful. Many urban Hasidim were no longer devoted to a single *shtibl* or group, and many participants in the *shtiblekh* were now actually non-Hasidim. These were, of course, related phenomena. "Hasidim and half-Hasidim, followers of Mizrahi [a religious Zionist party], and followers of Agudah [an Orthodox party]," writes one observer, "were able to pray side by side."[49] It became easier for Piaseczno Hasidim to pray with other groups and simultaneously more common to attract congregants who were only loosely affiliated to the group with whom a given *shtibl* was identified. Taken together, the postwar demographic shift, the crisis of Hasidism in general, and the rise of "à la carte Hasidism" make social historical measures such as "number of *shtiblekh*" or median distance from the dwelling place of the tsaddik less illustrative than when they were applied to Hasidic groups of one or two generations earlier. More important, these factors also help to explain the social limitations new Hasidic groups and their leaders, such as R. Shapira, had to face while trying to develop their social visibility at the time of the Great War and in its aftermath. These factors do not just represent a methodological limitation to my study, in other words, but also illustrate difficulties in public activity that R. Shapira and others had to face.

At the same time, we should not overlook the new avenues for success that opened up for twentieth-century Hasidim. We must consider, for example, the undeniable influence of the *Da'at Moshe* yeshiva that R. Shapira founded in 1923. At the peak of its popularity, more than three hundred students would study there.[50] It was, in fact, the second-largest yeshiva in Warsaw, superseded only by the yeshiva of the Ger Hasidim.[51] This was a novel and potentially ambivalent development. Shaul Stampfer has shown that Hasidim were resistant to the idea of yeshiva education throughout the nineteenth century. Only a small number of Hasidic yeshivot were in existence by the end of the nineteenth century, and all of these were closed during World War I. It was only when several of the yeshivot reopened and experienced a rich regrowth after the war that the idea of yeshiva education for Hasidic youth really took hold.[52]

For the Hasidic world, this represented a radically new situation, in which a *rosh yeshivah* (head of school) became an alternate and possibly subversive source of authority to the tsaddik and his dynasty. In the late twentieth century, this fragmentation of power indeed resulted in several heads of yeshivot challenging the traditional father-to-son succession of Hasidic leadership.[53] Although this was not yet the case in R. Shapira's day, R. Shapira clearly derived social influence from his role as one of the more successful Hasidic educators and the head of a sizable yeshiva. Evidence includes the position he was given at various rabbinical gatherings, fundraising campaigns organized on behalf of his yeshiva, and attention given to him by the Jewish media.[54] The Warsaw-based middle-class daily *Unzer Leben*, co-edited by Elchanan Zeitlin and Lazar Kahn, paid disproportionate attention to the activities of R. Shapira and his yeshiva. Thus, even though R. Shapira did not have a large number of full-fledged followers or *shtiblekh*, he does seem to have gained influence beyond what might have been expected for a traditional leader of a relatively small Hasidic group.

Toward Counter-Reformation

Given these realities, what can we say about the impact of the social, cultural, and political context on the shape and activities of interbellum

Hasidic communities, including Piaseczno? How can we accurately distinguish Hasidic life during this period from its golden age in the nineteenth century? And how can this context help us to better understand R. Shapira himself, his life, ideas, and activities?

As we have seen, the crisis unleashed by World War I had demographic, material/economic, and ideological dimensions. The loosening of social norms, a growing tolerance for hybrid positions, limited loyalty, and behavior teetering on the border between the Hasidic and secular worlds all became possible and even widespread, with increasing numbers of "cold Hasidim," "half-Hasidim," Hasidim who did not visit their tsaddik, and Hasidim who adopted an "à la carte" attitude.[55] Many of the writings and activities of the Piaseczner Rebbe may be seen as responding to these phenomena and to increasingly fluid forms of social identification (Seeman, this volume). His call for creating Hasidic confraternities that would revitalize participation in the Hasidic group by recalling the "founding fathers" of the movement is just one example. As Leshem (this volume) emphasizes, "it is important to understand that his work [of planning the fraternities] was related to the deterioration of the Hasidic movement."

By this call to "return to the sources," R. Shapira and some other contemporary leaders both diagnosed the crisis and attempted to resolve it (see Evan-Mayse, this volume). This might even be described as a kind of Hasidic "counter-reformation," as it bears numerous parallels to the paradigmatic case of an organized, militant—and successful—response to the crisis of a once-dominant religious formation.[56] Sometimes this took the form of political activism meant to protect or revitalize the community. Political activity had already constituted a form of Hasidism's engagement with modernity in the nineteenth century, with several tsaddikim active as political intercessors as early as the 1820s.[57] But it was only in the interwar period that Hasidism entered the stage of mass electoral politics, with thousands of followers involved in political activism and tsaddikim as party leaders. R. Shapira became involved in the Agudat Yisrael party, but some of his Hasidim made other choices. In Warsaw in 1936, Piaseczno Hasidim, together with the followers of the tsaddikim of Sokołów, Parysów, and Radzymin, formed an anti-Agudah block.[58] In Kielce, a group of Piaseczno Hasidim led by Hillel Oberman, together with Aleksander, Radomsk, and Chęciny Hasidim, supported Mizrahi (the religious Zionists) against Agudat Yisrael and Ger.[59] The specifics of political affiliation are less important for our purposes than the fact of heightened involvement in mass political organizations as an attempt at revival under modern conditions. R. Shapira also participated in various attempts to create new institutional frameworks, including political or professional organizations.[60]

More centrally, the core of the "Hasidic counter-reformation" was educational: a defensive attempt to strengthen Hasidic self-awareness, especially among young people, while urging more effective resistance to secularizing tendencies. The tsaddik of Bobowa, R. Ben-Zion Halberstam, voiced a powerful call for this sort of cultural resistance and succeeded in recruiting numerous young followers to the network of yeshivot he established.[61] Similar work was carried out by tsaddikim of Radomsko, Ger, and Aleksander.[62] R. Shapira was also deeply involved in this educational mission. His first such enterprise, the publication of his pamphlet *Benei mahshavah tovah*, describing his plan to recruit secret Hasidic fraternities, turned out to be a failure (at least by his own estimation), but it none-theless testifies to his attempt to create new forms of engagement among highly committed young cadres of Hasidim. As mentioned above, his next major project, the Da'at Moshe yeshiva, turned out to be a major success. The spread of such Hasidic yeshivot in Poland between the wars can be compared to the Counter-Reformation efforts of Jesuit and Piarist schools in the sixteenth and seventeenth centuries.[63] As in Counter-Reformation Catholicism, a network of schools aimed at shaping groups of future elites turned out to be the key tool for responding to crisis. Da'at Moshe was certainly part of this educational vanguard.

The success of R. Shapira's new school was accompanied by the educational tracts and weekly sermons that he not only delivered on a regular basis but also prepared for publication. There was nothing new about the publication of Hasidic sermons, to be sure, but unlike his predecessors, R. Shapira wrote these sermons with a clear diagnosis of acute crisis and a goal of renewing the very fabric of Hasidic community. As Ora Wiskind-Elper has noted (this volume), "Shapira's promotion of books here can be seen as the call of the hour. The old Hasidic world is gone forever; communities have been uprooted, their faithful scattered to the winds." Renewal required a radical revaluation of old strategies. "Despite everything," she writes, "a living encounter with the tsaddikim, a rebbe, a spiritual mentor, is still possible—now, paradoxically, through the written word. This, to be sure, is a revision of traditional values suited to the modern condition."[64] Traditional magical and miracle-working elements of Hasidic life had been reduced (see Idel, this volume), while new forms of spiritual leadership, mediated by modern print media and formal educational institutions, came to the fore.[65]

The new Hasidic community that R. Shapira envisioned was to be deeply self-conscious, spiritually developed, well organized, and clearly focused on long-term goals and objectives. If we want to view him from the standpoint of later social and intellectual trends, I would argue that he was as much the forerunner of Neo-Hasidism (see Idel, this volume) as he was part of the "counter-reformation" turn toward contemporary Hasidic fundamentalism. This is evidenced by his focus on institutional aspects of new forms of Hasidic community (fraternity, yeshiva, publications as a form of virtual community), his political involvement, his educational activities, and his communal vision. R. Shapira developed an "antimodernist modernity" through the use of modern tools in defense of premodern values and modes of life, a turn that eventually gave rise to the Hasidism we know today.

Conclusions

Though he was neither the most important tsaddik of his time nor even the only tsaddik active in the insignificant town of Piaseczno, R. Shapira distinguished himself through his penetrating diagnosis of the crisis in the Hasidic community and his tireless efforts toward revival. In this sense, his ideas and activities heralded what later Hasidic leaders would attempt: institutional revival and self-organization, a new emphasis on education and political activism, the creation of virtual community via effective use of mass media, and spiritual awakening. He also provides a representative example of the new emerging form of Hasidic leadership, which was based not only on a core group of followers but, increasingly, on the educational authority of the head of the yeshiva. It seems right, therefore, that his innovative writings have increasingly become the focus of both scholarly and popular interest. In this sense, R. Shapira is a fascinating example of a minor tsaddik but a major Hasidic innovator, who long after his death became one of the most prominent figures of Polish Hasidism.[66]

Notes

I am most grateful to the editors of this volume, Don Seeman, Ariel Evan Mayse, and Daniel Reiser, for their kind offer to include my contribution to this volume, then their patience, and finally, their outstanding work on making this piece readable. I also immensely appreciate their many queries, comments, and critiques, which allowed me to sharpen and clarify the article and its thesis.

1. My programmatic introduction to the anti-elitist, egalitarian study of Hasidism is to be found in Marcin Wodziński, *Hasidism: Key Questions* (New York: Oxford University Press, 2018), xxi–xxxi; much of this essay is based on ideas and interpretations offered in this volume. For an overview of the state of research on Hasidism more generally, see the bibliographical essays in David Biale et al., *Hasidism: A New History* (Princeton: Princeton University Press, 2017), 813–46; David Biale, "Hasidism," in *Oxford Bibliographies in Jewish Studies*, ed. Naomi Seidman (New York: Oxford University Press, 2015); Moshe Rosman, "Changing the Narrative of the History of Hasidism," in *Hasidic Studies: Essays in History and Gender*, ed. Ada Rapoport-Albert (Liverpool: Littman Library of Jewish Civilization, 2018), 1–19. See also Marcin Wodziński, "*Ad fontes*: Introduction," in *Studying Hasidism: Sources, Methods, Perspectives*, ed. Marcin Wodziński (New Brunswick: Rutgers University Press, 2019), 1–17.

2. Unofficial reports gave an even higher number of 686 Jews in Piaseczno in 1856, which would comprise 56 percent of the town's population. See Archiwum Główne Akt Dawnych (henceforth: AGAD), collection: Centralne Władze Wyznaniowe (henceforth: CWW), file no. 1761, pp. 159–209. For the general history of Piaseczno and its Jewish population, see Tadeusz Jan Żmudziński, *Piaseczno, miasto królewskie i narodowe, 1429–1933*, vol. 1, *Od XX. Mazowieckich do odrodzenia Polski* (Piaseczno: Zarząd Miasta Piaseczna, 1933); J. Antoniewicz, ed., *Studia i materiały do dziejów Piaseczna i powiatu piaseczyńskiego* (Warsaw, 1973); Ewa Bagieńska and Włodzimierz Bagieński, *Szkice z dziejów miasta Piaseczna* (Piaseczno: Oficyna Księgarska Mucha-Uchmanowicz, 2001); Ewa Bagieńska and Włodzimierz Bagieński, *Drugie szkice z dziejów Piaseczna i okolic* (Piaseczno: Oficyna Księgarska Mucha-Uchmanowicz, 2008).

3. AGAD, CWW, file no. 1761, pp. 4–266; Archiwum miasta Warszawy, Oddział w Grodzisku, collection: Magistrat m. Piaseczna, file no. 16 (copy in Central Archives for the History of the Jewish People, HM3675).

4. See AGAD, collection: Komisja Rządowa Spraw Wewnętrznych, file no. 6643, folio 144. See also Archiwum miasta Warszawy, Oddział w Grodzisku, collection: Magistrat m. Piaseczna, file no. 155 (copy in Central Archives for the History of the Jewish People, HM3680).

5. See Archive of the YIVO Institute for Jewish Research, RG27, Eliyahu Guttmacher (1796–1874), box 12, folders 643–44. Ten *kvitlekh* represent some 5 percent of the Jewish families of Piaseczno. For more on this, see Marcin Wodziński, *Historical Atlas of Hasidism*, cartography Waldemar Spallek (Princeton: Princeton University Press, 2018), 95–103.

6. See Regina Lilientalowa, *Pisma etnograficzne*, ed. Piotr Grącikowski (Kraków and Budapest: Austeria, forthcoming).

7. AGAD, CWW, file no. 1457, p. 579.

8. Ibid.

9. For a broader analysis of this stage of Hasidic communal development and the special role of the fight for rabbinical position, see Marcin Wodziński, *Hasidism and Politics: The Kingdom of Poland, 1815–1864* (Oxford: Littman Library of Jewish Civilization, 2013), 233–40.

10. See David Assaf, " 'Money for Household Expenses': Economic Aspects of the Hasidic Courts," in *Studies in the History of the Jews in Old Poland*, ed. Adam Teller (Jerusalem: Magnes, 1998), 14–50; and David Assaf, *The Regal Way: The Life and Times of Rabbi Israel of Ruzhin*, trans. David Lauvish (Stanford: Stanford University Press, 2002), 285–309 on *pidyonot* and *ma'amadot* (forms of financial contribution by Hasidim to their tsaddik) and on the financial aspects of the Hasidic courts more generally.

11. See Archiwum Państwowe w Łodzi, collection: Akta miasta Łodzi, file no. 150–51; collection: Anteriora Piotrkowskiego Rządu Gubernialnego, file no. 2491. For the case of R. Shalom of Bełz, who was forced into bankruptcy by his teacher, R. Ya'akov Yitzhak Horowitz of Lublin, so that he would become a rabbi, see Moshe Menahem hakohen Walden, *Sefer Nifle'ot ha-rabi* (Bnei Brak, 2005), no. 33.

12. See *Pinkas ha-kehilot: Polin*, vol. 4, *Varshah veha-galil* (Jerusalem: Yad Vashem, 1989), 346–47.

13. For essential biographical information on this tsaddik, see Yitzhak Alfasi, ed., *Entsiklopediyah la-hasidut: Ishim* (Jerusalem: Mosad Ha-rav Kook, 2000), 2:597; Yitzhak Alfasi, *Ha-hasidut mi-dor le-dor* (Jerusalem: Makhon Da'at Yosef, 1995), 394; Avraham I. Bromberg, *Mi-gedolei ha-hasidut: Ha-admorim le-veit Vurke ve-Amshinov* (Jerusalem: Mosad Bet Hillel, 1982), 184. See also Yekhiel Kamiel, "Mayn ershte nesiye tsum reben," in *Seyfer kalushin: Gehaylikt der khorev gevorener kehile*, ed. Arye Shamri et al. (Tel Aviv, 1961), 287.

14. See Alfasi, *Entsiklopediyah la-hasidut*, 3:73–74.

15. See Yekhiel Yeshaia Trunk, *Poyln: Zikhroynes un bilder* (New York: Farlag Undzer Tsayt, 1949), 4:155.

16. I am indebted to Daniel Reiser for bringing to my attention documents related to the houses possessed by R. Shapira in Piaseczno. For a brief biography of R. Shapira, see the introduction to this volume.

17. On this phenomenon, see Samuel C. Heilman, "What's in the Name?: The Dilemma of Title and Geography for Contemporary Hasidism," *Jewish History* 27 (2013): 221–40.

18. For more on the metropolization of the Hasidic leadership in the time of the Great War, see Wodziński, *Hasidism*, 259–65.

19. See also Marcin Wodziński and Uriel Gellman, "Towards a New Geography of Hasidism," *Jewish History* 26 (2013): 171–99.

20. For such comments on the settlement of Ya'akov Yitzhak Horowitz in Lublin, see, e.g., Moshe Menahem Walden, *Nifle'ot ha-rabi* (Warsaw, 1911), 13, 75,

86; Tsevi Meir Rabinowicz, *Bein Pshiskha le-Lublin* (Jerusalem: Kesharim, 1997), 110–12. For documents on the opposition to Yitzhak Meir Alter's activities in Warsaw, see Zofia Borzymińska, "Sprawa Rabiego Icchaka Meira Altera," *Biuletyn Żydowskiego Instytutu Historycznego* 52 (2001): 367–77; *Hasidism in the Kingdom of Poland, 1815–1867: Historical Sources in the Polish State Archives* (Kraków: Austeria, 2011), 429–39.

21. See, e.g., Efraim Shedletski, "Dem rebes 'letst-gelt,'" in *Seyfer Minsk-Mazovietsk: Yizker bukh nokh der khorev-gevorener kehile Minsk-Mazovietsk*, ed. Efraim Shedletski (Jerusalem, 1977), 157–60.

22. Ita Kalish, *A rabishe haym in amolikn Poyln* (Warsaw: Gmina Wyznaniowa Żydowska w Warszawie, 2009), 94. There is an inaccurate English translation in Ita Kalish, "Life in a Hassidic Court in Russian Poland toward the End of the Nineteenth Century," *YIVO Annual of Jewish Social Science* 13 (1965): 277.

23. Yehiel Poznanski, "Zikhroynes fun der fergangenhayt," in *Sefer-izkor li-kehilat Radomsk veha-sevivah*, ed. L. Losh (Tel Aviv, 1967), 58–59.

24. Pinhas Tsitron, *Sefer Kielts: Toledot kehilat Kielts mi-yom hivasdah ve-ad hurbanah* (Tel Aviv, 1956/1957), 176.

25. See Aharon Zeev Aescoly [Eshkholi], *Ha-hasidut be-Polin*, ed. David Assaf (Jerusalem: Magnes, 1998), 126–27.

26. On modern strategies for defending premodern values in Hasidism, see Marcin Wodziński, "How Modern Is an Anti-Modernist Movement?: The Emergence of Hasidic Politics in Congress Poland," *AJS Review* 31, no. 2 (2007): 221–40; Wodziński, *Hasidism and Politics*, 165–265.

27. On traditional relations between the Hasidic movement and the Jewish community and its institutions, see Shmuel Ettinger, "Hasidism and the *Kahal* in Eastern Europe," in *Hasidism Reappraised*, ed. Ada Rapoport-Albert (London: Littman Library of Jewish Civilization, 1996), 63–75; Yohanan Petrovsky-Shtern, "Hasidism, Havurot, and the Jewish Street," *Jewish Social Studies* 10, no. 2 (2004): 20–54; Marcin Wodziński, "The Hasidic 'Cell': The Organization of Hasidic Groups at the Level of the Community," *Scripta Judaica Cracoviensia* 10 (2012): 111–22.

28. For examples of accounts stressing the collective nature of interest in the tsaddik visiting the town, which typically involved all Jewish and non-Jewish segments of the local community, see, e.g., Israel Joshua Singer, *Of a World That Is No More: A Tender Memoir* (New York: Vanguard, 1970), 135–36; Martin D. Kushner, *From Russia to America: A Modern Odyssey* (Philadelphia: Dorrance, 1969), 10–12.

29. See Isaac Even, "Chassidism in the New World," in *The Jewish Communal Register of New York City, 1917–1918* (New York, 1918), 341–42.

30. This phenomenon, in different contexts and in its radical form, has been called "à la carte religion" or "religious *bricolage*" and is one of the most typical phenomena of contemporary religious life; see Reginald Bibby, *Fragmented Gods: The Poverty and Potential of Religion in Canada* (Toronto: Irwin, 1987).

31. See Ben-Zion Gold, *The Life of Jews in Poland before the Holocaust* (Lincoln: University of Nebraska Press, 2007), 103–16.

32. Ibid., 91, 93.

33. See, e.g., Shaul Miler, *Dobromil: Zikhroynes fun a shtetl in Galitsye in di yohren 1890 biz 1907* (New York, 1980), 11; Joseph Margoshes, *A World Apart: A Memoir of Jewish Life in Nineteenth Century Galicia*, trans. Ron Margolis and Ira Robinson (Boston: Academic Studies Press, 2008), 159.

34. For more on this, see Wodziński, *Historical Atlas of Hasidism*, 115–37. See also Wodziński, "Space and Spirit: On Boundaries, Hierarchies, and Leadership in Hasidism," *Journal of Historical Geography* 53 (2016): 63–74.

35. See Wodziński, *Historical Atlas of Hasidism*, 115–37. Representativeness at the level of ca. 70 percent, more than adequate for any analysis, has been confirmed by several control data.

36. See Wodziński, *Historical Atlas of Hasidism*, 118–19.

37. For a general analysis of limitations of memorial books as a source for historical research, see Monika Adamczyk-Garbowska, Adam Kopciowski, and Andrzej Trzciński, "Księgi pamięci jako źródło wiedzy o historii, kulturze i Zagładzie polskich Żydów," in *Tam był kiedyś mój dom . . . Księgi pamięci gmin żydowskich*, ed. Adamczyk-Garbowska, Kopciowski, and Trzciński (Lublin: Wydawnictwo Uniwersytetu Marii Curie Skłodowskiej, 2009), 11–86; see also Avraham Wein, "Memorial Books as a Source for Research into the History of Jewish Communities in Europe," *Yad Vashem Studies* 9 (1973): 255–72; Jack Kugelmass and Jonathan Boyarin, "Introduction," in *From a Ruined Garden: The Memorial Books of Polish Jewry*, 2nd ed., ed. Kugelmass and Boyarin (Bloomington: Indiana University Press, 1993), 1–48. The newest bibliography of the memorial books is to be found in Adam Kopciowski, ed., *Jewish Memorial Books: A Bibliography* (Lublin: Wydawnictwo Uniwersytetu Marii Curie Skłodowskiej, 2008). Many of the books are available online at http://yizkor.nypl.org.

38. I. B. Alterman, ed., *Megiles Gritseh* (Tel Aviv, 1955), 31; Meir Shimon Geshuri, "Khsidim shtiblekh," in *Seyfer Radom*, ed. Yitzhak Perlow and Alfred Lipson (Tel Aviv, 1961–63), 46; Mordekhai V. Bernshtayn, ed., *Pinkes Zhirardov, Amshinov un Viskit; izker-bukh tsu der geshikhte fun di kehiles: Zhirardov, Amshinov un Viskit; fun zayer oyfkum biz zayer khurbn durkh di natsis, yimakh shemam* (Buenos Aires, 1961), 93, 192–96.

39. See Tsitron, *Sefer Kielts*, 109.

40. The interviews have been recently digitized and are now available online; see https://dlc.library.columbia.edu/lcaaj.

41. See, for example, Arye Mencher, ed., *Sefer Pshemishl* (Tel Aviv, 1964), 141; Eliezer Sharvit, ed., *Sanok: Sefer zikaron li-kehilat Sanok veha-sevivah* (Tel Aviv, 1970), 103–108.

42. See, for example, Arthur Ruppin, *Pirkei hayyai* (Tel Aviv, 1944), 1:217–19.

43. See, for example, Leo Baeck Institute Archives, MM93, pp. 160–61.

44. See, e.g., Zeev Rabinowicz and Nahman Tamir, eds., *Pinsk: Sefer edut ve-zikaron li-kehilat Pinsk-Karlin* (Tel Aviv, 1966), 1:352–53, on the lesser dynasty of Horodok; David Shtokfish, ed., *Sefer Pshitik: Matsevet-zikaron li-kehilah yehudit* (Tel Aviv, 1973), 45, on the tsaddik of Opoczno.

45. See Meir Shimon Geshuri, ed., *Undzer shtot Volbrom* (Tel Aviv, 1962), 197; Hayim Volnerman, Aviezer Burshtin, and Meir Shimon Geshuri, ed., *Sefer Oshpitsin* (Jerusalem, 1977), 95.

46. On R. Meir Yehiel Halshtok of Ostrowiec, famous for his intellectual sharpness and ascetic practices, see M. Grosman, "Zikhroynes fun Ostrovtse," in *Ostrovtse* (Buenos Aires, 1949), 43–44. For a more extensive analysis of these other models, see Wodziński, *Hasidism*, 190–97.

47. Mordechai V. Bernshtayn, "Di geshikhte fun Yidn in Pulav," in *Yisker-bukh Pulav*, ed. Mordechai V. Bernshtayn (New York, 1964), 31.

48. On demography of interwar Hasidism, see Wodziński, *Hasidism*, 156–58.

49. Menakhem Baynvol, "Basey-medresh, khsidim shtiblekh un politishe organizatsye," in *Kehilat Sherpts: Sefer zikaron*, ed. Efraim Talmi (Wloka) (Tel Aviv 1959), 168.

50. We do not know enough about the yeshiva beyond the fact that it was a major educational success. For the basic information, see Nehemia Polen, *The Holy Fire: The Teachings of Rabbi Kalonymus Kalman Shapira, the Rebbe of the Warsaw Ghetto* (Northvale, NJ: Jason Aronson, 1994), 6; Daniel Reiser, Introduction, in Kalonymus Kalman Shapira, *Sermons from the Years of Rage* [in Hebrew], ed. Daniel Reiser, 2 vols. (Jerusalem: Herzog Academic College, 2017), 14, 337. For the number of students see, e.g., *Unzer-Ekspres*, January 11, 1932, 7. Interesting information on the fundraising activities, publicity, and educational practices can be found in the Jewish press of interwar Warsaw, e.g., *Der Moment*, May 27, 1927, 10; *Haynt*, August 7, 1937, 11; *Unzer-Ekspres*, September 16, 1931, 5; January 11, 1932, 7; April 21, 1933, 7; February 27, 1935, 9; March 1, 1936, 10; February 4, 1937, 7 (all available at Historical Jewish Press).

51. Shimon Huberband, *Kiddush Hashem: Jewish Religious and Cultural Life During the Holocaust* (New York: Yeshiva University Press, 1987), 175–76.

52. As noted by Shaul Stampfer, creation of Hasidic yeshivot was usually an expression of a consciousness of crisis. See Shaul Stampfer, "Hasidic Yeshivot in Inter-War Poland," in Stampfer, *Families, Rabbis, and Education: Traditional Jewish Society in Nineteenth-Century Eastern Europe* (Oxford: Littman Library of Jewish Civilization, 2010), 252–74.

53. On such a conflict in the Bobov dynasty, see Samuel C. Heilman, *Who Will Lead Us?: The Story of Five Hasidic Dynasties in America* (Oakland: University of California Press, 2017), 96–151.

54. See, e.g., *Unzer-Ekspres*, September 16, 1931, 5; January 11, 1932, 7; March 1, 1936, 10; February 14, 1936; February 16, 1936; February 4, 1937, 7.

55. See Yitshok Zandman, "Gostininer Idn," in *Pinkes Gostynin: Yisker bukh*, ed. Y. M. Biderman (New York, 1960), 174; Aaron Diamant, "Kolbushov a mokm khsides," in *Pinkes Kolbushov*, ed. Y. M. Biderman (New York, 1971), 389; "Khsidim un misnagdim shtiblekh," in *Sefer Bialah-Podlaskah*, ed. M. Y. Feigenbaum (Tel Aviv, 1961), 260.

56. For a broader explanation of the parallels between fundamentalization of Hasidism at the beginning of the twentieth century and the Catholic Counter-Reformation, see Wodziński, *Hasidism*, 269–75. For more on the Counter-Reformation itself, see, e.g., Robert Bireley, *The Refashioning of Catholicism, 1450–1700: A Reassessment of the Counter-Reformation* (Washington, DC: Red Globe, 1999).

57. See Wodziński, *Hasidism and Politics*, esp. ch. 5.

58. See *Haynt*, August 7, 1937, 11. On controversy between Ger and Piaseczno, see also *Unzer Leben*, September 16, 1931, 5.

59. See Tsitron, *Sefer Kielts*, 109. The wider context of this political conflict is unknown to us.

60. See, e.g., *Der Moment*, May 27, 1927, 10.

61. See, e.g., Yehudah Kinderman, "Khsides in Ushpitsin," in *Sefer Ushpitsin*, 261.

62. On this, see Moria Herman, *Ha-yahas li-venei no'ar ba-hasidut bi-tekufah she-beyn milhamot ha-olam: Ha-hidushim ha-hagutayim veha-ma'asiyim be-hasidut Polin li-venei ha-no'ar ki-teguvah le-azivat ha-dat 1914–1939* (PhD diss., Bar Ilan University, 2014).

63. Bireley, *The Refashioning of Catholicism*, 121–46.

64. Ibid.

65. See Daniel Reiser, *Imagery Techniques in Modern Jewish Mysticism*, trans. Eugene D. Matansky (Berlin: De Gruyter, 2018), 191–94. See also Moshe Idel, "The Rebbe of Piaseczno, or Two Lines in Hasidism," this volume.

66. In Piaseczno, however, few traces of R. Shapira remain. The rundown building of the former synagogue was demolished and turned into a parking lot in 1978. Except for a fragment of one brick wall, R. Shapira's house and his prayer house on 15 Niecała Street no longer exist. At the cemetery, only several dozen tombstones survive. Former prayer houses at 1 and 4 Nadarzyńska Street are still standing but bear no traces of their past function. Only the small building housing the nineteenth-century mikveh commemorates its former function with a modest plaque. For a brief description of the Jewish sights in Piaseczno, see https://sztetl.org.pl/en/towns/p/593-piaseczno; http://www.studnia.org/piaseczno/historia.htm; accessed: 12 Iyar 5779. For more, see Marcin Wodziński, *Chasydzki szlak Mazowsza* (Warsaw: Fundacja Chai, 2019), 86–87.

2

The Rebbe of Piaseczno

Between Two Trends in Hasidism

MOSHE IDEL

Kalonymus Kalmish Shapira, known as the Rebbe of Piaseczno, has become more closely identified with the Holocaust. He experienced it firsthand, reflected on its horrors and reacted to it from *inside* the catastrophe until he was killed with many of his followers. His sermons from the Warsaw Ghetto, originally published as *Esh kodesh*, represent one of the few attempts to understand the problem of suffering in real time, from the midst of the Holocaust, in light of kabbalistic and Hasidic traditions. Sermons delivered orally in Yiddish and then committed to writing in Hebrew were probably the most important genre by which Hasidic leaders communicated with their disciples. Like many other forms of Jewish mystical writing, these sermons tend to demonstrate a certain "conceptual fluidity," less concerned with intellectual coherence than with articulating a particular way of life or coping with perennial human questions (see Reiser, Seeman, this volume). Daniel Reiser's new critical edition of *Derashot mi-shenot ha-za'am* (*Sermons from the Years of Rage*) dramatically illustrates the process of ongoing elaboration, hesitation, and thematic development that accompanied these sermons during the last three years of R. Shapira's life, before the liquidation of the ghetto and the murder of its inhabitants.[1]

Despite their obvious importance, however, these ghetto sermons should not be allowed to eclipse R. Shapira's distinctive prewar literary corpus, which was devoted to a Hasidic revival that is reminiscent, I will argue, of modern Neo-Hasidism. Unlike sermons, whose themes are to some extent forced upon the writer by circumstance or by the liturgical calendar, some of these prewar tracts focus in a systematic way on questions of Hasidic education, renewal, and spiritual practice that can be difficult to discern in the ghetto sermons.[2] My goal in this chapter is therefore to situate some of the ideas and ideals described in these earlier works within the historical context of Hasidism and kabbalah more broadly. Since most of these prewar tracts are devoted to the training of younger disciples rather than accomplished Hasidic adepts, it is possible that there were other dimensions of Rabbi Shapira's teaching that he did not commit to writing.

Between Ecstasy/Prophecy and Magic

Though considered the founder of Hasidism, Israel Baal Shem Tov did not operate as a tsaddik, despite the fact that he embraced a mystical-magical model.[3] He did have several followers, but he was best known in popular circles as a wonder worker, popular healer, or magician, as we learn from the famous hagiography *Shivehei ha-Besht*. However, it is possible to discern in the testimonies about his life—some of them legendary, to be sure—two types of activities: the preaching of an intense religious life on the one hand and his profession as a magician on the other. Both seem to be related to the historical Baal Shem Tov, despite many exaggerations in the available testimonies. The two types of activities, different though they are, should not be understood as wholly distinct, as it is possible to detect throughout his teachings the vestiges of magical terminology inherited from the Kabbalah of Moshe Cordovero and his followers, which deals with the process of drawing down supernal power and distributing it to the community.[4] In my opinion, we should speak of a "mystical-magical model" alongside the more practical magical activities related to the Baal Shem Tov's profession.[5] The mystical element, which can have ecstatic valences, is expressed in some cases by the term *prophecy*, which was already common among Jewish writers from the Middle Ages and from time to time in Hasidism.[6] It is my opinion that some of the most extreme testimonies concerning the Besht's dual forms of activity were downplayed in Hasidic writings from the generation following his death, due to controversies with the mitnagdim, whose main target of criticism in the 1770s was the Besht himself.[7] They resurfaced only after the 1790s, when Hasidic masters felt more secure. The publication of the Besht's hagiography and the extreme mystical teachings preserved by Aharon Hakohen of Apta are both examples of his new confidence.[8]

It is undeniable that the development of Hasidism as a movement was predicated on the emergence of the institution of the holy man, the *tsaddik,* or "righteous one," as the leader of a specific group who cultivates an intense religious life but is also responsible for helping his constituency with more concrete matters. Operating between heaven and earth, a pontifical or Janus figure, the Hasidic leader was conceived of as essential for the well-being of his group, since he was deemed to constitute the channel, or pipeline, for the descent of divine power, which he distributed after ascending to the source of power.[9] This model entails devotion to the tsaddik, pilgrimages to the Hasidic courts on the Jewish holidays or other occasions, financial contributions, and the emergence of a new and important dimension to the figure of the rebbe: that of spiritual and economical counselor, combined in some important instances with magical qualities. Rabbi Israel Baal Shem Tov, his grandson Moshe Chaim Ephraim of Sdilkev (Sudylkov),[10] Elimelekh Weisblum of Lizhensk,[11] his two main disciples, Israel ben Shabbatai Hopstein, known as the Maggid of Kozhnits,[12] and Jacob Isaac Halevi Horowitz, the Seer of Lublin,[13] and, in a more theoretical manner, Kalonymus Kalman Halevi Epstein of Kraków, are only outstanding examples of this wonder-worker model of the tsaddik. The practice of blessing by the Hasidic leader was another important facet of this magical activity, which has continued through most of the main phases of Hasidism to this very day.[14] Unlike regular magicians, who developed a transient clientele, the Hasidic rabbis created a generally consistent group of followers, or a "court," who sought both spiritual guidance and material blessing.

Alongside this well-known wonder-working or magical model, however, the landscape of Hasidic leadership also included a more "spiritual" model, represented by tsaddikim such as R. Dov Baer (the Great Maggid of Mezritsh), R. Nachman of Bratslav, R. Shneur Zalman of Liady, R. Jacob Isaac of Pshiskhe (the Holy Jew), R. Menahem Mendel of Kotsk, and R. Mordechai Leiner of Izhbits, who were better known for their distinctive teachings than for their powers of blessing. The diversity and flexibility of Hasidic devotional forms allowed different tsaddikim to adopt distinctive paths and to attract Hasidim based on spiritual or intellectual proclivities as well as family affiliation. The institution of the tsaddik innovated by Hasidism and expressed in most cases by a living charismatic figure was thus more responsible than any other single factor for the continuity and diversification of Hasidism between the eighteenth and twentieth centuries.

Rabbi Shapira's place within this admittedly somewhat schematic typology of Hasidic leadership is fascinating. On the one hand, he was a direct descendent of the most magically oriented tsaddikim in Poland, whom he cites by name many times in his books. Moreover, he married a woman from the Kozhnits dynasty and was proud of his relation to the Hasidic master Israel of Kozhnits. Yet in his own leadership, he seems to have had more in common with the spiritual school or with later Neo-Hasidic figures I will mention below. He tended to emphasize spiritual guidance or techniques and to relegate some of the more magical and institutional aspects of Hasidic leadership to the margins.[15] This tendency may have begun with his father, R. Elimelekh of Grodzisk, whose books seem, on perusal, to downplay the ability of the tsaddik to draw down blessing relative to other Polish Hasidim.[16] R. Elimelekh does not, however, seem to have shared his son's strong interest in spiritual techniques or cultivation of prophecy. Careful analysis of the various factors that might have contributed to R. Shapira's model of leadership—such as his father's influence or the influence of other members of the more introversive "spiritual" school mentioned above, or indeed the maskilic critique of Hasidism with which R. Shapira would have had to contend[17]—remains an unfulfilled scholarly desideratum.

Spiritual Techniques and Prophecy

Naturally, the attenuation or even elimination of certain magical aspects of Hasidic leadership would have heightened the importance of the devoted spiritual life and the need to forge specific paths to its realization. Steps in this direction can already be found in late-thirteenth-century Kabbalah, especially in the ecstatic Kabbalah of Abraham Abulafia and his followers.[18] Such texts and were later taken up by kabbalists in early-sixteenth-century Jerusalem,[19] along with other techniques related to imagining colors in the context of letters of the divine name during prayer,[20] and in the Safedian Kabbalah of Moshe Cordovero and Hayyim Vital,[21] and thus also in early Hasidism. Some of the techniques mentioned above—Abulafia's combi-

THE REBBE OF PIASECZNO 57

nation of letters,[22] the drawing-down technique,[23] and the technique of
visualizing colors[24]—are well represented in the same major compendium
of Kabbalah, Cordovero's *Pardes rimmonim*, but the kabbalists practiced,
de facto, only the first two.[25] Kabbalists also associated prophecy with the
technique of drawing down divine influx.[26]

Despite this background, the early Hasidic masters did not forge a
detailed and widely accepted technique for the attainment of peak experience, and much of their practice was related to intensification of oral
rituals, especially prayer.[27] Though discussions of practices designated as
hitbodedut, hishtavut, devekut, hitpashut ha-gashmiyut, or *hitbatlut* (soli-
tary concentration, equanimity, cleaving, divestment of corporeality, and
self-nullification, respectively) stemming from earlier kabbalistic sources[28]
abound in Hasidic writings, they were not elaborated into a stable mystical
path. Few instructions from Hasidic works have been preserved and claims
of having achieved prophecy were also extremely rare.

Nevertheless, Rabbi Shapira was certainly aware of spiritual techniques, including visualization.[29] He was acquainted, for example, with
Moshe Cordovero's book and twice quotes a passage about visualizing
colors, though he probably did not adopt it.[30] Parallels between Abraham
Abulafia's discussions of prophecy and spiritual techniques and those in R.
Shapira's writings have also been suggested.[31] More specifically, in his study
of Shapira, Ron Wachs has pointed out a specific parallel to ecstatic Kabbalah, on which I would like to elaborate.[32] Wachs refers to a passage from
Shapira's *Benei mahshavah tovah* (see Leshem, this volume)[33] describing a
person's visualization of himself standing before the divine throne, which
may be compared with two passages from prophetic Kabbalah: one from
Yehudah Albotini's *Sullam ha-aliyyah* and another, shorter passage from
Abulafia's *Hayyei ha-olam ha-ba*.[34] All three sources use the verb *tsayyer*
to refer to the exercise of envisioning oneself standing in the presence of
supernal beings.[35] However, while Albotini's book, written in Jerusalem
at the beginning of the sixteenth century, is extant only in a few Eastern
manuscripts not available in Europe,[36] Abulafia's book is extant in dozens
of manuscripts, including some dated to eighteenth-century Poland,[37] a
few of which belonged to the libraries of Hasidic rabbis.[38] Moreover, an
important figure in the late eighteenth century, Pinchas Eliyahu Horowitz,
who belonged to the camp of the mitnagdim, wrote a short commentary
on this book in his youth, a copy of which is still extant.[39]

Abulafia's *Hayyei ha-olam ha-ba* is a detailed description of a technique for attaining prophecy. It begins with a poem whose first line is:

"Send a created hand in order to attain prophecy."[40] In this book, various forms of the root *TSYR*, referring to visualization, occur no fewer than two hundred times.[41] For example:

> Prepare your true thoughts to visualize [*le-tzayyer*] the Name, may he be blessed, and with it the supernal angels. And visualize them in your heart as if they were human beings standing and sitting around you, and you were among them as a messenger. . . . And after you have visualized this entirely, prepare your mind and your heart to understand the thoughts whose matters are brought to you by the letters you have thought of in your heart.[42]

There is no doubt that this is an outstanding case of active imagination. Moreover, according to this book of Abulafia's, the final aim of the mystical path is to attain a state of union with God. No drawing down of divine power is mentioned in this context.[43]

However, while in this passage from Albotini's book one has to imagine oneself sitting on high—indubitably reflecting the influence of Abulafia—Abulafia himself repeatedly speaks about standing before God,[44] as does Shapira, bringing Abulafia's and Shapira's books much closer to each other. Moreover, another passage in Shapira's book also seems to be close to Abulafia: "In a flash you will see yourself standing before his glory, amidst the great camp of the fiery angels; you are one of them."[45] Thus, we may speak of at least four instances in this one small book (Shapira's *Benei mahshavah tovah*) that deal with a type of visualization close to Abulafia's. This means that it is difficult to separate the ideal of prophecy from the techniques that may induce it, according to both the kabbalist and the Hasidic master. Reiser has also pointed out a possible impact of Abulafia's visualization of the divine name on Shapira.[46] It should be mentioned that Abulafia's attitude toward divine names was related to a critique of magical uses of those names.[47]

Shapira's emphasis on prophetic experiences is reminiscent of the prophetic ideals cultivated by Abraham Abulafia, and to a certain extent also by Joseph ben Shalom Ashkenazi.[48] These ideals could, at least in principle, have been known to a kabbalist and Hasidic master in the twentieth century, especially via Hayyim Vital's influential *Sha'arei kedushah*, which deals with visualization and prophecy.[49] A few passages influenced by this treatise can be discerned in early Hasidism.[50] A description of

prophecy that is strongly related to Abulafia's Kabbalah and was probably directly influenced by *Hayyei ha-olam ha-ba* appears in a popular
Hasidic commentary on the Pentateuch entitled *Or ha-ganuz la-tsaddikim*,
by Aharon Hakohen of Apta. In this commentary, only the prophetic/
ecstatic experience is mentioned, without any magical implication.[51] This
is the context in which we should view the efforts of Shapira in his early
treatise *Benei mahshavah tovah* to create a small elite group of Hasidism
with prophetic pretensions (see Wodziński, Leshem) whom he refers to
as *benei aliyah*,[52] which is reminiscent of Abulafia's studying with his
companions in Messina in the early 1280s.[53] While it would be overly
simplistic to reduce Shapira's interest in spiritual techniques and prophecy
to an assumed encounter with one specific book, the impact of Abulafia's
discussions of prophecy and visualization on Shapira, whether direct or
indirect, seems to have been significant.

Interesting parallels to Shapira's concern with techniques and prophecy
can be seen in Gershom Scholem's practicing Abulafia's techniques while
writing his first PhD thesis in Munich in 1919, and in David Hakohen
(Hanazir)'s interest in these techniques during the same period.[54] Though
Gershom Scholem and David Hakohen knew each other since 1923, their
interest in these techniques started somewhat earlier and probably independently. I assume that Shapira was unaware of these parallel interests
of his contemporaries, and unlike them, he never mentions the prophetic
thirteenth-century kabbalist or any of his writings, though a few of them
had already been in print for several generations due to Aharon Jellinek's
editions. These seem to be manifestations of a much more longstanding,
if somewhat vaguely conceived, interest in prophecy in Jewish thought,
especially in the Ashkenazi provinces.[55]

I wonder whether, in the case of Shapira, we can separate the initial
yearning for prophecy from the subsequent search for a technique for
attaining it. Perhaps the two originate in the same book: Abulafia's *Hayyei
ha-olam ha-ba*.[56] Abulafia, like Shapira after him, was not interested in
magic at all, and, thus, Abulafia's approach is much closer to Shapira's than
to that of Hayyim Vital in *Sha'arei kedushah*. The latter wrote, in the vein
of the mystical-magical model:

> He should imagine himself as if his soul departed [from the
> body] and ascended on high, and he should visualize the
> supernal worlds as if he stood within them. And if he performs
> a *yihud*, he should ruminate on it in order to draw light and

influx by it in all the worlds and should direct [his thought]
in order to receive his share at the end as well.[57]

Let me point out, however, that the ideal of prophecy, including discussions
of visualizations and the ascent on high culminating in drawing down
divine effluence, is central to Vital's treatise. Both the drawing forth of
this vitality and the mention of the share someone receives thereof are
part of what I have called the mystical-magical model. Abulafia was much
more concerned with individual redemption or perfection by means of
intellection, following the more universalist path of the Greek, Muslim,
and Jewish philosophers.[58] The mystical-magical model is also very much
concerned with perfecting others, including the community, divinity, and
the worlds, by means of particular deeds, that is, the commandments.

To what extent this surge of interest in spiritual techniques had to do
with the visits of Swami Vivekananda to Europe and the dissemination of
forms of Yoga less than a generation before remains an open question.[59]
In any case, Hillel Zeitlin, Shapira's contemporary and compatriot, was
acquainted with Buddhism (see Seeman, this volume), as were his older
contemporary Abraham Yitzhak Hakohen Kook, who became interested in
Buddhism at the beginning of the twentieth century while still in Eastern
Europe, and Kook's companion David Hakohen.[60] It should be mentioned
that some acquaintance with Tibetan religion is evident in a Hebrew
text published in 1814, by the very same publisher as the hagiography of
the Besht.[61] We may thus surmise a more complex explanation for the
emergence of an unparalleled interest in paranormal spiritual phenomena
induced by a technique sometimes referred to as prophecy: there was
not only a feeling of independence from critiques that inhibited claims
of prophecy earlier in the history of Hasidism[62] but also a general rise in
interest in cultivation of spiritual techniques.[63]

In any case, this surge of interest in spiritual techniques and prophecy in traditional circles beyond academia, which began in the late 1920s,
reached its apex at the end of the twentieth century with the publication
of Abraham Abulafia's writings and those of his followers. The printers and
publishers rooted in traditional circles in Jerusalem were in most cases
connected to Hasidic camps. Again, one may ask whether this interest had
to do with the surge of interest in India among modern Israelis. But the
possible influence of Hindu material on twentieth-century Judaism relates
to Shapira's work only in that it contributed to the cultural ambiance of
the time; it did not influence Shapira directly, as Abulafia's book did.

On Hasidism before and after Shapira: Some Observations

The Holocaust—and the murder of almost the entire Piasezno community—coincided with the end of several decades of dramatic growth of
Hasidism in many communities in eastern Europe, especially in Poland
and in Warsaw (see Wodziński, this volume). The Ger and Aleksander
courts, in particular, were flourishing, as to a lesser extent Hasidism in
general was thriving beyond its previous boundaries. Hasidism had confronted new intellectual and social challenges, from the older Lithuanian
mitnagdim and the maskilim to the newer Bundist ideology and Zionist
movement.[64] But the various Hasidic courts managed to conquer vast
parts of the Jewish population in a relatively short period of less than
two centuries.[65] The widespread embrace of Hasidism was not limited to
abstract faith in the various tsaddikim, changing modes of prayer, and
enthusiasm for the ideal of union with God. It also involved concrete
attachment to the leading figures of Hasidism.

We can extrapolate from the immense success of the first two centuries
of the history of Hasidism, in which it attracted ever-larger segments of
the Jewish population into its orbit, to what might have happened if the
Holocaust had not violently cut off the growth of the movement. Today,
Hasidism would represent the largest religious group in Judaism. The
main effect of Holocaust was the extermination of large parts of European
Jewry, and the cruelest blow was inflicted on the members of Hasidic
groups. The Polish, Hungarian, Bukovinian, and Bessarabian forms of
Hasidism were much more severely affected than other parts of the Jewish
population in those areas. Even those who survived were dislocated and
had to rebuild everything. In other words, the Nazi and Fascist crimes
against the Jews not only inflicted genocide but changed, at least for a
while, the direction of a religious development that might have generated
a spiritual renaissance for a major part of modern Judaism. This aspect
of the Holocaust still calls for further investigation, and here I can only
delineate some of its major points.

First and foremost, the Holocaust destroyed not only the most
important demographic Jewish centers but also the most creative centers
of Jewish spirituality that had developed in the two centuries preceding
the Holocaust. This included not only the proliferating Hasidic courts but
also many forms of secularist Judaism found in centers such as Warsaw
and Odessa. This change was, unfortunately, final. The total destruction of
the many small rural centers of Hasidim, and of all its urban centers in

eastern Europe, generated a new sociology of postwar Hasidism: almost completely urban and active in the new centers of Israel, the United States, and, to a lesser degree, western Europe.

My speculation regarding the growth of Hasidism and the potential it would have had to become one of the most vital trends in modern Judaism is supported by developments that occurred after the Holocaust. Many Hasidic groups were decimated by 1944, with some actually reduced to ashes, but they reemerged, like the phoenix, in the generations after the Holocaust. Hasidism proved capable of reestablishing some of the destroyed courts in Israel, the United States, and even western Europe, and it attracted large numbers of believers. Since the 1970s, some of these groups have attracted even greater numbers. These include Satmar, Ger, Belz, Vizhnits, and Lubavitch, as well as, more recently and dramatically, the followers of Nachman of Bratslav.[66] This is evident not only from the numbers of members of these groups but also from the construction of luxurious buildings, yeshivot, and synagogues; more conspicuous involvement in public life in Israel; and the new role of Chabad emissaries (*sheluhim*) in many centers throughout the world and on numerous American university campuses. The new role played by women, as *sheluhot,* in the activities of this Hasidic branch is also significant.

More recently, the massive pilgrimages of tens of thousands to Nachman of Bratslav's tomb in Uman, Ukraine; hundreds of thousands to Meron in the Galilee, in which Hasidic groups play quite a substantial role; and huge numbers to Brooklyn, the home of the last Rabbi of Lubavitch, before and after his death, are another indication of the revival of some aspects of Hasidism on the contemporary scene. The participation of Hasidic groups in Israeli elections since 1988 and the seating of Hasidic members of the Israeli parliament in government offices have become regular phenomena. The role of Jacob Litzman as the minister of health—though he formally refuses to participate in a secular government—is a sign of the growing influence of Hasidic groups on Israeli politics since the early 1990s.

Even after the growth mentioned above, the various Hasidic groups constitute only a small part of the Jewish people, perhaps less than 5 percent.[67] However, to extrapolate again: the growth of the Hasidic population is incomparably greater in comparison to that of secular Jews, which is an aspect of the vitality of this movement. Hasidic groups have entered urban centers and started to dictate a new form of traditional life, as in the case of the Ger Hasidim in the Israeli town of Arad, with the help of the above-mentioned cabinet minister Litzman. The demonstrations of

Hasidic groups, especially Satmar and Toledot Aharon, against showing movies on the Sabbath in Jerusalem ended in the victory of the Hasidim. It culminated in an anti-Zionist rabbi of a branch of Satmar, Rabbi Aaron Teitelbaum, flying from New York to Jerusalem (on Lufthansa, not EL AL) to celebrate the demolition of the theater and the construction of a complex of dozens of apartments for the growing Satmar Hasidic community. This is only an individual incident, but it is emblematic of a much broader phenomenon: the transformation of the small Hasidic groups from persecuted entities into organizations that are able to confront—efficaciously, from their point of view—larger audiences and eventually prevail, due to their dedication, tenacity, fanaticism, and sometimes even violent behavior.[68]

This is part of the zealous fight to preserve traditional modes of spirituality and identity, conceived of as more important than knowing or even practicing the details of Hasidic ways of life (communal customs and garments aside). Though it would be simplistic to portray entire communities as engaged in purely mimetic behavior, it appears to me that the new emphasis on institutionalization has become more prominent in the last two generations at the expense of spiritual aspirations and conceptual innovation. With the major exception of the leadership of the last Rabbi of Lubavitch, what we see is stark routinization of the charisma of Hasidic rabbis.[69]

Major recent concerns of some Hasidic groups relate to problems of succession of leadership and continual schisms and quarrels, as in the cases of the Satmar Hasidism and Shomer Emunim/Toledot Aharon, as well as heated controversies and competitions among the various Hasidic courts. Though certainly not a new phenomenon in the history of Hasidism, these conflicts seem to be more frequent in the present day. Moreover, the rise of ascetic behavior, which was not characteristic of early Hasidism, in some forms of contemporary Hasidism, especially Ger and Satmar, is part of an effort to counteract the impact of the strongly secular environments in which the Hasidic groups are living; this is akin to the emergence of nineteenth-century Jewish Orthodoxy.

Quite different, however, is another development related to the Hasidic movement: so-called Neo-Hasidism. Here we have an inverse process: the institutionalization that was so central to the emergence of Hasidism—along with the spiritual creativity intended for both the elite and the masses—has been abandoned in favor of a search for a more experiential type of Judaism for a relatively small number of elite young intellectuals, most of them educated in other areas of culture and religion (see Seeman, this volume). This is part of the more recent New Age turn to various forms of mysticism (be they Buddhist, Hindu, or kabbalistic) in an eclectic and syncretistic manner, while avoiding traditional Hasidic institutions, especially the tsaddik, as much as possible. In many cases the New Age turn fails to emphasize the centrality of Yiddish or Hebrew, even sometimes preferring English. Diminishing emphasis on belief in the magical power of language as well as that of the extraordinary human leader, is evident in depictions of early Hasidism by Neo-Hasidic scholars.[70]

These developments have much to do with the earlier attenuation of the role of the Hasidic leader as the quintessential center of a well-defined group of Hasidim and the total, though implicit, rejection of his magical powers in modern theologies that emanate mainly from scholars dealing with Hasidism, as mentioned above. This rejection is characteristic of some of the writings of Hillel Zeitlin,[71] Martin Buber, Abraham Joshua Heschel,[72] Elie Wiesel,[73] and, more recently, the various activities of Shlomo Carlebach,[74] Zalman Schachter-Shalomi, and Arthur Y. Green. Even Rivka Shatz Uffenheimer, a scholar who was also a critic of Martin Buber's understanding of Hasidism, has, implicitly at least, discounted the role of magic in early Hasidism. There is an evident leaning toward some forms of philosophy in some of these writings, as part of an effort to distill a central spiritual "message" in Hasidism capable of inspiring modern audiences beyond the traditional Hasidic groups, with the goal of igniting a Jewish renewal movement in the future.[75] On the other hand, both the magical aspect of a leading person and the violent behaviors of some Hasidic courts are totally absent. In a way, the role of a close-knit community as the main locus of popular aspects of Hasidism has been attenuated in comparison to earlier forms of Hasidism, though it does not totally disappear. On the other hand, these writers believe that traditional Hasidic sources are a major resource for the revitalization of Jewish life in modern times, the decadence evident in some traditional Hasidic developments notwithstanding. It should be emphasized that though the major developments of Neo-Hasidism—not to mention Jewish Renewal—took place in the United States, its beginnings were, as Arthur Green has noted, in Europe, that is, in the Ashkenazi communities from which some of its main figures came, including Hillel Zeitlin, Abraham Joshua Heschel, Zalman Schachter-Shalomi, Shlomo Carlebach, and Elie Wiesel.[76] In many cases, these individuals came from urban backgrounds. Had Shapira survived the Holocaust, he would likely have contributed to Neo-Hasidism, even though he was not a universalist per se.

Let me emphasize that I have no problem with the existence of Neo-Hasidic phenomena, since I do not reify Hasidism or reduce it to a primary message. My concern here relates only to the Neo-Hasidic type of scholarship, which reshapes, sometimes anachronistically, the earlier forms of Hasidism in the mold of Neo-Hasidism, for example, turning the eighteenth-century Hasidic masters into contemplative mystics.[77] Scholars may, perhaps, strive to reshape the future, but it is less advisable to reshape the past by relegating the uncomfortable, magical, or miraculous Hasidic beliefs to the margin.[78]

To return to the proposal articulated above: the different forms of twentieth-century Hasidic renewal do not stand alone, and they should be viewed in much wider contexts, not merely as internal developments. This is also true of the growing interest in Kabbalah, which has turned global, in both Jewish and non-Jewish circles, as the astonishing success of Philip Berg's and Michael Laitman's propagandist forms of Kabbalah amply demonstrates. The translation of Berg's and Laitman's biased presentations of Kabbalah into many languages is another indication of this economic success. The same can be said of the renewed interest in topics such as constellation of ideas, legends, and techniques relating to the "Golem." In fact, we may speak of a global "re-enchantment" concerning mystical, mythical, and magical phenomena, as is found, for example, in practical Kabbalah.[79] Max Weber's famous concept of "disenchantment" described a relatively narrow development that took place in middle and western Europe and affected the attitude of only a small part of the global population there, and even fewer elsewhere.[80] We may now speak about the recent re-enchantment of the world, after disillusions of both elite figures and larger masses from the optimism of the Enlightenment, with its reliance on reason, and of modernity, as well as the dissipation of some dominant ideologies.

This phenomenon is even more fascinating since it coincides with a long series of major developments in a variety of sciences, related to both the cosmos and human beings, which evidently did not dissipate earlier myths, anxieties, or expectations. As far as Judaism is concerned, this re-enchantment is evident and takes many forms, including the abrupt renaissance of interest in Hasidism, Kabbalah, and magic, as well as massive pilgrimages and intense cults of religious personalities encompassing much wider audiences than ever before in modern times, a massive return of the repressed, which reiterates and appropriates, mutatis mutandis, medieval and early-modern types of behavior.[81]

To put it in even broader terms, the renascence of Jewish mysticism on the global scene comes immediately after the similar interest in Hinduism and Buddhist forms of religiosity, including techniques like the various Yoga practices during the first part of the twentieth century and also, later, Transcendental Meditation. In fact, in some cases, as, for example, in the English writings of Aryeh Kaplan and Pearl Epstein relating to Kabbalah, technical elements of Jewish meditation have been expressly presented as an antidote to the surge of interest of young American Jews in Eastern forms of religiosity.[82] In this case, it is not a matter of conjecture regarding the vagaries of possible osmosis, as mentioned in the context of possible Eastern influence on Shapira. Here, there is more concrete and verifiable contact, considered positive by some and negative by others. On the other hand, the Jewish Renewal movement strove for a more ecumenical type of religious dialogue, as is evident in Schachter-Shalomi's approach, as metamorphosed in the *Penei 'or* (lit. "faces of light") phase. The difference between the two modes of Hasidism is between a being world apart and being part of the world.

In a way, the distinction between ecstasy and magic, which is also evident in some traditional Hasidic circles, influenced Neo-Hasidism and thus also the Renewal movement, but the nexus between the two has remained in the traditional forms of Hasidism operative today. They are two different Hasidic reactions to the challenges of modernity and to the urban situation, or two ways of shaping identity: one more universalist, opening toward fresh developments and adapting, and the other particularistic, with the concomitant insulation and inertia.[83] Let me emphasize that by using terms such as "opening," "insulation," and "inertia," I neither stake a claim in one of these Hasidic alternatives nor pass judgment on these different attitudes. Neo-Hasidism and its reverberations are more concerned with a community that shares ideas, attitudes, and a richer and more variegated intellectual and spiritual life, while the older forms of Hasidism represent a community that is more interested in producing what I call "performing bodies," with a lesser emphasis on belief and striving for an intense spiritual life.[84] The difference between the numbers of children belonging to these communities is an important criterion for predicting their future. The intense communal religious life that developed in the early history of Hasidism is related to life in small communities in modest *shtetlekh*, prayers in small *shtiblekh*, and celebrating the Sabbath and holidays together, including the widespread Hasidic custom of *tish* and the presence of the tsaddik. It differs from the mode of life prevalent in Neo-Hasidism, though both Hasidic modes share the religious and experiential importance of songs and singing. In this last case, the contribution of Shlomo Carlebach's music is outstanding. The divergence between these modes of contemporary Hasidism is the reason why the question of how long such a dichotomy in the phenomenology and sociology of Hasidism will last is hard to answer, given such an accelerated progression of history, especially in the case of modern Jewry, as it evolves both in Israel and in the United States.[85] Traditional forms of Hasidism lasted for more than two and one-half centuries, and the question is how long Neo-Hasidism will remain a viable, and not merely theoretical, option for modern-oriented minds.

The above discussions should be seen as part of a more comprehensive effort to understand Hasidism not only in the wider context of the history of Kabbalah since its beginning, or as merely a continuation of Lurianic Kabbalah or Sabbateanism, or as a reaction to them—a methodological approach that I call "proximism"[86]—but also as emerging and operating in much wider contexts. Such contexts—the plural is essential—would include Sufism, Christianity (especially Orthodox Christianity), and Altaic tribes (Turks or Tatars),[87] not to mention some elements that stem from Hinduism.[88] This global situation is not entirely a product of recent decades but was already reflected in movements that have been accelerating since the Middle Ages.

Given these realities, no single method of research and analysis can be considered sufficient. This includes the classical historical/philological method that was applied in a quite unilinear manner with respect to the sources of Hasidism as well as their later development.[89] A fresh history of Hasidism that considers questions related to the oscillation between the mystical-magical and the purely mystical, as mentioned above, remains a desideratum. Such a history would also consider other religious topics, such as the religious dimension of magic, to which some parts of the population—Jewish and non-Jewish—who believe in the miraculous are attracted. Shapira would be viewed as a complex figure who stands at the crossroads of the two tendencies in Hasidism, as a descendent of the wonder-working Hasidic leaders who was himself much more concerned with an experiential type of spirituality and prophecy and with the techniques for attaining it. Modern scholarship must operate with a more phenomenological analysis and a greater appreciation of historical complexities stemming from multiple religious contexts. At the same time, researchers considering Hasidism must attend to the different types of interaction—intellectual, social, and economic—which are constantly changing. These have not yet been taken sufficiently into consideration.[90]

Notes

1. See Kalonymus Kalman Shapira, *Sermons from the Years of Rage* [in Hebrew], ed. Daniel Reiser, 2 vols. (Jerusalem: Herzog Academic College, 2017).

2. See Don Seeman, "Ritual Efficacy, Hassidic Mysticism, and 'Useless Suffering' in the Warsaw Ghetto," *Harvard Theological Review* 101 (2008): 465–505; and Isaac Hershkowitz, *Rabbi Kalonymus Kalmish Shapira, the Piasechner Rebbe: His Holocaust and Pre-Holocaust Thought, Continuity or Discontinuity?* [in Hebrew] (master's thesis, Bar-Ilan University, 2005), 17–18. On Shapira, see, e.g., Nehemia Polen, *The Holy Fire: The Teachings of Rabbi Kalonymus Kalman Shapira* (Northvale, NJ: Jason Aronson, 1999); and Shaul Magid, *Piety and Rebellion: Essays in Hasidism* (Boston: Academic Studies Press 2019), 237–62.

3. On this model as far as the Besht is concerned, see Moshe Idel, *Vocal Rites and Broken Theologies: Cleaving to Vocables in Israel Ba'al Shem Tov's Mysticism* (New York: Crossroad, 2019, forthcoming), ch. 9; Moshe Idel, "The Besht as Prophet and Talismanic Magician" [in Hebrew], in *Studies in Jewish Narrative: Ma'aseh Sippur, Presented to Yoav Elstein*, ed. Avodov Lipsker and Rella Kushelevsky (Ramat Gan: Bar-Ilan University Press, 2006), 122–33; and in more general terms, Moshe Idel, *Hasidism: Between Ecstasy and Magic*, 103–45. On the magical stories about the Besht, see Immanuel Etkes, *The Besht: Magician, Mystic, and Leader*, trans. S. Sternberg (Waltham, MA: Brandeis University Press, 2005); Gedalyah Nigal, *Magic, Mysticism, and Hasidism* [in Hebrew] (Tel Aviv: Yaron Golan, 1992); and Jonatan Meir, "Marketing Demons: Joseph Perl, Israel Baal Shem Tov, and the History of One Amulet," *Kabbalah* 28 (2012): 35–66. My point is that in addition to the Besht's functioning as a magician, there is a magical component to some of the teachings in his name and to the way the role of the Hasidic tsaddik has been imagined.

4. See Idel, *Hasidism*, 147–208.

5. On this model, see also Phillip Wexler, *Holy Sparks: Social Theory, Education, and Religion* (New York, 1966), 125–29; Phillip Wexler, *The Mystical Society: An Emerging Social Vision* (Boulder: Westview, 2000), 35–39; Jonathan Garb, *Shamanic Trance in Modern Kabbalah* (Chicago: Chicago University Press, 2011), 75–77, who prefers the term *shamanic* to mystical-magical (89); Uriel Gellman, *The Emergence of Hasidism in Poland* [in Hebrew] (Jerusalem: Merkaz Zalman Shazar, 2018), 85.

6. See, e.g., H. W. Hines, "The Prophet as a Mystic," *American Journal of Semitic Languages and Literature* 40–41 (1923–24): 37–71; Robert Wilson, "Proph-

ecy and Ecstasy: A Reexamination," *Journal of Biblical Literature* 98, no. 3 (1979): 321–37; Benjamin Uffenheimer, *Classical Prophecy: The Prophetic Consciousness* [in Hebrew] (Jerusalem: Magnes, 2001), 59–61, 71–79. Compare, however, the somewhat different approach of Abraham J. Heschel, *The Prophets* (New York: JPS, 1962), who prefers to separate prophecy from ecstasy. In the Middle Ages, prophecy was a vague category that sometimes included ecstasy. See, e.g., Moshe Idel, *The Mystical Experience in Abraham Abulafia*, trans. J. Chipman (Albany: State University of New York Press, 1987), 73–78; Moshe Idel, "On Prophecy and Early Hasidism," in *Studies in Modern Religions, Religious Movements, and the Babi-Baha'i Faiths*, ed. M. Sharon (Leiden: Brill, 2004), 48–49, 58–64, 68–69; Haviva Pedaya, *Vision and Speech: Models of Revelatory Experiences in Jewish Mysticism* [in Hebrew] (Los Angeles: Cherub, 2002), 47–89.

7. See Idel, "Prophecy and Early Hasidism," 64. Let me remark that the available descriptions of early Hasidism hardly reflect the wild, anarchic nature that I assume it had, which was tempered in most of the available descriptions stemming from Hasidic sources, but which is still evident in the testimonies of the mitnagdim.

8. See Moshe Idel, *Vocal Rites*, appendix A. On problems with the use of the category of prophecy in the Middle Ages, see Moshe Idel, "Lawyers and Mystics in Judaism: A Prolegomenon for a Study of Prophecy in Jewish Mysticism," Straus Working Paper 10/10 (New York: New York University Law School, 2010), 14–18.

9. See Idel, *Hasidism*, 189–207, 211. The institution of tsaddik in Hasidism has been addressed by many scholars. See, e.g., Gershom Scholem, *On the Mystical Shape of the Godhead*, trans. J. Neugroschel (New York: Schocken, 1991), 120–39; Arthur Green, "Typologies of Leadership and the Hasidic *Zaddiq*," in *Jewish Spirituality*, ed. A. Green (New York: Crossroad, 1989), 2:127–56; Arthur Green, "The *Zaddiq* as *Axis Mundi* in Later Judaism," *Journal of the American Academy of Religion* 45 (1977): 328–47; Samuel H. Dresner, *The Zaddik: The Doctrine of the Zaddik According to the Writings of Rabbi Yaakov Yosef of Polnoy* (New York: Schocken, 1974); Rachel Elior, "Between *Yesh* and *Ayin*: The Doctrine of the Zaddik in the Works of Jacob Isaac the Seer of Lublin," in *Jewish History: Essays in Honor of Chimen Abramsky*, ed. Ada Rapoport-Albert and Steven Zipperstein (London, 1988), 393–455; and Ada Rapoport-Albert, "God and the Zaddik as the Two Focal Points of Hasidic Worship," *History of Religions* 18 (1979): 296–325. See also Shaul Magid, *Hasidism Incarnate: Hasidism, Christianity, and the Construction of Modern Judaism* (Stanford: Stanford University Press, 2014); and Shaul Magid, "The Case of Jewish Arianism: The Pre-Existence of the Zaddik in Early Hasidism," reprinted in Shaul Magid, *Piety and Rebellion*, 23–36. See also below, n. 78.

10. Alan Brill, "The Spiritual World of a Master of Awe: Divine Vitality, Theosis, and Healing in the *Degel Mahaneh Ephraim*," *Jewish Studies Quarterly* 8 (2001): 27–65.

11. Idel, *Hasidism*, 54.

12. See Simon Dubnov, *History of Hasidism* (Tel Aviv, 1927), 217–18 [in Hebrew]. See also Idel, *Hasidism*, 190–91.

13. See Gellman, *Emergence of Hasidism*, 146–62; David Biale et al., *Hasidism: A New History* (Princeton: Princeton University Press, 2018), 152–53.

14. On blessing as magic, see Idel, *Hasidism*, 425, index, under "blessing/ berakhah."

15. See Daniel Reiser, *Imagery Techniques in Modern Jewish Mysticism*, trans. Eugene D. Matanky (Berlin: De Gruyter, 2018), 191–94; Zvi Leshem, *Between Messianism and Prophecy: Hasidism According to the Piazecner Rebbe* (PhD diss., Bar-Ilan University, 2007), 118–28.

16. See Elimelekh of Grodzisk, *Divrei 'Elimelekh and 'Imrei Elimelekh*.

17. Justin Jaron Lewis, " 'Such Things Have Never Been Heard of': Jewish Intellectuals and Hasidic Miracles," in *Vixens Disturbing Vineyards: Embarrassment and Embracement of Scriptures; Festschrift in Honor of Harry Fox leVeit Yoreh*, ed. Tzemah Yoreh et al. (Boston: Academic Studies Press, 2009), 480–95; and Marcin Wodziński, *Haskalah and Hasidism in the Kingdom of Poland: A History of Conflict*, trans. S. Cozens and A. Mirowska (Oxford: Littman Library of Jewish Civilization, 2005).

18. See Moshe Idel, *Kabbalah: New Perspectives* (New Haven: Yale University Press, 1988), 74–111; Idel, *Mystical Experiences*, 13–72, which is a translation of a chapter of my 1976 PhD thesis, "On the Metamorphoses of an Ancient Technique to Attain a Prophetic Vision in the Middle Ages" [in Hebrew] *Sinai* 86 (1980): 1–7; and Idel, *Enchanted Chains, Techniques, and Rituals in Jewish Mysticism* (Los Angeles: Cherub, 2005).

19. See, e.g., Jonathan Garb, "Techniques of Trance in the Jerusalem Kabbalah" [in Hebrew], *Pe'amim* 70 (1997): 47–67.

20. Idel, *Kabbalah*, 103–11; Moshe Idel, "Kabbalistic Prayer and Colors," in *Approaches to Judaism in Medieval Times*, ed. David Blumenthal (Atlanta: Scholars Press, 1984–1988), 3:17–27; Moshe Idel, "*Kavvanah* and Colors: A Neglected Kabbalistic Responsum" [in Hebrew], in *Tribute to Sara: Studies in Jewish Philosophy and Kabbalah Presented to Professor Sara O. Heller Wilensky*, ed. Moshe Idel, Devorah Dimant, and Shalom Rosenberg (Jerusalem: Magnes, 1994), 1–14; Moshe Idel, "An Anonymous Kabbalistic Commentary on *Shir hayihud*," in *Mysticism, Magic, and Kabbalah in Ashkenazi Judaism*, ed. Karl Erich Grözinger and Joseph Dan (Berlin, 1995), 147–48. See also below, nn. 21, 28.

21. See J. Zwi Werblowsky, *Joseph Karo: Lawyer and Mystic* (Oxford: Oxford University Press, 1962), 38–83.

22. See Cordovero, *Pardes rimmonim*, Gate 21, especially ch. 1, where a passage of Abulafia's *Or hasekhel* has been copied, and Gate 30. In this passage, the visualization of letters is mentioned, using the verb *TZYR*. For more on this verb, see below.

23. It is discussed in several instances in this book but especially in Cordovero, Gate 32, ch. 3.

24. Cordovero, Gate 10.

25. The mystical-magical, which is related to prayer, and that of Abulafia. See Moshe Idel, *Studies in Ecstatic Kabbalah* (Albany: State University of New York Press, 1988), 139–40.

26. Cordovero, *Pardes rimmonim*, 21, ch. 1; and see Moshe Idel, "Prophecy and Early Hasidism," 53–54.

27. See Moshe Idel, "*Adonay Sefatay Tiftaḥ*: Models of Understanding Prayer in Early Hasidism," *Kabbalah* 18 (2008): 7–111; Moshe Idel, "Prayer, Ecstasy, and Alien Thoughts in the Besht's Religious World" [in Hebrew], in *Hasidism and the Musar Movement*, vol. 1 of *Let the Old Make Way for the New: Studies in the Social and Cultural History of Eastern European Jewry Presented to Immanuel Etkes*, ed. David Assaf and Ada Rapoport-Albert (Jerusalem: Merkaz Shazar, 2009), 57–120.

28. See Idel, *Hasidism*, 55–56, 60–62, 64; and Garb, *Shamanic Trance*.

29. For techniques of active visualization in modern Jewish mysticism, see Reiser, *Imagery Techniques*; Ron Wachs, *The Flame and the Holy Fire: Perspectives on the Teachings of Rabbi Kalonymus Kalmish Shapira of Piuczena* [in Hebrew] (Alon Shevut: Tevunot, 2010); Jonathan Garb, *Kabbalist in the Heart of the Storm: Moshe Hayyim Luzzatto* [in Hebrew] (Tel Aviv: Tel Aviv University Press, 2014), 112–13; Garb, *Shamanic Trance*; Tomer Persico, *Jewish Meditation: The Development of Spiritual Practices in Contemporary Judaism* [in Hebrew] (Tel Aviv: Tel Aviv University Press, 2016). On R. Shapira in particular, see Reiser, *Imagery Techniques*, 133–37.

30. See *Hovat ha-talmidim* (Tel Aviv, ND), 23; and *Mevo she'arim* (Jerusalem, 1962), fol. 25a. See Reiser, *Imagery Techniques*, 235n132.

31. See Reiser, *Imagery Techniques*, 439, under "Abulafia, Abraham."

32. See Ron Wachs, *Holy Fire*, 235–37.

33. *Benei mahshavah tovah* (Tel Aviv, 1989), 19.

34. *Hayyei ha-olam ha-ba*, ed. A. Gross (Jerusalem, 2001), third edition, 67. On this passage, to be translated immediately below, see Idel, *Mystical Experience*, 31.

35. Compare, however, Reiser, *Imagery Techniques*, 235.

36. See Gershom Scholem, *Kitvei yad be-kabbalah* (Jerusalem: National Library of Israel and The Hebrew University of Jerusalem, 1930), 225–30; Gershom Scholem, "Chapters from *Sullam ha-aliyyah*, by Yehudah Albotini" [in Hebrew], *Qiryat sefer* 22 (1945–46): 162–71.

37. Idel, "Prophecy and Early Hasidism," 66–67.

38. Ibid., 68.

39. Ibid., 67. See also See also Moshe Idel, "Menahem Mendel of Shklov and Avraham Abulafia" [in Hebrew], in *THE VILNA GAON and His Disciples*, ed. Moshe Hallamish, Yosef Rivlin, and Raphael Shuhat (Ramat Gan: Bar-Ilan University Press, 2003), 173–83.

40. *Hayyei ha-olam ha-ba*, ed. Gross, 3. See also ibid., 114, "The spirit of prophecy teaches masters of knowledge," which is the first line of the closing poem of this book, as well as ibid., 5, 10, 16, 20–21, 22, 27, 33, 59, 69, 77, 112, etc.

41. Let me point out that this verb is also used in another kabbalistic school as part of another technique of visualizing letters of the tetragrammaton, in different colors. See my "Visualization of Colors, 1: David ben Yehudah he-Hasid's Kabbalistic Diagram," *Ars Judaica* 11 (2015): 31–54.

42. See *Hayyei ha-olam ha-ba*, ed. Gross, 67; Idel, *Mystical Experience*, 31.

43. See Idel, *Studies in Ecstatic Kabbalah*, 16.

44. *Hayyei ha-olam ha-ba*, ed. Gross, 68, 73, 82.

45. *Benei mahshavah tovah*, 25. See also ibid., 18, 42. Compare also to ibid., 32.

46. See Reiser, *Imagery Techniques*, 239–40.

47. Moshe Idel, "Between Magic of Divine Names and the Kabbalah of Names: Abraham Abulafia's Critique" [in Hebrew], *Mahanayyim* 14 (2002): 79–96. This does not mean that he did not assume the possibility that the prophet could make some changes to reality, but he considered such changes far inferior to spiritual attainment and not a necessary outcome of cleaving to the supernal world. See Idel, *Ecstatic Kabbalah*, 63–65.

48. Idel, *Enchanted Chains*, 228–32.

49. For the significant influence of Vital's booklet on Hasidism, see Idel, *Hasidism*, 38, 99, 105, 297–98, 303, 339, 346, 378. This book deals also with visualization, mainly under the influence of Abulafia, and it is quoted by Shapira. See *Sermons from the Years of Rage*, 251, 261, 309. However, none of these references from Vital's book refer to visualization. On visualization in Vital's book, see Werblowsky, *Joseph Karo: Lawyer and Mystic*, 69–70; Elliot R. Wolfson, *Through a Speculum that Shines* (Princeton: Princeton University Press, 1995), 320–23; and Moshe Idel, *Ascensions on High in Jewish Mysticism: Pillars, Lines, Ladders* (Budapest: CEU, 2005), 52–53; Idel, "Prophecy and Early Hasidism," 54–55.

50. See Idel, "The Besht," 122–33, and "Prophecy and Early Hasidism," 41–75.

51. See Idel, "Prophecy and Early Hasidism," 68–69; Garb, *Shamanic Trance*, 87–88, 122; Reiser, *Imagery Techniques*, 215–17.

52. Leshem, *Between Messianism and Prophecy*, 76–91; Wachs, *Holy Fire*, 210–39; Daniel Reiser, " 'To Rend the Entire Veil': Prophecy in the Teachings of Rabbi Kalonymus Kalman Shapira of Piazecna and its Renewal in the Twentieth Century," *Modern Judaism* 34 (2014): 334–52; Reiser, *Imagery Techniques*, passim.

53. See Moshe Idel, *Abraham Abulafia's Esotericism: On Secrets and Doubts* (Berlin: De Gruyter, 2019, forthcoming), ch. 5.

54. See Moshe Idel, "Abraham Abulafia, Gershom Scholem, and David Hakohen (Hanazir)" [in Hebrew], in *Derekh ha-ruah: Jubilee Volume in Honor of Eliezer Schweid*, ed. Yehoyadah Amir (Jerusalem: Hebrew University and Van Leer Institute, 2005), 2:787–802.

55. See Moshe Idel, "Prophets and Their Impact in the High Middle Ages: A Subculture of Franco-German Jewry," in *Regional Mentalities and Cultures of Medieval Jews*, ed. J. Castano, T. Fishman, and E. Karnafogel (London: Littman Library of Jewish Civilization, 2018), 285–337. For a survey of the various phenomena described as prophecy in twentieth-century Judaism, most of them in central Europe, see Eliezer Schweid, *Prophets to Their People and Humanities: Prophecy and Prophets in 20th Century Jewish Thought* [in Hebrew] (Jerusalem: Magnes, 1999).

56. Compare to Reiser, *Imagery Techniques*, 248–49.

57. *Shaʾarei kedushah* 3:8; *Sefer shaʾarei kedushah ha-shalem*, ed. A. Gross (Israel, 2005), 128.

58. See Idel, *Abraham Abulafia's Esotericism*, ch. 9.

59. Christopher Isherwood, *Meditation and Its Methods According to Swami Vivekananda* (Hollywood: Vedanta Press, 1976). On the significant affinity between Abulafia's tripartite techniques of breathing and Yoga, see Idel, *Mystical Experience*, 14, 24–25, 39. See also Gershom Scholem, *Major Trends in Jewish Mysticism* (New York: Schocken, 1974), 139, 144, 146. On the history of interest in Buddhism among Western philosophers, such as Hegel, since the late eighteenth century and especially in the nineteenth century, see Roger-Pol Droit, *Le culte du néant: Les philosophers et le Bouddha* (Paris: Seuil, 1997).

60. See Amir Mashiach, "Rabbi Kook and Buddhism" [in Hebrew] *Daat* 70 (2011): 81–96.

61. See Moshe Idel, *Golem: Jewish Magical and Mystical Traditions on the Artificial Anthropoid, An Augmented Edition* (New York: Ktav, 2019, forthcoming), 407–12. See also Moshe Idel, *Ben: Sonship and Jewish Mysticism* (London: Continuum, 2007), 575–76n69.

62. Reiser, "To Rend," 345.

63. In any case, Abraham Joshua Heschel's strong interest in biblical prophecy and its possible reverberations in the Middle Ages is well known. See his collection of articles on this topic: Abraham J. Heschel, *Prophetic Inspiration after the Prophets: Maimonides and Other Medieval Authorities* (Hoboken, NJ: Ktav, 1996). In my opinion, it is not accidental that scholarship dealing with prophecy was initiated by a Neo-Hasidic thinker with profound familiarity with Hasidism. See Seeman, "Ritual Efficacy," 465–505.

64. Let me clarify that my assumption is not that Hasidism emerged as a response to modernity but that the various Hasidic denominations emerged for a variety of different reasons, including to confront various forms of modernity. See Moshe Rosman, "Hasidism: Traditional Modernization," *Simon Dubnow Institute Yearbook* 6 (2007): 1–10.

65. See, e.g., Glenn Dynner, *Men of Silk: The Hasidic Conquest of Polish Jewish Society* (New York: Oxford University Press, 2008); Gellman, *Emergence of Hasidism*; or Gellman, *Hasidism*, 272–82.

66. Zvi Mark, "The Contemporary Renaissance of Braslav Hasidism: Ritual, Tiqqun, and Messianism," in *Kabbalah and Contemporary Spiritual Revival*, ed. Boaz Huss (Be'er Sheva: Ben Gurion University Press, 2011); Eliezer Baumgarten, "Between Uman and Morocco: Ethnic Identities in Bratslav Hasidism" [in Hebrew], *Pe'amim* 131 (2012): 147–78.

67. Marcin Wodziński, *Historical Atlas of Hasidism*, cartography by Waldemar Spallek (Princeton: Princeton University Press, 2018), 192.

68. See Stephen Sharot, *Messianism, Mysticism, and Magic* (Chapel Hill: University of North Carolina Press, 1982), 189–205.

69. See Ibid., 155–88.

70. Nicham Ross, *A Beloved-Despised Tradition: Modern Jewish Identity and Neo-Hasidic Writing at the Beginning of the Twentieth Century* [in Hebrew] (Be'er Sheva: Ben Gurion University Press, 2010); Joanna Steinhardt, "American Neo-Hasids in the Land of Israel," in *Nova Religio: The Journal of Alternative and Emergent Religions* 13, no. 4 (2010): 22–42; Tomer Persico, "Neo-Hasidic Revival Expressivist Uses of Traditional Lore," *Modern Judaism* 34 (2014): 287–308; Perisco, *Jewish Meditation*, 244–71.

71. Arthur Green, "Three Warsaw Mystics," in *Kolot Rabbim: Essays in Honor of Rivka Schatz-Uffenheimer*, ed. Rachel Elior (Jerusalem, 1996), 1–58 [English section].

72. Arthur Green, "Abraham Joshua Heschel: Recasting Hasidism for Moderns," *Modern Judaism* 29, no. 1 (2009): 62–79; M. Idel, "Abraham Joshua Heschel on Mysticism and Hasidism," *Modern Judaism* 29, no. 1 (2009): 80–105.

73. Arthur Green, "Wiesel in the Context of Neo-Hasidism," in *Elie Wiesel: Jewish, Literary, and Moral Perspectives*, ed. Steven T. Katz and Alan Rosen (Bloomington: Indiana University Press, 2013), 51–58; Nehemia Polen, "Yearning for Sacred Place: Wiesel's Hasidic Tales and Postwar Hasidism," in *Elie Wiesel*, ed. Katz and Rosen, 69–82.

74. See Yaakov Ariel, "Hasidism in the Age of Aquarius: The House of Love and Prayer in San Francisco, 1967–1977," *Religion and American Culture* 13, no. 2 (2003): 139–65.

75. Arthur Green, "Renewal and Havurah: American Movements, European Roots," in *Jewish Renaissance and Revival in America: Essays in Memory of Leah Levitz Fishbane z"l*, ed., Eitan P. Fishbane and Jonathan D. Sarna (Waltham, MA: Brandeis University Press, 2011), 145–64. See also Hava Tirosh-Samuelson and Aaron Huges, eds., *Arthur Green: A Hasidism for Tomorrow* (Leiden: Brill, 2015).

76. Regarding the encounter between Zeitlin and Shapira, see the newspaper report in *Davar*, November 11, 1931, 2.

77. See, e.g., Rivka Schatz, "Contemplative Prayer in Hasidism," in *Studies in Mysticism and Religion Presented to Gershom G. Scholem*, ed. Efraim Elimelech Urbach, J. Zwi Werblowsky, and Chaim Wirszubski (Jerusalem: Magnes, 1967),

209–26; Arthur Green, *Your Word Is Fire: Hasidic Masters on Contemplative Prayer* (Mahwah, NJ: Paulist Press, 1977); and see my discussion of this trend in Idel, *Vocal Rites*, ch.13.

78. See also Lewis, "Such Things." *En passant*, my attitude toward magic, including Hasidic magic, is not positive, as Lewis assumes (487), nor is it negative; I am attempting to do justice to religious phenomena of the past.

79. Yuval Harari, "Three Charms for Killing Adolf Hitler: Practical Kabbalah in WW2," *ARIES* 17 (2017): 171–214; Jeffrey H. Chayes, "Rabbis and Their (In) Famous Magic: Classical Foundations, Medieval and Early Modern Reverberations," in *Jewish Studies at the Crossroads of Anthropology and History: Authority, Diaspora, Tradition*, ed. Ra'anan S. Boustan, Oren Kosansky, and Marina Rustow (Philadelphia: University of Pennsylvania Press, 2011), 58–79, 349–58; Gideon Bohak, "How Jewish Magic Survived the Disenchantment of the World," *ARIES* 19 (2019): 7–37.

80. Jason Ānanda Josephson-Storm, *The Myth of Disenchantment: Magic, Modernity, and the Birth of the Human Sciences* (Chicago: University of Chicago Press, 2017). See also Wouter J. Hanegraaff, *New Age Religion and Western Culture: Esotericism in the Mirror of Secular Thought* (Albany: State University of New York Press, 1998).

81. See Jeffrey H. Chajes, "'Entzauberung' and Jewish Modernity: On 'Magic,' Enlightenment, and Faith," *Jahrbuch des Simon Dubnow-Instituts* 6 (2007): 191–200.

82. To what extent Neo-Hasidism is reactive to the vivid interest in Hindu and Buddhist practices among some Jews requires more investigation. However, in any case, Schachter-Shalomi's longstanding involvement with Buddhist and Sufi meditation is well known. See Don Seeman and Michael Karlin, "Mindfulness and Hasidic Modernism: Towards a Contemplative Ethnography," *Religion and Society* 10 (2019): 44–62.

83. To be sure, intellectual and spiritual background does not always dictate a particular reaction. So, for example, the two major forms of Hasidism coexisted in Warsaw and the United States, and to a certain extent in Israel. This does not mean that the particularistic attitude does not undergo some changes or adaptations after its dislocation from eastern Europe. It should be mentioned that even in the strictest Hasidic camps, such as Satmar, there are conversions to Christianity, as we know from recent news. The complexity of life does not allow for simple answers.

84. See Moshe Idel, "On the Performing Body in Theosophical-Theurgical Kabbalah: Some Preliminary Remarks," in *The Jewish Body: Corporeality, Society, and Identity in the Renaissance and Early Modern Period*, ed. Maria Diemling and Giuseppe Veltri (Leiden: Brill, 2009), 251–71.

85. See, e g., the picture offered by Shaul Magid, *American Post-Judaism: Identity and Renewal in a Postethnic Society* (Bloomington: Indiana University

Press, 2013); and Magid, *Piety and Rebellion*, 263–310. How "postethnic" American "society" actually is, with the "renewal" of what is called *primavera latina* and the intensification of the white supremacy movement, to take just two more recent examples, is quite a difficult question that only the remote future may be able to answer. Not being a prophet, I have my doubts, especially regarding the will or capacity of most of the traditional Hasidic groups in the United States to transcend ethnic divisions and embrace a new American "postethnic" identity that would flower in neighborhoods like Boro Park and Williamsburg. See Janet S. Belcove-Shalin, ed., *New World Hasidim: Ethnographic Studies of Hasidic Jews in America* (Albany: State University of New York Press, 1995).

86. See Idel, *Hasidism*, passim, especially 4, 6–9. The nonlinear histories of Hasidism have not considered the possible impact of a series of pre-Lurianic forms of kabbalah, which is why I have called for a panoramic understanding of the sources of Hasidism, taking a much greater variety of such sources into consideration. See, e.g., the discussions of the material that comprises *Sefer raziel hamal'akh*, a collection of mainly magical texts from a variety of kabbalistic schools that do not include Safedian forms of kabbalah at all, and its influence on early Hasidism, in Moshe Idel, "R. Nehemiah ben Shlomo's Commentaries on the Alphabet of Metatron: Additional Inquiries" [in Hebrew]; *Tarbiz* 85 (2018): 549–52; Moshe Idel, "*Sefer razi'el hamal'akh*: New Inquiries," in *L'eredità di Salomone la magia ebraica in Italia e nel Mediterraneo*, Testi e Studi del Meis, ed. Emma Abate (Florence: Giuntina, 2019), 143–68; and see also Jonatan Meir, "Enlightenment and Esotericism in Galitzia: The Writings of Elyakim Getzl Milzhagi," *Kabbalah* 33 (2015): 306–308. Likewise, Cordoverian types of kabbalah, which add much complexity to existing scholarly analyses, have hardly affected scholarship of Hasidism and deserve to be taken into serious consideration.

87. Moshe Idel, "Early Hasidism and Altaic Tribes: Between Europe and Asia," *Kabbalah* 39 (2017): 7–51. To what extent the emergence of some aspects of the institution of the tsaddik in late-eighteenth-century Hasidism also owes something to the confrontation with the Tatar shamans, who were active in the immediate vicinity of some of the earliest small Hasidic groups, deserves additional consideration and differs from the more Eurocentric interpretations of the emergence of early Hasidism.

88. Moshe Idel, "R. Israel Ba'al Shem Tov 'In the State of Walachia': Widening the Besht's Cultural Panorama," in *Holy Dissent: Jewish and Christian Mystics in Eastern Europe*, ed. G. Dynner (Detroit: Wayne University Press, 2011), 104–30. Compare also to Reiser's observations in *Imagery Techniques*, 401–5.

89. See, e.g., Garb, *Shamanic Trance*; Moshe Idel, "'The Besht Passed His Hand over His Face': On the Besht's Influence on His Followers; Some Remarks," in *After Spirituality: Studies in Mystical Traditions*, ed. Philip Wexler and Jonathan Garb (New York: Peter Lang, 2012), 79–106. On the influence of Mesmerism on

the interwar Hasidic mystic in the case of Menahem Mendel Ekstein, see Reiser, *Imagery Techniques*, 348–59, 369–73. On the need for more complex academic methods for investigating Jewish mysticism, see Idel, *Ascensions on High*, 1–13.

90. Compare to the more factual thrust of the narratives in the essays in Biale et al., *Hasidism*.

3

The Devotional Talmud

Study as a Sacred Quest

ARIEL EVAN MAYSE

When I was a tender youngster, seeking the wisdom of Torah, I learned the ways of casuistry (*pilpul*) from my teacher. At the age of ten, I was coming up with my own creative interpretations (*hiddushim*). But later on, after I entered the sacred *beit midrash* of the Kotzker Rebbe, the source of wisdom and understanding, I learned the ways of penetrating insight (*iyyun*). He helped me understand true creativity in Torah, for not all sophistry is truly novel.

—Rabbi Avraham Borenstein, *Eglei tal*

In studying Torah, we become attached to the Teacher of the Jewish people—to the God of Israel. But one must know how to study Torah!

—Rabbi Kalonymus Kalmish Shapira, *Hovat ha-talmidim*

This chapter explores Talmud study as a devotional practice and a search for mystical self-expression in the teachings of Kalonymus Kalmish Shapira of Piaseczno. I will argue that Rabbi Shapira sought to inspire his readers—and listeners—to see the Talmud, the backbone and core of rabbinic Judaism, as a vital textual gateway through which to explore the infinite expanse of the heart's kingdom. Shapira's teachings reframe the study of Talmud as a spiritual quest, one undertaken by the scholar in order to reveal the deepest elements of the self and to attain an intimate vision of the Divine.[1] This may be seen as part of a broader attempt at religious and spiritual renewal among Hasidim and others in interbellum Warsaw (see the preceding essays of Idel and Wodziński).[2] The simultaneous flourishing of *mussar* yeshivot may have been viewed as both competition and inspiration for the relatively new Hasidic yeshivot, including the one Shapira founded. This might even suggest a pointed—if subterranean—polemical edge to Shapira's teachings on the necessity of integrating positive emotive and spiritual experience with scholarly pursuits.[3]

Talmudists often cloak innovation and creativity in the mantle of tradition. Recent scholarship has challenged the view of the great talmudic academies of nineteenth- and twentieth-century Eastern Europe as bastions of antimodernizing Orthodox traditionalism. The embrace of highly abstract conceptual analysis in Lithuanian talmudism may, for example, be understood as a revolutionary break with the patterns of study cultivated hitherto in Eastern Europe.[4] Similar arguments have been made regarding the talmudists of Central Europe and Galicia, many of whom bespoke a traditionalist ideology but were highly creative in their formulation of new modes of interpretation and legal formulation. Although these scholars were staunchly opposed to all religious or communal reform, their works evince strikingly original and innovative intellectual positions.[5] It is thus noteworthy that the talmudic methodologies of the mostly Hasidic scholars in Congress Poland have received significantly less scholarly attention. The legal writings of central figures such as Yehudah Aryeh Leib Alter of Ger (1847–1905), Yosef Engel (1858–1920), Yosef Rosen (1858–1936), and Aryeh Tsevi Frumer (1884–1923), to name but a few, have yet to be the subject of any sustained critical analysis.[6]

This is the context in which I seek to examine Kalonymus Kalman Shapira's attempt to integrate Talmud study with the mystical teachings and contemplative techniques for which he is better known.[7] My particular focus will be his stirring depictions of studying rabbinic texts as a spiritual quest to reveal the innermost creativity of the individual self and as a journey toward the Divine sparked by the encounter with the folios of the Talmud. In this I hope to contribute to a broader, more phenomenologically compelling narrative than the one that views historical-critical styles of scholarship and unflagging secularization as the exclusive harbingers of modernity.[8]

Renewing the Talmud

Shapira's thinking on the study of Talmud represents a jostling eddy of cultural and intellectual contexts. Polish talmudism had long struggled against *pilpul*, a form of legal sophistry that many Polish scholars accused of doing violence to the talmudic text and swiftly collapsing into baseless casuistry.[9] Shapira was also shaped, in part, by descriptions of Talmud study found in some kabbalistic texts in which preference is given to experiential devotion in studying the "inner dimensions" (*penimiyyut*) of Torah—that is, mystical theosophy—rather than talmudic dialectics.[10] Some of these texts, including the significant Lurianic corpus that emerged from the hand of Hayyim Vital, describe studying the casuistic patterns of Jewish law as useful only in order to break through the "husks" (*kelippot*) that obscure and surround the holy sparks, or divine wisdom, hidden deep within Scripture.[11]

Hasidism absorbed many elements of the kabbalistic approach to engagement with Torah, though in doing so, Hasidic thinkers subtly shifted their orientation away from mystical metaphysics or theosophy and toward the devotional elements of sacred study.[12] Teachings from the Baal Shem Tov on immersion in Torah study underscore the experiential and affective dimension of religious scholarship.[13] To a certain degree, this impulse flattens the distinctions between various kinds of sacred texts. "The entirety of our Torah, both written and oral, includes nothing—not even a single letter—that speaks of anything other than sacred service of God," claims one source. "I heard my holy teacher the Maggid [of Zlotshev] say that he saw absolutely no difference between the books before him; whether [studying] Talmud or Kabbalah, he saw nothing other than how to serve God."[14] Hasidic thinkers also seem to have understood that not only Talmud but Kabbalah, too, could become the focus of arid, dry, and soulless scholarship.[15] Rather than isolating and prioritizing the study of one particular corpus, whether rabbinic literature or mystical texts, these early Hasidic leaders argued that the devotional "how" of sacred study should outweigh the question of "what" corpus forms the subject of inquiry.

The Hasidic emphasis on *devekut* as the pinnacle of religious service, in study as well as in prayer, sparked the ire of the Lithuanian rabbinate.[16] Their polemics criticized the Hasidim for disdaining scholars and, in more extreme cases, for neglecting and even deriding Talmud study as a hindrance to the true goals of the spiritual life.[17] This backlash might have inspired the Hasidim to reinforce their study of halakhah and tighten up on certain matters of ritual practice, though they maintained their critique of narcissistic scholars and abstract sophistry.[18] By the nineteenth century, however, a significant number of Hasidic thinkers who were also *poskim* (rabbinic jurists) emerged in Galicia, Congress Poland, and White Russia.[19] The Hasidic world had, to a large degree, joined forces with the traditional rabbinate and staked out a fiercely antimodern stance, refusing to compromise on issues of changing customs, including dress and language, and utterly resisting all forms of educational reform. In many communities, this focus on performance of the law and the study of halakhah took pride of place over mystical quest.[20]

Shapira was a direct descendent of Rabbi Yisra'el Hapstein (c. 1734–1814), the Maggid of Kozhnits, an early Hasidic leader whose fame for charismatic piety and wonder-working was complemented by his reputation for rabbinic erudition and legal prowess.[21] Sacred study of a variety of religious texts was, for Shapira, a crucial element of the spiritual path. Some of his teachings highlight the devotional potential of *all* such study, regardless of the topic or genre;[22] such homilies seek to inspire Shapira's students to embrace the affective, emotional elements of study together with its intellectual component.[23]

Suggesting that studying rabbinic literature allows for a singular kind of encounter with God, Shapira notes that talmudic scholarship also presents unique challenges. In his effort to highlight the spiritual dimensions of reading Talmud, Shapira did not in any way depreciate the power and authority of Kabbalah; rabbinic sources along with Jewish mystical texts represent a coherent and complementary literary inheritance.[24] This paradigm follows that of late medieval and early modern Jewish intellectuals such as Rabbi Isaiah Horowtiz (c. 1555–1630), whose classical book *Shenei luhot ha-berit* sought to reintegrate the esoteric and exoteric dimensions of Jewish thought into a coherent whole. But Shapira's nuanced approach separates him from more recent thinkers such as Hayyim of Volozhin on one hand and from the more cognitively inclined talmudic study of Hasidic groups like Kotsk and Ger on the other.

In 1923, Shapira founded a yeshivah called Da'at Moshe (see Wodziński, this volume), which, with perhaps some three hundred students, represented a significant institution of talmudic learning in interbellum Warsaw.[25] The educational philosophy outlined in *Hovat ha-talmidim* makes it clear that holistic spiritual education was the purpose of this institution, but the heart of the curriculum of Da'at Moshe was the Babylonian Talmud.[26] Shapira also evidently formed an advanced group of talented students, apart from the younger disciples in the yeshivah, to study the intricate laws required for ordination as a rabbinic judge (*dayyanut*).[27] Shapira also encouraged one of his disciples to establish a *beit midrash* for the study of Talmud and Hasidic sources in Lodz.[28]

The decision to establish a yeshivah was a deliberate step in Shapira's project of reforming Jewish education to contend with modern challenges.[29] Da'at Moshe was to be an insulated space for spiritual development, an environment in which the students were to focus on communion with the Divine in single-minded devotion to study and on their own personal religious journeys.[30] In a fundraising address on behalf of the Council for Aid on Saving the Yeshivot of Poland and Lithuania, he noted that times had changed: "The salvation of Israel, in spiritual and physical matters, depends on the yeshivah. The yeshivah will receive your children, and after some years it will return them to you—full of Torah and fear of heaven."[31] Yet the point of the yeshivah was not simply to protect its students from the changing times while allowing the rest of the generation to flounder. Shapira hoped that his students would become the heart of a religious revival, eventually producing a new cadre of intellectually talented and spiritually engaged rabbinic leaders.[32]

In his role as founder and *rosh yeshivah* of Da'at Moshe, Shapira was an Orthodox thinker, a Hasidic leader firmly committed to providing a spiritual alternative to the draws of secular culture and political life in twentieth-century Warsaw.[33] Key to this were creating a new way of approaching traditional texts and training a new generation of students—and teachers—who saw the study of Talmud as an immersive spiritual experience. Shapira understood that for many people, including some individuals within the Hasidic fold, Talmud study had lost its ability to command the heart and mind. His development of meditative techniques was one strategy for suffusing the modern world with an élan of spiritual renewal, but so was his attempt to re-envision talmudic study as a quest to unearth the mysteries of the human soul and to stand in the presence of God.

Sacred Study

Rabbi Shapira understood that Hasidic theology had sometimes been viewed as supplanting the study of Talmud with an exclusive emphasis on reading kabbalistic or ethical-spiritual literature. Such devotional works inspire the mind and heart more easily than intricate rabbinic dialectics. Shapira tackled this issue head-on, noting that the intent of Hasidic spirituality is to fundamentally change the student's relationship to *any* element of Torah they might study:

> O Jewish student, do not think that with our words in this book we wish to exempt you from studying Talmud, Midrash, the *Shulhan arukh,* and the other holy works that instruct us in the holy way of ascending to God—heaven forfend that we say thus!
>
> On the contrary, our intention is to correct you (*le-takken et atsmekha*), so that you may look into them and imbibe their holy words into your soul and into your body, drenching all of your limbs with the font that emerges from the house of God and the holy palaces.[34]

The goal of Hasidism is not to supplant the traditional centrality of Talmud and other rabbinic sources. The aim of Hasidic piety, argues Shapira, is to cultivate such a rigorous sense of spiritual attunement that the study of these texts cannot fall into mental sophistry, abstraction, and dry intellection. Instead, Talmud study reveals the bodily practices and intellectual gateways through which a serious student might step into the presence of the Divine. According to this view, Hasidism seeks to enliven scholars and whet their longing for God, thus revealing the Divine precisely within the intricacies of legal exegesis.[35]

Attaining communion with the Infinite is the ultimate goal of all sacred learning, claims Shapira, but this rung cannot be reached through intellectual immersion in talmudic texts alone. One must also be prepared for the experiential dimensions of this scholarship.

> According to one's degree of preparation, becoming fit (*mitkasher*) for God's revelation, so will be one's faith, awe, and love and the arousal (*hitpa'alut*) of one's character traits (*middot*) to God. So too will be one's understanding of Torah—each person grasps some sense of the Divine in exoteric and esoteric [subjects] (*nigleh ve-nistar*), for the Blessed One is found in the Torah.
>
> When one understands a page of Talmud, such as "two individuals are holding onto a garment,"[36] one grasps the

portion of divine illumination in that page,[37] even though his external mind (da'ato ha-niglah) thinks that these are matters of this world—Reuven, Shimon, a garment, a disagreement, and so forth.[38]

To the untrained eye, the study of Talmud is nothing more than dialectical attention to the boring and mundane elements of human life. But for the individual who has undergone spiritual preparation, cultivating the soul and developing the emotional faculties, the Talmud comes alive as a soul-document revealing a unique portion of the Divine.[39] Moreover, Shapira emphasizes that the student of rabbinic literature must come to see that the intricate details of the talmudic deliberations actually disclose God's presence. Just as the seemingly ordinary phenomena of the physical world reveal the divine majesty in palpable and almost tactile terms, so too do the concrete details of the talmudic page.

The nuanced spiritual message of a 1942 sermon, for example, is a tender meditation on the power of talmudic aggadah to bring people together by illuminating the teacher as well as the student. Unlike some elements of religious experience that are irretrievably personal and incommunicable, attentive study of rabbinic aggadah alongside halakhah opens the mind and heart. This spiritual openness, Shapira says, is the pulsing core of Torah, its deepest and innermost essence.[40] Accessing the "secret" of Torah (sod, raz, or sitrei oraita), long understood by the Jewish mystics as the highest mode of Torah study, does not necessarily entail opening up the Zohar or works of Safed Kabbalah.[41] These books have long since been printed and their once esoteric ideas await the eager scholar (see Seeman, this volume). For Shapira, the greatest mysteries to be unlocked in study are those hidden within the human soul. Many of these cannot be accessed except through the penetrating study of rabbinic texts.

A related, but distinct, conception of Talmud study appears in a short essay that was evidently a sort of prolegomenon to Shapira's commentary (or notes) on the Zohar.[42] The essay begins with the story of the biblical leader Ezra, who, upon returning to the land of Israel, sees that many of the Israelites—including priests—have abandoned the Torah (Ezra 9:1–15). Only a few righteous individuals have remained faithful to God. Immediately, Ezra understands that the Torah has become foreign to them; they have been standing outside of it, without internalizing its spiritual and moral message. Ezra therefore realizes that in addition to cognitive Torah study, he needs to find a new way of drawing Torah down into their emotional and spiritual lives. The answer is the project of the Oral Torah:

> How is it possible to bring the Torah, its soul and spirit, which are broader in measure than the earth, into the gateway of the heart of the human being, when the aperture is not that of a wide hall, as it is for the few elites of great spiritual stature? . . .
>
> God instructed him [Ezra], awakening him with the holy spirit—as well as the other *tsaddikim* who were with him—to reveal the Oral Torah. [He sought not just to share] the concise laws and decisions (*dinim ketsarim u-maskanot*) but, from the Torah, to reveal intellect and emotion that fit those of the human being. This enables [the Torah] to cross the threshold of the person and dwell within him, becoming one with him. . . .
>
> They taught them not only the laws, but the reasoning (*pilpul*) and dialectics (*shakla ve-tarya*), so that each person—according to his state—could understand it and bring it into his mind.[43]

It would have been misguided for Ezra to simply condemn his generation for their spiritual ills and disobedience—they were alienated from the written Torah's teaching, which had seemed to have become irrelevant. Talmudic dialectics and the quest to understand its intricate textual workings, approached properly, allow the very essence of Torah to penetrate into one's being and to stir one's mind and heart.

> Perhaps this is how we are to understand [the question]: why has the Gemara of the times of the Mishnah not remained? In giving us the Gemara, they [i.e., Ezra and the sages] intended to give us the intellectual [element] of Torah so that we might grasp ahold of it. When the reasoning (*pilpul*) of the Gemara was revealed by the Amoraim, that of the Tannaim was hidden. And when one delves deeply into the intellect of the Torah, the knowledge and will of God . . . then Torah has already entered one's mind. Y-H-V-H, God of Israel, dwells within one.
>
> But if the sages spoke to the mind through the Gemara [i.e., the legal sections of the Talmud], bringing the Torah into the person, through midrash and aggadah [they spoke] to the emotions. . . . The sages focused (*tsimtsemu*) their own

feelings into these words, into the words of the midrash; [these teachers shared] how they attained uplift in each and every *mitzvah,* and in all the other words of Torah, so that every person—each according to his state—might reach [this same type of] ecstasy and feeling, becoming ignited when studying and speaking aloud the words of the Midrash.[44]

The Talmud of the Tannaim (the sages of the Mishnah) is no longer necessary, suggests Shapira, because the explanations of the Amoraim—full of complexities and conceptualization as well as details—come alive for the reader in an immediate sense as they are recited aloud and interrogated. These rabbinic teachings, he claims, are vessels that hold the spiritual experiences of generations past, and connecting to them unites the Torah with the quality of the Divine that dwells within the human being. Rather than privileging either halakhah or aggadah, Shapira notes that the intellectually challenging legal sections of the Talmud awaken the mind (*sekhel*), while the rabbinic legends and theological musings arouse the heart or "feeling" (*hargashah*). The nomian or praxis-oriented domains of Talmud are thus fused with the emotive in order to generate a fully integrated religious experience.

Earlier generations, Shapira claims, needed less cerebral instruction because the deeper reasons and meaning that undergird the life of devotion were grasped more easily. The integration of the self was more organic, the human connection to the Divine more intuitive, and practices were observed spontaneously—though consistently—in response to the immediacy of the divine command. By the time of Ezra's return to the land of Israel, however, the community had reached a point of crisis. Leaders and teachers were thus required to adopt new strategies for meeting the spiritual challenges of the hour, which they did by joining "each murmur of the whispering of their soul to the details of every verse in the Torah."[45] The greatness of rabbinic exegesis, thus construed, lies in their attempt to translate what had once been an intuitive connection to God into an active interpretive and ritual journey. The present-day student may access spiritual uplift through traversing the verdant exegetical canopy of practices rooted in the fertile ground of the sacred text.

Reframing the discourse of halakhah as a spiritual quest of self-discovery and divine revelation is a central feature of Shapira's innovative take on Talmud study, although his approach surely demands equal sensitivity to the abundant sections of aggadah. He has no truck with the claim that such texts are only for those whose minds are not keen enough for hal-akhah. "Should a disciple of Torah (*ben torah*) who studies Talmud skip over this homily?!," he asks. "Even were we all sages, all knowledgeable in the Torah, it is a commandment for us to study these words . . . [for] it is aggadah that draws forth the heart."[46] Talmudic aggadah can no more be eliminated from religious study and practice than the throbbing heart can be excised from the human body; without the theological and spiritual core, the skeleton of legal structures and the mind to which they adhere are doomed to become ossified and desiccated. The attempt to imbricate aggadah and halakhah should be seen as an important part of Shapira's approach to Talmud study, a step that is necessary—though not itself sufficient—for sparking a spiritual awakening through scholarship.

This process of expanding the reach of Torah through both legal and theological interpretation, thus overcoming the rift between the reader and the sacred texts, stretches beyond the Talmud and classical midrashim. For Shapira, at least in this essay, the process reaches its zenith in the exegesis of the *Zohar*.

> Through the words of midrash, the sages sought to bring the Torah, along with its master—the Master of the world—into a Jew's innermost realm through the gateways of their hearts and emotions. They accomplished this by focusing their pas-sionate excitement and holy spirit, derived from every verse of commandment, into the words of ordinary people, making "handles" (*oznayim*) [through which to grasp] their ecstasy and the sacred visions that they witnessed, such that the heart could understand.
>
> In the *Zohar*, by contrast, their ecstasy and prophetic spirit appear nearly unclothed, just as they are. . . . Even the exegesis (*derush*) in the *Zohar* is different from that of the aggadah and Gemara. It goes beyond the walls of human understanding; the fiery holy spirit that burns within it is naked, untethered by the person's intellect or understanding. This is a matter of the heart, but so are the intellectual matters that we find from time to time in the *Zohar* or Kabbalah; they, too, are matters of the heart and the spirit.[47]

The playful spirit of Zoharic exegesis, claims Shapira, amplifies the cre-ative, evocative impulse of the Midrash; the study of kabbalistic texts thus reminds one of the soulful form that all religious study must take.

In the *Zohar*, he notes, the reader witnesses an uninhibited fire of textual interpretation that is passionate and nearly erotic in its intensity. But the Talmud and classical midrashim are able to reach a much wider audience precisely because they do not speak this way. The quotidian concerns of the rabbinic literature are an accessible lens through which the interior dimensions of Torah and religious spirit may be projected and conveyed. Therefore, properly interweaving halakhah and aggadah—law and theology—arouses the mind and heart to the service of God and revives an intuitive, even prophetic spiritual connection to the Divine that has been lost. The disposition that results from enfolding aggadah back into halakhah, Shapira argues, allows the reader to see even the most quotidian debates in the Talmud and the most obscure kabbalistic theosophy as spiritually relevant to one's immediate situation and existential concerns.

In reading Shapira's imagined historical narrative about Ezra's quest to make Torah relevant for his community, one cannot help but wonder whether the rebbe is making a point about his own contemporary reality. Many Hasidic leaders in interbellum Warsaw were content to wall themselves off within their courts and educational institutions, ignoring the fate of those Jews for whom Torah and tradition were becoming increasingly irrelevant. In this lies a subtle criticism of their routinized piety, performed not out of intense conviction but because of political or social goals.

Shapira, by contrast, saw himself as duty bound to search for a spiritual language that would bring the Torah into the hearts and minds of a wide variety of listeners. There was a time, perhaps also imagined, when the place of God in one's life was easy to locate, when piety was organic and devotion intuitive. This changed with the disenchantment and secularization of the modern world, which widened the gulf between humanity and the Divine like never before. The way to greet such a challenge, Shapira argued, was to reclaim the power of study through creative and impassioned exegesis (see Wiskind, Polen, this volume). The *Zohar* is the heart of this renewal, and aggadah is its right hand. But its legs are the nomian practices of rabbinic Judaism and the talmudic text from which they stem. The rabbinic corpus must be studied not as dry dialectics of legal formalism but as a text suffused with divinity (see Maayan, Seeman, this volume) that awakens the soul of the reader and commands a response through sacred deed.

Shapira's emphasis on aggadah as a means of enkindling the soul was surely meant as a corrective to contemporaneous modes of Torah study prevalent in Lithuania but also found in Poland, in which aggadah was disregarded in favor of halakhah. Like other early-twentieth-century thinkers, such as Rabbi Abraham Isaac Kook and Hayyim Nahman Bialik, who underscored the crucial place of aggadah in Jewish cultural and spiritual development, Shapira saw rabbinic aggadah as linking together multiple modes of devotional literature, seamlessly integrating the fires of Kabbalah and the penetrating insight of talmudic discourse. Even in moments in which he describes Kabbalah as the highest subject of study, the Piasec-zner argues for a kind of midrashic simultaneity in which the various strata of the Torah are all true, each speaking to different people—and to different elements of the self within the same person.[48] Among these, the Talmud provides an intellectual thrust that illuminates the power of the commandments and reveals deeper reservoirs of inspiration that are drawn forth through their fulfillment.

Sacred Knowing

The study of Talmud is, for Shapira, an opportunity to glimpse the Divine as visible in the seemingly mundane questions regarding practices and law that concern much of rabbinic exegesis. This is true for all of the scholarly disciplines of Torah study, but Shapira notes that the concrete, mundane subjects of talmudic inquiry, reflecting the rabbinic sages' concern with the realm of the ordinary, particularly attunes scholars to seeing *all* aspects of the world as manifestations of the Divine.[49] The discourse of rabbinic law represents divine wisdom precisely as translated into the language of ordinary situations involving civil disputes between "lenders and borrowers"; when unpacked correctly, the Talmud infuses the lived human experience and daily life with sanctity and spirituality.

Studying Talmud demands that one bring together mind and heart, because intellection and knowledge are necessary but insufficient grounds for spiritual uplift. The complex embodied praxis of rabbinic Judaism, derived from and joined to the study of legal precepts, has the power to infuse ritual with new devotional energy:

> This is an essential teaching of Hasidism *(ikkar be-torat ha-hasidut)*: do not be satisfied with the mind alone being formed through worship. The connection [to God] that remains in the intellect alone cannot endure. One can subjugate it and know something with full cerebral clarity, [realizing] that

one is serving only God in all the details of one's thought, speech, and deeds, and nevertheless one's heart and entire body are far.[50]

One must connect the entire soul and fullness of one's physical vitality, penetrating into the soul and raising it up, arousing it to become like a flame—in every *mitzvah*, in Torah, and in worship.[51]

Though knowledge alone is not enough to bind one to the Divine, the contemplative mind links together various emotive faculties. Inspiration that is compartmentalized, whether in the mind alone or in the emotions alone, cannot endure. This integrative push is one of the fundamental theological watchwords of Hasidism: one must unite all elements of the self in the service of God. Doing so, Shapira argues, enables the worshipper to see rabbinic texts as far more than manuals for practice or books of obtuse casuistry. For scholars primed to search for unified, embodied knowledge, the Talmud provides a critical key for transforming every element of one's spiritual praxis.

In this way, Shapira's description of Talmud study is directly connected to his many teachings on the role of halakhah and the centrality of physical *mitzvot* to the spiritual life and cultivation of inner piety. Scholars often paint Hasidism as an anomian—or even antinomian—movement of renewal, but current research argues that Hasidism has, from the eighteenth century to the present day, offered a wide variety of different models in which the performance (and reformulation) of law, mystical eros, and impassioned religious devotion have been fused in novel forms of Jewish legal method and discourse.[52] Shapira's attempt to revive Talmud study as a spiritual practice, inclusive of sections dealing with halakhah as well as aggadah, should be seen against this backdrop of a Hasidic ethos that engages with the study and performance of quotidian jurisprudence as a devotional exercise.

Integration of mind and heart lie at the very core of a short essay on the power of exegesis printed in Shapira's prewar sermons, *Derekh ha-melekh*.[53] Shapira argues in that essay that Kabbalah and Hasidism reveal that sacred study is not simply about amassing knowledge but rather about "drawing forth, summoning a cascade" (*hamshakhah ve-hishtalshelut*) of divine vitality and wisdom.[54] The goal of this knowledge is to awaken the emotive faculties and unite them with wisdom (*hokhmah*) and knowledge (*yedi'ah*), thus allowing the intellect to function as a part of a whole being.[55]

> As we engage in study [of Torah], a portion of God's illuminated wisdom and blessed will are drawn forth from the supernal worlds into our minds and our hearts. But this only happens if one has transformed the different parts of one's very being into a "throne" (*merkavah*) [i.e., a dwelling for the divine Presence].
>
> If one has performed one's divine service, taking strength and eliciting a divine revelation through one's form, then when one approaches the Torah, studying [the subject of] "an ox that gored a cow" [the fifth chapter of tractate Bava Kamma], carefully examining it with one's mind for some time, then one will find oneself lifted up. God's spirit will beat within one [like a heart], for the divine dwells within one.[56]

The inner contemplative life, fostered within the heart as well as the mind, shapes the manner in which a student approaches a sacred text. We might do well to compare this passage with the fifth chapter of Shneur Zalman of Liady's *Likkutei amarim—Tanya*. This book, which had a significant impact on Shapira, offers a spiritual vision that prizes the intellect above the emotions and demands that the worshipper allow his mind to "rule over the heart" and only thus propel spiritual uplift.[57] For Shneur Zalman, the mind communes with God directly during study of halakhah. Shapira, inheriting a very different stream of Hasidic thought, argued that talmudic study can—and should—generate a holistic transformation, but only if it includes the emotional faculties. The scholar achieves unity with the Divine through engaging with the talmudic text to the extent that the various dimensions of the self have become integrated.

Shapira claims that the talmudic sages attempted to draw the light of Torah into the human intellect. This does not mean, however, that rabbinic discourse should be misconstrued as the fruit of pure human reason. By arguing that that the ancient rabbis sought to explain God's laws in human terms, Shapira charted an interesting third position that complements the stance of several well-known Lithuanian talmudists.[58] He argues that key legal ideas or precepts, such as the rabbinic law requiring an oath from one who admits part of a monetary claim, may indeed conform to human reason, but they are not ultimately bound to it:[59]

They [the sages] all knew that the Torah does not enjoin its commandments because of human reason, God forbid. Even if a dazzlingly brilliant person were to come along and give other intellectual reasons, we will not alter, heaven forfend, even the dot of the *yod* from the laws of the Torah as they are received.[60]

Why, then, should the sages struggle to express divine logic in terms of human reason? Because doing so awakens the "intellect and mind, and the light of prophecy in the Torah will thus be revealed."[61] Talmudic explorations of logic and reason bring prophecy out of abstraction and into the embodied commandments, rendering the intellectual realm more attainable.[62] Moreover, Shapira claims, the concrete and mundane subjects of talmudic inquiry, reflecting the Talmud's overall concern with the realm of the quotidian, attune us to seeing *all* aspects of the world as manifestations of the Divine.

Shapira thus expands the Baal Shem Tov's teaching on divine immanence in the cosmos and in human language, a bedrock theological message of early Hasidism, by turning it into a call to find God in the most ordinary, recondite, and seemingly irrelevant talmudic discussions. The matrix of the talmudic text represents an opportunity for revelation in which the hidden self may disclose itself through encounter with the Divine. The Baal Shem Tov renewed Jewish life at the beginning of the Hasidic movement by expanding the theater of experience through sanctification of mundane deeds such as eating, walking, or even sleeping, and through a newly devotional approach to the study of both rabbinic and kabbalistic literature. Surrounded by talmudic sophistry but also by waves of promising intellects who were appalled at the aridity of contemporary Orthodox talmudism in his own day, the Piaseczner Rebbe extended this call to divine immanence even to talmudic discussions anchored in the most mundane subjects of loans, oaths, and damages.[63] Such quotidian debates witness a unique manifestation of the divine revealed through the contours of the text and in so doing reveal a unique element of the student's own spiritual self.

Sacred Self

Among the cornerstones of Shapira's educational philosophy is the notion that Torah cannot be well understood if the text is held at a distance from the human being. This refers not just to apathy or disinterest but also to holding Torah at arm's length in order to maintain an avowedly scholarly abstraction or objectivity. The student or scholar must invest all parts of the self, with unadulterated intellectual and emotional presence, in the encounter with the text in order to summon forth new meaning from its words:

> Not only was the Torah given to Israel, but Israel was given to the Torah . . . there must be a mutual exchange in all acts of commerce (*kinyan*). What must we give to the Torah? Our very selves (*et atsmeinu*). We should not stand outside of it and glance upon it but rather give all of our very essence to the Torah; our souls must be brought into it. . . .
>
> When one studies with the soul and thus comes to reveal it, this is the study of the secrets of Torah, the secret of the "pledge" (*sod ha-eravon*; Gen 38:20)—even when one studies the laws "partial admission of claim" (*modeh be-miktsat*), or [the laws] of an ox goring a cow . . . in this too one can study the secrets of Torah, revealing the innermost soul that is concealed and hidden.[64]

As we have seen, Shapira recasts the notion of esoteric study into a devotional key. Even one who does not study Kabbalah must pay close attention to the deepest riddles of the human soul. At times, these rise to the surface through the study of Jewish mystical sources, and at others they are unearthed through impassioned prayer.[65] In this case, however, it is the confrontation with the difficult and seemingly banal discussions in rabbinic literature that are the key to unlocking the personal inner realm.

What is the "pledge" to which Shapira elliptically refers? This turn of phrase reveals his capacity for deft and creative exegesis. Hearkening back to the biblical account of Judah and Tamar, Shapira notes that Judah, having just slept with the mysterious stranger at the crossroads in a fit of lust, admits to at least partial wrongdoing by sending along his comrade "to receive the pledge from the woman's hand." Shapira then suggests that one who studies the talmudic laws of partial admission will reveal the soul that has been vouchsafed within him by God, a mysterious "pledge" deposited with a human being that must be developed and called forth in the act of study.

The quest to grasp the ideational core of the talmudic text is in fact a journey to come to know one's innermost self. "All the holiness rests in the Torah, and in it you will become connected to the holiness of the Infinite One," writes Shapira. "But you must know how to study Torah. First of all, you must reveal your soul that is hidden within you, sleeping and faint, and enter the Torah with it."[66] Addressing his young disciples, Shapira argues that to become a unique self is nothing less than a "duty from which none of you can be exempted."[67] Through studying Hasidic works, and through engagement in prayer and other devotional activities, one is readied to meet the divine and the self in the act of reading the Talmud. In this confrontation with the text, creativity and self-formation go hand in hand.

> When you first started to study Talmud, you were taught the first chapter of Bava Metsia [beginning with the words]: "Two individuals are holding onto a garment." This subject is easy for a child to grasp. But is it truly so simple? Haven't the Tosafot and the other sages, early and late (*rishonim ve-aharonim*), toiled mightily [in the text] and plumbed its depths?
>
> You, too, have a place to make your own. As you exert yourself in study, more and more will be revealed. In every place, in every subject, you can strive and delve deeply [into its words], revealing a greater measure of your power, your vital animating force (*nafshekha*), and your soul, connecting them to the Torah and to the Infinite One who lies within.[68]

Some talmudic passages seem quite easy to understand, but this effort-lessness is actually a sign that the student has not paid ample attention to the processes of self-discovery and innovation. Indeed, as Shapira avers in the continuation of this chapter, talmudic texts become threadbare when read so many times that the illumination and intellectual engagement fades away.[69] Scholars throughout the generations have applied themselves to tilling the canonical texts with discipline and aplomb, and thus sowing seeds through exegesis, have yielded bountiful harvests of meaning. Every person who confronts the text will find hidden ideas concealed therein, and, perhaps of even greater importance, will conjure up and unveil new elements of their own soul and spirit.

Talmud study, thus construed, is an intensely personal devotional journey. "One can," writes Shapira, "recognize one's own spiritual state in the new interpretations one finds in the Torah."[70] Ideas that are truly novel and truly anchored in the divine nature of the text will illuminate everyone who comes in contact with the scholar; these ideas raise up students spiritually as well as intellectually. "When we study Talmud or another work written by a holy person, even though we are learning the laws of the ox that gored the cow, we feel the infusion of holiness long afterward."[71] Other ideas may excite the listener for a short period, but ultimately all textual interpretations—including talmudic ones—that are not rooted in the exegete's soul are no more than fabrications foisted upon the text: "[N]o holiness, no extra soulfulness (*neshamah yeterah*) has been drawn down. We do not feel the holy spirit lingering afterwards."[72]

Studying Talmud with the intensity and presence needed to reveal hitherto concealed dimensions of the self requires significant preparation. It cannot be accomplished in a single moment, and the scholar cannot wait until the talmudic source lies open on the table. The process begins with awakening the self to the spirit of prophecy—that is, to the spark of inner potential for spiritual growth, attunement, and actualization—and only then training one's eyes upon the talmudic text itself.[73] Only thus, with the search for the self, do the words of the talmudic rabbis begin to bear fruit.

Given this difficulty, Shapira acknowledges that one might be tempted to turn to books whose spiritual message is easier to access. He was well aware, as noted above, that one might interpret the legacy of the Baal Shem Tov as a call to study the devotionally inclined books of Kabbalah and Hasidism. Yet Shapira insists that this would not by itself elide the fundamental issue at the heart of his concern: that the study of *any* text must become a matter of sacred attention.

> Sometimes one may feel that one has become a different person, as if one has been joined to an angel, feeling that one has ascended and been raised up from the body, enjoying the most sublime delight and longing and becoming impassioned to ascend heavenward toward God. This realization may even come about after studying a page of Talmud, such as the laws of partial admission, or "one who switches a cow with a donkey."[74]
>
> And so it is with the opposite: at times one may gaze into all the ethical books and yet remain just as before—a rock that cannot be overturned, sunken in corporeality without a feeling of uplift.
>
> The reason for this is that in truth, one's holy essence has not [yet] been born. The only essence that has been brought forth is the same as before, [expressed] in those debased mat-

ters, in the lowest of things. Holy matters are only a garment
without any essence or soul . . .

If one brings one's self to the Torah and *mitsvot* with
all one's soul, as a Jew, then the portions of one's essence are
born through this.[75]

Shapira is speaking of Hasidic disciplines of reading and spiritual arousal
designed to reveal the soul through the encounter with rabbinic literature,
but his point is articulated in expansive terms: illumination in scholarship
is a product of focused attention, presence, and open-heartedness rather
than the particular subject of inquiry.

The broader context of the homily is critical for understanding Shapira's point. He describes Rosh Hashanah as more than a time of rebirth
for the cosmos. On this day, the worshipper is called to enter a new state
of being, making such great strides in the spiritual quest that he or she
is essentially reborn. Accomplishing this type of fundamental, qualitative
shift means more than collecting accolades or achievements—more prayer
or study in the same hackneyed modality—while the self remains in its
preexisting form. Rosh Hashanah, correctly approached, demands a radical
inner transformation, through which one's authentic self is born.

Encountering and being shaped by the ethos of Hasidic texts is a
crucial part of this process of self-discovery. The same is true of Lurianic
Kabbalah and the *Zohar*, read for their devotional significance rather than
their theosophical speculation. But, Shapira says, spiritual uplift may be
gleaned from even difficult or seemingly irrelevant aspects of the Talmud.
One who cannot find a vision of God in rabbinic literature will be equally
blind to the divine presence in even the most spiritually rich and exciting
words. The key is approaching the text with a sense of openness, excite-
ment, and newness. Thus prepared, the reader may become transformed
and reborn in the encounter with the rabbinic text.

We have noted that Shapira refers to Talmud study as a journey that
is both intellectual and emotional, a quest requiring the integration of all
fundaments of one's being. But it is also shot through with the thrill of
self-discovery:

Israel yearns for the Torah. One is pained if one does not
understand something [in one's studies], and one rejoices
and delights in discovering its meaning. The search and the

previous suffering [in not knowing] are like, for example, a
person who is looking for a lost object. The Talmud says that
a person will strive to recover his lost item[76]—[in our case, the
student] is searching for a part of the self, and delights in the
union [when it is recovered]. The student is united [with the
lost aspect] of his own essence. . . .

If a person studies Torah with his mind alone, he will err
in his judgment and argue that an unclean creature is ritually
pure with 150 warped reasons [in support]—but in addition to
this, his comprehension will be no more than fleeting happen-
stance rather than true [integrated] knowledge. Such a person
will have tasted nothing of its deeper meaning.[77]

The study of Talmud with the mind alone is far worse than insufficient.
Cerebral exegesis that lacks the necessary counterbalance of the emotions
is skewed and distorted. Such interpretations cannot take root in the soil
of the soul, and the illumination—such as it is—is fleeting and transitory.
Torah study that is founded in yearning and love as well as intellectual
longing, by contrast, sparks a search for the Divine that is pleasurable
and full of delight, though it may indeed be unending. But the study of
Talmud is in fact two quests that appear to be coterminous: the search
for God among the ordinary markers of human experience expressed in
talmudic dialectics and the hunt for hidden elements of the self that are
revealed in this encounter with the ancient text.

Conclusion

Did Shapira's spiritual approach to studying rabbinic texts influence his
mode of talmudic exegesis? Lacking any firm evidence in the form of
hiddushim, the kind of rabbinic novellae often published by talmudists,
we cannot say for sure.[78] His sermons are peppered with references to
classical midrashim and talmudic discussions, which he interprets for
their devotional significance through a Hasidic lens rather than the textual acrobatics appearing in classical talmudic scholarship. The homilies
in his Ghetto sermons, in particular, are filled with rabbinic aggadah,
surely meant to open the heart and awaken the soul amid the sadness,
destruction, and pain of the Warsaw Ghetto (see Leib-Smokler, Abramson,

Seeman, this volume). In this crushing environment, the spirit of talmudic and midrashic sources—and of aggadah in particular—offered a way of transcending time and entering the world of illuminated exegesis rather than temporal suffering.[79]

Shapira's remarks at a ceremony marking the completion of a cycle of studying the entire Talmud certainly speak to this point. His homily demonstrates his exegetical technique and his belief in the transformative power of talmudic study when such scholarship emerges from spiritual preparation. In a move characteristic of sermons at the end of a study cycle, he joins the final lines of the Talmud with the opening words of its very first tractate. In doing so, he highlights the transformative power of the study of halakhah, noting, however, that one must be correctly prepared in order for the study of Talmud to lift one beyond the confines of the world:

> "One who studies (*shoneh*) halakhot [every day] is assured to be worthy of the world to come (*ben olam ha-ba*)."[80] We must understand: don't all Israel have part in the world to come?[81] We have already discussed that the Torah becomes our intellect, as our mind is garbed in it. What is this intellect? The divine intellect, which becomes ours, for we, through our mind, enter it. Thus, it is not that one who studies Torah will, in the future and after his life, become worthy of the world to come—this is attained as soon as he begins to study! . . .
>
> Its end is embedded in the very beginning—the final lines of ShaS [the Talmud] in the opening [mishnah]: "When [do we recite Shema in the evenings?] From the time that [the priests enter] to eat their terumah."
>
> The Mishnah is telling us how we must study the Torah: with holiness and purification of body and soul. The allusion is as follows: Thus shall you know when it is permitted to recite Shema and study—when it is permitted for the priests to enter and eat terumah. When is this? Once they have cleansed themselves of any impurity.
>
> You might object: Why do we require such purity when studying [the mundane laws of] partial admission or an ox that gores the cow, which is such and such?
>
> You must know, however, that "one who studies halakhot . . . is assured to be worthy of the world to come"—such

a person immediately enters the Garden of Eden and must therefore first become pure.

Understand this.[82]

Notes

1. On this question, see David Maayan, "The Call of the Self: Devotional Individuation in the Teachings of Rabbi Kalonymus Kalman Shapira of Piaseczno" (master's thesis, Hebrew College, 2017), and Maayan's essay in the present volume.

2. Glenn Dynner, "Replenishing the 'Fountain of Judaism': Traditionalist Jewish Education in Interwar Poland," *Jewish History* 31 (2018): 229–61.

3. My thanks to Glenn Dynner for suggesting this line of inquiry.

4. Paul E. Nahme, "*Wissen Und Lomdus*: Idealism, Modernity, and History in Some Nineteenth-Century Rabbinic and Philosophical Responses to the Wissenschaft des Judentums," *Harvard Theological Review* 110, no. 3 (2017): 393–420. See also Eliyahu Stern, *The Genius: Elijah of Vilna and the Making of Modern Judaism* (New Haven: Yale University Press, 2013); Chaim Saiman, "Legal Theology: The Turn to Conceptualism in Nineteenth-Century Jewish Law," *Journal of Law and Religion* 21, no. 1 (2005): 39–100; and Shai Wozner, *Legal Thinking in the Lithuanian Yeshivoth: The Heritage and Works of Rabbi Shimon Shkop* [in Hebrew] (Jerusalem: Magnes, 2016).

5. Michael K. Silber, "The Emergence of Ultra-Orthodoxy: The Invention of a Tradition," in *The Uses of Tradition: Jewish Continuity in the Modern Era*, ed. Jack Wertheimer (New York: Jewish Theological Seminary of America, 1992), 23–84; and more recently, Maoz Kahana, *Me-ha-Noda bi-Yehudah le-ha-Hatam Sofer: Halakhah ve-hagut le-nokhah etgare ha-zeman* (Jerusalem: Merkaz Zalman Shazar, 2015).

6. See Israel Ori Meitlis, "Scholarship (*Lamdanut*), *Hassidut* and *Kabbalah*: On Hassidic and Kabbalistic Influences on the Scholarship of Joseph Rosen" [in Hebrew], *Sidra* 30 (2015): 93–119.

7. See my remarks on this subject in Ariel Evan Mayse, "Like a Blacksmith with the Hammer: Talmud Study and the Spiritual Life," in *The Quest for Meaning*, ed. Martin S. Cohen and David Birnbaum (New York: Mesorah Matrix, 2018), 369–409.

8. See the lucid and insightful discussion of the thorny terms *secularism* and *secularization* in the editors' introduction to Ari Joskowicz and Ethan B. Katz, eds., *Secularism in Question: Jews and Judaism in Modern Times* (Philadelphia: University of Pennsylvania Press, 2015), 1–24; and, more broadly, Charles Taylor, *A Secular Age* (Cambridge: Harvard University Press, 2007), 3–4; and the critique in Susannah Heschel, "Religion and Its Discontents," *AJS Perspectives* (Fall 2011): 6–7; Louis Dupré, "Spiritual Life in a Secular Age," *Daedalus* 111, no. 1 (1982):

21–31; and Leigh Eric Schmidt, "The Making of Modern 'Mysticism,'" *Journal of the American Academy of Religion* 71, no. 2 (2003): 273–302. In making this point, I hope to contribute to the ongoing scholarly debate regarding the multiple pathways of Jewish modernity. See Shmuel N. Eisenstadt, *Multiple Modernities* (New Brunswick: Transaction, 2002).

9. Elhanan Reiner, "Changes in Polish *Yeshivot* in the 16th and 17th Centuries and the Debate over *Pilpul*" [in Hebrew], in *Studies in Jewish Culture in Honour of Chone Shmeruk*, ed. Israel Bartal, Ezra Mendelsohn, and Chava Turniansky (Jerusalem: Magnes, 1993), 9–80.

10. Melila Hellner-Eshed, *A River Flows from Eden: The Language of Mystical Experience in the Zohar*, trans. Nathan Wolski (Stanford: Stanford University Press, 2009), 155–228.

11. See Jacob Katz, "Halakhah and Kabbalah and Competing Disciplines of Study," in *Divine Law in Human Hands: Case Studies in Halakhic Flexibility* (Jerusalem: Magnes, 1998), 56–87; Lawrence Fine, *Physician of the Soul, Healer of the Cosmos: Isaac Luria and His Kabbalistic Fellowship* (Stanford: Stanford University Press, 2003), 207–19.

12. See Abraham Joshua Heschel, "Hasidism as a New Approach to Torah," in *Moral Grandeur and Spiritual Audacity*, ed. Susannah Heschel (New York: Farrar, Straus and Giroux, 1996), 33–39.

13. Immanuel Etkes, *The Besht: Magician, Mystic, and Leader* (Waltham: Brandeis University Press, 2005), 113–51.

14. Mushallam Feibush Heller, *Yosher divrei emet*, ed. Avraham Kahn (Jerusalem: Toledot Aharon, 1974), no. 24, fol. 123b.

15. This idea is found in the early Hasidic story in which the Baal Shem Tov refers to a kabbalistic explanation given by Dov Baer of Mezritsh as "utterly without soul." See Dan Ben-Amos and Jerome Mintz, eds., *In Praise of the Baal Shem Tov: The Earliest Collection of Legends about the Founder of Hasidism* (Northvale, NJ: Jason Aronson, 1993), 81–84. See also Heller, *Yosher divrei emet*, no. 11, fol. 122a.

16. See Mordecai L. Wilensky, "Hasidic-Mitnaggedic Polemics in the Jewish Communities of Eastern Europe: The Hostile Phase," ed. Gershon Hundert (New York: New York University Press, 1991), 261–66; Rivka Schatz-Uffenheimer, *Hasidism as Mysticism*, trans. Jonathan Chipman (Princeton: Princeton University Press, 1993), 310–25; Norman Lamm, *Torah Lishmah: Torah for Torah's Sake in the Works of Rabbi Hayyim of Volozhin and his Contemporaries* (New York: Yeshiva University Press, 1989), 230–324; and Allan Nadler, *The Faith of the Mithnagdim: Rabbinic Responses to Hasidic Rapture* (Baltimore: Johns Hopkins University Press, 1997), esp. 51–60, 151–53, 160–64.

17. See the summary in Wilensky, "Hasidic-Mitnaggedic Polemics," 244–71.

18. Joseph Weiss, "Torah Study in Early Hasidism," in *Studies in East European Jewish Mysticism and Hasidism*, ed. David Goldstein (London: Littman Library of Jewish Civilization, 1997), 66–67.

19. Scholem's claim that Hasidism "developed independently of the rabbinic tradition" for nearly a century requires serious revision; see Gershom Scholem, *Major Trends in Jewish Mysticism* (New York: Schocken, 1974), 345.

20. See Benjamin Brown, "Substitutes for Mysticism: A General Model for the Theological Development of Hasidism in the Nineteenth Century," *History of Religions* 56, no. 3 (2017): 247–88.

21. For one example of Hapstein's legal work, see the controversial *'Agunat yisra'el* (Warsaw, 1880).

22. See Kalonymus Kalman Shapira, *Benei mahshavah tovah* (Jerusalem: Va'ad Hasidei Piaseczno, 1989), 52.

23. On this point, see Don Seeman, "Ritual Efficacy, Hasidic Mysticism, and 'Useless Suffering' in the Warsaw Ghetto," *Harvard Theological Review* 101, no. 3/4 (2008): 469–70. On the mystical dimensions of Shapira's approach to study more broadly, see Daniel Reiser, *Vision as a Mirror: Imagery Techniques in Twentieth-Century Jewish Mysticism* (Los Angeles: Cherub, 2014), 145–46.

24. See Kalonymus Kalman Shapira, *Mevo ha-she'arim* (Jerusalem: Feldheim, 2001), 186–87.

25. See Shimon Huberband, *Kiddush Hashem: Jewish Religious and Cultural Life in Poland during the Holocaust* (Hoboken: Ktav, 1987) 178; Nehemia Polen, *The Holy Fire: The Teachings of Rabbi Kalonymus Kalman Shapira, the Rebbe of the Warsaw Ghetto* (Northvale, NJ: Jason Aronson, 1994), 1–2. Estimating the size of Shapira's yeshivah remains a thorny problem. Daniel Reiser has published a document preserved in the Yeshiva University Archive listing the income and expenditures of Da'at Moshe, which lists three hundred students of ages ten to twenty-five. See Kalonymus Kalman Shapira, *Sermons from the Years of Rage* [in Hebrew], ed. Daniel Reiser (Jerusalem: Herzog Academic College, 2017), 1:337. However, according to The Mark Wischnitzer Papers housed at the YIVO Institute in New York (YIVO RG 767), there were 176 students at Da'at Moshe in 1938.

26. See Aharon Sorski, *Marbitsei torah me-olam ha-hasidut* (Benei Berak, 1988), 6:182–86. See the advertisement placed in *Der Moment*, 26 Tishrei, 5695; and the description of an opening ceremony (*hanukat ha-bayit*) published in *Haynt*, 9 Heshvan, 5689 (October 23, 1928), no. 247, 6.

27. See *Toledot yosef tsevi* (Jerusalem, 2000), 347.

28. See *Sippuro shel ha-hasid ha-aharon: Yisrael Yitzhak Kihn*, ed. Shahar Zeev Kihn (Jerusalem, 2017), 60–61.

29. Two all-Hasidic yeshivot with similar goals were established in interwar Poland: the Metivta (or "Academy") in Warsaw and *Hakhmei Lublin* in the city of that name. See Shaul Stampfer, "Hasidic Yeshivot in Inter-War Poland," *Polin* 11 (1996): 3–24; and David Biale et al., *Hasidism: A New History* (Princeton: Princeton University Press, 2018), 602–605.

30. Polen, *Holy Fire*, 3, describes the educational philosophy of Shapira's yeshivah as follows: "imbuing the child with a vision of his own potential great-

ness and enlisting him as an active participant in his own development." See Shapira's comment in his *Derekh ha-melekh* (Jerusalem: Va'ad Hasidei Piaseczno, 1995), 441: "When you are in yeshivah, do not simply loiter around. Sit yourself down in awe and dignity before the Divine, who is to be found there." The short Yiddish text in which this appears evidently served as one of the foundations of Shapira's book *Hovat ha-talmidim*.

31. *Derekh ha-melekh*, 461.

32. Ibid., 462. Compare the remarks in *Mossad ha-yeshivah ha-gedolah metivta* (1922), no. 7, 5, as quoted in Biale et al., *Hasidism*, 602.

33. See also the remarkably bold statements by his students in the "To the Reader" preamble of the first volume of *Ha-kerem* (Kislev 5691). This short passage celebrates the power of talmudic exegesis—intellectual and evocative—as well as the authors' unwillingness to brook any compromise with modernity, revealing the journal's complicated commitments to twentieth-century Hasidic Orthodoxy and rabbinic creativity.

34. *Hovat ha-talmidim*, ch. 7, 66.

35. See also Emmanuel Levinas, *Nine Talmudic Readings*, trans. Annette Aronowicz (Bloomington and Indianapolis: Indiana University Press, 1990), esp. 5, 14, 32, 55.

36. B. Bava Metsi'a 2a.

37. See the formulation of the Kotsker Rebbe preserved in *Amud ha-emet* (Bnei Brak: Pe'er, 2000), 210: "The light of a commandment rests within the talmudic tractate in which it is discussed."

38. *Sermons from the Years of Rage, parashat bo* 5702 (1942), 1:255.

39. See *Zohar* 1:103b; and *Sermons from the Years of Rage, parashat bo* 5702 (1942), 1:254–55.

40. *Sermons from the Years of Rage, parashat bo* 5702 (1942), 1:255.

41. Here Shapira cites, and develops, the experiential understanding of *sod* suggested by Kalonymus Kalman Epstein of Krakow (after whom he was named). See Kalonymus Epstein, *Ma'or va-shamesh* (Jerusalem: 1992), *parashat tavo'*, 2:629–30. See also Heller, *Yosher divrei emet*, no. 22, fol. 122a; Kalonymus Epstein, *Keter shem tov ha-shalem* (Brooklyn: Kehot, 2004), no. 240b; and Moshe Idel, *Hasidism: Between Ecstasy and Magic* (Albany: State University of New York Press, 1995), 174.

42. Nothing further from this work remains.

43. "Mesirat moda'ah," in *Derekh ha-melekh*, 426–27.

44. Ibid., 427.

45. Ibid., 428.

46. Ibid., 429. This formulation of "even were we all sages" draws upon the Passover Haggadah.

47. Ibid., 431.

48. *Mevo ha-she'arim*, 186, 188–89.

49. See, for example, ibid., 211–12.

50. On this element of Shapira's project, see James Jacobson-Maisels, "Embodied Epistemology: Knowing through the Body in Late Hasidism," *Journal of Religion* 96, no. 2 (2016): 185–211.

51. Introduction to *Hovat ha-talmidim*, 21–22.

52. For a recent study, see Maoz Kahana and Ariel Evan Mayse, "Hasidic Halakhah: Reappraising the Interface of Spirit and Law," *AJS Review* 41, no. 2 (2017): 375–408.

53. *Derekh ha-melekh*, "*Derekh ha-iyyun ha-meyuhad*," 435–40. This essay is evidently the only extant fragment of the projected *Hovat ha-avreikhim*.

54. Ibid., 339.

55. My own understanding of this passage as an integrated knowledge differs slightly from that of Jacobson-Maisels, "Embodied Epistemology," 188, who cites it as an example of Shapira's occasional emphasis on the power of the intellect.

56. *Hovat ha-talmidim*, ch. 5, 228.

57. See Schneur Zalman of Liady, *Likkutei amarim–Tanya*, revised bilingual ed., trans. Nissan Mindel (Brooklyn: Kehot, 1998), fol. 9a–10a. Hillel Zeitlin dismisses the influence of Schneur Zalman's writings on Shapira, a surprising move given the obvious affinities as well as Zeitlin's own intellectual and spiritual commitments to Chabad. See Seeman, "Ritual Efficacy," 472, n. 26.

58. Here I have in mind Hayyim of Brisk, who argued that halakhah operated according to abstract and immutable divine principles, and Shimon Shkop, whose writings emphasized the human logic of halakhah. Given the close links between the Jewish communities of Warsaw and Vilna and their rabbinic leaders in the interbellum period, it is certainly not beyond the pale to assume that Shapira was aware of these thinkers and their intellectual legacies. In addition to the sources cited above, see Shimon Gershon Rosenberg, *Be-torato yehegeh: Limmud gemara ke-vakashat elokim*, ed. Zohar Meor (Mekhon Kitvei Rav Shagar, 2009), 46–104; Shai Wozner, "On the Duty to Obey the Law in Halakhik Thought: Reflections on the Thesis of Shimon Shkop," *Jewish Law Association Studies* 20 (2010): 353–60; and Yosef Lindell, "A Science Like Any Other?: Classical Legal Formalism in the Halakhic Jurisprudence of Rabbis Isaac Jacob Reines and Moses Avigdor Amiel," *Journal of Law and Religion* 28, no. 1 (2013): 179–224.

59. B. Bava Metsi'a 2a–3b.

60. *Mevo ha-she'arim*, 190.

61. Ibid., 192.

62. Ibid., 198.

63. Compare *Mevo ha-she'arim*, 214–15.

64. *Derekh ha-melekh, rosh ha-shanah*, 197. See also Shapira, *Derekh ha-melekh, parashat be-shalah* 5690 (1930), 98.

65. *Sermons from the Years of Rage, parashat ki tetse* 5700 (1940), 1:150.

66. *Hovat ha-talmidim*, ch. 12, 118–19.

67. Author's introduction in ibid., 35. See also Shapira, *Tsav ve-zeruz* (Jerusalem: Feldheim, 2001), no. 10, 331–32, where the cultivation of the self is presented as an explicit alternative to philosophical notions of determinism that were gaining traction in that time. There, Shapira further notes that the voice of this unique self becomes embodied in one's theological writings; this mode of anchoring the spiritual quest in the text complements the argument of the present study. My thanks to Don Seeman for bringing this crucial passage to my attention.

68. *Hovat ha-talmidim*, ch. 2, 126.

69. Ibid., 126–27.

70. Shapira, *Derekh ha-melekh, parashat mikets* 5730 (1929), 56.

71. Ibid., *sukkot* 5690 (1929), 280.

72. Ibid., 280.

73. Ibid., *shavuot 2* 5689 (1929), 406.

74. M. Bava Metsi'a 8:4.

75. *Derekh ha-melekh, rosh ha-shanah* 5686 (1925), 194–95.

76. B. Kiddushin 2b.

77. *Derekh ha-melekh, parashat va'era* 5689 (1929), 94.

78. In a 1926 letter, Shapira laments the loss of his *hiddushim* on the tractate Berakhot, which took him the better part of a year's labor. His choice to begin with this tractate may suggest that Shapira wanted to author a commentary on the entire Talmud, but I believe it more likely that he was interested in writing on Berakhot because of the tight interweaving of its aggadah and halakhah. Reiser cites the letter in *Sermons from the Years of Rage*, 1:42. To my knowledge, Shapira's Talmudic novellae did not appear in the journal *Ha-kerem*, so in the theft of this document, we lost whatever we might have had.

79. See his remarks on precisely this point in *Sermons from the Years of Rage, parashat bo* 5702 (1942), 1:253–59. And yet, as Don Seeman, in "Ritual Efficacy," 465–505. has argued, Shapira's Ghetto writings emphasize the element of divine vitality that is identical with divine suffering far more than the quest to reveal the self and soul that undergirds so much of his prewar corpus.

80. B. Niddah 73a.

81. M. Sanhedrin 10:1.

82. *Derekh ha-melekh, siyyum ha-shas*, 442.

4

Mystical Fraternities:
Jerusalem, Tiberius, and Warsaw

A Comparative Study of Goals, Structures, and Methods

Zvi Leshem

Introduction

The first book of R. Kalonymus Kalmish Shapira, *Benei mahshavah tovah*, was probably composed in the early 1920s.[1] It was a secret handbook for the establishment and running of secret Hasidic mystical fraternities, a work that both dealt with group guidelines and detailed various mystical techniques and meditative exercises for expanding consciousness and achieving prophetic inspiration. The book also served as a blueprint for much of R. Shapira's later writings, in which he expanded upon these ideas and techniques. The idea of the group itself is discussed at length in some of R. Shapira's later works, although it was no longer veiled in secrecy.

I will explore the historical context of the Hasidic fraternity itself and how earlier mystical fraternities may have influenced the Piaseczner's plan and program. I propose to analyze the "structural" aspects of the plan laid out in *Benei mahshavah tovah*, including group meetings, study, confession, and the relationships among members of the group, in comparison with two prior examples and one contemporary one. First, I will examine testimonies and documents pertaining to the Ahavat Shalom fraternity in the Bet El Kabbalistic Yeshiva in Jerusalem in the mid-eighteenth century. Second, I will look at letters dealing with similar topics from the early Tiberius Hasidic groups of R. Menachem Mendel of Vitebsk and R. Abraham of Kalisk. My claim is that these letters, published early in the nineteenth century, probably served as a direct source for R. Shapira as he planned *Benei mahshavah tovah*. Additionally, I believe that he may have received oral and written traditions pertaining to the above groups via his father-in-law, R. Yerahmiel Moshe Hapstein of Kozhnits, who received them from the rebbes of Karlin. The work *Maor va-shemesh*, by his great-grandfather R. Kalonymus Kalman Epstein of Kraków, which placed great emphasis on the centrality of community in Hasidic life, may have also inclined him in this direction.[2]

This should also be examined through the prism of earlier mystical fraternities in Judaism, such as the group of R. Shimon bar Yochai described in the *Zohar*, the students of R. Yitzhak Luria in sixteenth-century Safed, and the students of R. Moshe Hayyim Luzzatto in eighteenth-century Padua. These, however, are not a major focus of this research, since I wish to deal only with historically documented fraternities that were in close historical proximity to R. Shapira, although the others no doubt loomed large in his imagination. My interest is to define and analyze the major components of the mystical fraternities in Jerusalem and Tiberius and determine to what extent they influenced R. Shapira's vision. Furthermore, I wish to clarify in what ways the goals and methods of *Benei mahshavah tovah* differ from the earlier models and why. Finally, I will contrast R. Shapira's model for Hasidic fellowships with those of his Warsaw contemporary Hillel Zeitlin and close with a chilling account of R. Shapira's participation in a fraternity of sorts prior to his martyrdom in November 1943.

In doing so, I hope to make a novel contribution to the understanding of the communal aspect of Hasidism. This is important in light of the individualist and existentialist trend that has characterized research on Hasidism in recent years.[3] This more communal approach, while significant in its own right as a counterbalance to much of current research, has methodological implications as well, leading toward a more interdisciplinary approach to Hasidic studies, in which the tools of "Jewish thought" or "intellectual history" are combined with those of "social history" (Wodziński, this volume).[4]

The Goals of *Benei Mahshavah Tovah*

Before addressing R. Shapira's plan for renewal, it is important to understand that his work was related to the deterioration of the Hasidic movement (see Idel, Mayse, this volume). In his opinion, certain aspects of Hasidic life had fallen into disregard, including the crucial institution of Hasidic fellowship, the *Hevraya qadisha,* which first appears in the context of the *Zohar.*[5] Drastic educational reform and spiritual revolution were needed. As part of his program, he strove to reinstitute spiritual societies, an effort first outlined by R. Shapira in his short treatise *Benei mahshavah tovah.*

The book's target audience was the Hasidic spiritual elite. Its goal was to help engender small fraternities of like-minded Hasidim interested in holistic spiritual service, the experience of intimacy with the divine, and ultimately the soul's "melting." Members would seek to achieve a heightened state of consciousness that went beyond special times of prayer or Torah study. It was meant to be a total revolution in the religious persona of the individual, who would learn to think constantly of God, living in a state of intense concentration and powerful emotion bordering on prophecy.[6] Much of this book, and of R. Shapira's other works, is dedicated to practical guidance in this area (see Idel, Seeman, this volume).[7] The fraternity would provide a framework within which each individual member could learn how to properly serve God. Significantly, the group was meant to serve the individual, and not the other way around.[8] R. Shapira gives practical instruction on the topic of *mahshavah* (consciousness) and how to achieve the state of *mahshavah tovah,* or heightened consciousness.[9]

Benei mahshavah tovah concludes with a list of "bylaws." Each society must maintain a notebook with the names of its members and its records. Included in the notebook (in the script used for a Torah scroll) is the *nusah ha-kabbalah,* a document in which the new member accepts upon himself the terms of the group by affixing his signature.[10] What follows is the text of the agreement. Since I will be comparing it to similar documents, I quote it here almost in full:

> In free will and volition, in alignment with the deepest desire of my heart, life, psyche, and soul, I take it upon myself to become a member of this devoted group . . . to clean and clear my body and mind and to offer them in holiness to the holy God. I devote to God's holy purposes my intentions, thoughts, speech, and deeds, in a binding and immutable commitment. . . . I stand before God and declare myself holy and devoted—body, heart, and mind—I am his. . . . May his holiness enter my being. At every moment and at every level, wherever I may be, there may I be surrounded by God. May

the glory of his presence encompass me from this moment on through eternity.

> I pray to God with all my heart and soul: If my urges overpower me . . . if I stray from the will of God in my intentions, in my awareness, in my speech or deeds, please God, for the sake of your great mercy, do not despise me . . . I know your holy hand is always open wide to accept the strays who return—accept me, for my remorse is sincere. When you are in my heart, I am whole . . . I go forth to enter the presence of God. I commit my 248 organs and limbs to the 248 positive commandments. I accept the 365 negative commandments in my sinews and my flesh. By this declaration, I accept upon myself to carefully observe every aspect of my behavior, intentions, and speech, in a manner appropriate for a person who has made a commitment to holiness and elevation. . . . I know that the Holy One will support me with his unflinching righteousness and guide me on his holy path. . . . Amen.[11]

It is worth noting R. Shapira's repeated stress on a "holistic" service of God. This is seen in phrases such as "body and mind" and "intentions, thoughts, speech, and deeds." The document also expresses a strongly immanent worldview, in which the devotee not only is "surrounded by God" but also longs to be entered by "his holiness" (on "incarnational" themes, see also Maayan, this volume). Yet even as the text emphasizes striving for spiritual perfection, the inevitable failure of the imperfect human being is recognized and finds its place.

The Society: Structure and Activities

The fraternity is meant to remain egalitarian and apolitical, with no officers or honors. Members are instructed to emphasize the biblical mandate to love all fellow Jews (*ahavat yisraˀel*), inflected with kabbalistic nuance, and must not cause any conflict with those who are not members. The members of the society must meet at least three times each week.[12] During meetings, they are told, it is crucial to refrain from frivolous discussion. Each member can study whatever he pleases, such as Mishnah or Gemara. At least once a week, however, all members must study together, especially works of Hasidic guidance, including R. Shapira's tract itself. In doing so, they should "study slowly and in depth, applying the topic to themselves, how they will fulfill the advice of the book . . . any member who thinks of a good idea . . . should discuss it with his friends, and they should listen, for even if the matter is insignificant nine times, the tenth time there may be some importance." R. Shapira continues with practical instructions:

> It is proper for them to occasionally drink together, not to get drunk and act frivolously, God forbid, but in the way of Hasidim to connect with each other, and also to arouse the animal soul from its laziness. . . . After they drink, they should sing a spiritually arousing song . . . and if they are inspired and wish to dance together, they should dance, so long as they don't spend all of the time just drinking, singing, and dancing.[13]

Regarding relationships within the society, R. Shapira gives guidance based on the idea that "the holy society is based on three principles: the connection of friends, the love between friends, and the cleaving of friends. . . . They must all love each other with powerful love." Despite the deep connection among them all, it is also important for each to have a particular friend and study partner:

> Each should choose one special friend, before whom he can reveal all of the secrets of his heart, in both spiritual and physical matters, his concerns and his joys, his failures and successes. His friend should then comfort and advise him and cause him to rejoice as much as possible, also in spiritual matters, according to his understanding of the situation, and then they should reverse roles.[14]

Nonetheless, there is collective responsibility for the needs of all members: "If there is one member for whom no one wishes to be a spiritual discussion partner, the fraternity must provide one for him." It is also crucial that the members hold each other in great esteem. It is, however, completely forbidden to reveal matters of the society in public: "Do not discuss or publicize matters of the holy society in the market or the streets; don't brag about it in front of others. . . . All of Kabbalah is called 'secret' (*sod*); so too, all service involving the revelation of the soul is opposed to publicity, preferring secrecy."[15]

This short tract includes a complete and self-contained Hasidic system in the service of God, education, and spiritual guidance. Since R. Shapira later wrote openly of these societies in his other prewar works, *Hakhsharat ha-avreikhim* and *Mevo ha-she'arim*, I surmise that he eventually decided to open the ranks of the societies to the wider Hasidic community. Practically speaking, however, the groups that would coalesce around *Benei mahshavah tovah* would no doubt remain the inner circle of the elite Piaseczner Hasidism, those closest to R. Shapira.[16] While the Holocaust cut this noble experiment short, leaving us with little data with which to evaluate its successes or failures, we must admit that no evidence has yet been uncovered to indicate that the kinds of fraternities envisioned by this book were ever widespread (see Wodziński, this volume).

Pre-Hasidic Mystical Fraternities

The phenomenon of mystical fraternities can be traced back to the biblical institution of *Benei ha-nevi'im*, neophyte prophets who engaged in mystical techniques, including music and meditation, in order to achieve prophetic inspiration. This group directly influenced R. Shapira's vision.[17] In the early rabbinic period, furthermore, one encounters the story of R. Akiva and his students entering the *Pardes* ("garden"); this was also when the circles that produced the *merkavah* mysticism arose, as well as the imagined circles described in *merkavah* literature.[18] Yehuda Liebes has pointed out that in the classic period of Kabbalah, the *hevraya kedosha* of R. Shimon Bar Yohai and his students, the heroes of Zoharic literature, may in fact have mirrored an actual mystical fraternity active in late thirteenth-century Spain, centered around the personality of R. Moshe de Leon. This circle, according to Liebes, may have authored the *Zohar*, spiritually or imaginatively transplanting themselves in the land of Israel of the second century.[19]

The tradition of mystical fraternities continued into the early modern period, with the circle of the Safadian Kabbalists centered on R. Yitzhak Luria (the Ari) in the sixteenth century.[20] Following in the footsteps of the Lurianic Kabbalah and its groups were the circles of Rabbi Moshe Hayyim Luzzatto (Ramchal) in early eighteenth-century Padua[21] and R. Shalom Sharabi (Rashash) at Yeshivat Bet El in eighteenth-century Jerusalem.[22] The Bet El group is significant for this study, since we have the pact document signed by its members. It will be instructive to compare this document (*shtar hitkashrut*), signed in 1754 and 1758, with the document signed by members of R. Shapira's groups as well as with other instructions he gave to group members. The original Hebrew document was printed by Moshe Yair Weinstock and translated into English, published, and analyzed along with another testimony by Louis Jacobs.[23]

Jacobs opens with a description of Bet El and its mystical inner circle, *Ahavat Shalom* (whose members are also known as *mekhavnim*, or "those with intentionality"), penned by Ariel Bension, the son of a later member of his group.[24] Bension describes the community as being centered on the performance of the prayer intentions of the Ari and R. Hayyim Vital as understood in the Sephardic tradition. Like R. Shapira, Bension stresses the centrality of "brotherly love" within the community. Concentration in prayer was to be attained through inner joy aroused through introspection and the use of special melodies, interspersed within the prayer services, "suggestive of the form which the meditation was to take." In Bension's words, "under the magic of these tunes, *mekhavnim* and listeners, animate and inanimate objects, became one in the true pantheistic sense." Bension also discusses the "pact of friendship," which he says is "filled with expressions of the deep and abiding love of man for his neighbor . . . striving after complete union."[25]

This document opens by positing the desire of the signatories to "become as one man, companions, all for the sake of the unification of the Holy One, blessed be he, and his *shekhinah*." Thus, the pact is signed with binding conditions. The initial group of signatories numbered twelve, corresponding to the twelve tribes. They bound themselves to each other with great love: "That all of us should love each other with great love, both spiritual and physical." The goal was that "the twelve of us will be as one man" in order to provide mutual assistance out of a feeling of complete identification. "Each of us will rebuke his associate when, God forbid, he hears of any sin the latter has committed." This mutual responsibility is to continue even in the world to come, and the pact stipulates the relinquishment of any spiritual benefit that may have accrued to one member at the expense of another.

The egalitarian nature of the fraternity is also stressed: "never to praise one another even if it is clear to everyone that one associate is superior. . . . None of us will rise fully to his feet before any other associate. . . . We shall conduct ourselves as if we were one man, no part of whom is superior to any other part." Finally, it is important to note that the pact also demands secrecy, just as R. Shapira's did: "We further take upon ourselves the obligation never to reveal to any creature that we have resolved to do these things."[26]

At this point, it is crucial to note the comment of Israeli scholar Meir Benayahu, who writes, "It seems, based upon this copy, that it was disseminated by the Galilean Hasidim to the communities in Poland and Ashkenaz."[27] Benayahu's assertion, though unsourced, is highly significant, because it points to a direct link from Jerusalem to Tiberius and from there to the eastern European Hasidim. However, even if Benayahu is incorrect, we have direct evidence of the presence and influence of a different fraternal pact, that of the students of R. Hayyim Vital in Safed in the sixteenth century after the death of R. Isaac Luria. In 1940, Zeev Rabinowitz published descriptions of several manuscripts found in the genizah[28] of the Karlin-Stolin Hasidic masters in Stolin, Belarus. Among them was a contract between the students of R. Isaac Luria and R. Hayyim Vital, which was signed in Safed in 1565. In it, they pledge themselves to serve God and study Torah as directed by Vital and not to reveal his kabbalistic teachings without permission. In response, Gershom Scholem discussed the document in detail and speculated as to how and when it may have reached Stolin.[29] Scholem states that he initially believed that the Hasidic leader R. Abraham Kalisker purchased the document on a visit to Safed and sent it to his friends in Russia, from where it reached one of the early rabbis of Karlin. This theory, similar to Benayahu's claim regarding the Jerusalem document, was subsequently rejected by Scholem based on information about the pact in R. Hayyim David Azulay's *Shem ha-gedolim*. Scholem ultimately speculates that "perhaps the document arrived in Stolin at a later time, and one of the tsaddikim of the House of Stolin purchased it in the nineteenth century from Italy." As we shall see, Scholem's intuition was partially correct; the document was purchased by a tsaddik of Karlin-Stolin in the nineteenth century, but directly from Palestine, not via Italy.

Abraham Avish Shor has published two articles on the Luria-Vital pact documents in the Stolin genizah.[30] He cites a letter of R. Asher the Second of Stolin to R. Shmuel Heller, the Chief Rabbi of Safed, dated 1861, in which he discusses the purchase of such documents and their delivery to Stolin and thanks him for documents already received. In addition to the pact of Vital's students, the genizah held a similar document from the students of R. David ben Zimra (Radbaz) from Egypt dated 1565. These documents were very beloved to the rabbis of Karlin-Stolin, as Shor writes: "At opportune occasions the Young Rebbe [R. Asher] would enjoy looking at these pact documents." He also quotes from a notebook penned by R. Yerahmiel Moshe of Kozhnits, stepson of R. Asher, who was raised in Stolin in the presence of R. Asher and Asher's father, R. Aharon the Second of Karlin: "Once the rebbe showed the holy signatures on this document to some people, pointing out the holy signatures of the Radbaz and the Ari's students, and said, 'That is the signature of the Radbaz and eleven students who made a covenant to serve God with no ulterior motives.'" The Karliner also made a point of showing them to another well-known Hasidic personality, R. Yizchak Isaac of Komarno, on the occasion of a journey that the two made together. This testimony is highly significant, since R. Yerahmiel Moshe was R. Shapira's [older] nephew and later became his father-in-law. After R. Shapira was orphaned at a young age, he was effectively raised in the court of R. Yerahmiel Moshe in Kozhnits and trained by him to be a rebbe (see Idel, Wodziński, this volume).[31] When R. Yerahmiel Moshe died, R. Shapira became the new rebbe for many of his Hasidim. It is thus reasonable to assume that the traditions regarding fraternities and pacts of this kind would have been passed on from R. Yerahmiel Moshe to R. Shapira. I thus posit a clear chain of tradition regarding these fraternities. Their documents traveled from Egypt and Safed to Stolin, in Poland, and from there on to Kozhnits, and finally to Piaseczno.[32] Although we do not yet know of similar mystical societies in Stolin or in Kozhnits, their absence would only make R. Shapira's activities even more remarkable, as it would mean that he was not engaged in an act of continuity from his most proximate Hasidic context but rather in a great restorative project stretching across time and space to eighteenth-century Jerusalem and Tiberius, sixteenth-century Safed, and, in his mind, even to the *hevra kadisha* of the *Zohar* in second-century Galilee (see Idel, this volume). This is remarkable indeed.

Hasidic Mystical Fraternities
in Eighteenth-Century Tiberius

Returning to the early Hasidic community, much has been written about the Baal Shem Tov and the Maggid of Mezritsh and their mystical circles.[33] I will focus on the Hasidic mystical fraternities in Tiberius at the end of the eighteenth century, which seem to have served as one model for the Benei mahshavah tovah groups. Our information regarding these groups is contained in letters from R. Menahem Mendel of Vitebsk and R. Abraham of Kalisk to their followers in Europe. These letters were published in the early nineteenth century and were very likely read by R. Shapira.³⁴

These two students of the Maggid arrived in Tiberius in 1777. Their oeuvre includes the aforementioned letters as well as Hasidic sermons: *Peri ha-arets*, by R. Menachem Mendel, and some material published in *Hesed le-Avraham*, by R. Abraham, the son of the Maggid. The first scholar to analyze the letters that are relevant to our discussion was Joseph Weiss in his 1955 article "Kalisker's Concept of Communion with God and Man."³⁵

R. Abraham stresses the importance of the state of *ayin* (mystical "naught"). Unlike the Maggid's system, in which *ayin* is a spiritual state, for Kalisker, it is "an attitude of social humility." *Ayin* "is divested by Abraham of its mystical sense and is . . . self-annihilation in terms of human relationships." He writes that "the relationship between man and man is the pivot round which the thoughts of Abraham revolve." Of course, this does not have to be a zero-sum game, and I question Weiss's dichotomy between *ayin* as a mystical state and *ayin* as a social attitude. It is equally possible that the two can coexist and even strengthen each other. This would, in fact, appear to be the attitude of R. Shapira, who writes that by annulling one's ego before one's friends, one will succeed in doing so in his relation with God as well. (For a somewhat contrary view, see Maayan, this volume.)³⁶ Kalisker's approach, however, is predicated on his definition of *devekut* (cleaving) and of the lower state of *devekut be-qatnut*, or cleaving while in a limited spiritual state. *Qatnut* is recognized in Hasidism as the condition in which one is not able to connect deeply with the divine. R. Abraham presents an understanding in which *katnut*, the time when concentration upon God is not possible, offers an opportunity for concentration upon one's fellowman, "the choicest opportunity for 'loving one's neighbor,' *devekut* with the neighbor.'" This serves two purposes: First, connecting with God vicariously, via members of the fraternity who are in a state of *gadlut*, and second, a degree of divine providence normally available only when in a state of cleaving or *devekut*.³⁷

Weiss entertains the possibility that Kalisker is referring to a relationship of *devekut* with the tsaddik rather than directly with God, which, if correct, would return R. Abraham's perspective to a more common Hasidic one. However, he rejects this possibility, stressing the egalitarian spirit of the group: "This theory of *devekut* . . . proves to be a special case within the general theory of *dibbuk haverim*, i.e. close association of friends of equal stature . . . the *tsaddik* plays a very unimportant role . . . the first time in the history of Hasidism that clear expression is given to the idea of the value of the Hasidic community per se as distinct from its dependence on the *tsaddik* . . . a new value: that of the contemplative community whose members are bound together by the emotional values of sympathy and brotherhood."

Weiss compares R. Abraham's letter to a letter of R. Menachem Mendel to the community in Bieshika. The novelty here is "individual confession between friends," in which Weiss sees a break in "the exclusive tradition of collective confession . . . so characteristic of Judaism."[38] He takes pains to explain the difference between the confession recommended here and confession before the tsaddik as an initiation rite, which was found in early Bratslav Hasidism. What we have here is "between equals; neither is it part of an initiation ceremony, but rather a daily custom." Weiss translates, "Let him hold converse with them every day for about half an hour, and engage in self-reproof for the evil ways he sees in himself. His companion should do likewise . . . and truth will begin to shine." We are not dealing with a confession before the group but rather "an individual confession between two companions." Another noteworthy point in the letter of R. Menachem Mendel is the following instruction, similar to that found in *Benei mahshavah tovah*: "have a set daily time for the study of ethical works such as *Reshit hokhmah*, *Sefer ha-yasher* of Rebbenu Tam, and *Sefer haredim*. And especially the Holy Zohar."[39]

In contradistinction to Weiss, Zeev Gries sought to demonstrate the mystical underpinnings of Kalisker's approach and to show its antecedents in earlier kabbalistic myth and practice, which culminated in the mystical group centered on R. Abraham's own teacher, the Maggid of Mezritsh. For our purposes, it is interesting to note the comparison that Gries makes between the mystical fraternities in Tiberius and those of Bet El. Gries quotes R. Hayyim David Azulay, who had been a member of the *Ahavat Shalom* group in Bet El, who states that "the holy *Zohar* strongly warned regarding the love of friends, and so, too, our master the Ari (R. Isaac Luria), of blessed memory."[40]

In comparing Benei mahshavah tovah with Bet El, we encounter some obvious differences but also many striking affinities. In Bet El, the main focus was on prayer with Lurianic *kavvanot* within a full-time prayer and study group whose lifestyle was both exclusivist and ascetic. R. Shapira's fraternities, on the other hand, were forbidden from withdrawing from their regular synagogue communities. In Bet El, there was a hierarchical structure, led by the *rosh yeshivah,* whereas *Benei mahshavah tovah* was completely egalitarian. Finally, the Bet El friendship pact includes otherworldly elements, such as the connection between living and dead members. In *Benei mahshavah tovah,* these factors are not present.

On the other hand, both groups have a document that must be signed by all members. Both groups also demand absolute secrecy regarding group activities. Both groups stress the use of *niggun* (melody) in the context of group activity. Both groups also place great emphasis on the spiritual goal of *devekut* (cleaving) both to God and to the other members, who aid each other in cleaving to God. In this context, the two groups use similar language: Bet El has "*ahavah rabbah, ahavat nefesh, ve-ahavat ha-guf*" (great love, spiritual love, and physical love). Benei Mahshavah Tovah has "*hithabberut haverim, ahavat haverim, hitdabbekut haverim*" (the connection of friends, the love of friends, and the cleaving of friends). Both groups also emphasize ongoing dialogue among the members, but Bet El stresses rebuke, whereas R. Shapira urges peer counselling. In Bet El, furthermore, the members pledge not to lavishly praise one another but rather to demonstrate moderate respect, as if they were all equal, while in Benei Mahshavah Tovah, each member is urged to view the others (and himself) as members of the spiritual elite (*benei aliyah*). The Bet El agreement binds the members to follow any *takkanah* or good custom that the majority agrees upon, while *Benei mahshavah tovah* instructs its members to share and discuss ideas pertaining to divine service, with the aim of applying them to practical observance.

Comparing *Benei mahshavah tovah* to the Hasidim in Tiberius, I find both differences and similarities, with the similarities far outweighing the differences. Among the contrasts is the absence of the two models of *devekut be-gadlut* and *devequt be-katnut* in *Benei mahshavah tovah.* There, *devekut* is always a vehicle for connecting with God, and the individual member utilizes the group setting to achieve this *devekut.*[41] R. Abraham's concept that one achieves constant *devekut* by cleaving to others who are cleaving to God is also absent in *Benei ahshavah tovah.* In terms of affinities, we should note that both the directives of the rabbis from Tiberius and *Benei mahshavah tovah* place great stress on *devekut* between fraternity members. Both groups are egalitarian, and the tsaddik is not a central figure in the group.[42] The stress on humility as a central character trait is found in both. Both groups strongly emphasize the importance of group discussions regarding personal issues and difficulties. According to R. Abraham, the very act of verbal communication works to draw mercy upon the individual.[43] In the letter of R. Menachem Mendel, we find a directive to engage in individual confession between friends within the group. This is similar to the practice in *Benei mahshavah tovah,* although the word *confession* is not used there. However, in *Benei mahshavah tovah,* the focus is on mutual counseling and advice. Perhaps for both groups, this practice also strengthens mutual dependence due to the sharing of secrets. R. Menachem Mendel instructed his followers to set a daily time to study *sifrei mussar.* Similarly, *Benei mahshavah tovah* ordains that the group must study works of Hasidism, and both texts suggest the study of the *Zohar.*

As I have demonstrated, significant parallels exist between the guidelines for *Benei mahshavah tovah* and those of both the Bet El fraternity and the directives of R. Menachem Mendel and R. Abraham to their followers. While according to Benayahu it is possible that Hasidim had access to information regarding the *Ahavat Shalom* fraternity in Jerusalem, it is unlikely that this information would have been known to R. Shapira.[44] On the other hand, it is reasonable to assume that R. Shapira had read the letters of R. Menachem Mendel and R. Abraham, which had been published in early Hasidic works. It is certainly possible that these had direct influence on the planning of Benei Mahshavah Tovah. Furthermore, there is a good possibility that R. Shapira was exposed to the idea of these fellowships and to pact documents originating from Safed via his father-in-law R. Yerahmiel Moshe, who received this tradition from the rebbes of the Karliner Hasidim. Even if it is not possible to demonstrate direct textual influence connecting Warsaw to the antecedent in Tiberius, from a phenomenological perspective the similarities are extremely significant.

Hillel Zeitlin and his Mystical Fraternities

There is at least one very important Neo-Hasidic parallel to Shapira's attempt to foster Hasidic mystical fraternities in Warsaw in the 1920s, namely, the Benei Yavneh and Benei Hekhalah societies proposed by the Warsaw-based author, publicist, and mystic Hillel Zeitlin in his work *Safran shel yehidim.*[45] This comparison is quite poignant, as both of these unique visionaries of interbellum Warsaw were later martyred in the Holocaust.

Zeitlin was born in the Russian town of Korma in 1871 and murdered in Warsaw on the eve of Rosh Hashanah 1942.[46] He was raised in a Habad Hasidic family, and as a youth, he studied Kabbalah and Hasidism in addition to traditional talmudic studies. As a young man, he began to study general literature and philosophy as well, undergoing a spiritual crisis. He later returned to his Hasidic roots, delving deeply into Kabbalah, particularly the *Zohar* and Hasidism, focusing on the schools of Habad and Bratslav. It is important to note that he published an enthusiastic review of R. Shapira's *Hovat ha-talmidim* when it appeared in 1932, under the title *Admor—Amon Pedagogue*.[47] In the 1920s and '30s, Zeitlin tried to establish several mystical fraternities under various names, including Benei Yavneh and Benei Hekhalah, and his *Sifran shel yehidim* was dedicated to this topic. The project was by and large a failure, as is hinted at by Zeitlin himself in various places and as discussed by his student Simha Bunim Urbach.[48]

We can glean information regarding Zeitlin's goals from two letters that he sent to Palestine (1925 and 1938).[49] The first was sent to Nehemia Aminah, one of the leaders of the *Ha-po'el ha-mizrahi* religious labor organization.

> I think that there is a need to establish a small group of "Yavneh" in Jerusalem, that is to say, a group of laborers who live according to our guidelines[50] . . . here in Warsaw there already is a group like that, but I think that Jerusalem (or the Land of Israel in general) is its true location. The members of "Yavneh" can be affiliated with any political party they want, but they must be cognizant of the holiness of Israel and the true loftiness of Israelite religion and band together to according to the religious rules I have established . . . and to gather at least once a week for mutual study and discussion of true religion. Here I mainly study the Tanya . . . Kuzari . . . Maharal.

Here, Zeitlin expresses his ambition to disseminate his idea of religious fraternities in the Holy Land. He viewed the religious workers in Palestine as prime candidates for the new type of socioeconomic Hasidism that he wished to build. It is also instructive to note which religious tracts Zeitlin studied with his group in Warsaw.

The second letter was written almost fourteen years later, on the eve of World War II, to an unidentified recipient in Jerusalem.

> Horrific judgments are descending but also great loving-kindness. We must sweeten the judgements. . . . We need to join together in apolitical groups, but not mere Torah groups . . . and not even groups of regular kabbalists who engage in intentional

prayer and mystic unifications . . . rather, small groups of individuals who feel all of the pain of the world at this terrible time, all of the pain of this birth . . . groups of this sort are as essential to us as air to breathe.

In this letter, we sense both Zeitlin's acute awareness of impending catastrophe and his sense that the moment was pregnant with messianic potential. He ends his letter by emphasizing that only the prayers of such special groups in the Holy Land have the potential to save the Jewish People: "certainly such prayer in the Holy Land will break through the heavens."

Zeitlin quotes a wide variety of sources, including Kabbalah (mostly the *Zohar*), Hasidism, "secular" Jewish and non-Jewish thinkers, as well as medieval Jewish philosophy and ethics. This stands in sharp contrast to R. Shapira, who never mentions non-Jewish or secular sources and cites only Hasidic works from the modern period.[51]

Recall that *Benei mahshavah tovah* was composed in the early 1920s and distributed to a small group of Hasidim, who were prohibited from disseminating it beyond their group. *Sifran shel yehidim* was published openly in 1928. Thus, while R. Shapira was presumably aware of Zeitlin and his activities, there is no reason to assume any influence from him.[52] On the other hand, Zeitlin was certainly influenced by R. Shapira, but perhaps only at a later stage. While I cannot discount the possibility that Zeitlin somehow saw a copy of *Benei mahshavah tovah*, this seems unlikely. It is more reasonable to assume that both authors drew on common sources and traditions from the kabbalistic and Hasidic tradition, which inspired a kind of parallel evolution.

Both thinkers were acutely aware of the spiritual dangers facing Orthodoxy in Poland from secularization and of the decline of the Hasidic movement, which had strayed far from its original path. They both proposed strategies to contend with this situation. R. Shapira's work in this direction was primarily educational. He served as a Hasidic rebbe, a local rabbi, and *rosh yeshivah* of the yeshiva that he founded. He advanced a detailed educational/spiritual path for young students and advanced *avreikhim* alike. In Warsaw, he worked actively within the religious establishment to combat Shabbat violation and to strengthen yeshivot.[53] Zeitlin, on the other hand, was a public figure and a polemicist who wrote concerning current political, social, and religious issues. While both turned to the Hasidic spiritual elite, proposing fraternities stressing (at least) weekly meetings dedicated to common study and emotional service of God, there are significant differences as well. Regarding the stated goals of the groups, R. Shapira turns to the Hasid who is pained over his perceived distance from God and offers him a clear and graduated program to purify his thoughts and achieve closeness to the Divine. This takes place in a group setting, together with others who face similar spiritual challenges and have similar goals. While ultimately these elites would presumably have an impact on the wider Hasidic community, the overt goal is that of individual spiritual perfection, albeit achieved through work within the group.

Zeitlin expresses wider goals. Identifying his time period as that of the "birth pangs of the Messiah," he wants to hasten the final redemption. He turns not to those who feel spiritually distant from God but rather to those who feel the pain of "Israel in exile" in order to bring the messiah and redeem the world. Zeitlin's messianism seems to be more acute than that of R. Shapira, for whom it is a less overt theme in his writings, and certainly in *Benei mahshavah tovah*.[54] Another significant difference is Zeitlin's emphasis on socioeconomic issues, a theme largely absent from the writings of R. Shapira. The universal themes and openness to secular studies that are central to Zeitlin's writing are also foreign to his Hasidic contemporary R. Shapira.[55] Whereas R. Shapira demanded strict secrecy regarding his fraternities and their handbook, Zeitlin published his book as well as newspaper articles in which he urged interested parties to contact him. Zeitlin also wrote to his followers in Palestine, urging them to establish societies. In the published letters of R. Shapira to his Hasidim in Palestine, this topic is not discussed. The literary styles of the two works are quite different as well. *Benei mahshavah tovah* sets out a detailed program for the groups, including bylaws. The main focus, however, is on practical guidance in mystical practices and meditation. *Sifran shel yehidim*, on the other hand, while opening with a call for people to band together in fraternities, also discusses a wide range of philosophical topics, offering little guidance as to the actual functioning of the proposed societies. If R. Shapira offers us a practical spiritual handbook, Zeitlin provides us with a work of philosophy and mystical thought.

While both thinkers aspire to renew and revitalize the Hasidic community in light of their vision of original Beshtian Hasidism, their long-term visions differ greatly. R. Shapira proposes a return to the earlier Hasidic path of intense divine service predicated on kabbalistic panentheism and mystical practices as the path to ecstatic mystical experience and even prophecy. Zeitlin's vision is more modern, stressing universalism, socialism, and the enrichment of Torah study by adding arts, sciences, philosophy, and psychology to the religious curriculum. All of these themes are absent from R. Shapira's more traditional and particularistic worldview. While both thinkers exhibit a certain radicalism in their methods and visions, there remain significant differences as well. In the final analysis, it is worthy of note that Warsaw's Hasidic society in the interwar period produced two outstanding Hasidic leaders and thinkers, both of whom saw the importance of reestablishing mystical fraternities.[56]

Postscript and Conclusions

Before concluding, I would like to discuss a unique fraternity of sorts that R. Shapira took part in at the end of his life. Nehemia Polen concludes his book *The Holy Fire* with a riveting account of R. Shapira's final months after having been deported from the Ghetto.[57] Based on the testimony of survivor Simhah Rotem, Polen learned that representatives of the Jewish Underground smuggled themselves into Trawniki in the summer of 1943 in order to smuggle out prisoners, including R. Shapira. Instead, they discovered that a group of some twenty prisoners, including "artists, well-known physicians, communal leaders, leaders of various parties," had made a pact that none of them would leave the camp unless all of them could leave. Thus, R. Shapira refused to leave, and he and most or all of the others were murdered the following November.[58] In Polen's view, this pact represents "mystically permeated solidarity" on the part of R. Shapira.

> The pious hasidic master joined hands with nominally secular figures: political activists, lawyers, intellectuals, artists, and others, sweeping aside all ideological differences in an act of solidarity that reached the core of their shared Jewish identity . . . to turn down a rescue attempt in such circumstances was a compelling act of faith, a concrete articulation of the soul-to-soul binding that he had preached all his life, an ultimate expression of the unity of Israel.

Building on Polen's words, I believe that I can also add that the Trawniki "fellowship" can also be viewed as a new and radical twist on the *Benei mahshavah tovah* ideal as expressed in the ultimate absurdity of life in the shadow of impending death (see Reiser, this volume). This, then, is perhaps the highest ideal of "Hasidic fellowship" that we have encountered: commitment to group martyrdom together with one's fellows.

Influenced by the fraternities of sixteenth-century Safed, the mid-eighteenth-century Bet El Yeshiva, and late-eighteenth-century Tiberian Hasidism, R. Shapira reworked all of these in a manner that he felt was appropriate for his modern context. He had two main goals. The first was to empower an elite cadre of Hasidic *avreikhim* (advanced students) as part of his attempt to strengthen Hasidic society and fortify it against the corrosive influences of secular modernity (see Wodziński, Seeman, this volume). Second, as part of his messianic vision, he wished to enable these elite devotees to deepen and intensify their spiritual experiences and to achieve some level of prophecy. This was to be done within the setting of the fellowship, for "the individual cannot achieve alone what he is capable of achieving within the group."[59]

Notes

This article is dedicated to the memory of Rabbi Natan Siegel. R. Siegel was one of the earliest teachers of Piaseczner Hasidism and the first to introduce me to the works of R. Shapira. I wish to thank Professors Moshe Hallamish and Nehemia Polen for suggesting this topic to me and the editors of this book for their helpful comments.

1. See Zvi Blobstein (Leshem), "'Iyyunim be-shitato ha-ruhanit shel ha-'admor mi-Piasezneh" (master's thesis, Touro College, 2002), 38–39. See also Kalonymus Kalman Shapira, *Sermons from the Years of Rage* [in Hebrew], ed. Daniel Reiser (Jerusalem: Herzog Academic College, 2017), 1:38–41. The first official edition was published by the Piasezner Hasidim, Tel Aviv, 1973.

2. See Kalonymus Kalman Epstein, *Ma'or va-shemesh*, at the beginning of *parashat Kedoshim*.

3. This has been a very common approach to Bratslav Hasidism and in research regarding Mordekhai Yosef Leiner of Izhbits. Regarding Shapira, the recent dissertation of James Jacobson-Maisels, "The Self and Self-Transformation in the Thought and Practice of Rabbi Kalonymus Kalmish Shapira" (PhD dissertation, University of Chicago, 2014) is a good example.

4. See Zvi Leshem, "Questions and Cartography: Recent Trends in Hasidic Historiography," *Tradition: A Journal of Orthodox Jewish Thought*, 51, no. 2 (2019) 116–21.

5. Kalonymus Kalman Shapira, *Hakhsharat ha-avreikhim* (Jerusalem, 1966), 58b–63a. On R. Shapira's attitude toward the *Zohar*, see Zvi Leshem, "Between

Messianism and Prophecy: Hasidism According to the Piaseczner Rebbe" [in Hebrew] (PhD diss., Bar-Ilan University, 2007), 136–42.

6. On Prophecy in R. Shapira's writings, see Leshem, "Between Messianism and Prophecy," 76–88; Ron Wacks, *The Flame of the Holy Fire* [in Hebrew] (Alon Shvut: Tevunot, 2010), 209–39; Daniel Reiser, *Vision as a Mirror: Imagery Techniques in Twentieth Century Jewish Mysticism* [in Hebrew] (Los Angeles: Cherub Press, 2014), 194–221.

7. For a brief article on this approach, see Nehemia Polen, "Sensitization to Holiness: The Life and Works of Rabbi Kalonymos Kalmish Shapira," *Jewish Action* (1989–90): 30–33.

8. Kalonymus Kalman Shapira, *Tsav ve-zeruz* (Jerusalem: 1962), 52; and *Hakhsharat ha-avreikhim*, 62b.

9. The literal translation of the phrase is "children of good (or positive) thinking."

10. *Benei mahshavah tovah*, 54.

11. Ibid., 54–55.

12. Shapira, 56. In *Hakhsharat ha-avreikhim,* 61a–61b, R. Shapira insists on daily meetings as well as a communal "third meal" (*se'udah shelishit*) every Shabbat.

13. *Benei mahshavah tovah*, 56–57. On music, dance, and drinking in the works of R. Shapira, see Leshem, "Between Messianism and Prophecy," 167–69, 188–94.

14. *Benei mahshavah tovah*, 56–57. See Shalom Dov Schneersohn (Rashab), *Sefer Ha-ma'amarim tarna"t* (Brooklyn: Kehot, 1984), 60–61, who also discusses group work.

15. Shapira, *Benei mahshavah tovah*, 56–58.

16. These are not necessarily mutually exclusive options. R. Shapira probably wanted to promote his ideal of Hasidic fraternity on two parallel tracks, with parallel groups for the spiritual elite. His decision to write about them in a work addressed to the wider community indicates a willingness to widen the ranks of the groups to all interested parties.

17. Shapira, *Benei mahshavah tovah*, 58.

18. On the Pardes story, see Yehuda Liebes, *Het'o shel Elisha: Arba'ah she-nikhnesu le-fardes ve-tiv'ah shel ha-mistikah ha-talmudit* (Jerusalem: Akadamon, 1990). On merkavah mysticism, see Gershom Scholem, *Jewish Gnosticism, Merkabah Mysticism, and the Talmudic Tradition* (New York: Jewish Theological Seminary, 1965); Rachel Elior, *The Three Temples: On the Emergence of Jewish Mysticism* (Oxford: Littman, 2004); and Peter Schafer, *The Origins of Jewish Mysticism* (Princeton: Princeton University Press, 2009).

19. See Yehuda Liebes, "The Messiah of the Zohar: On Simeon bar Yohai as a Messianic Figure" and "How the Zohar was Written," in *Studies in the Zohar*, trans. Arnold Schwartz, Stephanie Nakache, and Penina Peli (Albany: State University of New York Press, 1993), 1–84, 85–138.

20. Regarding the Safedian group, see Emanuel Etkes, *The Besht: Magician, Mystic and Leader* (Waltham: Brandeis University Press, 2005), 154–55. See also Lawrence Fine, *Physician of the Soul, Healer of the Cosmos: Isaac Luria and His Kabbalistc Fraternity* (Stanford: Stanford University Press, 2003). For a more psychological reading, see Jonathan Garb, "The Psychological Turn in Sixteenth Century Kabbalah," in *Les mystiques juives, chrétiennes et musulmanes dans l'Égypte médiévale (VIIe–XVIe siecles)* (2013), 109–24.

21. See Meir Benayahu, *Kitvei ha-kabbalah she-le-Ramhal* (Jerusalem: Meir Benayahu, 1979); Isaiah Tishby, *Messianic Mysticism: Moses Hayim Luzzatto and the Padua School* (Oxford: Littman, 2008); Jonathan Garb, *Mekubbal be-lev ha-se'arah* (Tel Aviv: Tel-Aviv University, 2014). The pact document of the group was published in Mordechai Shriki, ed., *Igrot Ramhal* (Jerusalem: Mahon Ramhal, 2001), 5–11.

22. Pinchas Giller, *Shalom Shar'abi and the Kabbalists of Bet El* (Oxford, 2008). See also S. H. Kook, "Le-toledot havurat ha-meqqubalim be-Yerushalayim," *Luah Yerushalayim* (Jerusalem: Mosad HaRav Kook, 1944); and Joseph Weiss, "The Kavvanoth of Prayer in Early Hasidism," in *Journal of Jewish Studies* 9, no. 3-4 (1958): 163–92.

23. Moshe Yair Weinstock, ed., *Siddur ha-ge'onim ve-ha-mekkubalim* (Jerusalem: Shai Weinfeld,1970), 1:38–39. Jacobs used this version in preparing the translation in Louis Jacobs, *The Schocken Book of Jewish Mystical Testimonies* (New York: Schocken, 1996), 192–207.

24. Ariel Bension, *The Zohar in Moslem and Christian Spain* (London: Routledge, 1932), 242–46. Bension had already published the Hebrew version in his Hebrew work *Sar Shalom Sharabi* (Jerusalem: Zutot, 1930), 87–91. Yaakov Shalom Gafner published the three extant pacts from Bet El in his *Or ha-shemesh* (Jerusalem: Helkat Mehokek, 1970), 40–51. He also mentions the fourth document, which is not extant.

25. In his use of the word *introspection,* Jacobs seems to be thinking of the term *hitbonenut,* but this is speculative. Bension's language is flowery and dramatic, and his intention is not always clear. Another example is his use of the word *pantheistic.*

26. Among the signatories are the Rashash himself, as well as the Hid"a, R. Hayyim Joseph David Azulai ("the young"). According to Giller, the original manuscript is in the Hid"a's handwriting. Giller surmises that he was also the driving force behind *Ahavat Shalom.* Giller, *Shalom Shar'abi,* 87. On this group, see also Laurence Fine, *Judaism in Practice* (Princeton: Princeton University Press, 2001), 210–13.

27. Benayahu, "Shtere hitkashrut she-le-meqqubale Yerushalayim," *Asufot* 9 (1995): 11–127. This quote is from p. 16.

28. A genizah is a storage space for sacred books and manuscripts that are forbidden to discard.

29. Zev Rabinowitz, "Min ha-genizah ha-stolenit," *Zion,* year 5, vol. 2, 125–26. Gershom Scholem, "Shtar hitkashrut shel talmide ha-Ari," *Zion,* year 5, vol. 2, 133–60. Scholem was very interested in this document, and through the agency of Rabinowitz, he received a copy of the signatures on tracing paper. The document had been published previously in R. Shlomo David Eybeschutz, *Levushe serad* (Krakow: Druk and Verlag 1881), 15–16.

30. Abraham Avish Shor, "Shtare hitkashrut she-be-ginze hatser ha-kodesh Stolin-Karlin," *Kovets bet Aharon ve-Yisrael* 7 (1987): 85–105; and "Al ha-otsar she-be-hatser ha-kadosh be-Stolin," *Kovets bet Aharon ve-Yisrael* 7 (1997): 129–36. Shor communicated to me that in the 1860s, Heller's nephew, Moshe Leib Heller, traveled to Karlin and Stolin to be in the presence of Aharon, thus strengthening the connection between Safed and Stolin-Karlin.

31. On R. Yerhamiel Moshe and R. Shapira, see Aharon Surski, "The History of the Holy Rebbe Kalonymus Kalmish Shapira of Piaseczno" [in Hebrew], appended to Kalonymus Kalmish Shapira, *Esh kodesh* (Jerusalem: Va'ad Hasidei Piaseczno, 1960), 5–7, 12–13; Leshem, "Between Messianism and Prophecy," 3; Malkah Shapiro, *The Rebbe's Daughter: Memoir of a Hasidic Childhood,* trans. Nehmia Polen (Philadelphia: Jewish Publication Society, 2002).

32. Thus, R. Shapira emerges as the last in a chain of Jewish mystics who privileged the institution of spiritual fraternities in their spiritual systems.

33. Parallel to this time, one can mention the circle of the Gaon of Vilna, and in the twentieth century, that of R. Abraham Issac Kook. On the Baal Shem Tov, see (in addition to Etkes, *The Besht*) Abraham Joshua Heschel, *The Circle of the Baal Shem Tov* (Chicago: University of Chicago, 1985); Moshe Rosman, *Founder of Hasidism: A Quest for the Historical Ba'al Shem Tov* (Oxford: Littman, 2013). On the Maggid, see Solomon Maimon, *An Autobiography* (Urbana: University of Illinois, 2001); and Ariel Even Mayse, "Beyond the Letters: The Question of Language in the Teachings of Rabbi Dov Baer of Mezritch" (PhD diss., Harvard University, 2015). On the Kabbala of the Vilna Gaon, see *Daat* 79–80 (2015): *Lithuanian Kabbalah from the Vilna Gaon to Rabbi Kook.* See also Yosef Avivi, *Kabbalat ha-Gra* (Jerusalem: Kerem Eliyahu, 1993). On Rav Kook, see Semadar Cherlow, *Tsaddik yesod olam: Ha-shelihut ha-sodit ve-ha-havvayah ha-mistit shel Ha-rav Kook* (Ramat Gan: Bar-Ilan University, 2012).

34. Menahem Mendel Me-Vitebsk, *Pri ha-arets* (Kapust: Yafeh, 1814); Menahem Mendel Me-Vitebsk, *Sefer igrot kodesh (Lekutei amarim)* (Lemberg: S. Tzverling, 1911). The letters were reprinted in Yisrael Halpern, *Ha-aliyot ha-rishonot shel ha-hasidim le-Erets Yisrael* (Jerusalem: Schocken, 1947); Yaakov Barnai, *Igrot hasidim me-Erets Yisra'el me-ha-mahzit ha-sheniah shel ha-me'ah ha-shemonah esre* (Jerusalem: Mahon Ben Zvi, 1980); and Yehiel Greenstein, *Talmidei ha-Ba'al Shem Tov be-Erets Yisra'el* (Tel Aviv: Maor, 1982). Regarding the authenticity of the letters, see: Raya Haran, "In Praise of the Rav: On the Question of the Authenticity of

Hasidic Letters from the Land of Israel" [in Hebrew], *Qatedra* 55 (March 1990): 22–58; and Raya Haran, "On the Night of Each Letter: Regarding the Process of Copying Hasidic Letters" [in Hebrew], *Zion*, year 56, no. 3 (1991): 300–20. See also Yehoshua Mondshine, "The Authenticity of Hasidic Letters from the Land of Israel" [in Hebrew], *Qatedra* 63 (April 1992): 65–97.

35. Reprinted as Joseph Weiss, "Kalisker's Concept of Communion with God and Man," in *Studies in Eastern European Jewish Mysticism and Hasidism* (London: Littman, 1997), 155–69. Our citations are from the latter edition.

36. Shapira, *Tsav ve-zeruz*, 45.

37. On this point, according to Weiss, R. Abraham is following in the footsteps of Maimonides, *Guide for the Perplexed*, part 3, ch. 51. Regarding R. Abraham's use of the *Guide*, see Yisraėl Yaakov Deinstag, "The Guide for the Perplexed and Sefer Ha-mada in Hasidic Literature" [in Hebrew], in *The Jubilee Volume for Rabbi Professor Abraham Weiss* (New York: Vaad Sifrei HaYovel, 1964), 307–29.

38. While the Safed kabbalists had advocated confession by the individual to a small group, Weiss is convinced that there is not a direct historical connection between the two cases.

39. Gershon Hundert, "Toward a Biography of Abraham Kalisker" (master's thesis, Ohio State University, 1971) essentially follows Weiss, stating, "Kalisker has created a kind of 'mystical sociology.' " Hundert is more cautious in dismissing the idea that Kalisker may in fact be focusing on cleaving to the tsaddik and not only to the members of the group. See also Jeffrey Dekro, "Love of Neighbor in Later Jewish Mysticism," *Response: A Contemporary Jewish Review*, no 41–42, vol. 13, no. 1–2 (Fall–Winter 1982): 74–83.

40. Zeev Gries, *Me-mitos le-etos: Kavim le-demuto shel Avraham me-Ka-lisk*, in *Umah ve-toeldotehah: Be-ikvot ha-kongres ha-olami ha-shemini le-madaè ha-yahudut*) Jerusalem: Zalman Shazar, 1984), 2:117–46. For a parallel to this idea in R. Abraham's sermonic writings, see *Hesed le-Avraham* (Jerusalem: Siftei zadikim, 1995), 110.

41. See *Tsav ve-zeruz*, 45, which emphasizes that the group exists to help the individual in his spiritual path and not the other way around. I would also like to question Weiss's non-ecstatic reading of R. Abraham in light of his famous practice of performing public somersaults. These acrobatics may have helped to inspire those of the Piaseczner Rebbe in the twentieth century. See Zvi Leshem, "Flipping into Ecstasy: Towards a Syncopal Understanding of Mystical Hasidic Somersaults," *Studia Judaica* 17 (2014): 1 (33), 157–84.

42. I should, however, note that in the later discussion of the groups, there does appear to be a role for the rebbe within the group (*Mevo ha-she'arim* 45b).

43. Weiss calls this "an early attempt at group therapy."

44. And certainly not the pact, which was first published well after the R. Shapira's death.

45. Warsaw 1928. For a detailed comparison of the two figures, see Leshem, "*Between Messianism and Prophecy*," 196–221. There were also additional attempts to form spiritual groups in Poland at this time.

46. On Zeitlin, see Simha Bunim Urbach, *Toledot neshamah ahat: Hillel Zeitlin ha-ish u-mishnato* (Jerusalem: Shem V'Yafet, 1953); Zvi Harkavi and Yeshayahu Wolpsburg, eds., *Sefer Zeitlin* (Jerusalem: Mosad HaRav Kook, 1945); Shraga Bar Sela, *Ben sa'ar le-demamah: Hayyav u-mishnato shel Hillel Zeitlin* (Tel Aviv: HaKibutz HaMeuhad, 1999); Arthur Green, "Three Warsaw Mystics," in *Rivka Schatz-Uffenheimer Memorial Volume* (Jerusalem: 1996), 2:1–58; and Arthur Green, ed., *Hasidic Spirituality for a New Era: The Religious Writings of Hillel Zeitlin* (New York: Paulist Press, 2012). See also Jonatan Meir, ed., *Rabbi Nahman of Bratzlav: World Weariness and Longing for the Messiah; Two Essays by Hillel Zeitlin* [in Hebrew] (Jerusalem: Arna Hess, 2006); and Arthur Green and Ariel Even Mayse, "The Great Call of the Hour: Hillel Zeitlin's Yiddish Writings on Yavneh," *Geveb* (March 8, 2016), https://ingeveb.org/articles/the-great-call-of-the-hour-hillel-zeitlins-yiddish-writings-on-yavneh.

47. Republished in the Jerusalem 1979 edition of Hillel Zeitlin, *Safran shel yehidim*, 241–44.

48. Urbach, *Toledot neshamah ahat*, 168–69. For more on the groups, see also Yitzhak Gush-Zahav, "Israel and the Nations in His Perspective" [in Hebrew], in *Sefer Zeitlin*, ed. Harkavi and Wolpsburg, 80–96.

49. Harkavi and Wolpsburg, eds., *Sefer Zeitlin*, 128–29, 131–32.

50. Zeitlin refers to several religious and socioeconomic rules that he published in an earlier article. They include engaging in physical labor, avoiding luxuries, sexual and dietary purity, avoiding politics, remembering the "three loves" of the Besht (God, Israel, and Torah), and propagating the activities of "Yavneh."

51. The one exception is in *Zav ve-zeruz*, 45, where he mentions Aristotle as quoted in *Sefer ha-ikkarim* in order to bitterly attack his position.

52. Recently, a newspaper article from the period has surfaced that gives evidence that both were once present at a gathering of Warsaw rabbis. See "Kav le-kav," *Dvar*, Wednesday, November 11, 1931, 2.

53. See the speech given before the Committee to Save the Yeshivot in Poland and Lithuania, *Derekh ha-melekh*, 418–20.

54. On the messianism of R. Shapira, see Ofer Schiff, *Messianic Fervor and Its Application in the Sermons of the Piaseczner Rebbe during the Holocaust Period* [in Hebrew] (master's thesis, Tel Aviv University, 1987). For a comparison of the messianism of the two figures, see Eliezer Schweid, *Bein horban li-yeshuah* (Tel Aviv: HaKibutz HaMeuhad, 1994), 107–109.

55. The three themes of universalism, social justice, and secular studies are central to Zeitlin's vision of "futuristic Hasidism" delineated in Zeitlin, *Safran shel yehidim*, 43–48.

56. It is worth noting that Zeitlin's writings influenced the development of modern Neo-Hasidism, both in its Orthodox formulation in Israel and in its liberal interpretation in the United States. On Israel, see Yoav Sorek, *Shalhevet be-terem or* (master's thesis, Touro College, 2006), 114. Regarding the United States, see, for example, Green, *Hasidic Spirituality*, xi–xii; and Arthur Green and Ariel Evan Mayse, eds., *A New Hasidism: Roots* (Philadelphia: Jewish Publication Society, 2019).

57. Nehemia Polen, *The Holy Fire: The Teachings of Rabbi Kalonymus Kalman Shapira, the Rebbe of the Warsaw Ghetto* (Northvale, NJ: Jason Aronson, 1994), 152–56, 185–86nn27–28. Polen assumes that R. Shapira was murdered in Trawniki. This is a matter of dispute; see Leshem, "Between Messianism and Prophecy," 4n11.

58. This can be seen as a continuation of R. Shapira's well-documented earlier refusals to escape from the Ghetto. See Polen, *Holy Fire*, 7. See also Leib Bein, *Me-pinkaso shel itona'i hasid* (Jerusalem: 1967), 34. However, from David Zilbershag, ed., *Zikhron kodesh le-va'al esh kodesh* (Jerusalem: Vaad Hasidei Piaseczna–Grodzisk, 1994), 70, it seems that R. Shapira did want to escape from Trawniki. Perhaps this was before the agreement with the other inmates.

59. *Benei mahshavah tovah*, 8.

5

Self-Creation through Texts

Kalonymus Kalman Shapira's Incarnational Theology

DAVID MAAYAN

The Piasecnzer Rebbe, R. Kalonymus Kalman Shapira, articulated a vision of reality as filled with divine immanency and called upon his readers to recognize and live their lives in *devekut,* or "cleaving" to the Divine. As Ariel Evan Mayse (this volume) makes clear with respect to his study of Talmudic texts, however, Shapira also insisted on the imperative for each person to articulate and make manifest his or her unique, human individuality. For this reason, I will argue that Shapira rejects the model of *bittul* (self-nullification) as the means to intimacy with God, articulating instead an incarnational theology in which God enters into the articulated form of the body and soul of the devotee.[1] Rather than "saturating" reality, as in some forms of Hasidism, causing the specific articulations of this-worldly reality to fade or be dissolved into undifferentiated oneness, Shapira teaches that God enters into and fills the unique forms, movements, and moments of each individual. Needless to say, this incarnational theology carries significant implications for Shapira's textual hermeneutics as well as his interpretation of lived experience in terms of objects, self, body, and other selves.

Holy Stones, Divine Bodies

In a lengthy sermon for the Sabbath of *parashat vayyeshev,* December 28, 1929, Shapira considers a biblical passage in which the future patriarch

Jacob "took from the stones of the place (*vayyikah me-avnei ha-makom*)" while he was fleeing from his brother and placed them beneath his head to sleep (Gen 28:11).[2] Shapira begins by citing unnamed "holy books" that ask why the verse does not more simply state that Jacob took stones *from* the place rather than stones *of* the place. Then Shapira offers an answer of his own: "The Holy One, blessed be he, is called *makom* (literally, "the Place"), and our father Jacob took divine holiness and devotional service even from stones." This is possible because Jacob recognized that he was taking stones from *avnei ha-makom*, now read as "the stones of the *makom*," that is, the divine. The first, "simple" meaning of this response is that Jacob was able to take holiness from corporeal things (*divrei ha-olam*). But Shapira also reminds us that the classical kabbalistic work *Sefer yetsirah* uses the term *stones* to refer to letters.[3] Thus, in consonance with a Hasidic teaching commonly attributed to the Baal Shem Tov (Seeman, this volume), Jacob was able to "take holiness and devotional service also from them, from the letters."[4]

Shapira's teachings affirm the irreducible value of corporeal reality as well as the letters and forms of the Torah. These twin affirmations depend upon one another: "In truth, these two are one matter. One who is able to take in 'light' from the letters is able to receive light from the things of this world as well, and if he receives light from the things of this world, he receives light from the *letters in themselves* aside from the *words* and the *intention* that is in the words of the Torah."[5] The letters in themselves (*be-atsmam*) have (or, perhaps better, *are*) an inherent holiness and intrinsic value that is not exhausted by the lexical meanings that can be derived from them through words and articulable intentions.

Shapira grants supreme value to letters as well as embodied actions. We must avoid seeing letters, or embodied actions, he teaches, as merely *means to an end* rather than ends in themselves. He urges that "devotional service (*avodah*) is not merely like service to a human king—may the difference be preserved!—which provides only an intermediary (*emtsa'i*) to the fulfillment of the king's will, though the servant [herself] remains at a distance. Instead, [the service of God] is *in itself* a cleaving to the supreme King of kings, the Holy One, blessed be he!" And how does this embodied service itself constitute a cleaving to God? Shapira immediately explains: "For the Holy One, blessed be he, 'alone has done, is doing, and will do all actions.'[6] All actions that are done, even now in the world—he alone is the doer."[7]

For Shapira, all activity in the world thus expresses divine vitality. In botanical growth, he explains, "the power of divinity wants to expand, and [therefore] the plant actively grows." Human activities that are directed entirely toward the person's own expansion, including in the most literal sense of eating "so that his body may grow and expand," or engaging in trade, also express divine vitality. There is also an additional level of divine vitality, which is at work in the performance of the *mitsvot* (commandments) and devotional service.

Just as the "simple" divine vitality within a plant pushes it to grow, so too a human being with "the vitality of holiness" within him engages in bodily actions and performance of the mitsvot. God is the agent, the doer, who acts through the person. The call to cleave to God cannot be understood abstractly; rather, we must "cleave to his attributes—just as he is compassionate, so you should be compassionate."[8] However, "it is not in the feeling of compassion in the heart alone, but rather in the compassionate action: 'Just as He visits the sick, etc.,' as our rabbis (may their memories be a blessing) have said.[9] By giving a coin to a poor person, [a person] cleaves to God's attributes, because God is doing this action through him, and holy vitality is revealed in this activity."[10]

This is a far cry from the idea of *imitatio dei* explored by Maimonides, for example, on the basis of the same rabbinic texts (see also Diamond, this volume). In this formulation, Shapira has moved from the notion of a person walking in God's ways to that of God becoming incarnate through human activity. Thus, the fundamental affirmation of God acting through the person applies not only to the ethical precepts given as examples but to the entirety of religious life. "The performance of the commandments and the Torah engaged in by a human being alone would not cause such supernal effects; rather, it is God who acts through the [person of] Israel." The person must "prepare himself" for God to act through him. Shapira notes the rabbinic claim that God fulfills the *mitsvot* of the Torah[11] and that this statement applies to all of the *mitsvot*. Even the *mitsvot* of "the eating of matzoh and bitter herbs, God fulfills *through* [or *by means of*] (*al yedei*) the [person of] Israel." For Shapira, the opening word of the Decalogue is the divine "I" (*anokhi*) because this "I" applies to all of the Torah. It is as if God were saying that in "all of the Torah and the *mitsvot*, I, the Lord your God, am the active agent."

It is not that we wish to cleave to God and therefore God provides us with the *mitsvot* as a means of achieving or earning this end. Rather, God wishes to become *manifest* in holy activity. The *mitsvot*—and the Jewish bodies that perform them—provide God with the material and locus for achieving this goal. Thus, the activity prescribed by the commandments has inherent value, because the purpose of eating matzoh is to make it possible for God, as it were, to eat matzoh. This purpose is *identical* with the very act itself. If cleaving and proximity to the divine remains a human goal of the performance of the *mitsvot,* this incarnational understanding asserts that it is in the act of performing a *mitsvah* that a person achieves the greatest possible cleaving to the divine.

Irreducible Letters, Irreducible Bodies

As we have seen, Shapira contrasts the letters of the Torah with "the words and intentions that are in the words of the Torah." Just as the physical performance of the *mitsvot* should not be seen as the means to a transcendent, spiritual end, we should not view the letters of the Torah as simply the means to an end that transcends them. In a remarkable reading, Shapira presents the dispute between Joseph and his brothers in Genesis 37 as relating precisely to this point. Citing Rashi's comment on Gen 37:3,[12] Shapira notes that Jacob gave over "all of his Torah" to Joseph, including his understanding of how to take holiness "not only from the words and statements alone but also from the letters and their combinations." Joseph's brothers were not, however, on this exalted level. "*Their* entire service to God was only to receive statements and [articulable] intentions from the words." Joseph brought "*dibbatam* (their words/ reports) *ra'ah* (bad) *el avihem* (to their father)" (Gen 37:2). According to Shapira's reading, this means that Joseph understood his brothers' words as "bad to their father"—that is, for one on Jacob's level of understanding, the focus on words and lexical meaning alone and consequent devaluing of concrete reality and letters was "bad."[13]

Continuing in this vein, Shapira notes that Joseph's reward for his level of understanding was that his father gave him a *ketonet passim,* usually understood as a striped or colored cloak. Shapira notes that the midrash claims that *passim* is a way of conveying the meaning *pass yad* (the palm of the hand), for the garment was so fine—so delicate and thin—that it could be condensed and concealed in the palm of one's hand.[14] Shapira asks how the midrash could see *passim* as standing for *pass yad*—after all, the final letter is a *mem,* not a *dalet.* He answers that "it is known that the form of the final *mem* letter is a *dalet,* a *dalet* which has been doubled," with the second *dalet* turned upside down and attached to the other side. "Therefore, for one whose service is only in words and statements, the [only] hint [in the word] is *passim.* But since they [Jacob and Joseph] learned how to receive from the forms of the letters as well, and the form of the final *mem* is a *dalet, passim* also hints at *pass yad.*"[15]

This unusual reading of a relatively obscure midrash discloses the essence of Shapira's hermeneutics. One who is focused on the meaning of the words in the Torah is carried away from the concrete particularity and physical form of the letters. However, when one contemplates the very letters of the Torah in their embodied form, new meanings and interpretations pour forth that are only available to one who approaches the text in this way. Although Shapira does not make the point explicitly, it may be that the image of the subtle, fine, and hidden nature of the cloak—which is itself the interpretation that emerges from the *pass yad* reading—as that which emerges only from a concrete focus on the visible, material form of the letters is illustrative of his view. The most subtle and hidden interpretations, the finest garments of Torah, are what emerge from a hermeneutic that insists on the intrinsic holiness of the letters themselves as incarnational vessels for the divine.

A teaching in Shapira's interbellum mystical tract *Benei mahshavah tovah* (see Leshem, this volume)emphasizes the direct link between one's view of physical reality and one's view of texts, particularly kabbalistic texts.[16] Shapira explains that a kabbalist sees the "truth and the essence" of the things of the world, "that they are entirely [divine] names, and souls."[17] In truth, this sense of the inherent holiness of the things of this world must come prior to the proper learning of Kabbalah, because one then turns to the Kabbalah not to gaze into some "other" spiritual world but rather to understand the details of the holy structure of the very world one sees and inhabits. However, one who is not awakened to the inherent holiness of the world "and comes to learn Kabbalah—then only confusion and contradictions will swirl within him." This is because he sees, for example, "physical bread—to eat and satisfy" the body, yet the Kabbalah describes how three names of Y-H-W-H emanated down into this aspect of "bread."[18] He then wonders: How could these spiritual, transcendent realities have become so corporealized as to become physical bread? Recoiling from any incarnational thinking, he will resolve his own confusion by supposing that the kabbalists intended only to "make a hint" here. Yet, even so, he wonders, "Why did they even hint at supernal matters with corporeal things? Why did they associate the name of the King with a lowly and disgraceful thing?"[19]

Shapira's "confused" would-be kabbalist sees conceptual meanings and mystical intentions as higher realities than bread. But in truth, the bread itself surpasses any meaning or intention that can be articulated. The profound meanings that flow forth from the bread (which are disclosed through the study of Kabbalah), and from the letters of the Torah, are affirmations of the inherent holy essence of their source. However, just as bodies remain irreducible, the letters of the Torah and the things of this world remain inexhaustible, their meaning never fully plumbed or able to be articulated in concepts or verbal intentions.

Engraving the Self

For Shapira, the essence of the Torah is the divine self. This idea has roots in Nahmanides's famous description of the Torah as composed entirely of divine names[20] and much subsequent kabbalistic speculation. In particular, Hasidic authors are fond of quoting the rabbinic interpretation of the first word of the Decalogue, the divine "I" (*anokhi*), as an acronym for *ana nafshay ketavit yehavit* (see Wiskind, this volume).[21] The simple reading of this phrase is as an emphasis on God as the giver of the Torah: "I myself wrote and gave [the Torah]."[22] Hasidic authors often read the phrase as "I wrote and gave myself [in the Torah]"—as teaching that the Torah is divine self-revelation.

For Shapira, the "Torah" that expresses the divine self is not only the words and intentions that can be derived from its study but also, indeed primarily, the letters themselves, which embody this self (see, however, Seeman, this volume). In fact, the greater revelation—and ultimate incarnation—of the divine self is in human embodied actions, particularly the performance of the *mitsvot*: "And from the beginning of the giving of the Torah, God said, 'I (*anokhi*) am Y-H-W-H, your God,' and the *anokhi* is said in reference to *all* of the Torah, [e.g.,] 'Remember the Sabbath day, to sanctify it,' etc., for 'I, Y-H-W-H, your God, am the doer' of all the Torah and *mitsvot*."[23]

Shapira's emphasis here on the divine as the true agent or self that is at work in human actions may seem to imply that the goal of the human devotee should be *bittul*, or self-nullification, which allows this divine self to manifest.[24] However, just as the particular articulation of an individual human body—or an individual Torah scroll—serves as the ideal locus for divine incarnation, so too the uniqueness of the human self should by no means be erased in his or her divine service. In fact, Shapira urgently insists that every act of divine service should manifest the unique individuality of the human being who is performing it.[25] There is a harmonic interdependence in the revelation of the human and divine selves.

Shapira is also interested in the function of writing as a means of transmitting the unique human self. In the opening reflection to his "spiritual journal," *Tsav ve-zeruz*, Shapira contemplates the tragedy of human mortality. After cultivating a unique self over the course of a lifetime, how tragic it is that this person must cease to be! If only we had just one more lifetime on this earth to live again, starting from the fully cultivated self we had attained![26] He then turns with hope to the act of writing as an attempted solution to this problem of death:

> It is good for a person to record all of his thoughts. Not in order to make a name for himself as an author of a book but rather to engrave himself *(laharot et atsmo)* on paper, to preserve all of the movements of the soul, *its fallings and its risings.* All of its being, its form, its cognitions, and all that it acquired for itself in the expanse of its lifetime should remain alive.[27]

Through his writings, Shapira is striving to preserve the unique self, the individual self in its full form, created through the narrative of its particular experiences. This opening paragraph could have ended with a declaration that a person should record his "pearls of wisdom," those thoughts and insights that occurred to him during inspired moments, for future generations. Yet Shapira does not want merely to preserve wisdom in an abstract sense; he wants to preserve the self he has cultivated. Thus, the voice of the self's "fallings" must be recorded as well, for it is not some impersonalized "highlights" that he wants to preserve but the full force of his selfhood. Scholars who have worked on Shapira and who feel moved (as I do) such that they wish for their work to contribute, in some small way, to the fulfillment of Shapira's stated wish to live on through his work should reflect on his own stated intent to convey his soul's "fallings" as well as its ascents. The rabbi's own words here can serve as a reminder to his readers and interpreters that an overly hagiographic approach (however understandable and well intentioned) may frustrate his own deeply stated desire to be permitted to "live on" in the fullest, richest sense possible after death.

Self-Creation through Writing

For Shapira, writing is not merely a means of conveying the self to others but a process of self-discovery and ultimately of self-creation. Once again, a primary source for this material is the 1929 sermon we have been considering.

True thought, which focuses consciousness, is the coming into being of a new aspect of self or essence. Shapira presents this in an innovative discussion of *mahshavot zarot* ("strange" or "foreign" thoughts).[28] The Baal Shem Tov taught that "inappropriate" (archetypically, though not exclusively, sexual) thoughts that arise during devotional service should be viewed as "holy sparks" yearning to be reconnected to their source through the "rectification" allowed by prayer and holy deeds.[29] Some earlier approaches had treated such thoughts as intrusions of the demonic upon the world of sanctity.[30]

In marked contrast to both of these approaches, Shapira suggests that *mahshavot zarot* reflect neither sin nor a craving for sin, nor indeed anything supernatural, but simply a "natural deficiency" (*hisaron tevi'i*). It is the nature of thought that it is "unable to rest," states Shapira; thus, if consciousness reflects for some time on a particular thought and sees no newness in it, it leaves this thought aside and moves on to others. Idel's comments (this volume) on the importance of contemplative technique to Shapira's oeuvre would seem very apposite here. Shapira's writings reflect a constant urgent interest in increasing the ability of the human mind to remain focused and cleave to a single thought.

In Shapira's analysis, the problem at the root of the fleeting nature of thought is captured well in the term *mahshavot zarot*. For "thought is not able to be grasped by and made to cleave to a matter foreign to itself (*davar zar*)." However, when a person exercises his human creativity and produces a *hiddush*, a new Torah interpretation or teaching, "it is just the opposite!"

> He wants always to think of this matter, another time, and another time—until he needs to turn his thought forcibly away from it [if he wants to think of something else]. The reason for

this is that in every original intellectual insight (*hiddush*), a new portion is born in the essence of the intellect of the originator, only it is enclothed in the form of the understanding that he is reflecting upon. And since the essence of his intellect is unified with the matter that he is reflecting upon (in keeping with the comment of Rashi, of blessed memory, on "and they became one flesh"[31] that in the child, they [the two parents] become one flesh), his thought becomes bound to the matter that he is reflecting upon and does not fly from thought to thought.[32]

Torah interpretation is thus not a matter of divine self-revelation alone but also of human self-revelation and self-creation. This is not restricted to some "elevated" manifestation of Torah study but applies even to the attempt to study and interpret the simple meaning of a Torah text. "Every plain meaning of the Torah (*peshat ha-torah*) that a person understands . . . is not the essence of the Torah (in itself); rather, it is that which the Torah hints to him, the Torah that is enclothed in *his* soul, *his* mind, and *his* will. A person is [therefore] able to recognize the situation of his own soul in his original Torah insights."[33] Shapira's emphasis on Torah as self-revelation means that Torah as divine revelation cannot demand the erasure of the human individual. In fact, engagement in Torah here is the very process of writing and birthing a unique self.

The Ingathering of Alterity

We have seen that, for Shapira, the new articulable insights that are born in the creatively interpreting mind enclothe "a new portion . . . in the essence of the intellect of the originator."[34] It is not only that the same essence—or self—has brought forth a new articulation of itself but that there is a new portion of self that has come into being. This new being is not born naked but rather comes garbed in its expression as a new insight or interpretation (*hiddush*).[35] It is this that the mind is then able to contemplate with focused attention—indeed, it requires effort to pry its attention away—precisely because it recognizes that it is not a matter foreign to itself but rather a new portion of its own being that has been, or is in the process of being, born. This is a significant new interpretation of the relationship between literary and psychic process described in this volume by Wiskind and Seeman.[36] The mind's steady attention represents the circular fascination of the self giving birth to itself, contemplating its own being. How does Shapira articulate the relation between this self-contemplation and other ultimate values—empathy, altruism, and devotion to the divine?

In a teaching marked as being from Rosh Hashanah 5686 (correspond-ing to September 19–20, 1925), Shapira introduces the centrality of the ability to recognize alterity, and empathy, at the beginning of a discussion of how thought (*da'at*) can actualize (*po'el*). He asks rhetorically, "If a person thinks that day is night, is [the time] affected by his thought?" However, thought that is itself a new "created essence" (*etsem nivra*) can indeed be a creative force. For Shapira, this higher type of thought always has an element of self-recognition (which is simultaneously a self-actualization) to it—yet this very self-recognition is impossible outside a recognition of that which is other than the self: "For example, when a person recognizes something other than himself (*davar zulato*), it is not only the other that he recognizes. He also recognizes himself by means of this, for the one who recognizes (*ha-ba'al makir*) has also been revealed."[37] This rather abstract philosophical point is immediately rendered by Shapira in terms of being able to recognize, and empathize with, other human beings:

> If a person wants to know whether he is wise, then he needs to [demonstrate the capacity to] grasp the mind of another. If he desires to know whether he is a compassionate person, he is able to know this if he feels the suffering of another; and if he does not grasp the other, then he fails as well to apprehend himself. However, it is not only wisdom or com-passion themselves which are revealed—rather, the one who has wisdom and the essence of the soul of the one who has compassion are revealed.[38]

Pursuing this thought further, Shapira urges that true self-knowledge is defined precisely as the taking-in and ingathering of alterity: "For all recognition is the ingathering of that which is other. When one knows a matter, then there is found, now, in his mind a matter foreign to itself (*davar zar*)." That which "was not in him before, he now has apprehended and understood."[39] Now, it is possible to conceive of this process as a kind of conquering of alterity, which has now become absorbed and incorpo-rated into the self. However, this manner of thinking, which pictures self and other as in a competitive rather than interdependent relationship, is precisely what Shapira emphatically resists with his careful formulation.

Shapira describes that which has entered the mind as still retaining its otherness (*davar zar*). In effect, the other truly enters one's mind. To the extent that it—or, more poignantly, he or she[40]—does not, one is displaying not a capacious mind but rather a lack of self-realization. Shapira explains that he speaks of the faculty of "recognition" (*hakarah*) rather than of the intellect (*sekhel*) because "recognition encompasses within itself both knowledge and feeling."[41] It makes no sense to speak of empathy as taking in the other's pain and "making it one's own" if this means that one feels the pain entirely as one's own and forgets about the other. Rather, the pain entering the self must be recognized as transcendent, belonging to the other person. Shapira formulates this crucial point: recognition is an ingathering of alterity. This true recognition of the other is simultaneously a basis for creation and recognition of self. Any other form of "self-realization" is actually nothing more than a counterfeit masquerading under that term, like the supposed "wisdom" of one who cannot apprehend the wisdom of others or the "compassion" of one who cannot feel another's pain.

Alterity and the Body

Shapira's insistence on the cardinal importance of recognizing the alterity of the other may also be tied to his positive evaluation of bodies and physicality. His approach should be contrasted with that of R. Shneur Zalman of Liady (1745–1812), the founder of Chabad Hasidism, whose teachings are referenced in Shapira's writings. In chapter 32 of *Likkutei amarim*, R. Schneur Zalman writes:

> Fulfilling that which was mentioned above—viewing his body with scorn and revulsion and having his joy be only the joy of the soul—is a direct and easy way to come to fulfill the commandment "You shall love your fellow as yourself" (Lev 18:19) toward every soul of Israel, both great and small. That is, since his body is despised and loathed by him, while as for the soul and spirit—who can comprehend their greatness and excellence in their root and source in the living God? And

[considering] also that all [Israel] are of a kind and all have one Father, such that all of Israel are truly called brothers in terms of the root of their souls in the One God, and only the bodies are separated . . . [42]

For Shneur Zalman, the disparaging of the body is the surest road to being able to love one's fellow Jews. This is because the body is the source of separation, distinction, and individual identity.[43] Since the souls of all Israel are all "of a kind" (mat'emot—a word related to the Hebrew term for "twin"), one who values only the soul will be drawn to love his fellows, for there will be nothing dividing him from them. However, one who focuses upon the body will have no true basis for love. Shneur Zalman continues: "For those who consider their bodies of principle importance (ikkar) and their souls secondary (tafel), therefore, it is impossible for there to be genuine love and brotherhood between them. [For such persons, there can be] only that [love] which is dependent on a [transitory] thing."[44]

The basis of love, in this model, is precisely sameness. Persons who are focused upon their bodily difference and individuation are separated from, and cannot truly love, their fellows. Even the lower level of "love" that such persons may manifest is "dependent upon a thing," that is, some form of mutual interest or benefit, allowing only for a bond based upon this sameness. But this sameness, being transitory and inessential, cannot serve to produce true love. Eventually, the alterity between the two will assert itself once again, and the temporary connection forged between them will shatter.[45]

An essential difference between Shapira's thought and Shneur Zalman's here is that Shapira does not see the body as that which distinguishes between individuals. The lifetime project he advocates is one of continually articulating a unique self, a unity of body and soul, that is as infused with the divine as it is unique in its own particularity.

Self-Creation and the Divine Creator

I have shown that, for Shapira, a new "portion" of self is born together with each new sacred insight. In fact, he goes farther and describes the entirety of one's self and even one's body as being created anew through one's developing consciousness. Shapira writes that the "person of Israel creates his own essence"[46] and that through this process "his entire body is created anew."[47] How does this vision of "self-creation" present itself in Shapira's thought, and how does he relate it to the concept of God as Creator? A continued close reading of his 1925 sermon for Rosh Hashanah may help to answer this question.

Shapira begins his transition to the more explicit terminology of self-creation by making use of a phrase in rabbinic literature that he interprets as introducing a role for the creature's *da'at* in the process of his or her own creation. *Da'at*, often translated as "knowledge," can also denote "consciousness," "intent," "opinion," and "consent." As this multiplicity of meanings is at play in Shapira's text here, I will leave the term untranslated:

> The midrash hints that "all the works of creation were created . . . according to their *da'at*."[48] That is, God asked each one for its *da'at* as to how [it would like] to be created. We find that their *da'at* is prior to their creation and that the essence of each one was created according to its *da'at*.[49]

The rabbinic teaching that Shapira draws upon is talmudic, but his citation is only partial, and his interpretation differs from that of the most prominent previous Jewish commentators on the passage: "R. Yehuda ben Levi said: All the works of creation were created according to their height,[50] according to their *da'at*, and according to their form[51] (*le-tsivyonam*), as it says, 'And the heavens and the earth were completed, and all of their hosts (*tseva'am*)' (Gen 2:1)—do not read 'their hosts' but rather 'their forms' (*tsivyonam*)."[52]

Together with the suggestive phrase "according to their *da'at*," the original teaching also includes two other phrases: everything was created according to its "height" and according to its "form." Commentators on the passage have seen it as teaching that God created the first living beings already at their "complete" stage. Thus, Rashi comments that "the fruit tree was ready to produce fruit immediately."[53] Similarly, Rashi explains "their form" as implying that each thing was created, as it were, in its "mold" (*defus*). God is in control, creating each creature in its appropriate fullness, according to the archetypal form that God has in mind for each.

But what of the phrase "according to their *da'at*?" Although this phrase is open to interpretation, most medieval commentators interpreted it along similar lines to "height" and "form." Thus, Rabbeinu Hananel (990–1053) writes that this means "not like the *da'at* of children, but rather with the *da'at* of those fully mature."[54] Similar readings are found in Maimonides and the medieval Jewish philosopher Joseph Albo (1380–1444).[55] Albo renders the phrase "according to their *da'at*" as "with their consent," framing this reading as metaphorical. "If, metaphorically (*al derekh mashal*), they had been asked whether they would consent to exist in the form, that is, the beauty, stature, and excellence which is to be found in them, they would have agreed to be created."[56]

Rashi also interprets the phrase in terms of consent: "He [God] asked them whether they desired to be created, and they said 'Yes.'"[57] This brings us closer to Shapira's reading, but the differences are crucial. For Rashi, the form of the creature is predetermined by the Creator. The creature is asked to consent to being created but is not consulted about its form or attributes, which are determined by God. The consent determines *whether* the creation will take place, but the *how* is determined entirely by God.

Shapira reads *da'at* quite differently here, as indicating that not only the creature's *consent* but the creature's own *opinion* is being sought by the Creator—and the form in which the creature is created is thus fashioned *by the creature itself* in the realm of *da'at*. An interesting precedent for Shapira's reading is found in Levi Yitzhak of Barditshev's (1740–1809) influential early Hasidic collection *Kedushat Levi*, a work that is referenced multiple times in Shapira's own writings. There, we read:

> Now we will expound upon a speculative question. It is known that the Holy One, blessed be he, creates his world anew with each and every breath. We perceive and see this each day (as is formulated in the liturgical poem: "for like the clay in the hand of the potter, so are we in your hand"), and the entire world is likewise in His hand, and he creates them anew each moment. Why, then, does it not happen that a [creature] transforms from a human into an animal, or from an animal into a human, or from a farm animal into a wild beast, and so on?
>
> The matter must be as follows: Just as at the beginning of the works of creation, "they were created in their likenesses,[58] their *da'at*, and their forms"—as is found in Rosh Hashanah 11a, and see there Rashi's commentary c.v. *le-da'atan*: "He [God] asked them whether they desired to be created, and they said, 'Yes'"—so it is always, certainly, that each and every creature's will is to remain thus, as it was created before, and not to change from its [original] creation. Therefore, even though it is true that the Holy One, blessed be he, creates his world

anew at each moment, since it is the will of the created creature that it stay [in its form,] thus it remains. For he renews
his lovingkindness and each moment fulfills for his creatures
their desire: that they should be as they were created. And for
this we praise him.[59]

Placing this teaching alongside Shapira's, we can note some significant ways in which it is closer to his than the medieval interpretations
reviewed above. For one thing, this teaching reflects the notion, so
frequently emphasized in early Hasidic texts, that God's generous act of
creation is a never-ending, constantly renewing process rather than a one-
time event. Reflections on "the works of creation" thus provide insight
into the workings of the present moment. In addition, Levi Yitzhak here,
although citing Rashi, clearly understands the "consultation" process with
the creature about to be created (or created anew) as involving not just
whether to be created but *how* and *in what form* to be created. Remarkably, Levi Yitzhak introduces this element of "self-creation" to explain and
establish a principle of continuity and sameness in the world rather than
to propose a possibility of change.

Shapira, by way of contrast, is proclaiming that human beings have
the possibility to inaugurate change in their very being, indeed to create
themselves (including their material reality) anew. By means of new acts
of "recognition"—those acts of consciousness that include both cognitive
awareness and depth of feeling—the human being provides the Creator
with a new *da'at*, and he or she is then created in accordance with this
da'at. Shapira recognizes the kind of radical freedom implied in this notion,
for one is not constricted even by one's own essence: one's *da'at* precedes
the creation of one's essence.

This is a remarkable parallel to one of the famous slogans of French
existentialism, the claim that (at least in humans) "existence precedes
essence" (see Reiser, this volume). This view was given early and forceful
expression in Jean-Paul Sartre's 1945 lecture *L'existentialisme est un human-
isme*. Sartre explicitly presented his existential philosophy as dependent
upon his atheism. For Sartre, the theistic notion of God as creator meant
that God was seen as creating human beings based upon an essence, a
"certain conception which dwells in the divine understanding."[60] Even as
philosophic atheism emerges in the eighteenth century, claims Sartre, the
remnants of this notion of an essence linger on in philosophical assump-
tions about the existence of a universal "human nature." For Sartre, this

notion deprives human beings of full freedom, as they are trapped by their own essence, and of their individuality, since "human nature" is posited as a universal essence. For Sartre, only "atheistic existentialism" declares the human free (although thus also, as Sartre emphasizes, responsible), able to create her own essence through her existence. That is, "he will be what he makes of himself. Thus, there is no human nature, because there is no God to have a conception of it."[61]

Shapira draws on the midrashic expression that God created creatures "according to their *da'at*" to grant each human being an indispensable role in creating his or her own essence. God turns away, as it were, from God's own ideas and "asks each one for her own *da'at*." Initially, Shapira still explicitly names God as the Creator, who consults with the creature regarding its own creation. However, summarizing the insight derived from this reading, Shapira says only that "their *da'at* is prior to their creation and that the essence of each one *was created* according to its *da'at*."[62] Two paragraphs later, we find the following formulation: "*The person of Israel creates his own essence* by means of holy recognition. We find that the [act of] recognition is itself a holy essence, a reality unto itself, a holy form (*guf kadosh*) with a holy essence in it—and this essence, this awareness, has an active capacity."[63] Shapira's passionate advocacy of human freedom, manifesting in the active creation of one's own unique self, comes through in these passages.[64]

Conclusion

Although I have focused primarily on just two of Shapira's many recorded sermons, I hope that these have been sufficient to exemplify the range and subtlety of his writings. I would like to conclude by noting one characteristic tendency of his thought. The teachings I have cited here are wrestling with the interrelationship of several commonly paired concepts, including body and soul, word and meaning, physicality and spirituality, self and other, human and God. Frequently, these are construed as having a hierarchical and oppositional relationship to one another. Yet Shapira does not follow this path. Instead, with remarkable consistency, he seeks to articulate a notion of absolute interdependence between supposed antipodes. At times, this leads him to emphasize the inherent holiness of the body, the irreducible holiness of the letters, and the indispensable value of the other person. The soul does not *make use of* the body, meanings do not *emerge* from letters, and self neither *overcomes* nor *frees itself* from other. In place of hierarchy, we have ontological interdependence. The fundamental human religious activity in Judaism, the bodily performance of the commandments, is attributed to divine agency. The most uniquely divine activity of creation, on the other hand, is attributed to human beings! Human and divine activity, human and divine being, cannot be divided into compartmentalized realms.

However, we have also seen that rather than simply asserting the unity of opposites, Shapira attempts to articulate and even prove the truth of their interdependence. In addition to citing and interpreting earlier sources, he advances rational arguments that attempt to convince the reader of his views, appealing also to the reader's ethical sense.[65] These expositions are at times highly abstract, concerned with nuances of definition and precise conceptual analysis, yet Shapira consistently intersperses these with this-worldly parables and frequent appeals to the reader's own lived experience, resulting in a uniquely Hasidic religious phenomenology (see Seeman, this volume). Shapira's precise and nuanced descriptions of the interrelationship of body and mind, awareness of self and other, and divine and human agency are not just descriptive in intent but also seek to instantiate a dynamic and radical unity of human experience.

Notes

1. On the question of the application of the term *incarnational* to Jewish theologies, see Alon Goshen-Gottstein, "Judaisms and Incarnational Theologies: Mapping Out the Parameters of Dialogue" in *Journal of Ecumenical Studies*, 39, no. 3–4 (2002): 219–47; Shaul Magid, *Hasidism Incarnate: Hasidism, Christianity, and the Construction of Modern Judaism* (Stanford: Stanford University Press, 2015); Elliot R. Wolfson, "Judaism and Incarnation: The Imaginal Body of God," in *Christianity in Jewish Terms* (Boulder: Westview, 2000); Moshe Idel, *Ben: Sonship and Jewish Mysticism* (New York: Continuum, 2007), esp. n180 on 99–101.

2. Kalonymus Kalman Shapira, *Derekh ha-melekh* (Jerusalem: Va'ad Hasidei Piaseczno, 1995), 5690 (1929), 47–55.

3. *Sefer yetsirah*, 4:16, where letters are termed "stones" and words (or combinations of letters) are termed "houses"; thus, "two stones build two houses, three stones build six houses, etc."

4. Shapira, *Derekh ha-melekh, parashat vayyeshev* 5690 (1929), 47.

5. Ibid.

6. Shapira is quoting here from the liturgical "I believe" (*Ani ma'amin*) credo, itself based upon Maimonides's thirteen principles of faith, found in many traditional prayer books to be recited after morning prayers.

7. Shapira, *Derekh ha-melekh, parashat vayyeshev* 5690 (1929), 47.

8. Ibid., 48. Shapira's formulations here reflect a construction widespread in earlier Hasidic literature. In b. Ketubot 111b, R. Eliezer is quoted asking and answering the question of how we may "cleave to" God, whereas b. Sotah 14a records R. Hama ben R. Hanina's question and answer about how we may "walk after God." As here, R. Eliezer's question was often combined with R. Hama's answer, thus rendering "walk after his attributes" definitional of *devekut*. Shapira also draws on the teaching of Abba Shaul recorded in b. Shabbat 133b and the top of y. Pe'ah 3a.

9. See previous note.

10. Shapira, *Derekh ha-melekh, parashat vayyeshev* 5690 (1929), 48.

11. Shemot Rabbah 30:9.

12. Rashi is drawing on Bereshit Rabbah 84:8.

13. Shapira, *Derekh ha-melekh, parashat vayyeshev* 5690 (1929), 54.

14. Bereshit Rabbah 84:8.

15. Ibid.

16. Kalonymus Kalman Shapira, *Benei mahshavah tovah* (Israel: Va'ad Hasidei Piaseczno, 1999), 31–32.

17. This should not be taken to mean that the substantiality of the world dissipates and is seen to be "only" names and souls, for in the same breath (and in consonance with his teachings throughout his works), Shapira emphasizes that names and souls are themselves more substantial than we sometimes imagine them to be—thus, letters can be called "stones," and that same sense of a chunk of reality applies equally, as we have seen, to letters per se and to all corporeal things.

18. This is because the Tetragrammaton is numerically 26 and *lehem* (bread) is three times this, 78.

19. Shapira, *Benei mahshavah tovah*, 32.

20. In his introduction to his commentary on the Pentateuch.

21. B. Shabbat 105a.

22. See Rashi loc. cit. Of course, it is also possible to read the unnamed reference more restrictively, that the "given" here refers to just the Decalogue, for example. See Pesikta Rabbati 21 for such a reading. For obvious reasons (including the pressure of the "heretic" who distinguished the divine revelatory nature of the Decalogue from the rest of the Torah and its commandments, as implied in b. Berakhot 12a), later Jewish exegesis tended to interpret the phrase here more expansively. See Isaiah Horowitz's *Shenei luhot ha-berit* (Jerusalem: Oz ve-hadar, 1993), 3:57, *masekhet Shavu'ot, perek Torah Or,* 3:3, which interprets

ketavit as a reference to the Divine as author of the written Torah and *yehavit* as a reference to the Divine as interpreter of the written Torah, through the giving of the oral Torah.

23. *Derekh ha-melekh, parashat vayyeshev* 5690 (1929), 48. For the idea that the embodied Torah of Israel is superior even to the letters of a Torah scroll as a locus of divine presence, see *Derekh ha-melekh, parashat noah,* 8–9, and the discussion in my thesis, "The Call of the Self: Devotional Individuation in the Teachings of Rabbi Kalonymous Kalman Shapira of Piaseczno" (Newton: Hebrew College, 2017), 69–71.

24. Although Shapira's critique of this understanding of *bittul* comes through most clearly in his explicit rejection of it, as in the sources cited in the previous note, he also engages in significant reinterpretation of the term in pieces in which he does adopt it positively, such as in the sermon from *parashat Vayyetse* 1930 [5691]. In her discussion of this sermon in this volume, Wiskind's emphasis on its continuity with the teachings of the Maggid of Mezritsh about self-nullification and *ayin* (nothingness) risks obscuring the innovation of Shapira's deployment of the Maggid's teaching. By the time he is done, Shapira has shifted the Maggid's mystical teaching about ontology and nothingness to an existential key about epistemology and radical self-doubt: "A person must establish times for himself to extricate himself from all the forms of his divine service, standing like a naked *golem* without a garment, and to doubt: 'Perhaps, God forbid, I am mistaken about everything. Who knows, it is possible that all of my devotional service that I have engaged in for all the years of my life was in vain and for nothing, and who knows whether after 120 years [when I die] . . . I will see that I have [lit., "there is here"] no Torah, no service; my entire life was a life of error, and what can I do then? All was lost" (*Derekh ha-melekh, parashat vayyetse* 5691 [1930], 36). Shapira's presentation of the positive uses of doubt here has much in common with the great existentialist Polish line of the Hasidic schools of Pshiskhe-Izhbits/Radzin-Kotsk, a subject that I hope to expand on in future work. At any rate, I submit that the absence of this quote, or even the central term *doubt,* from Wiskind's summary of this sermon risks obscuring the originality of Shapira's teaching here, and particularly its discontinuity with the original context of the teaching attributed to the Maggid that is his starting point.

25. Shapira, *Tsav ve-zeruz,* no. 10, in Kalonymus Kalman Shapira, *Hakhsharat ha-avreikhim, Mevo ha-she'arim, Tsav ve-zeruz* (Jerusalem: Va'ad Hasidei Piaseczno, 2001), 331–32, and cf. my discussion and summary in my thesis (cited in n. 23), 14–16.

26. Ibid., no. 1, 321. This yearning for more embodied life, and the sense of the unmitigated tragedy of death, perhaps speaks more eloquently than any of his more theoretical statements about Shapira's true positive valuation of the corporeal.

27. Ibid.; emphasis added.

28. Shapira, *Derekh ha-melekh, parashat vayyeshev* 5690 (1929), 49.

29. See the sources and discussion in Louis Jacobs, *Hasidic Prayer* (New York: Schocken, 1973), 104–20.

30. Indeed Jacobs, ibid., shows the relatively rapid retreat, even among Hasidic authors, from the Baal Shem Tov's teaching on this point to this earlier model, which was declared as advice intended only for great tsaddikim. Rabbi Yitzhak Ayzik Yehudah Yehiel Safrin of Komarno (1806–1874) stands out for his forceful defense of the ongoing universal applicability of the Baal Shem Tov's approach; see the sources cited by Jacobs.

31. Gen 2:24 and Rashi there.

32. Shapira, *Derekh ha-melekh, parashat vayyeshev* 5690 (1929), 49.

33. Ibid., 56. In the same paragraph, Shapira states this in terms of recognizing other selves as well: "So too, it is possible to recognize the soul [of the person] in the *hiddushei torah* that each individual understands."

34. Ibid., 49. The passage was quoted at some length in the preceding section.

35. Note that this formulation concords with the emphasis we have already seen in Shapira on the inherent holiness of the letters (and physical reality). On the one hand, it is true that the letters "garb" an essence, which we may therefore legitimately construe as "deeper." Yet, since the essence does not preexist the letters (that is, the "new portion" of essence, in Shapira's words), we cannot think of the essence as having simply put on a garment, which may perhaps then be taken off or switched for another. Rather, there is an intrinsic being-together of the letters with the portion of essence that they garb. The next *hiddush* will not simply be a new garment placed on the same essence but will announce instead the birth of a new portion of essence, and so on.

36. See the masterful analysis of Shapira's visionary practices in Daniel Reiser, *Imagery Techniques in Modern Jewish Mysticism*, trans. Eugene D. Matanky with Daniel Reiser (Berlin: De Gruyter, 2018), especially in relation to the process of the revelation of the soul/self (*hitgalut ha-nefesh*), 209–13. On the interrelationship between Shapira's literary and psychic process, see Don Seeman, "Ritual Efficacy, Hasidic Mysticism and 'Useless Suffering' in the Warsaw Ghetto," *Harvard Theological Review* 101, no. 3–4 (2008): 465–505. See also Don Seeman and Michael Karlin, "Mindfulness and Hasidic Modernism: Towards a Contemplative Ethnography," in *Religion and Society: Advances in Research* 10 (2019): 44–62 on Hasidic mindfulness practice. The authors explore the various conceptions of self that underlie the approaches to such practice in both Hasidic and non-Hasidic (e.g., Buddhist) contexts.

37. *Derekh ha-melekh, rosh ha-shanah* 5686 (1925), 193.

38. Ibid.

39. Loc. cit.

40. Shapira's notion of the "ingathering" certainly includes the nonhuman world, as his works attest. (See, e.g., his advice about finding times to commune

with nature, head into the woods and see oneself as "a simple creature amongst the creatures of God" in *Tsav ve-zeruz*, no. 18, in *Hakhsharat ha-avreikhim, Mevo ha-she'arim, Tsav ve-zeruz*, 331.) However, it is equally clear that, for Shapira, it is the lived experience of other persons that calls for our deepest acts of empathy and understanding. Note also his likening of creation itself to the image of a profound *tsaddik* deep in contemplation of supernal mysteries, whose silent cleaving to God inspires us to tremble in awe of the Divine and opens up possibilities for our own intimacy with God. Ibid., no. 29, 346–47.

41. *Derekh ha-melekh, rosh ha-shanah* 5686 (1925), 193.

42. Shneur Zalman of Liady, *Likkutei amarim—Tanya*, 41a.

43. See the discussion of (Jewish) souls and bodies in Moshe Cordevero, *Pardes rimmonim* 4:6. Cordevero states that human differentiation and uniqueness is only possible due to the partnering of souls with bodies, for bodies exhibit differences and variation of which souls are incapable. I am grateful to Eitan Fishbane, whose paper "Personal Identity and the Ontology of the Soul in Sixteenth-Century Kabbalah," presented at the 2017 Conference of the Association for Jewish Studies, brought this source to my attention. Accessed online February 12, 2019, at https://www.academia.edu/37120253/Personal_Identity_and_the_Ontology_of_the_Soul_in_Sixteenth_Century_Kabbalah.

44. Loc. cit. The distinction to which Shne'ur Zalman refers between the transitory love that is dependent upon a thing and the sustaining love that is not is found in m. Avot 5:16.

45. In asserting this, I am drawing upon the emphasis in m. Avot 5:16 that a love that is dependent upon a thing will, in the end, cease to be. On the interpretation of this passage from *Likkutei amarim* in Chabad Hasidism, see the selections compiled in Yehoshua Korf, ed., *Likkutei bi'urim be-sefer ha-tanya* (Brooklyn: Kehot Publication Society, 1968) [in Hebrew and Yiddish]), 1: 195–97.

46. Shapira, *Derekh ha-melekh, rosh ha-shanah* 5686 (1925), 194. This brief quote will be explored in its fuller context below.

47. Ibid., 195. That this self-creation through consciousness has a corporeal dimension is evident, Shapira continues, for "we see: one who learns Torah for a number of years, his entire body transforms, until 'the wisdom of a man illuminates his face' (Eccl 8:1)."

48. B. Rosh Hashanah 11a, and B. Hullin 60a, in the name of R. Yehoshua ben Levi.

49. Shapira, *Derekeh ha-melekh, Rosh Hashanah* 5686 [1925], 193.

50. Some have the text "in their height" here.

51. Or "beauty." See b. Rosh Hashanah 11a, the commentaries of Rashi s.v. *be-tsivyonam* and Tosafot s.v. *le-qomatan*.

52. b. Rosh Hashanah 11a. On the question of the justification for including height and *da'at* together with form when the homiletic reading seems only to

relate to the latter, see the commentary of Baruch Ha-Levi Epstein in his *Torah temimah* ad. loc., who claims that the former two are encompassed in the concept of the full "form" or "beauty" of that which is created.

53. B. Rosh Hashanah 11a, Rashi s.v. *be-qomatan nivra'u*. This interpretation of R. Yehoshua ben Levi's words is in fact implicitly suggested by the flow of the talmudic discussion, which sees his teaching as of use in interpreting the apparently redundant phrase "fruit trees which produce fruit" in Gen 1:11.

54. B. Rosh Hashanah 11a, Rabbenu Hanenel ad. loc.

55. Maimonides, *The Guide of the Perplexed*, translated and annotated by Shlomo Pines (Chicago: University of Chicago Press, 1963), Vol. 2, 355; and Albo, *Sefer ha-iqqarim* Ma'amar 2, 22:3.

56. Loc. cit.

57. b. Rosh Hashanah 11a, Rashi c.v. *le-da'atam*.

58. The text has *be-demutan* in place of *qomatan* here.

59. Levi Yitzhak of Barditshev, *Kedushat Levi* (Warsaw: 1876), *kedushat purim, kedushah 3*, 21.

60. Jean-Paul Sartre, "Existentialism is a Humanism," trans. Philip Mairet, in *Existentialism from Dostoevsky to Sartre*, ed. Walter Kaufmann (New York: Meridian, 1956), 290.

61. Ibid., 290–91.

62. *Derekh ha-melekh, rosh ha-shanah* 5686, 193; my emphasis.

63. Ibid., 194; my emphasis.

64. Obviously, given Shapira's strong traditional Hasidic Orthodoxy, he does not promote absolute liberty. Rather, he suggests, in the spirit of m. Avot 6:2, that the commandments graven (*harut*) on the tablets themselves provide freedom (*herut*). If poorly developed, this rabbinic formulation may serve only as Orwellian doublespeak. In Shapira's thought, his emphatic insistence that each individual cultivate an utterly unique approach to every aspect of Torah observance and study reveals him to be an enthusiastic advocate of creative freedom, within a Hasidic form; see the sources cited above in n25.

65. For example, Shapira's impassioned definition of compassion as the ability to truly grasp the pain of another, discussed above in section VI. This functions not only as a logical definition of terms but also as a rhetorical appeal to the reader's ethical sense, urging her not to allow a vague and self-absorbed feeling to pass itself off under this moniker.

6

Hasidism in Dialogue with Modernity

Rabbi Kalonymus Shapira's *Derekh Ha-Melekh*

Ora Wiskind

Until now, Rabbi Kalonymus Kalman Shapira has been best known to scholarship for his Warsaw Ghetto sermons, and secondarily for his important prewar mystical and educational tracts, such as *Hovat ha-talmidim* (see Mayse, Seeman this volume) and *Benei mahshavah tovah* (Leshem, this volume). His collection of sermons from between the wars (1925–1936), meanwhile, has been mostly neglected. These homilies were apparently delivered orally (probably in Yiddish) on Sabbaths and festivals and then recorded in Hebrew, in his own hand, shortly thereafter.[1] They were preserved in manuscript form and later posthumously published as *Derekh ha-melekh*, "The King's Way." Not surprisingly, these sermons display important continuities with R. Shapira's other, better-known works: an acute historical consciousness, strikingly modern psychological and phenomenological insights, a clear pedagogical orientation, and mystical attunement. Yet they also deserve study in their own right, not least for what they convey of his impressive exegetical and literary accomplishments. This chapter (and this volume) therefore contribute to a partial shift in focus from the radical, charged tropes of suffering and the catastrophic end of meaning that dominate scholarly discourse on his Warsaw Ghetto *Sermons from the Years of Rage*. I intend to underline some more nuanced elements of his prewar thought and to offer some comparisons between his

interbellum and later Holocaust sermons (see also Seeman, this volume).
Among the themes that recur in R. Shapira's writings are self-awareness,
emotion, the need for inner psychic unity, empowerment, the urgency of
communication, and an endless desire for divine presence. There are striking consonances between these concerns and innovative trends emerging
in the same years in psychology, educational philosophy, phenomenology,
and nascent Neo-Hasidism.[2] I will consider some of these in the following
pages and will also suggest certain lines of continuity between R. Shapira's two collections of commentaries or *derashot*. A closer look at the
early sermons collected in *Derekh ha-melekh* offers new perspective on
the relationship between hermeneutics and mysticism, and promises to
shed new light on R. Shapira's conception of Hasidism and its mission of
redemption and renewal.

The Historical Backdrop

A circumspect reading of *Derekh ha-melekh* requires some attention to the
historical setting of the sermons. As Wodziński (this volume) describes
in greater detail, the period of R. Shapira's creativity was in the aftermath
of the Great War that consumed Europe between 1914 and 1918, along
with "the revolutions, civil wars, and new nationalisms that came in its
wake." These "shattered the world of the nineteenth century and ushered in
momentous ideological, cultural, and social changes that would shape the
interwar period and beyond." Mass expulsions reduced millions of eastern
European Jews to homeless refugees and concentrated others in urban
areas. The traumas of war, relocation, poverty, and anti-Semitic violence
all took their psychic toll. The following passage, an entry in R. Shapira's
spiritual diary, *Tsav ve-zeruz* (also cited by Seeman, this volume), reflects
his sense of the Jewish experience in interwar Poland. It was written in
the late 1920s in response to a wave of suicides in the Jewish community:

> Mourn—but not only for those who have done away with
> their lives. Weep bitterly for the walking dead. . . . They have
> not killed themselves, yet they are dead all the same. Life is
> cheap. To be or not to be, it makes no difference any more.
> In former times, the evil inclination had to make an effort to
> bring a person to apostasy, to lose faith in God—it was not
> easy, and he did not always manage. But now, I look around

and I see people . . . whose selfhood [*ha-anokhi*] has become worthless to them. Live or die, heaven or hell—for whom? Only for their pitiful selves—what an utterly pitiful and meaningless thing to care about. "So it happened, along the way"—he froze your soul, chilled your whole being.[3]

Equally alarming, in R. Shapira's eyes, was the rapid corrosion of the old Hasidic world of faith. Wodziński outlines some major historical factors at work: "The destruction of courts and *shtiblekh* and the deaths of tsaddikim shook the very foundations of Hasidic socio-religious life and dealt an incomparably heavy blow to the functioning of the tightly knit Hasidic communities. With no access to the tsaddik, with no place for prayer and daily gatherings, Hasidism lost much of its essential experience for many."[4] The dislocation and migration of huge populations, rapid urbanization, poverty, revolution, and new intellectual currents were dramatically transforming traditional Jewry.

Beyond Hasidic circles, however, questions of identity were central to the modern Jewish experience as a whole: "The highly polarized Polish Jewish community fought a vicious internal battle over the hearts and minds of its young people and who could provide them with the best means to cope with both their Jewish identity and the challenges of modern society."[5] The educational theory and practice that R. Shapira developed in the interwar period was therefore one tactic for confronting problems of Jewish identity, especially with respect to young people (Evan Mayse, Seeman, this volume).[6] In a broader sense, R. Shapira's oeuvre as a whole evidences his desire to renew Jewish spirituality by way of Hasidic teaching, an endeavor with clear messianic undercurrents. Yet alongside his other works, his sermons constitute a unique medium with its own specific social context and hermeneutical power. The homiletic is arguably the classic and most enduring genre of discourse in Jewish literary tradition. Preachers in all historical periods and places have served as agents of culture: their sermons bring sacred texts to life by making them relevant to contemporary concerns.[7] And so R. Shapira's interwar discourses can yield important new insight onto his deepest convictions about Hasidic teaching and the ethos it embodied at a crucial historical juncture; they may also illuminate aspects of his own lived experience.

Derekh ha-melekh (to offer an associative gloss on the title of this work, "The King's Way") addresses this core concern: How might a sense of inner majesty be restored? Can some spark of honor be salvaged, enthroned

again, within the Hasidic world? (See also Evan Mayse, this volume.)
Understood literally, "The King's Way" might mean the "highroad," or a
manner of living that befits true "sons of the King"—that is, every Jewish
soul.[8] Kingship—a mien of dignity and quiet greatness—is manifest in R.
Shapira's authorial persona as well. As a writer and as a religious leader,
he asserts himself in these discourses as an agent of empowerment. What
he teaches is a way to discover inner resources and unleash the power of
self-transformation, to break a path of religious authenticity, to struggle for
spiritual wholeness. In the midst of all this, a dialogue ensues. Traditional
Jewish sources, read imaginatively through the prism of modern culture
and contemporary discourse, speak in new voices for a new reality.[9] My
aim is to explore that dialogue and its far-reaching implications.

Facets of the Self

The concept of the self and its emergence figures prominently in *Derekh
ha-melekh*. In many and varied contexts, R. Shapira stresses the importance of self-awareness, self-knowledge, and a sense of personal identity;
achieving them is posed as an ethical and religious imperative.[10] The cypher
he uses to speak of selfhood is the biblical Hebrew term *anokhi* (as in
"I [*anokhi*] am the Lord your God"). Its negative counterimage is called
anokhiyut, meaning self-absorption, selfishness, an egotistical concern for
one's own well-being, with an implicit defacing of others. Two discourses
on the portion *vayyetse* (Gen 28:10–32:3), dated to the winters of 1929
and 1930 respectively, probe the meaning and importance of selfhood
with striking originality (see also Maayan, this volume).[11]

    The biblical scene that incites R. Shapira's reflection follows Jacob's
flight from his brother Esau: "Jacob departed from Beersheba and went
toward Haran. He came to the place and rested there, because the sun
had set. He took from the stones of that place and arranged them around
his head and lay down there. And he dreamt." The vision of Jacob's ladder
follows, with angels ascending and descending from heaven. God declares
his promise to Jacob: "I am with you; I will guard you wherever you go,
and I will return you." Finally, Jacob wakes from his slumber and says,
"Surely God is present in this place and I did not know!" (Gen 28:10–16)

    Let me highlight some of most innovative features of R. Shapira's
sermon (1929) on these verses. He deconstructs Jacob's admission "and I

did not know," reordering its syntax to mean "for I was unaware of my self (ve-anokhi–lo yadati)." He then describes a range of human experiences called "knowing," all of them related in one way or another to self-knowledge and apprehension. (Maayan, this volume, explores the vital role of da'at in self-creation.) One form is intellectual, abstract knowledge of unrelated units of information—a disembodied, disinterested, and essentially static mental state. A second is affective knowledge, linked to the sensory organs. A third kind of knowledge, the most valuable and all-encompassing, is bound up with actual self-awareness and interiority. Significantly, though, it is incited by an external source, as R. Shapira writes: "So, for instance, a new interpretation or Hasidic insight [eizeh derekh hadash be-drush o be-hasidut] that one sees in a book: that knowledge moves one profoundly . . . it strikes to the soul's depths and reverberates through one's consciousness, affecting everything one already knew" (see Diamond, this volume).

The exegetical lynchpin for all these reflections is the revelation at Sinai: "Anokhi [I] am the Lord" (Exod 20:2), with its famous rabbinical gloss to the effect that "I [God] have given you something of myself in these words [the Torah]."[12] More than a heteronomous force prescribing instrumental action (the commandments) or voicing a theology, the Torah is here conceived as a locus of intimate encounter with the Divine (Evan Mayse and Maayan, this volume). On R. Shapira's reading, anokhi thus signals a deeply vulnerable, embodied mode of knowing. He concludes the sermon with a bold analogy: In the human realm as well, words spoken in holiness are a vehicle of self-revelation. The mandate, then, is to discover one's own selfhood, to emerge from "not-knowing" as a conscious, empowered individual.

> Now, what Jacob really experienced—that is beyond our comprehension. But [from these verses we learn that] every Jew must discern what the Torah hints about one's own self and personal state. Thus, Jacob said, "Truly, God is in this place"—that I knew [intellectually]. . . . "But I, I did not know myself"—that knowing had not penetrated to my inmost being, had not yet informed my own sense of self. . . . "And so he vowed: May God be with me"—and grant me knowledge . . . not for my benefit alone, but that I may convey my understanding to others. For this is the essence of a Jew.[13]

Note the uncommon rhetorical force of this passage, albeit presented here in translation. With psychological acumen and rich emotional language, R. Shapira charts a process of self-transformation. Its effects are meant to radiate outward, beyond the personal dimension. These lines give voice to an ethos of communication, empathy, and authenticity, to the social concerns that underlie his grand vision of a unified spiritual community.[14] Perhaps more strikingly still, in this sermon, R. Shapira performs the very mode of being that he describes. His engagement with the biblical narrative is a gesture of sharing his own "self" with his listeners, enacted through the sermon. I will return to this autobiographical facet of his writing later.

The second sermon on this same biblical passage, here from the year 1930, begins with the same verse, "And I did not know. . . ." Jacob, in the biblical narrative, falls asleep. Metaphorically, R. Shapira adds, he is reduced or returned to a state of formlessness, becoming a *golem* (literally, a lifeless lump). Drawing on a powerful kabbalistic motif, R. Shapira refers to that surreal, unwilled state of slumber as *dormita*.[15] It is an essential, flickering moment of "ego-annulment," a letting-go of the self (*bittul atsmuto me'at*). Essential because only then can true change take place: a metamorphosis that penetrates the core self. Here, the prooftext that enables this exegetical leap from the mystical to the psychological plane is an early Hasidic teaching, which R. Shapira cites in the name of the Maggid of Mezritsh. Avot 5:9 reads, "Seven things characterize a wise person . . . and as for a clod, all of them are the reverse (*hilufeihen ba-go-lem*)." R. Shapira explains, "That is, for something to be transformed or transmuted (*hilufin*) . . . it must first revert to being a *golem*. Its separate, individual form has to be stripped away and voided, become nothing."[16]

A series of metaphors illustrate the point. Among them are the metaphor of a seed that must disintegrate in the earth for new life to sprout from it, and the metaphor of silver that must first be smelted if new vessels are to be forged. This sermon, in a basic sense, is about personal development: it envisions self-transformation as the overarching goal of religious life (see Maayan, this volume). Yet a subtext seems to inform this discourse as well. Shapira notes the difficulties that trouble and confuse his listeners and acknowledges their power to obstruct emotional and spiritual growth. One ever-present factor is a destructive kind of self-absorption that impedes any possible awareness of divine presence. He names it by alluding to a teaching by the Baal Shem Tov: "On the verse 'I [*anokhi*] stand between God and you' (Deut 5:5): self-centeredness [*anokhiyut*] is what alienates you from God. And so, the more one casts off egotism, the closer one can come to wholeness and to holiness."[17]

A second problem, on an ostensibly opposite pole, is a terrifying sense of emptiness, as if one's soul were "arid or petrified, a heart of stone that feels nothing, a hollow human being," broken and bereft of anything sacred. Both deficiencies, R. Shapira suggests, may be resolved by a willful act: "To reach a higher level, one must first become a formless *golem,* struggle free of all one's presuppositions and conclusions, cast off everything. This enables one to look at things objectively, with a 'naked intellect' (*sekhel arum*), unencumbered. Then it is possible to see clearly and to renew oneself as never before."[18] Personal growth, on this model, plays out in an ongoing dialectic of fragmentation and mindful reconstruction. It is a positive, yet profoundly unsettling, process. The final section of the sermon addresses the sense of vulnerability and uncertainty that must be endured for the work of self-renewal.

R. Shapira revisits the experience of the patriarch Jacob, superimposed now on that of Moses. Both biblical figures were driven by a yearning for divine presence. A midrash connects that yearning to the "pauses," or gaps, between moments of speech that punctuate any dialogue: "The pauses (*ha-hafsakot*)—what role did they serve? To give Moses time to reflect, in the silence between the words."[19] At issue is a paradox inherent, in effect, in every act of communication. The "pause" connotes a tenuous experience of absence. Here, God draws away, as it were, and addresses Moses no more. Yet those moments of cessation are vital for any true understanding to take place. In the silence, left alone with his thoughts, Moses has time to contemplate and to internalize what he has heard. The pauses, then, are a portal: they enable response and personal initiative, an "arousal from below"—that is, from the human side. With this in mind, R. Shapira returns to the opening scene of the Torah portion. Jacob journeys to Haran. For fourteen years, he had been sheltered safely in "the tent of Torah." Now, thrust into a lonely, alien landscape, fear suddenly overcomes him. How will he continue, even here, to strive for holiness? "And so he vows: 'May God be with me'—with my essential self—'and guard me' here as well—even in the silent spaces (*ha-hafsakot*). . . . Then, on his way back home at last, he could affirm: 'I dwelt with Laban,' and I upheld all the commandments—there, most of all, in the midst of the pauses."[20]

I have framed these two *derashot* in implicit dialogue with contemporary concerns (see also Seeman, this volume). Indeed, R. Shapira himself reads traditional Jewish sources in that light. Biblical figures, on his retelling, model the attentiveness to matters of the spirit that he recognizes as vitally important. Through these readings, he urges his listeners and his readers to discover their true, unique selves, to become autonomous individuals invested with choice and will. The human experiences dramatized in these passages effectively reframe the sense of emptiness and indirection that plagued many of his generation. When the suffering of the present moment can be envisioned on a broader horizon encompassing both "before" and "after," a fuller narrative might emerge. Hope remains, even now, of regaining a sense of divine presence. What is needed are tools for the work to be done (see also Seeman, this volume). I turn now to look more closely at the sensibility that R. Shapira sought to cultivate, as well as the literary techniques he used to teach that sensibility to others.

Developing a Language of Mindfulness

> A *hasid* exists beyond the margins (*lifnim mishurat ha-din*). . . . He perceives the world, but not with the constricted vision of someone who sees only base physicality. Rather, as we have said in the name of the Baal Shem Tov, "When you contemplate the world, you will see God, and God sees you."[21] . . . A *hasid*—he is totally unconfined by stricture (*din*), and so his vision, too, reaches beyond all manner of restriction (*tsimtsum*). The same is true of his study of Torah: the simple meanings of the verses, or even of Kabbalah, are not enough for him. In everything, he strives to apprehend with unlimited insight, with a gaze that knows no boundedness.[22]

These lines describe a spiritual stance and a vital mode of being. Key terms—*din, tsimtsum, hasid*—refer here to emotional and cognitive limitation and gesture toward a way that such forms of boundedness might be overcome. In rhetorical tone, this passage is infused with an aura of promise, with the endless potential of existential freedom.

In a Yom Kippur sermon from 1925, R. Shapira urges his listeners and readers to make an inner shift that might open them to a moment of transformative vision. In subject matter, the sermon concerns Yom Kippur. Its primary themes are traditional: return and repentance, asking forgiveness for one's wrongdoings, and pleading to be judged favorably, "to be inscribed in the Book of Life." The last section of the day's liturgy marks the culmination of a spiritual journey, the final stage when God's judgment will be "sealed."

> To understand something about Yom Kippur and the moment of its "sealing" (*hatimah*) and our request to be not only "written" but also "sealed" [in the Book of Life], and what this "seal" has to do with worlds beyond:
> *Tikkunei zohar* speaks of "the holy gate in which all forms are visible." The Assembly of Israel pleads: Master of the universe, even though I am in exile, far away from you, "Set me as a seal (*hotam*) upon your heart" (Song 8:6), and may your image not be removed from me—that is, your seal, your Presence—for this is what arouses remembrance in exile.
> Now, the meaning of God's seal, and our asking God to be "as a seal upon your heart"—all that is beyond our understanding. But what it teaches us about serving him, as the Baal Shem Tov revealed—this, perhaps, we can explain . . . [23]

R. Shapira recalls one of the Baal Shem Tov's most radical convictions, a controversial, founding tenet of Hasidism: that traces of God can be found everywhere in the world "as the image of the seal impressed upon it," an indwelling presence inscribed by absence.[24] The next lines of this sermon explore the nature of the "image" or "form" (*tsurah*) and how it may be apprehended. Unlike the physical manifestation of a person or of an object, the "form" is intangible and immaterial. Still, although it is invisible to the eye, R. Shapira suggests, the form of that entity permeates our awareness; it makes a mark on some level of consciousness. This impression is what ultimately enables us to recognize others and to claim our possessions—far more powerfully and convincingly than any external, objectively defined sign of identity.[25] At issue once again is an intuitive mode of knowing, a nonintellectual, nonrational faculty. By analogy, R. Shapira continues, a primary task of religious life is to contemplate the world with that same essential capacity: to look beyond appearances—all the disparate, partial, confusing phenomena that clamor for attention—and discern the "image," the traces of God that dwell secretly within it (see also Seeman, this volume). "Just as we can gaze into the face of another and sense that person's inwardness . . . so must we regard the world: not with our eyes but through our souls—to distinguish and recognize the Master of the seal in the impression left behind."

In theosophical terms, these lines describe the concept of divine immanence. R. Shapira names it otherwise. He recalls the kabbalistic notion called *memale kol almin,* the emanation of divinity that infuses the "vessels" and all of created reality.[26] Far more than an abstract category, it gives voice to a mystical sensibility charged with emotional resonances. Implicitly, this idea responds to a radically opposite perspective: that the world is a fractured place of limitation and darkness, in which the countenance of the Holy One is utterly hidden, while the sacred letters of creation have scattered chaotically, senselessly. That dialectic, Shapira suggests, is contained in an emblematic flash of perception:

> Adam, the first human, realized his failing: "I heard your voice and I hid" (Gen 3:10). What a profound confession those words utter! "Master of the Universe, I know, I see that it is not you who have concealed yourself from me after my sin." No. "I hid"—"I myself am responsible." Yet people imagine that it is God who hides from them. Everything is different, though, for one who discovers [or uncovers] one's soul.[27] Such a person, looking at the world through the soul, can discern the image of the Master impressed in the seal. Then, at last, the divine letters will join together once again, and God's holy name fills all of reality.[28]

Sin, on this retelling, casts a veil or husk over the soul, cutting it off from the light of holiness. To mitigate that state, one must first of all perceive oneself as a moral agent; then, one must willfully rend the veil and cast off the self-deceptions that separate one from God. Healing and repair, recovering a natural sense of holiness—all that is predicated on inner work. Its power is transformative, for the individual and for the world itself. And yet, R. Shapira notes in rhetorical counterpoint, there are those who ignore the summons, who would rather hide behind a false sense of powerlessness and cavil: "This doesn't have anything to do with me, it's beyond my power." His response is that you don't need to be a locksmith to open a door; though you understand little, the keys are in your hand. Anyone can unfasten the gates; the labor of every Jew has an effect above.[29]

This is an empowering message, to be sure. But R. Shapira concludes his sermon with an even stronger claim. He recalls the second half of the dialectic, that transcendent realm that kabbalists call *sovev kol almin*, which surrounds or envelops all spheres of existence. On this concealed other side, the same vital interrelationship between the seal and its impression is manifest, only in a paradoxical reversed order.

> Now the dimension called *sovev* [encompassment] is bound up with the Jewish people. For God conceived of Israel primordially, before creation. As Rebbe Dov [Baer, the Maggid of Mezritsh] taught, the world came into being "in the merit of the forefathers, who engendered your will to create it."[30] . . . Thus, in the very beginning, long before God's image came to be revealed in earthly reality, the impression—the essential soul of Israel—was already manifest in the Master of the seal, so to speak. . . . This, then, is the meaning of *Tikkunei zohar*. The Assembly of Israel is saying to the Holy One, "Even when I am far away from you, in exile, 'Set me as a seal upon your heart'—not only has your image been impressed on me, but may my image remain forever imprinted in you, on your heart, as it were, an eternal, present memory."
>
> And so Yom Kippur, a day that transcends all the worlds, a day on which the encompassing light emanates forth, when all the accusers are silenced and Satan cannot enter—this holy day ends with a moment of "sealing" (*hatimah*), in the sense of "set me as a seal upon your heart." So, too, may God become visible through his seal and bless us with all manner of goodness, as we pray, "Seal us for Life." Amen.[31]

The poetic metaphor of the "seal" here is richly allusive. It is rooted in the rabbinical notion that the Jewish people "arose in divine thought" (*alu be-mahashavah*) before the beginning of time—an abstract, virtual, potential existence not yet realized. R. Shapira couples this concept with a second, more tangible image drawn from mystical teaching. He signals the radical nature of his contention with traditional cautionary phrases: "as it were," "so to speak." Rhetorically, these lines return to the passage from *Tikkunei zohar* with which the sermon began. Here, though, the focus is on a hidden counterimage, the esoteric, second side of the dialectic. Israel—

the Jewish people—is carved, inscribed, in God's metaphysical essence, an embodied presence that cannot be removed or erased.[32] At issue, then, is a double sense of being: " 'Set me as a seal upon your heart'—not only has your [God's] image been impressed on me [Israel], but may my image remain forever imprinted in you, on your heart." Through his sermon, R. Shapira seeks to show a way to re-find that vital religious consciousness and to integrate it into life.

In a broader sense, this discourse forefronts his program of cultural and spiritual renewal by means of Hasidic tradition. That program has much in common with other contemporary calls for Jewish renaissance in a Neo-Hasidic spirit. One was Martin Buber's quest "to recover from historical Hasidism a message that might address the crisis of modern men and women, a crisis he defined as the radical alienation of the profane from the sacred."[33] Or, as Alan Brill describes Abraham Joshua Heschel's interwar agenda: he "sought to present the pre-modern texts on revelation as a means of reawakening the religious sense of revelation, as mediated through various modern idioms. . . . Rather than relying on traditional hierarchy, Heschel provides a kabbalistic and Hasidic sensibility that is mediated through his poetic imagination."[34] So, too, R. Shapira teaches how an encounter with holiness might still come about. His is a redemptive vision—a glimpse of the "light of the Messiah" soon to be revealed.[35]

Real Presence

R. Shapira's sermons, as we have seen, are deeply self-reflective. At times, he voices the awareness of a Hasid, guided and formed by his own religious mentors; at other times, he takes on the persona of spiritual mentor, his words suffused with the aura of tsaddikim of former days. In effect, Shapira's illustrious lineage burdened him with a heavy sense of responsibility: to bridge between the old, lost world of religious faith and a new reality; to communicate spiritual values to an estranged generation of Jewish youth; somehow to carry on the redemptive mission of Hasidic teaching.[36] He takes up the challenge. Countless rhetorical gestures throughout his works convey the sense that he has something momentous to bestow, that he must entrust his listeners and his readers with a sense of ongoing revelation. Beyond their clear dramatic force, the autobiographical aspects of such gestures and their *ars poetica* demand closer attention, with respect to the interbellum sermons in particular.

In the midrash Tanhuma, [*parashat*] *vayyehi*, on the verse " 'So
their father spoke to them . . . And then he instructed them:
I shall be gathered to my people' (Gen 49:28–29): He said to
them: if you are worthy, take care of my bones; if not, when
I depart from this world, I shall leave you and go to my forefathers." . . . The tsaddikim—their light is not for themselves
alone but for the whole world. Like sunlight: anyone who opens
a window is illuminated; so, too, all who draw near to them find
holiness. The light of the tsaddikim expands their souls—while
the tsaddik lives and onward, after he is gone. But if people
distance themselves, heaven forbid, then, when the tsaddikim
die, the light of their souls leaves this world. For it is known
that no soul can exist here below without a body to contain
it, as we learn from the Ruzhiner Rebbe.[37] . . . And so, when
we draw close to the tsaddikim, we come to be a "body" for
them: their souls and their light and their holiness dwell here
with us. Otherwise, their souls, disembodied, fade away and
disappear above. And so the midrash says: "If you are worthy,
take care of my bones/my essence (*atsamay*). If not, when I
depart from this world, I will leave you utterly."[38]

The frank, emotional language of this passage has the poignancy of a
spiritual testament. On this retelling of the midrash, it is the (Hasidic)
tsaddik who, on his deathbed, appeals to the living, "Take care of my
bones." At bottom, it is a plea for mercy. The dying, after all, are helpless;
they can only request that something of themselves be preserved and cher-
ished. Whether or not it will happen is a matter of choice, of will, and,
ultimately, a test of merit. Shapira dwells on this for some lines and then
countenances a second, alternative mode. No matter what, he avers, some
glimmer of spiritual brightness will always linger behind the tsaddikim.
It may also reappear without warning in secret ways.

Guided from the world beyond, a person walks an unknown
path, shrouded in deathly darkness. Suddenly, here—a flash
of illumination! Whence has it come? It is the soul-light of
a tsaddik. And so, in this world, any Jew might feel, from
deep within, a moment of ascent, an unexpected welling-up
of holiness and desire to serve God with all one's being. Such
an awakening—this, too, comes about when a tsaddik of old

reveals himself: an indwelling presence that augments one's own soul—as we learn from Joseph Sarug [a medieval kabbalist] in the notion of *ibbur ha-tsaddikim*. For the holiness of Israel is there, in every Jewish soul, although it lies concealed in a matted shroud, covered over with gross corporeality. . . . Truly, divine Presence is in exile, in our very midst. It can be aroused, though, in a single moment. The souls of the tsaddikim can set it free, can release it from its house of bondage.[39]

This passage resonates with esoteric allusions. Righteous individuals, long dead, might truly manifest themselves in one's inner life. They come in times of need, to guide and enlighten those who hope for them. Significantly, though, what R. Shapira portrays is not a rarified, mystical encounter reserved for a spiritual elite but something that can happen to "every Jewish soul." R. Shapira performs this crucial message in many of his sermons. (See also Maayan, this volume.) Consider, for instance, the following passage, and note how the narrative voice shifts for a moment from second to first person—a rhetorical gesture that seems to give voice to R. Shapira's personal experience.

As we know, "Three books are open on Rosh Hashanah. . . . The wholly righteous are inscribed for life; the wholly wicked for death; the mediocre, those in the middle—they hang in suspense from the New Year until the Day of Atonement."[40] . . .

The Gemara, Pesahim 112b, says: "R. Akiva said to Shimon bar Yochai: If you want to be strangled, go hang yourself on a big tree." Rashi explains: "If you want to say something that people will hear and accept, say it in the name of a great person." . . . Then, although your understanding reaches no higher than the lowest rung, even so, light from above, a ray of true light—from Rebbe Elimelekh or from the [Kozienicer] Maggid—is revealed *to me when I join myself* to their path, a path of holiness. . . . And because the true light of a great man speaks through you when you join yourself to him, if only to the lowest aspect of his teaching, your words contain holiness far more than you can know. As soon as they leave your mouth, others can sense their holiness, and so do you. Thus, "the mediocre"—they "hang themselves on tall trees": that is, on the tsaddikim and everything they have seen and understood from their holy books.[41]

Tongue in cheek, perhaps, but Shapira has placed himself squarely in the class of "those hanging," figuratively sustained by the power of his righteous forebears. Self-consciously, he voices the awareness of a receiver [Heb. *mekabbel*], a Hasidic follower, a latecomer of meager understanding. Listening more closely, however, what this passage really communicates is an ethos of reciprocity.[42] The soul-light of the tsaddikim endures in this world as an imperceptible, still un-actualized force. To draw their presence down, back into the phenomenal world, is the task of the living—a task entrusted to all those willing to answer the summons, "If you are worthy, take care of my bones."

Readers and Authors, Bones and Books

There is one more dimension of *ars poetica* that needs to be addressed. We have seen that "the holy books" of Hasidic masters from generations past were a formative part of R. Shapira's identity and self-awareness.[43] Reflections on reading, writing, and the power of books pervade his own works (see also Seeman, this volume). A sermon on *parashat Shemot* (1929) forefronts these themes. I will read it as an ego-document or self-revelation of singular importance.[44]

R. Shapira begins his discourse with some reflections on reading practices. Books, he asserts, embody the whole essence of their authors, and so dedicated readers must strive to discern the author's unique spiritual form (*shi'ur komah*), which is revealed/concealed in his work. R. Shapira then turns to the authorial persona, modeled here after the figure of the Hasidic tsaddik. The author (*mehabber*, literally, "connector") is an emissary. Like prophets of times past, he is charged to draw divine light and holiness, the word of God, down into the human realm; through his writings, he must also try to restore channels that join earth with heaven, to teach his readers how to serve God. True, prophets no longer have the power to foresee the future, "but prophecy in the form of guidance, bringing illumination—that has never ceased. Revelation continues: we see it still, in the Oral Torah, the *Zohar*, the holy Ari, the Baal Shem Tov, of blessed memory." In the course of the sermon, the narrative voice becomes more personal:

> An author, then, must reveal his own spiritual form. He does
> so limb by limb: one holy thought, another word of guidance,
> a Torah insight, a moment of intent. Each is a part of himself;

combined, they are his spiritual stature, and through him prophetic insight, unencumbered by corporeality, may be revealed
to Israel. Such a person, then, must speak and write down his
thoughts, must share them with others. For this is not a private
matter; the holiness he has received is not meant for him alone
but for all of Israel. . . . Others, too, need to receive that light
and holiness from above, channeled through his being into
their hearts and souls. . . . He must shape it and give birth
to it. . . . And so, the book that contains this individual's discourses, insights, and novella is no mere collection of random
thoughts. Rather, his very essence and spiritual form, imbued
with holiness, comes to light through the book he has written.[45]

These lines seem quite transparently self-referential. I believe they
also require us to qualify Moshe Idel's claim (this volume) that R. Shapira
turned away from the "mystical-magical" model of Hasidic leadership
practiced by some of his most illustrious forebears in favor of a more
contemplative "experiential type of spirituality and prophecy." What we
see here (and in many other passages of his interbellum writing) is,
rather, that these two models were deeply intertwined in R. Shapira's
portrait of the tsaddik, in terms of his spiritual force and teachings. R.
Shapira frames the act of writing as a religious imperative and an ethical
obligation, in part because the text serves as a literal conduit for spiritual
vitality (which Idel refers to as "mystical-magical"). Whatever has been
granted from above—prophetic understanding and experience *as well as*
vital potency—must be shared with others, preserved in lasting form.[46]
Beyond the words, books embody their authors' spiritual form, and this
is their ultimate value.

In an immediate sense, R. Shapira's promotion of books here can be
understood as the call of the hour. The old Hasidic world is gone forever;
communities have been uprooted, their faithful scattered to the winds.
Despite everything, a living encounter with the tsaddikim, with a rebbe,
a spiritual mentor, is still possible—now, paradoxically, through the written word. This, to be sure, is a revision of traditional values suited to the
modern condition. By rhetorical means, R. Shapira fosters the vital sense
of presence that he describes. His discourses bear witness to his belief that
sharing of oneself is what engenders a community of faith. On a deeply
personal level, he adjures his listeners—present and future—to seek out
the undying vitality that lies hidden in his own works. R. Shapira's ethical

will, a few simple lines, among his last, penned in the Warsaw Ghetto (see Magid, this volume), attests cogently to this. He implores relatives and friends in far-off Palestine to publish his manuscripts after the war, to distribute them widely, and to preface every volume with this final request, that "every Jew should study my books."[47] Books, like bones, contain an impalpable essence. Words that an author has left behind still have the power to transform others and to repair the world—if only their readers are willing.

Notes

1. The earliest dated teaching is 1925 (Shavuot 5685), and the latest is 1936 (va'ethanan-nahamu 5696). On the transcription of R. Shapira's interwar sermons and the publication history of *Derekh ha-melekh*, see Kalonymus Kalman Shapira, *Sermons from the Years of Rage* [in Hebrew], ed. Daniel Reiser, 2 vols. (Jerusalem: Herzog Academic College, 2017), 1:36, 42–45.

2. Neo-Hasidism began at the turn of the twentieth century with the works of Martin Buber and Hillel Zeitlin. In very different ways, each of them aspired to engender a spiritual revival in European Judaism by reworking traditional Hasidic teaching to respond to contemporary needs. See Tomer Persico, "Neo-Hasidic Revival: Expressivist Uses of Traditional Lore," in *Modern Judaism* 34, no. 3,1 (October 2014): 287–308; Arthur Green and Ariel Evan Mayse, eds., *A New Hasidism* (Philadelphia: Jewish Publication Society, 2019). Also see Idel and Seeman (this volume).

3. *Tsav ve-zeruz*, 16 17, s. 25. A marginal note there links the wave of suicides to an economic crisis in the Jewish community between 1926 and 1928. See Seeman, "Ritual Efficacy, Hasidic Mysticism and 'Useless Suffering' in the Warsaw Ghetto," *Harvard Theological Review* 101 (2008): 489.

4. Wodziński, "War and Religion," 297–311. Shapira addressed many of these issues in a public speech delivered before a meeting of Orthodox leaders that took place in Warsaw in the early 1920s. It was published in *Derekh ha-melekh* (Jerusalem: Va'ad Hasidei Piaseczno, 1995), 460–62. On the deterioration of the traditional Hasidic world, see Benjamin Brown, *The Haredim: A Guide to their Beliefs and Sectors* [in Hebrew] (Tel Aviv, 2017), 33–82. See also Wodziński, this volume.

5. Gershon Bacon, "National Revival, Ongoing Acculturation," Simon Dubnow Institute Yearbook 1 (2002): 81. In this context, Bacon cites the pioneering work by Max Weinreich, *Der veg tsu undzer yugnt: Yesoydes, metodn, problemen fun Yidisher yugnt-forshung* (Vilna, 1935), one of the first "serious attempts at sociological, cultural, historical and psychological work on Polish Jewry." See

Bacon, "Woman? Youth? Jew?: The Search for Identity of Jewish Young Women in Interwar Poland," in *Gender, Place, and Memory in the Modern Jewish Experience*; Sean Martin, "Jewish Youth between Tradition and Assimilation: Exploring Polish Jewish Identity in Interwar Kraków," *The Polish Review* 46:4 (2001): 461–77. For a comprehensive review, see Glynn Dynner, "Replenishing the 'Fountain of Judaism': Traditionalist Jewish Education in Interwar Poland," *Jewish History* 31, no. 3–4 (2018): 229–61.

6. See Natanel Lederberg, "Bein emet Kotska'it leharmonia ahdutit: gishato hahinukhit shel ha-Imrei emet migur," *Akdamot* 23 (2009): 181–97.

7. On the historical role of sermons as a vehicle for disseminating ideology, see Marc Saperstein, *Jewish Preaching, 1200–1800: An Anthology* (New Haven: Yale University Press, 1989), 44–63; in Hasidic tradition in particular, see Mendel Piekarz, *The Beginning of Hasidism* [in Hebrew], 124, 163–70; Zeev Gries, "The Hasidic Managing Editor as an Agent of Culture," in *Hasidism Reappraised*, ed. Ada Rapoport-Albert (London, 1996), 141–55.

8. *Melekh* [king] is surely linked by association to R. Shapira's own Hasidic lineage—most immediately, to his father Elimelekh (whose name literally means "God is King" and who died during his son's youth); *melekh* also suggests the profound spiritual connection he felt to his forbear R. Elimelekh (known as "Rebbe Melekh") of Lizhensk.

9. Other prominent figures of the time had similar projects, such as Aaron Friedman (Ish Shalom), *Hokhmat ha-nefesh* (1909); Fischel Schneerson: see David Freis, "Journey to the Centre of the Soul: Fischl Schneersohn's Psycho-Expeditions between Modern Psychology and Jewish Mysticism" (paper presented at the 17th World Congress of Jewish Studies, Hebrew University of Jerusalem, August 8, 2017); and Hillel Zeitlin: see Green and Mayse, *A New Hasidism*, 1–50. Reiser has discussed theurgic aspects of "empowerment" (following scholar Jess Hollenback) in R. Shapira's notion of the mystic-prophet: "He is a mystic because his very essence is defined by a mystical attachment with the Divine; and empowered, since this personal, even individual, connection to God has a direct influence on society." Daniel Reiser, " 'To Rend the Entire Veil': Prophecy in the Teachings of Rabbi Kalonymus Kalman Shapira of Piazecna and its Renewal in the Twentieth Century," *Modern Judaism* 34 (2014): 338–39. I use the term *empowerment* here in its more down-to-earth psychological sense.

10. The concepts of the self, self-annihilation (*bittul*), and self-actualization and their relation to *devekut* have a complex legacy in Hasidic thought from its early days and are pronouncedly present in Polish Hasidism. As David Maayan notes, Shapira related to the traditional Hasidic notion of self-negation with some ambivalence; throughout his works, he developed an innovative view of the self in relation to the Divine. See Maayan, "The Call of the Self: Devotional Individuation in the Teachings of Rabbi Kalonymus Kalman Shapira of Piasec-

zno" (master's thesis, Hebrew College, 2017). For a contrasting approach to the place of *bittul* in R. Shapira's thought, see James Jacobson-Maisels, "The Self and Self-Transformation in the Thought and Practice of Rabbi Kalonymus Kalmish Shapira" (PhD diss., University of Chicago, 2014), 558–82.

11. *Derekh ha-melekh, parashat vayyetse* 5690 (1929), 29–33; ibid., *parashat vayyetse* 5691 (1930), 34–38. Cf. *Tsav ve-zeruz,* no. 45, 51: "As the Baal Shem Tov taught: 'I [*anokhi*] was standing between God and you' (Deut 5:5)—the egotistical self-interest [*anokhiyut*] that people have, concerned solely with their own needs—that is what stands between God and them. . . . But to overcome this self-absorption—the only way possible is through love of others; a person can't achieve it alone."

12. B. Shabbat 105a. The Rabbis decipher the word *anokhi* as an acronym that reads *ana nafshi katavit yehavet.* Translated more literally, the phrase could mean: "I myself write and give [the Torah]." An important pretext for this sermon (which R. Shapira cites, p. 29) is R. Elimelekh of Lizhensk, *No'am Elimelekh, likkutei shoshanah,* 105a.

13. *Derekh ha-melekh, parashat vayyetse* 5690 (1929), 33.

14. I draw here on Charles Taylor, *The Ethics of Authenticity* (Cambridge: Harvard University Press, 1991). Elsewhere in this sermon, R. Shapira cites Job 6:25, in which Job's friends are denigrated for their hollow presence and the cold, abstract comfort they proffered while withholding their emotions and inner "selves."

15. The image of the *golem* originates in the midrashic imagination: R. Shapira opens his sermon with a passage from Genesis Rabbah 24.2 on the verse "Your eyes saw my unshaped form (*golmi*)" (Ps 139:16). The Latin word *dormita* first appears in the *Zohar* (3.142b) referring to this primordial moment of engenderment. Adam, in the biblical narrative on which the midrash is based (Gen 2:21), is cast into slumber (*tardemah/dormita*), and a rib is removed and formed into his female "other side." The "mystery of *dormita*" develops further in Lurianic teaching. The concept of the *golem* (as hylic matter and as locus of transformation), however, stems from earlier kabbalistic sources; it is linked with the theosophical world of the *sefirot* through a radical rereading of Job 28:12: "Wisdom is formed in nothingness (*veha-hokhmah me-ayin timatseh*)." A more immediate source of influence here, though, linking the notion of *ayin* to the sefirah of *hokhmah*—perceived as the locus of contemplative mediation as well as inner transformation—is clearly the Maggid of Mezritsh. See Ariel Evan Mayse, *Speaking Infinities: God and Language in the Teachings of Rabbi Dov Ber of Mezritsh* (Philadelphia: University of Pennsylvania Press, 2020), 4–5, 62, 116–17, 272 n. 65. Finally, the ironic nuance of the Yiddish *golem*—a fool or klutz—was surely not lost on R. Shapira's audience.

16. A play on the root *h.l.f.,* meaning to change, transmute, reverse; or exchange; *Derekh ha-melekh, parashat vayyetse* 5690 (1929), 34. This reading of

m. Avot 5:9 is cited in many early Hasidic works, more often in the name of the Baal Shem Tov. C.f. Yitzhak Aizik Yehudah Yehiel Safrin, *Otsar ha-hayyim, kedoshim*, fol. 158a; *Notsar hesed*, m. Avot 5.7.

17. *Derekh ha-melekh, parashat vayyetse* 5690 (1929), 35. Compare *Tsav ve-zeruz*, 45 (see n12 above), where he stresses the need to combat selfishness and egotism by enhancing interpersonal relationships and building a united spiritual community.

18. *Derekh ha-melekh, parashat vayyetse* 5690 (1929), 35. Significantly, R. Shapira notes: "Only a *hasid* is able to leap out of his skin, to throw off all his worries along with his deficiencies and stand apart from them. . . . This is the spirit of a *hasid*—in a moment, he can free himself of his own ego (*ha-anokhi shelo*), of his very self." *Derekh ha-melekh, parashat yayyiggash* 5690 (1929), 71. For an earlier Hasidic reconception of the "Lurianic myth of restorative descent," as Zvi Mark puts it, see his " 'Katnut' [Smallness] and 'Gadlut' [Greatness] in the Teachings of Nahman of Bratslav and their Roots in the Lurianic Kabbalah" [in Hebrew], *Daat: Journal of Jewish Philosophy & Kabbalah* 46 (2001): 45–80.

19. Sifra, *vayyikra* 1.9; Bemidbar Rabbah 14:20.

20. *Derekh ha-melekh, parashat vayyetse* 5691 (1930), 38.

21. It was Maimonides who first drew the link between the individual called *hasid* and the mode of being "beyond the margins" or, on a more literal translation, being before or beyond the letter of the law (*lifnim mishurat ha-din*); see his Commentary on the Mishnah, Avot 6:1. R. Shapira cites this teaching in the name of the Baal Shem Tov often in his writings.

22. *Derekh ha-melekh, parashat vayyehi* 5690 (1929), 80–81.

23. *Derekh ha-melekh, motsa'ei yom ha-kippurim* 5686 (1925), 266. He cites *Tikkunei zohar, tikkun* 1, fol. 18a). See also *Zohar* 2:114a; 1:244b; other notable pretexts are Bemidbar Rabbah 5:6 (on Isa 48.9); b. Ta'anit 4b. R. Shapira revisits the motif of the seal in his *Sermons from the Years of Rage, shabbat hol ha-mo'ed pesah* 5700 (1940), 124.

24. *Derekh ha-melekh, motsaei yom ha-kippurim* 5686 (1925), 266. R. Shapira's formulation of this tenet, which I have translated nonliterally, is "the form of the Maker is in the made, the form of the Sealer is in that which is sealed" (*tsurat ha-po'el be-nif'al, ve-tsurat ha-hotem be-nehtam*. Early Hasidic works, drawing on kabbalistic sources, cite a slightly different key phrase. Its first half, "the power of the Maker is in the made"—*koah ha-po'el be-nif'al*—appears frequently in sermons of the Maggid of Mezritsh. On the image of the seal in earlier kabbalistic sources, see Michal Oron, "Set Me as a Seal upon Your Heart: The Poetics of the Zohar in *Sabba de-Mishpatim*" [in Hebrew], in *Masu'ot: Studies in the Literature of Kabbalah and Jewish Thought dedicated to the Memory of Prof. Efrayim Gottlieb*, ed. M. Oron and A. Goldreich (Jerusalem: Mossad Bialik, 1994), 1–24.

25. *Derekh ha-melekh, motsa'ei yom ha-kippurim* 5686 (1925), 267. R. Shapira alludes here to halakhic disputes concerning the optimal method of identifying lost objects and beloved ones—whether by external marks (*simanim*) or by a subtler

means of recognition based on a general impression of their form, called *tevi'ut ayin*. See b. Gittin 27b; b. Bava Metsia 23b; b. Hulin 96a. He rather consistently uses the term *nefesh* to refer to what we would call "consciousness." Thus, he speaks of an impression that "permeates our consciousness" (*over el nafshenu*). To illustrate the idea of parts forming a whole, he develops the kabbalistic notion of language: the metaphysical nature of letters, devoid of semantic content, that combine to form units of meaning. A possible influence here is R. Shneur Zalman of Liady's *Likkutei amarim–Tanya, sha'ar ha-yihud ve-ha-emunah*, ch. 1.

26. Cf., *Zohar* 3. 225a; the concept is developed in Lurianic teaching and further in Chabad Hasidim; for sources, see Roman Foxbrunner, *Habad: The Hasidism of Shneur Zalman of Lyady* (Tuscaloosa: University of Alabama Press, 1992), 292.

27. *Mi she-megaleh et nafsho*; translated literally, "one who reveals, or uncovers, or bares one's soul"; a second connotation of *megaleh* is "discover." Reiser remarks that the unusual terms *giluy hanefesh* or *nefesh geluyiah*, which figure prominently in R. Shapira's works, appear to be his invention. He cites the Lurianic work *Shaarei kedushah* as a possible source of inspiration: Reiser, *Vision as a Mirror: Imagery Techniques in Twentieth Century Jewish Mysticism* [in Hebrew] (Los Angeles: Cherub-Press, 2014), 194–98.

28. *Derekh ha-melekh, motsa'ei yom ha-kippurim* 5686 (1925), 268. The cypher at work here, of course, is the notion of *hester panim*—the hiddenness of the divine countenance. The notion of the form *tsurah* reappears in *Sermons from the Years of Rage, shevi'i shel pesah* 5701 (1941), 191.

29. *Derekh ha-melekh, motsa'ei yom ha-kippurim* 5686 (1925), 268–69.

30. "The forefathers, who engendered Your will (*she-as'u retsonekhah*)" is a creative reinterpretation of the phrase from the liturgy; its straightforward sense is that the forefathers fulfilled or carried out God's will.

31. *Derekh ha-melekh, motsa'ei yom ha-kippurim* 5686 (1925), 269. Compare his reflections on *or makkif—or penimi* in *Benei mahshavah tovah*, 32. In other sermons, R. Shapira explores the related motif of the trace or *reshimu/roshem*. See *Derekh ha-melekh, shavu'ot* 5689 (1929), 391–96. On *hotam* and *reshimu/roshem* in kabbalistic and early Hasidic sources, see Esther Liebes, "Reshimu (Imprint), Hylic Matter and Kadmut HaSekhel" [in Hebrew], in *The Latest Phase: Essays on Hasidism by Gershom Scholem*, ed. David Assaf and Esther Liebes (Jerusalem, 2008), 277–79. A probable source of influence is Schneur Zalman of Liadi's reading of the verse "Set me as a seal upon your heart" (Song 8:6); See *Likkutei Torah* 45a; 45d. For later developments in Chabad thought, see Elliot Wolfson, "Nekuddat ha-Reshimu—The Trace of Transcendence and the Transcendence of the Trace: The Paradox of Ṣimṣum in the RaShaB's Hemshekh Ayin-Beit," *Kabbalah* 30 (2013): 75–112.

32. This idea is based on a midrashic trope: "the image of Jacob is engraved in the Holy Throne." See b. Hullin 91b; see also *Zohar* 1:301 and *Zohar* 2:114a; Shneur Zalman of Liady, *Likkutei torah, shir ha-shirim*, and parallels.

33. David Biale et al., *Hasidism: A New History* (Princeton: Princeton University Press, 2018), 564. As Buber put it, "Hasidic teaching is the proclamation of rebirth. No renewal of Judaism is possible that does not bear in itself the elements of Hasidism." Martin Buber, *The Legend of the Baal-Shem* (1955), xii–xiii. Ariel Evan Mayse and Arthur Green chart the history of this rebirth in their two-volume *A New Hasidism*.

34. Alan Brill, "Aggadic Man: The Poetry and Rabbinic Thought of Abraham Joshua Heschel," *Meorot* 6, no. 1 (2006). On Heschel's overarching project, see Arthur Green, "Abraham Joshua Heschel: Recasting Hasidism for Moderns," *Modern Judaism* 29, no. 1 (2015): 62–79.

35. *Derekh ha-melekh, motsaei yom ha-kippurim* 5686 (1925), 268. R. Shapira's interwar theory of prophecy has also been compared with Heschel's. See Seeman, "Ritual Efficacy, Hasidic Mysticism and 'Useless Suffering,'" 475–77.

36. R. Shapira's paternal lineage stemmed from R. Elimelekh of Lizhensk, the Maggid of Kozniece (Kozhenits); and R. Hayim Meir Yehiel Shapira, the "Seraph of Mogielnica"; ancestors on his mother's side include R. Jacob Isaac, the Seer of Lublin; and R. Kalonymus Kalman Halevi of Kraków, author of *Maor va-shemesh*, his maternal grandfather, after whom he was named. His father was R. Elimelekh of Grodzisk Mazowiecki, an important Hasidic leader in nineteenth-century Poland.

37. The teaching he cites in the name of R. Israel of Ruzhin (on m. Avot 3:12) is based on the same analogy of container and contents. See *Irin kaddishin* (Warsaw: 1885), 48b; *Irin kaddishin Tinyana, pesah*, 15b–16a.

38. *Derekh ha-melekh, parashat yitro*, 5690 (1930), 104. R. Shapira often uses the word *atsmut* in the sense of "essence." The double reading that I suggest, although linguistically unorthodox, is supported by many other instances in his writings.

39. Ibid., 106. He attributes the concept of *ibbur ha-tsaddikim*—literally, "impregnation"—to Joseph Sarug, an early disciple of Rabbi Isaac Luria. An editorial note on this sermon in the Feldheim edition (Jerusalem: Feldheim, 2011), 153, refers to *Emek ha-melekh, shaar* 16:45, by Naftali Hertz Bachrach, a student of Joseph Sarug. An indirect source may have been writings from the Chabad school. See Nahum Grinwald, "Al kabbalat Mahari Sarug be-torat he-hasidut: "Reshimu," Malbush, vehatsimtsum she-lifne ha-tsimtsum ha-rishon be-hasidut Habad," *Heikhal ha-Besht* (2011–14).

40. B. Rosh Hashanah 16b.

41. *Derekh ha-melekh, shabbat teshuvah*, 5690 (1929), 255–56.

42. See also *Derekh ha-melekh, parashat shelah* (undated), 163–64.

43. R. Shapira's many references to teachings from his father's published sermons testify to the vital role of books in his personal formation. R. Elimelekh of Grodzisk, author of *Imrei elimelekh* (Warsaw, 1876) and *Divrei elimelekh* (Warsaw, 1890-1), died when the rebbe was nearly three years old. Notably, however, he sometimes argues the opposite: "The essence of Hasidism cannot be

engraved in a book, but only in the Hasidim themselves . . . *they* are the 'book of Hasidism,' their journeys and their deeds, their selves and their feelings . . .' *Mevo hashe'arim*, 39–40.

44. Ego-documents, in the widest sense, are sources that provide or reveal privileged information about the "self" who produced them. Writings of this nature include diaries, memoirs, letters, and ethical wills, in which the writer is continuously present, implicitly or explicitly, as a first-person "I." In *Hasidic Commentary on the Torah* (Oxford: Littman Library of Jewish Civization, 2018), 191, I consider other aspects of this sermon; on the nature of Hasidic homiletics and written texts, see my discussion in *Hasidic Commentary*, 16–22. Ariel Evan Mayse and Daniel Reiser analyze the nexus between orality, language, and print culture in Hasidism in their "Territories and Textures: The Hasidic Sermon as the Crossroads of Language and Culture," *Jewish Social Studies: History, Culture, Society* 24, no. 1 (2018): 127–60.

45. *Derekh ha-melekh, parashat shemot* 5689 (1929), 89–91. The motif of author/tsaddik connecting heaven and earth reappears in other works; c.f., *Mevo ha-she'arim* 3a–b; 4a–5a; 29b, etc. See David Maayan's insightful discussion of this sermon in *Call of the Self*, 57–64.

46. For other instances and their role in furthering R. Shapira's attempts during the 1920s and 1930s to reanimate Hasidism and restore its power as a living tradition, see Wiskind-Elper, *Hasidic Commentary on the Torah*, 174–77.

47. *Sermons from the Years of Rage*, unnumbered page; MSS, ŻIH, Ring. II/370. Reiser (ibid., 80) posits that R. Shapira's writings, along with his last testament, were entrusted to the "Oneg Shabbat" Archives in January-February 1943.

Part II

Text, Theodicy, and Suffering

7

A New Reading of the Rebbe of Piaseczno's Holocaust-Era Sermons

A Review of Daniel Reiser's Critical Edition

MORIA HERMAN

There are no words with which we can lament our woes. There is no one to chastise, no heart to awaken to the [divine] service and Torah. How many attempts does it take for a prayer to arise, and how much Sabbath observance exists even in one who truly wishes to observe it? A fortiori, there is neither spirit nor heart to weep for the future and the building of the ruins at such time as God in his mercy will deliver us. There is only God, may he pity us and deliver us in the blink of the eye, and may he build the ruins. Only through full redemption and resurrection of the dead can the Blessed One build and heal. Please, God, have mercy and do not be late in delivering us.

—From a note by the Rebbe of Piaseczno on his sermon for portion *ekev* in 1941

The Holocaust-era sermons of Rabbi Kalonymus Kalmish (Kalman) Shapira, the Rebbe of Piaseczno, are central to the study of Jewish thought in the Holocaust context. Unlike other thinkers who interpreted and coped with the Holocaust primarily in retrospect, the Rebbe reflected on and wrote about the cataclysm as it was transpiring. His sermons, delivered in the Warsaw Ghetto between 1939 and 1942, are a fascinating and unique historical and human document.

A community leader even before the Holocaust, R. Shapira made it his goal to use Ghetto sermons to bolster the morale of his flock and of others who might heed his teachings. On the nights following Sabbaths and festivals, he set down his sermons in writing. In early 1943, these texts, together with other documents, were placed in milk containers and buried in the Ghetto. In 1950, construction workers digging in the former Warsaw Ghetto area found the containers, which were then taken to the Jewish Historical Institute in Warsaw. The sermons were first published in Jerusalem by several of the Rebbe's followers who had immigrated to Israel—Rabbi Eliahu Hammer and his son, Abraham; Rabbi Elimelech Ben Porat; and Rabbi Elazar Bein—under the supervision of R. Shapira's nephew, Rabbi Elimelech Shapira in 1960. The editors titled the work *Esh kodesh*.[1]

Dozens of studies have been written about R. Shapira's Holocaust-era sermons.[2] All are based on this 1960 edition, despite its many flaws. R. Shapira's handwriting, difficult to decipher, caused many words to be mislabeled. The editors also sometimes revised the internal organization of the sermons, deleted words, and reordered a few sentences.

The two-volume *Derashot mi-shenot ha-za'am* (*Sermons from the Years of Rage*), edited by Daniel Reiser, rectifies these defects. Reiser's title preserves the expression that R. Shapira used to describe the sermons in a letter that he attached to his writings: "Torah innovations *mi-shenot ha-za'am* (from the years of rage)."[3]

In Volume One, Reiser deciphers the manuscript of the sermons anew by using high-quality scans and enlarging the text by hundreds of percent. The result is an accurate scholarly edition that includes the expansion of abbreviations and abridged words and the addition of numerous notes that track down R. Shapira's sources in Jewish literature, Bible, midrash, Hasidism, and the Kabbalah, along with explanations of and elaboration on kabbalistic concepts. At the end of Volume One is an index of sources, names, and topics that may be useful to anyone interested in what the Rebbe of Piaseczno had to say.

Apart from the painstaking deciphering and the notes in the new edition, Reiser's work is immensely important in an additional respect: R. Shapira's writings are hybrid texts, composed of many glosses and corrections, which Reiser successfully brings to light. Not only did R. Shapira produce his sermons in the midst of the Holocaust while coping with the many vicissitudes of Ghetto life, but he also continually proofed and corrected several other manuscripts that he had written before the war. Apart from the sermons that he delivered in the Ghetto, he revised his other as-yet-unpublished writings during this time, including *Hakhsharat ha-avreikhim* and *Mevo ha-she'arim*.[4]

R. Shapira sometimes erased entire sermons and augmented, amended, and proofed others, transforming them over time. Hardly a page in the manuscript version of the sermons is free of deletions and comments. Even the last sermons, delivered in the summer of 1942, shortly before the onset of transports from the Ghetto to the extermination camps, contain notes and deletions. Various kinds of proofing marks appear in the manuscript—deletions in the text proper with words added over them; arrows pointing to added text in the margins; and letters with lines drawn to added text above and below, with the addition marked with the same letter in boldface.

Some of the extra material was edited as well, evidently indicating that R. Shapira reviewed the sermons several times and amended them repeatedly.

These glosses were embedded without comment in the text of the 1960 edition. Those who study the accepted version therefore have no way of knowing that it is composed of different layers of corrections by the author. The 1960 edition rarely makes note of this. Furthermore, it includes paragraphs and entire sermons that R. Shapira had deleted (by crossing them out) from his handwritten manuscript.

In order to allow readers to appreciate R. Shapira's revisions, Reiser created a facsimile edition in Volume Two: a scanned image of the Rebbe's manuscript and, on the facing page, a deciphering of the handwriting that identifies the stages in which the sermons were written. The various proofing phases are highlighted in different colors, allowing researchers to track easily the various deletions and additions that followed.

Apart from the scholarly edition and the facsimile of the manuscript, Reiser begins Volume One with a far-reaching introduction that adds an important contribution to the research on R. Shapira. It begins with a series of milestones in the Rebbe's life. This is a serious and probing piece of research based on contemporary letters and newspapers, including many sources relating to the life of R. Shapira and his family, his medical training, his connections with the land of Israel, and his personality. The

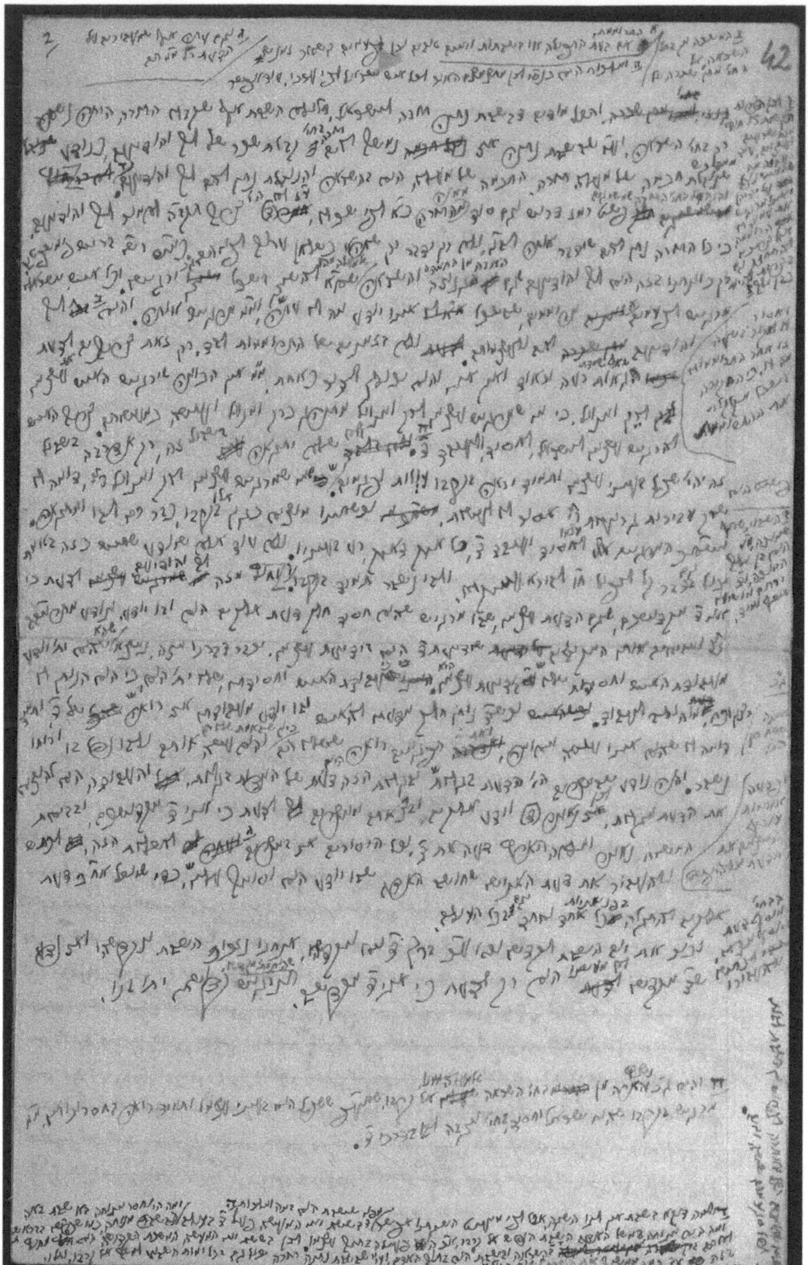

Figure 7.1. Sermon for Parashat Yitro, February 1942. Manuscript no. ARG II 15 (Ring. II/370). Courtesy of ŻIH (Żydowski Instytut Historyczny).

גנוך, בחי' וּמֵהוּ מַתַּן שְׂכָרָהּ, והכל מודים בשבת דבשבת ניתנה תורה לישראל, דלולא השבת אף שקבלו התורה היתה נשארה

רק בחי' השראה, וע"י שבשבת ניתנה תורה אז נוֹבַל חָכְמָה נמשך להם גָּ תורה בחי' קבלת שכר של לך והודיעם כנודע שֶׁנּוֹבַל

ממדרש שנובלת חכמה של מעלה תורה. החכמה של מעלה היא בהשראה והנובלת נתן להם לך והודיעם. ומפני שבתא הוא בינה ומלכות בּ ומלכות היא כנס"י ולמה

דוקא בשבת אין לנו השג, אבל לפי מיעוט השגתנו אפשר לכן מצטמצם האור לכל איש ישראל לפי ערכו, עוד אפשר דבשבת ימי המעשה פעל ד' בעולם (ובשבת)

ומה הי' חסר מנוחה באה שבת באה מנוחה, כמו שפרש"י בבראשית. ומה היא מנוחה, במשל האדם השבת

הנפש אל קרבו, א"כ היא פעולה בתוך עצמו. לכן בששת ימי המעשה המשכת הקדושה היא חוּץ מחוץ לאדם

בֵּין מִלְּמַעְלָה בֵּין מִלְּמַטָּה, לְמַעְלָה בהשראה ובשבת הוא בתוך האדם, וע"י שבשבת נתנה תורה יכול גם בכל

ימות השבוע למשיך אל קרבו, ותלוי בזה כָּמָּה עד כמה ממשיך את השבת לימות החול ּ וכמו שאומרים הצל

מאחרה לפרוש מן השבת לבלתי תהי' סגור מהם ששה ששה ימים. לֹא רָק חוּץ

מַה שֶּׁמַשִּׂיגִים חֵלֶק והנה על בחי' התורה שמשיגים פשט רמז דרוש וגם סוד (מהתורה) ממנו כ"א לפי שכלו, אמר (ד')

ע"ז לא ה' צריך הקב"ה לאמור לך והודיעם,

כי כל התורה נתן להם שידבר אותה לבני, ולא רק ידבר רק שתהא ערוך כשלחן כמ"ש רש"י בריש פ' משפטים.

רק כוונתנו בזה היא לך והודיעם מַן הארה מן החמדה הגנוזה והשראה שלמעלה מהם שא"א להשיג בשכל ישׁייִגּ גָ"כ

ירגישו. וכל איש ישראלי

מרגיש לפעמים וָמְנַּם בִּ התרוממות, אם בעת התפילה או בשבתות וימים טובים וכן לפעמים בשאר זמנים, מרוממים,

שבשכל אא"ל אינו יודע מה לו עתה ּ ואסור לו לחקור בשעה זו אחר התרוממותו מה לו, כי החקירה בשכל

מקלקלת את ההתרוממות, ומ"מ מרגיש אותה. והיא בַּתֵי' בּ המשכה מן בחי' השראה, אל בחי' מתן שכרה של לך

והודיעם מַתַּן שְׂכָרָהּ להם ולעצמות. לֹדַעַת ולא בזמנים של התרוממות לבד, רק זאת צריכים לדעת

שֶׁאַף שָׂמַדְתָּ הגאות רעה מאוד ואין אני והוא יכולין לדור כאחת, מ"מ אין הכוונה שירגיש האיש את עצמו

לְדַק לָרַק ומנוול, כי מי שמרגיש עצמו לרק ומנוול מתנהג כרך ומנוול ועושה כמעשיהם. צריך האיש

להרגיש עצמו מישראל, לחסיד, ולעובד ד'. וְהִיא ג"כ נִיצוֹ והארה מן ההַהִרוֹּם בחי' השראה שֶׁעָלָיו שלמעלה ממנו,

אל קרבו, שא"ע שׁשפל הוא בעיני עצמו ותמיד רואה בחסרונותיו, מ"מ מרגיש בקרבו שהוא ישראל וחסיד,

בחי' ויגבה לבו בדרכי ד'. וְלֹא בִּלְבַד וְלֹא רק שלא יתגאה עֵצֵּ בְּשֵׁכִל זה, רק אדרבה בשביל

זה יהי' שפל בעיני עצמו ותמיד יראה בקרבו עולות ופגמים. כַּ פְּשׁוּט הוא שמי שמרגיש עצמו לריק ומנוול ר"ל, דומה לו

שרק עבירות גרועות ר"ל אסור לו לעשות, מִשֶּׁאֵ"כ מִי וכשאינו מוציא כגן אֵלּוֹ בקרבו, כבר רם לבו ומתגאה.

מִשֶּׁא"כ המרגיש אצ"ע עצמו לחסיד ועובד ד', כל אבק דאבק רע בעיניו. ולא עוד אלא שידוע שאינו יכול בזה באמת

יכול גָּ בדבר קל ליפול ח"ו לבירא עמיקתא, ולבו נשבר תמיד בקרבו. לֹכֵן הצרות הקשות ר"ל חוץ מזה שרעים

לעצמם, עוד רע בזה מה שהאיש נופל בָּזֶה על ידיהן ואינו מרגיש את עמידתו הַגֵּ הרוממה, אבל צריכים

להתחזק גם בצרות להיות כבן מלך בַּ הַשְּׁבוּי, שאף שבוי שמוכה, מ"מ הוא בן מלך המוכה, ור' ירחם ויושיענו תיכף

ומיד Z. וְחוּץ מזה מִי שֶׁמַּרְגִּישׁ עַצְמוּ לך והודיעם לדעת כי

אני ד' מקרישכם, שגם הדעת עצמו, שבו מרגיש שהוא חסיד דעת אלקים הוא ובו יודע, ונודע מהרמב"ם

ז"ל ומביאים אותו המקובלים עַל יְדִיעָה גָּ' היא שבו יודע שידיעתו של עצמו, וכבר דברנו מזה, נמצא שְׁהָא שהוא ית' יודע

מעבודת האיש וחסידות שלו עַצְ גָ"כ בידיעתו עצמו הִיא. היינו כָּ כָּ בעבודת האיש וחסידותו, שלו ית' הוא, כי הוא הנותן לו

רצון וכח, הֵעַה גּוּמֵּ גְּמָה ולב לעבוד. וּכְשֶׁהָאִישׁ וכשד' נותן חלק מקדנתו להאיש ובו יודע מעבודתו אז רואה שַׁהַבֹּל ּ שאינה

שלו רק ד', ותמיד שלו רק ד', ותמיד

דומה לו שהוא אינו עושה מאומה, וְאַדְרַבָּה הפגמים רואה ששלו הם כיון שבאמת שלו הם הוא עשה אותם ולבו נופל בו ורוחו

נשבר. והנה נודע שבמצרים הי' הדעת בגלות ּ ופרעה אותיות עורף הצמצם את הדעת מלהתפשט ובגלות הזה היום,

דעת של המדות בגלות, אבל ּ והעבודה היא להוציא

את הדעת מגלות, אַ לֵן נאמר (ד') וידע אלקים, ובצאתם ממצרים לָך לדעת כי אני ד' מקדישכם, ובביאת

המשיח נאמר ומלאה הארץ דעה את ד', וכל היסודים אז במצרים וְעַתָּה לֹא גָּ וגם עתה אף שמעבירים על הדעת

ר"ל מ"מ הם לתכלית הזה, הֵם לכתש

ולהעביר את דעת האנושי שחושב האדם שבו יודע הוא וסומך עליו, לְ בבחי' ויוסיף דעת יוסיף מכאב, כָּדֵי

לכתש ולהעבירו, כדי שיוכל אח"כ דעת

אלקים להתגלות בפנימיות בְּכָל אחד ואחד וְגַם וְבָכֹל העולם.

זכור את יום השבת לקדשו וכו' ע"כ ברך ד' וכו' ויקדשהו, אנחנו נזכור השבת ונקדשהו ואז נדע

שד' מקדשנו לֹדַעַת הוא, רק לדעת כי אני ד' מקדישם, שהוא ית' מַקְדִּשׁ מקדשנו, ונרגיש קדושתו ית' בנו.

Figure 7.2. Reiser's decipherment for Parashat Yitro, February 1942. Reiser edition
volume 2, 99. Courtesy of Yad Vashem.

systematic biographic presentation that Reiser's effort yields elucidates details that previously had remained vague. For example, Reiser refutes the widely held claim among researchers that pharmacies in Warsaw accepted R. Shapira's autodidactic medical expertise and honored his prescriptions.[5]

Furthermore, in the introduction, Reiser describes the writings of R. Shapira and the process that led to their discovery and publication. His entire oeuvre is reviewed at length in terms of order of publication, different versions and copies, when written, when published, and how published. However, in this reckoning Reiser makes no reference, even briefly, to the contents of R. Shapira's prewar books, and this omission is a drawback.

The introduction also contains much about the burial and discovery of R. Shapira's manuscripts. Until now the research has been vague about the matter and has not examined it thoroughly. Some scholars state without any foundation that R. Shapira interred his writings personally.[6] Reiser rules this out, noting that the milk containers that held the Rebbe's writings were also found to harbor many additional documents belonging to the Oneg Shabbat Archives, which had functioned in the Warsaw Ghetto and had documented events during the Holocaust. Accordingly, Reiser contends that members of the archive project (rather than R. Shapira himself) buried the rabbi's manuscripts along with their own documents. The question, then, is how R. Shapira's manuscripts came into the possession of the Oneg Shabbat people in the first place. Some postulate that they had been handed over by Szymon Huberband, the Rebbe's cousin and a member of the Oneg Shabbat leadership.[7] Reiser disproves this conjecture, showing that Huberband had been murdered in August 1942, whereas R. Shapira's writings include paragraphs of later provenance. He suggests that it was another member of the Oneg Shabbat administration, Menachem Mendel Kohn, who had been in touch with the Rebbe and who had handed over the writings. He stresses, however, that this is merely speculation.[8]

Reiser convincing argument that that R. Shapira did not inter the manuscripts himself but somehow handed them over to the "Oneg Shabbat" people sheds light on his conscious intent to preserve his writings. It also attests to his historical consciousness and conviction that his sermons were important and meaningful not only to his congregation and his contemporaries but also to posterity. The fact that R. Shapira continued to edit and proof his writings during the Holocaust, even when it became unclear whether he and those around him would survive, lends support to this proposition. He appears to have considered his writing a sort of mission, as attested in a letter that he attached to his manuscripts:

> Please try to publish [these manuscripts], either together or separately, as in your beneficence you see fit. Please also try to disperse them among the Jews. And please print on every volume that I wish and beg every Jew to study my writings. Surely, the merit of my holy forebears will be at his [the person responsible for publication of the manuscripts] side and that of his entire family in this world and in the afterworld. May God pity us.[9]

The fact that R. Shapira delivered sermons, put them in writing, and even bothered to correct and proof them repeatedly amid the spiraling horror, and at a time when he was in no way confident that anyone would ever read the works, evokes amazement. R. Shapira himself writes about a coping process of this kind in his sermon for the portion *ha-hodesh* in 1942:

> Sometimes the man himself wonders about himself: Haven't I been broken? Do I not spend nearly all my time weeping and sometimes sobbing as well? How can I learn Torah and from where do I get the strength to produce Torah and Hasidic innovations? Sometimes he wonders if it is mere courage that I can strengthen myself and study [Torah] amid the so-numerous woes, my own and those of Israel. Again and again [he tells] himself: Am I not broken? How many are my sobs? My whole life is despondency and darkness. He is perplexed, this man, about himself.[10]

Although the passage is mostly written in the third person, its contents indicate that the Rebbe enunciated them from his own experience. The difficulty that he faced in continuing to engage in writing and studying Torah while surrounded by ongoing horror only sharpens the question of the meaning of this composition and its role in coping with suffering and catastrophe.

Taking up this topic at the end of the introduction, Reiser expounds on the meaning of writing in the shadow of death and presents several psychological models that may explain the phenomenon. One of them describes creative endeavor in the shadow of death as a form of denial or escape that allows the writer to disregard or distract himself from the encroaching death. Another model portrays creative work as the triumph of the spirit over death or, as Reiser writes, "the fulfillment of liberty in a world devoid of liberty."[11] According to a third model, writers produce texts for the sake of eternal life, because they have despaired of a reality that has become meaningless to them. Reiser does not decide which of these models, if any, fits R. Shapira's corpus. Reiser contends that R. Shapira's literary and oral teaching despite the cataclysm around him lends these sermons a universal significance in addition to their religious and philosophical meaning.[12]

Many studies have been written about R. Shapira's response to suffering. Some writers argue that his outlook evolved during the course of his torments.[13] These studies are all based on the 1960 edition, however, so that authors could not know about R. Shapira's own constant glosses and revisions. Reiser demonstrates the significance of this lacuna in several instances

In his sermon for portion *ki tavo* in 1940, R. Shapira expressed his expectation of supernatural intervention, such as miraculous deliverance. He sketched a small arrow over these words and wrote an addendum in the margins: "Even if a great supernatural deliverance comes afterward, do the Jews have the strength to endure such woes?"[14] This note attests that no matter what hope he may have held out for miraculous deliverance, R. Shapira was uncertain that the Jews could endure their afflictions. In the 1960 edition, this addendum appears in the sermon text proper, with no indication that it was added after the basic composition of the sermon.[15]

Another example appears in the sermon for portion *hukkat* in 1942, one of R. Shapira's last, delivered several weeks before the beginning of transports from the Ghetto to the extermination camps. In this address, he writes about the cruelty shown toward children:

> The cruelties of the haters of Israel always particularly targets Jewish children, either to kill them, Heaven forbid, or to force them into heresy, as is known from decrees imposed centuries ago, Heaven forbid.

A letter marked next to this sentence refers to a gloss in the margin:

As we see now, too, lamentably, the cruelties and murders against young children surpass all the cruelties and ghastly murders visited upon us, the House of Israel. Oh, what has befallen us?[16]

Once again, this addendum appears in the text of the 1960 edition proper, and is not marked in any way.[17] Reiser conjectures, on reasonable grounds, that the addendum is evidence of the immense suffering inflicted on children at the time of the transports from the Ghetto.[18] These examples of revisions that R. Shapira made in his writings—meaningful changes in reference to the topic of suffering—appear throughout the manuscript and should propel new research on this theme.

Reiser himself finds it hard to detect that R. Shapira had a well-formed and systematic outlook on coping with suffering and considers it difficult to speak of evolution in his views. One might, he suggests, find allegedly early views on coping with torment that recur later and allusions to an allegedly later outlook in early sermons. "After reviewing all the sermons," Reiser concludes,

I think it correct to say that the Rebbe does not have a clear and definitive statement to make, either about the essence of the afflictions or even about the purpose of the sermons. The sermons reflect a process and one who tracks them also tracks, as far as possible, the personal process that the Rebbe underwent.[19]

As for the purpose of the sermons, quotations presented by Reiser show that they were initially meant to encourage and comfort R. Shapira's listeners. Two years into the Holocaust, however, he admits that he no longer finds his own soothing remarks and sermons to be convincing:

Particularly as the woes continue, even one who has strengthened himself and the rest of the Jews from the very start tires of strengthening and laboring to comfort himself. Even if he is willing to strain and offer whatever comforting and strengthening words he may, he cannot find the words because during the lengthy days of woes he has already said and repeated everything he can say. The words have grown old and can have no further effect on him or his listeners.[20]

Again, despite being written in the third person, these remarks imply that R. Shapira is expressing his own experience. The change in his attitude toward the purpose of the sermons reflects his general state of mind as it comes through in the writings. The fact that, despite his corrections, he left intact both his initial and his later remarks on the topic, which express totally different approaches, is an example of his writing style. The sermons do not reflect an explicit approach and systematic doctrine but rather a personal process of coping.

Apart from researchers who deal with R. Kalonymus Kalman Shapira's teachings, the many people who are interested in his philosophy may find this new edition immensely useful. Volume One presents the sermons in a manner that is accurate and loyal to R. Shapira's guidelines for their publication in their final unexpurgated and noncorrected form. Volume Two introduces the revisions and deletions, displays R. Shapira's actual handwriting, and traces his states of mind and the immense thought that he invested in his writings.

A larger and broader index at the end of Volume One, with additional topics, might have been more useful to the reader. The index is insufficiently detailed; it lacks important themes that recur in R. Shapira's thinking and sermons, such as gentiles, Hasidism, passion, happiness, prophecy, non-Jewish thinking, creation, and destruction, to name only a few.

Furthermore, even though in his notes on the sermons Reiser presents many sources from the Bible, the Kabbalah, and Hasidism, he makes hardly any reference to R. Shapira's earlier writings, even though they presage many of the themes evoked by his Holocaust-era sermons. Particularly conspicuous are many potential parallels from R. Shapira's interbellum collection, *Derekh ha-melekh*.[21] R. Shapira often makes reference in these earlier sermons to the same topics, sources, and questions that he would invoke in similar liturgical contexts during the war. In his sermon on *parashat mishpatim* of 1938, for example, he asks exactly the same question that would later arise in his sermon for the same Torah portion of 1940.[22] In his sermon for *parashat naso* in 1940,[23] a question raised in regard to the same portion, in 1930, is asked again.[24]

Given the lack of reference to R. Shapira's other writings, one may get the impression that his Holocaust-era sermons are unrelated to the rest of his oeuvre. This is not so. R. Shapira's distinctive voice is reflected in all of his writings, as it is in his later Holocaust-era compositions. A comparison of R. Shapira's prewar refletions and those from the *Sermons from the Years of Rage*, accurately rendered for the first time in Reiser's edition, offers a vital context for ongoing research. To put it plainly, Daniel Reiser's edition of *Sermons from the Years of Rage* is an inspiring achievement. The extensive labor invested in the accurate deciphering of the Rebbe's handwriting through use of epigraphy and new technologies and the editor's clear and edifying, evidence-based presentations lift the study of this form of Hasidism to a whole new level. These volumes will undoubtedly be critical for understanding Orthodox Judaism's confrontation with the Holocaust.

Notes

We are grateful to the author and to the editors of *Yad Vashem Studies* for allowing us to reprint this review essay. It appears here in translation from Hebrew by Naftali Greenwood, with some emendations for style and consistency by the editors of the current volume.

1. Kalonymus Kalmish Shapira, *Esh kodesh* (Jerusalem: Va'ad Hasidei Piaseczno, 1960).

2. Nehemia Polen, *The Holy Fire: The Teachings of Rabbi Kalonimus Kalman Shapira, the Rebbe of the Warsaw Ghetto* (Northvale, NJ: Jason Aronson, 1994); Yitzhak Hershkowitz, "The Martyred Rabbi Kalonimus Kalman Shapira, the Piaseczno Rebbe: His Thinking Before and During the Holocaust, Continuity or Change?" [in Hebrew] (master's thesis, Bar-Ilan University, 2005); Mendel Piekarz, *The Last Hasidic Literary Document on Polish Soil: The Warsaw Ghetto Writings of the Rebbe of Piaseczno* [in Hebrew] (Jerusalem: Yad Vashem, 1979); Esther Farbstein; *Hidden in Thunder: Perspectives on Faith, Halachah, and Leadership during the Holocaust* (Jerusalem: Mossad Harav Kook, 2007), 479–509; Eliezer Schweid, *From Ruin to Salvation: The Haredi Response to the Holocaust as It Occurred* [in Hebrew] (Tel Aviv: Hakibbutz Hameuchad, 1994), 105–54.

3. *Sermons from the Years of Rage*, 1:328–29. A scanned image of the letter, which researchers sometimes term a "testament," is published as an appendix in Reiser's edition. It is also translated from Yiddish into Hebrew in the front matter to *Esh kodesh*.

4. Kalonymus Kalmish Shapira, *Hakhsharat ha-avreikhim, Mevo ha-she'arim, Tsav ve-zeruz* [in Hebrew] (Tel Aviv: Va'ad Hasidei Piaseczno, 1962).

5. *Sermons from the Years of Rage*, 1:15–16.

6. Ibid., 1:26n66.

7. Ibid., 1:30.

8. Ibid., 1:32.

9. Ibid., 1:328–29.

10. Ibid., 1:293.

11. Ibid., 1:78.

12. Ibid., 1:80.

13. Ibid., 1:59n206.

14. Ibid., 2:86–87, quoted in the introduction, 1:71.

15. *Esh kodesh*, 61.

16. *Sermons from the Years of Rage*, 2:236–37, also cited in the introduction, 1:71–72.

17. *Esh kodesh*, 186.

18. *Sermons from the Years of Rage*, 1:72.

19. Ibid., 1:57.

20. Ibid., 1:277, also cited in the introduction, 1:57.

21. Kalonymus Kalmish Shapira, *Derekh ha-melekh* (Jerusalem: Va'ad Hasidei Piaseczno, 1995).

22. Ibid., 108.

23. *Sermons from the Years of Rage*, 1:136.

24. *Derekh ha-melekh*, 148.

8

Creative Writing in the Shadow of Death

Psychological and Phenomenological Aspects of Rabbi Shapira's Manuscript "Sermons from the Years of Rage"

Daniel Reiser

Man should not cast aside from him the fear of the earthly; in his fear of death he should—stay.

—Franz Rosenzweig, *The Star of Redemption*

Sermons from the Years of Rage

There are few extant documents of rabbinic thought composed under the Nazi regime. As such, the collection of sermons authored by the Piaseczner Rebbe, R. Kalonymus Kalmish Shapira, in the Warsaw Ghetto[1]—effectively the final Hasidic work to be written in Poland, as noted by Mendel Piekarz—is among the canonical, if not the leading, work of Orthodox thought written during this period.[2] Like his prewar sermons (see Wiskind, this volume), they were probably first delivered orally in Yiddish and then recorded in rabbinic Hebrew.[3] It should be noted that they contain no direct references to current political or historical events, nor is there any direct mention of Germans or other key Ghetto figures, though there are numerous indirect references to specific occurrences: "evildoers," suffering, tribulations, physical and spiritual distress, the pain of losing loved-ones, and crises of religion and faith.[4] The book is primarily concerned with the religious and phenomenological significance of suffering.

These wartime sermons aimed to provide their audience with hope and self-respect as well as offer counsel, forge a religious path, and persuade listeners that spiritual gains and human dignity were still attainable, despite the German efforts to destroy them.[5] But that was not their sole purpose. One must recall that R. Shapira not only delivered the sermons orally but also took pains to preserve them in writing. It is evident from the sermons of the latter half of 1941 and onward that R. Shapira was well aware that his chances of survival—and those of the people around him—were steadily diminishing[6] and that the destruction wrought by war, including spiritual and religious crises, would never be fully healed:

> Who is not pained as they behold the suffering of Israel, in body and soul; and whose heart does not ache when they see that there are no *hadarim,* no *yeshivot,* no place of Torah or gathering of Torah scholars? This is not only the case at this moment, as the houses of the Lord are destroyed, but the [conditions of the] present will also be manifested in the future. For young men who are students of Torah will be lacking: some will be missing on account of unnatural deaths and starvation, God save us, and others will be compelled by circumstances to go out and seek sustenance for themselves. From where shall we lay hold of lads who are students of Torah if now there are none studying, and some of them have not withstood the test and, driven by hunger, have gone out to the market on the Sabbath in order to barter? Do we really think that such lads and young men who have spent years wandering about the marketplace and streets conducting business or begging for bread, whether on a weekday or the Sabbath—the Torah and Hasidic teachings acquired over several years in the *hadarim* and *yeshivot* having been forgotten—[do we really think] that when the opportunity arises, these ones will return to the *hadarim* and *yeshivot* like before?![7]

Given these circumstances, there is no doubt that the effort taken to preserve this sermon in writing—particularly in light of the difficult physical conditions prevailing at that time in the Ghetto—indicates a broader objective.[8] R. Shapira's request in his final testament that these sermons be published demonstrates that he did not perceive them as mere consolation speeches, nor were they addressed solely to his ill-fated contemporaries. R. Shapira understood his sermons to be religious writings of enduring significance addressed to future generations and others not party to the historical context in which they were originally delivered. One might even suggest that he refrained from addressing particular historical events in order that the significance of the sermons not be limited to any particular incident occurring within a specific context, time, and location. He sought to preserve the sermons for all time, "to scatter them throughout Jacob and divide them amongst Israel," as indicated in his final testament.[9]

This collection, which he titled *Sermons from the Years of Rage* in his handwritten manuscript, is distinguished by its willingness to confront the experience of suffering:

> When we studied the words of the prophets and of our sages of blessed memory regarding the tribulations of the destruction [of the temple in Jerusalem], we thought we had some grasp of these tribulations, even crying on occasion at that time. However, now we see how great the difference is between hearing about tribulations and seeing them, and all the more so suffering them—God save us—such that they are nearly incomparable . . . and as much as we discuss the tribulations, we are not able to describe them as they truly are, for knowledge and discussion of tribulations cannot be compared to experiencing them.[10]

R. Shapira shares his intimate doubts and misgivings with the reader,[11] producing a unique and moving document. An examination of these sermons does not reveal a clear and defined stance on either the meaning of suffering or the aim of the sermons themselves. Instead, R. Shapira invites the reader to join his own struggle to persist. In one of his first sermons, R. Shapira declares his aim to provide strength and encouragement, "that you [the future reader] might be strengthened through me"[12] and "when others see that I fortify myself despite my tremendous suffering, they too might issue an *a fortiori* ruling regarding their own suffering—which is not as bitter as mine—and be strengthened."[13] Yet two years later, R. Shapira admits that he is no longer persuaded by his own words of consolation:

> Particularly when the sorrows are unceasing, then even the one who had initially strengthened himself and the rest of Israel now ceases to be strengthened and is weary of being consoled. Even if he wanted to exert himself and utter some remarks of comfort and strength, he would have no words to say, for over these many long days of suffering he has already spoken and repeated once more everything there is to say. The words have grown old and have no further effect on him or on his listeners.[14]

Such honesty has few parallels in rabbinic literature. For two and a half years, R. Shapira preached, encouraged, and comforted. Now, as his sermons draw to a close and "the sorrows are unceasing," he publicly declares that he no longer has the strength to fortify and console himself—or the strength to fortify and console his readers. This obviously raises the question of why he exerted such energy to complete his manuscript, correcting the sermons and committing them to future publication.

A Philology of Suffering

A philological examination of the handwritten manuscript "Sermons from the Years of Rage," which I conducted for the critical edition, indicates that the sermons were produced sequentially, one proof succeeding another. Further evidence of this appears in a letter R. Shapira appended to the manuscript with instructions for the reader and publisher, including a system he had devised for proofing his text:

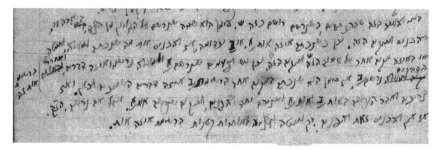

Figure 8.1. Manuscript no. ARG II 15 (Ring. II/370), page 4. Courtesy of ŻIH (Żydowski Instytut Historyczny).

I note herewith that in the writings, wherever a mark such as this ↓ appears, it means that what is written on the side of the page at this line should be inserted at this location. And also, when a letter such as *alef* or *bet* or the like appears, then what is written above, below, or somewhere else on this page should be inserted at the location where the notation is recorded. And sometimes an *alef* is recorded and sentences appear above, after which the letter *bet* is written. This indicates that written elsewhere in the text marked by *bet* are remarks that belong here. Then what is written at the letter *bet* should be connected to the letter *alef*, and both should be inserted together at the place where the letter *alef* appears. But if the word *hagaha* [proofreading] is written, then the text should not be inserted; it should only appear below in small letters and should be marked by some letter.[15]

In fact, initial proofing appears in the body of the manuscript text itself: words are deleted by being crossed out, and added words and sentences are placed atop existing or deleted words. Further proofing is done by adding arrows to indicate supplemental text in the margins of the page. Sometimes the author decides to delete an old "add" mark by crossing the words out; wherever this is done, the arrow is deleted in the same manner. Such deletion is evidence of at least one additional round of proofing, in which the author reviewed his comments and decided to delete some of them.

A further stage of editing was accomplished by adding letters to the body of the text: inscriptions in square (Assyrian) Hebrew letters, and underlining for emphasis. Each such letter is a reference to a note on the upper or lower margin of the page—not on the side margins, as with the arrow marking. The reference in the text proper appears again next to the added text (upper or lower), so that the proper location for each added text may be identified.

In general, I concluded that the notes marked with arrows are older than those marked with letters, because many marginalia that are referenced by arrows end with the appending of a letter that leads to an additional remark on the top or bottom margin of the page. Admittedly, the opposite sometimes occurs as well—a comment marked by a letter is added at the top or the bottom of the page, at which location an arrow directs the reader to an additional supplemental text alongside the first comment. This represents yet another level of proofing, in which R. Shapira reviewed the remarks that he had added and corrected them as well.[16]

I believe that careful investigation of the manuscript's archaeology, its layers and emendations over time, calls our attention to a human phenomenon worthy of discussion. Many of the marginal notes were actually written late in 1942, though R. Shapira was already aware by late 1941 (see Magid, this volume) that Polish Jewry was facing an unprecedented catastrophe from which it might never recover. By the time these last notes were added to the manuscript in 1942, in fact, the mass transports from the Ghetto to the death camps had already begun. R. Shapira must also have known that there was very little chance that he, his manuscript, or any of his immediate followers would survive. Under these circumstances, his commitment to painstaking, multilayered, and minute revision of his already finished text should not be taken for granted.

R. Shapira knew that he was going to die and had already lost all his family, and how did he occupy himself? With correcting and editing his sermons! Moreover, all of this was done without any certainty that these sermons would ever be found and published. Such literary activity is testimony to a life lived at two extremes: the bitter reality of death and the simultaneous vitality invested in writing, corrections, and stylistic editing. On one hand, there is calamitous death that destroys everything, while on the other hand, a new literary creation is produced that requires a great deal of concentration. Even before we consider the actual content of these sermons, their very existence should be treated as testimony to an extraordinary human endeavor. R. Shapira was himself aware of this tension, which sometimes provoked him to reflect on whether his own ability to write under these circumstances was a sign of indifference or apathy to his own suffering and that of others around him:

> There are times when a person is astounded by himself, exclaiming, "Am I not broken? Am I not nearly always in a state of tears, crying from time to time? How can I study Torah? By what means may I strengthen myself to produce new teachings of Torah and *hasidut*?" At times, his heart strikes him, as he declares: "Is it not my heartlessness that allows me to fortify myself in the study of Torah while my sorrows and the sorrows of the Jewish people are so great?" He will once more answer himself, "Am I not broken? How great are my tears; all of my life is woe and gloom." This person is perplexed by himself.[17]

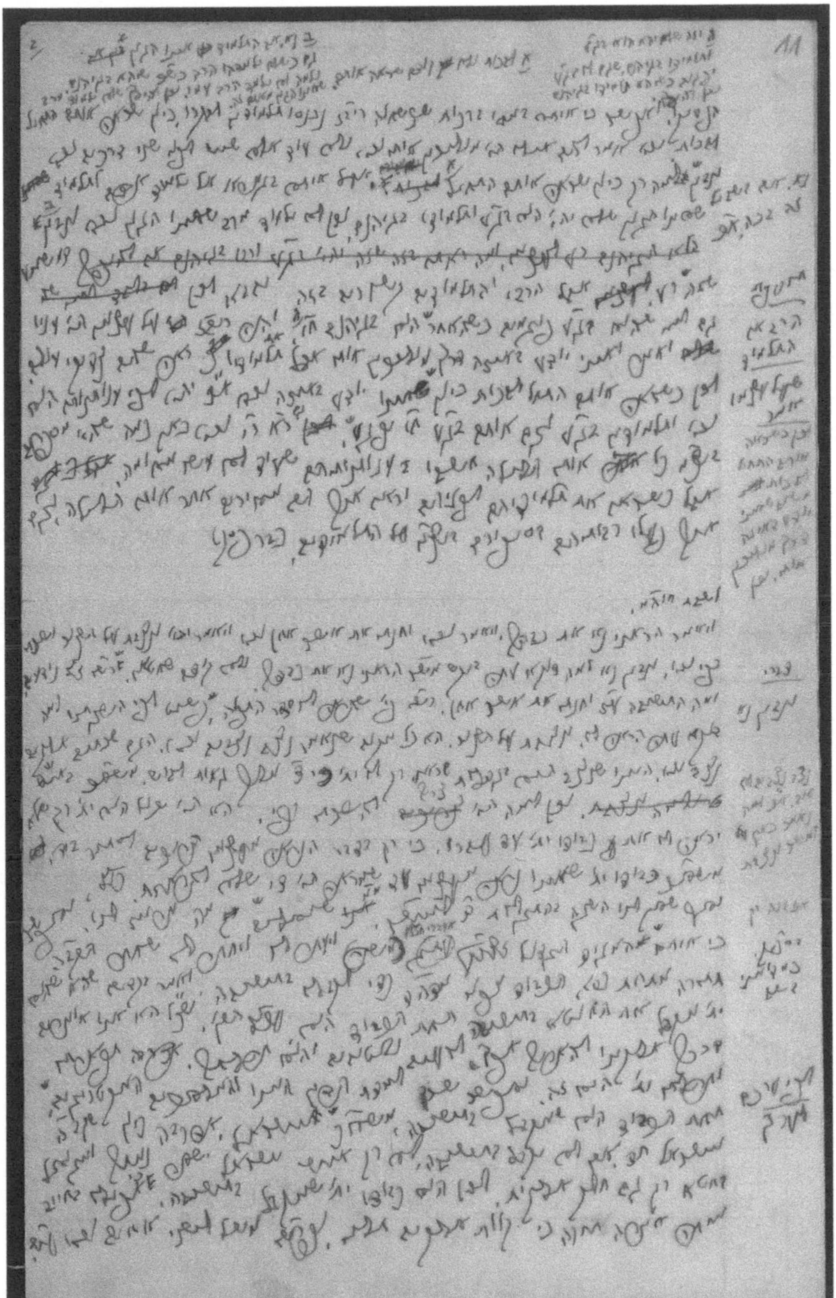

Figure 8.2. Sermon for Passover 1940. Manuscript no. ARG II 15 (Ring. II/370).
Courtesy of ŻIH (Żydowski Instytut Historyczny).

While this passage is framed in the third person, it is clear that the author, who "strengthen[s himself] to produce new teachings of Torah and *hasidut*," is actually testifying about himself. If my reading is correct, this passage represents a personal testament to the pangs of guilt that seized him ("his heart strikes him") because he was apparently able to remain creative despite the torments of his fellows, which "are so great." On the one hand, he feels great discomfort about allowing his routine of studying Torah and Hasidic teachings to continue as though nothing has happened; on the other, he expresses deep awareness of pain and rupture, so that he is "perplexed by himself." The ability to live in between these two opposing worlds—the world of literary creation and innovation, and the world of total destruction—is testimony to a special kind of resilience deserving description in its own right.

A Psychology of Suffering: Writing in the Shadow of Death

Beginning in the 1970s, a psychological theory was developed that was concerned with the influence of awareness of death on human cognition and behavior: terror management theory. The Jewish American writer and cultural anthropologist Ernest Becker claimed that all creative activity is directly related to the denial of death.[18] For him, culture and creativity supply a certain bulwark against the fear of death, while the denial of death motivates man to write and create. In other words, human creative activity is a form of escape from or ignoring of death, an attempt to prevent the inexorable end. According to this model, writing may have offered R. Shapira a mental reprieve from the bitter reality and death surrounding him, despite the fact that his sermons directly address death and suffering.[19]

A different approach suggests that human creativity contends with death and, rather than evading it, emerges victorious. There are matters more important than life, and engagement with them represents the victory of the spirit over death and the physical. When Socrates was sentenced to death by the court of Athens in 399 BCE, he was faced with the possibility of evading and changing his punishment. However, Socrates decided, for philosophical reasons, to bear his punishment and drink the cup of poison hemlock. His death was portrayed by Plato as a victory of the philosopher and of philosophy.[20] Socrates refused to desist from philosophy and stated in his defense, "On this point I would say to you, men of Athens: 'Whether you believe Anytus or not, whether you acquit me or not, do so on the understanding that this is my course of action, even if I am to face death many times.' "[21] Also, "death is something I couldn't care less about."[22] His engagement with philosophy overcame his instinctive fear of dying. This is a victory, not an escape.

It must be noted, however, that Socrates left behind no writings of his own and that Plato's dialogues were written as works of philosophical fiction after his death. This being the case, it is worth noting an authentic autobiographical work authored by an individual sentenced to death, *The Consolation of Philosophy*, by Anicius Manlius Severinus Boethius, which was written while its author was in prison awaiting his execution.[23] Boethius was a Roman consul at the beginning of the sixth century who was executed for treason in 524 CE, after two years of imprisonment. *The Consolation of Philosophy*, written in the shadow of his impending death, is not merely a depiction of his inner life but a manifestation of the philosophy that is, in the words of Kabbalah scholar Yehuda Liebes, "the triumph of the spirit of the individual over the reigning tyranny, and the victory of reason over suffering and emotion."[24] Like *Sermons from the Years of Rage*, this can be understood as a triumph of the spirit through the writing of a text. In this understanding, the writing does not escape or commemorate suffering—it overcomes it.

Viktor Frankl, the founder of logotherapy, wrote about his experiences in German concentration camps and maintained that he and his fellow prisoners succeeded in actualizing their spiritual freedom in the very place where they had been deprived of all human rights.[25] Frankl came to Auschwitz with a completed manuscript ready for publication, which was confiscated upon arrival. Realizing that the manuscript was lost, he began to reconstruct the work, an activity that gave meaning to his life and endowed him with physical and spiritual strength. "Certainly," he testifies, "my deep desire to write this manuscript anew helped me to survive the rigors of the camps I was in. For instance, when in a camp in Bavaria I fell ill with typhus fever, I jotted down on little scraps of paper many notes intended to enable me to rewrite the manuscript, should I live to the day of liberation. I am sure that this reconstruction of my lost manuscript in the dark barracks of a Bavarian concentration camp assisted me in overcoming the danger of cardiovascular collapse."[26] The writing of notes on scraps of paper and the desire to rewrite his book enabled Frankl to overcome his difficult surroundings and actualize his spiritual freedom. According to this model, R. Shapira's writing was an actualization of freedom in a freedomless world.

A third approach can be found in the writings of Martin Heidegger. His *Being and Time* (1927) addresses the meaning of death at great length.[27] According to him, death exposes the individual to his own mortality and the lack of meaning in his life, but it is this very lack of meaning that enables the individuation of the individual and is therefore true meaning. Death is devoid of substance; it is a pure emptiness, which contains all and hence brings forth the creation of the new. The mental renunciation of the everyday world gives birth to the new, as the universal meaning is abandoned and gives way to the personal creation of the individual.[28]

Similarly, Franz Rosenzweig utilized the existential fear of death to criticize rationalist Western philosophy, opening his *Star of Redemption* (1921) with the words, "*in philosophos!*"[29] As an existentialist, Rosenzweig positions existence as prior to all thought and places the earthly fear of death—which philosophical idealism, and Hegel in particular, attempt to deny—as the starting point of *Star of Redemption*. Rosenzweig wrote the book in light of his encounter with the horrors of World War I. For him, death establishes existence as prior to all thought. From the fear of death, man realizes his being; this fear is the source of all life.[30]

Another modern writer, Lev Shestov—born Yehuda Leyb Schwarzmann (1866–1938)—argued that meaninglessness and despair are primary human experiences ("Utter futility! All is futile!"),[31] which, however, point to an experience of faith beyond both knowledge and hopelessness.[32]

According to Shestov, the experience of doubt and the deepest uncertainty are continuous with the experience of "faith." The believer begins his path in the depths of despair, but it is from these very depths that he cries out to God: "Out of the depths I call you, O Lord."[33] What does he call? "My God, my God, why have you abandoned me?"[34] Faith is not a sense of contentment but rather a struggle with bitterness and a darkened spirit: "I say to God, my rock, 'Why have You forgotten me, why must I walk in gloom?' "[35] The individual finds himself in a constant struggle against reason and logic, against the "truth" thrust upon him; this struggle is the state of faith. Shestov's final work, *Athens and Jerusalem*, concludes with these words: "Philosophy is not *Besinnen* but struggle. And this struggle has no end and will have no end. The kingdom of God, as it is written, is attained through violence."[36]

Much like awareness of despair, which is the starting point of religious experience, awareness of death also serves a central function in Shestov's thought. Only death can shake off from man the false enchantments of knowledge and scientific truth.[37] "[Shestov's] philosophy seeks to instruct man to contend with the horrors of his historical existence, to live authentically with his despair without evasion, and to recognize the horrific reality of mortality and the lack of importance of an existence bound to end. All of these are meant to instruct him however in that spiritual strength which is faith, to lead him to God who will provide him not only with a primary meaning to his life, but with freedom."[38] Death exposes man to the end, and consequent meaningless nature, of his life and reminds him of his finality in order that he not be engulfed by a fabricated world devoid of meaning.[39] The fear of death shatters the illusion of our existence as independent and distinct beings. The possibility of faith thus develops in the very face of death.

The Neo-Hasidic thinker Hillel Zeitlin (see Leshem, this volume), who was acquainted with R. Shapira and even wrote a glowing review of his educational tract *A Student's Obligation*,[40] was also influenced by Shestov. In an essay titled "From the Depths of Doubt and Despair (On the Tremendous Striving of Lev Shestov)," Zeitlin addresses the extreme negation of all values and meaning in the world, which found expression in Shestov's thought.[41] "Friedrich Nietzsche came and rejected all that was human," writes Zeitlin, "conceiving by this to make room for the Übermensch. Lev Shestov . . . came and elevated the rejection of all things human to a degree of shocking and wondrous perfection in his recognition that the Übermensch too is but a 'human, all too human' conception." For Shestov, according to Zeitlin, "all that is human—even if it be decorated with the finest adornments of philosophy, science, and verse—is nothing but futility and pursuit of wind."[42] However, Zeitlin notes, Shestov's negations must be understood as continuations of "Hume's efforts in the critique of human perception; Schopenhauer's efforts in the negation of any value to life; Nietzsche's efforts in the critique of man and all that he has; Rousseau and Tolstoy's efforts in the negation of all that is called culture and civilization; Dostoyevsky's efforts in his groping about and prodding . . . and [that] it is from that very depth of nothingness that he calls out to God-Wonder."[43] Zeitlin puts all this into a familiar Jewish idiom: "Through recognizing the nullity of all that is human, he [Shestov] seeks 'the One who spoke and the world came into being.'"[44]

According to this third model, R. Shapira's writings are not a manifestation of a polarized life led between a mode of innovative creation and a reality emblematic of death and destruction. The bitter existence to which he was fated had already lost all meaning, and the works he wrote were a possession to bring before God, evoking the talmudic aphorism

"Praiseworthy is he who comes here with his teachings in his hand."[45]
R. Shapira did not record his sermons for others but rather for himself,
as he wrote elsewhere: "Behold, a person does not write solely for others . . . but also notes for himself";[46] "Every [personal] impression (*roshem*)
needs paper and space to be written (*yirshemu*) on."[47] The manuscript is
R. Shapira's offering for eternal life: "Fix yourself in the vestibule so that
you may enter the palace."[48]

In sum, the manuscript *Sermons from the Years of Rage* is a testimony to the phenomenon of creation in the shadow of death. Three
philosophical and psychological explanations have been given above for
this phenomenon:

1. Ignoring the world: the attempt to prevent inevitable death.

2. Triumph over the world: the actualization of freedom in a
   freedomless world.

3. Disillusionment with the world: through recognizing the
   nullity of all that is human, he seeks "He who spoke and
   the world came into being."

A Phenomenology of Suffering

The attempts I have suggested above to explain R. Shapira's "creative writing
in the shadow of death" should not be seen as three distinct approaches
that do not correspond. We should note that R. Shapira's sermons do not
contain a clear and decisive doctrine, and R. Shapira does not hesitate to
acknowledge that he himself is perplexed, as we saw above.[49] Therefore, it is
more likely that R. Shapira engages in all these three different approaches—
on different occasions. In practice, we can also approach this subject from
a completely different perspective: the phenomenological one. According to
this approach, his sermons are more of an attempt to refashion the question
of suffering in phenomenological terms, as a wandering journey rather than
a quest for "meaning" alone.[50] Don Seeman has argued, convincingly, that
this collection of sermons should be "approached as it was written, with a
view to ritual and hermeneutic strategies rather than foregone ideological
conclusions, and to lived experience in suffering rather than doctrine."[51]

Cultural anthropology tends to assume that ordered and coherent
meaning is the primary desideratum of social life. Both Max Weber and

Clifford Geertz associate religious rituals with the quest for meaning in suffering. According to Geertz, the purpose of rituals is to make suffering meaningful and therefore sufferable.[52] In contrast, Seeman uses the phenomenological account of Emmanuel Levinas, who argues that suffering is inherently "useless" and therefore resistant to meaning's claim. Seeman demonstrates how R. Shapira's Ghetto sermons constitute a denial that the insufferable can be made sufferable and "urge ritual fidelity *in spite of* meaninglessness, and not always as its antidote."[53] In a later article, Seeman expands and deepens his idea of "ritual in its own right" and deals with R. Shapira's quest for ritual efficacy in a reality of radical suffering. R. Shapira's response to crisis in the Warsaw Ghetto was not limited to making suffering meaningful but extended to the problem of efficacy, which precedes "meaning."[54] Seeman was the first to use this kind of language and to develop categories of experience as a key method for reading R. Shapira's sermons.

Nonetheless, Seeman does find a kind of meaning—not in the sense of meaningfulness with which anthropology remains preoccupied but rather in the sense of a purpose, sometimes pragmatic, for suffering. Such as: "bringing down blessing," "defending the cosmos," and "suffering for the other," which all derive from kabbalistic teachings: "I have argued that the impossible weight of suffering in Warsaw pushed ritual practice inexorably away from its meaning-making dimension and towards an increased emphasis on the essentially ethical gestures of bringing down blessing, defending the cosmos, and suffering for the other."[55]

With this perspective, I would like to look into what I have described as the tension of "writing in the shadow of death." There is no doubt that both preaching and writing down the sermons are ritual practices, which have the highest priority in halakhah and the deepest significance in Jewish mysticism.[56] Studying and teaching Torah are rituals that carry deep cosmological significance for Rabbi Shapira: "Innovative study and teaching of the sacred texts in their traditional form is a ritual activity that literally draws divine vitality down from above to support the integrity and existence of the cosmos, including the community of believers."[57] R. Shapira himself engages this problem through the study and teaching of Torah: "It is certain that Rabbi Shapira refers not just to the text of Scripture when he says 'Torah' in this context, but to the whole interwoven corpus of Jewish sacred textuality, including his own Hasidic sermons, whose production and study are without a doubt meant to be ritually efficacious in their own right."[58]

This concept of "ritual in its own right" can lead us to a more extreme approach and at once a very simple claim: R. Shapira wrote down his sermons as a plain act of learning Torah. He continued doing what he always did in his lifetime: teach and write—rituals in their own right—with no additional explanation, even not the pragmatistic one, and a fortiori the mystical motive. This explains the feelings of guilt and perplexity he expresses over the very act of writing these sermons. But at the same time, he expresses the feeling that he cannot put down his pen. To be clear, I do not underestimate the value of the concept of ritual efficacy developed by Seeman. However, I want to differentiate between teaching Torah by preaching a sermon to the public and writing it down afterward, especially given the layers of editing and proofreading explored above.

Rituals bring down divine blessing and defend the cosmos, according to Jewish mysticism. However, writing down the sermons may be an action of *torah lishmah,* learning Torah for its own sake, a value that has a long history in Jewish tradition.[59] The study of Torah outweighs, in Judaism, all other precepts (*mitsvot*),[60] hence we can approach it in a different manner from all other rituals. R. Shapira writes his sermons, then he proofreads them and writes corrections in the margins of a manuscript, then he adds another layer of corrections and additions, and so on, all alongside the bitter reality outside, because this is his way of learning Torah. Obviously, there is no certainty that these sermons will ever be found or published. However, this did not change R. Shapira's sense of obligation toward learning Torah, which became part of his DNA and which he could not disengage from, even in times of crises, just as he could not stop breathing oxygen.[61]

As Seeman points out, learning Torah in the Ghetto (like all other religious rituals) was not done in order to "make suffering sufferable," in Geertz's terms. It was a ritual efficiency, which, according to Ariel Evan Mayse, was "surely meant to open the heart and awaken the soul amid the sadness, destruction, and pain of the Warsaw Ghetto. In this crushing environment, the talmudic and midrashic aggadah spirit offered a way of transcending time and entering the world of illuminated exegesis rather than temporal suffering."[62] This is true for learning the sources that construct the homily and then teaching it aloud to the public. Nevertheless, R. Shapira could have stopped here. Why did he need to write his sermons, and why did he need to make changes—often very minor ones that have no effect on meaning? Moreover, R. Shapira stopped preaching just before the "Great Action," which began on July 22, 1942. Major parts of his proofreading were carried out after the Ghetto emptied.[63] It is clear that at that point, R. Shapira was not working on his Torah in order to provide hope or self-respect or for the sake of "suffering for the other," or even for "affective strategies that would allow his followers—and the cosmos itself—to resist collapse,"[64] since there was no longer an audience, or an "other," or followers, and the cosmos did collapse. It seems to me that his writing, under these circumstances, expresses the value of *torah lishmah* in its most extreme form, as a "ritual in its own right."[65]

We can never know with any degree of certainty how R. Shapira himself viewed this tension of creativity in the shadow of death—if he saw any tension at all—aside from the personal testimony that he recorded for various audiences, both immediate and less proximate, in these sermons. But I believe that critical examination of his manuscript together with openness to the psychological and phenomenological dimensions of suffering and creativity offers the best chance we have to do justice to his torment.

Notes

This research was supported by Herzog College, to which I would like to express my sincere and deepest gratitude. The present article is an updated and revised version of an earlier Polish draft which appeared as Daniel Reiser, "Pisarstwo w cieniu śmierci: rękopis rabina Szapiry 'Kazania z lat szału' w perspektywie psychologicznej i fenomenologicznej," *Zagłada Żydów: Studia i Materiały* 15 (2019): 62–88.

1. For more extensive biographical information, see Aharon Sorsky, "Rabbi Kalonymus Kalmish Shapira, of Blessed Memory," in Kalonymus Kalmish Shapira, *Esh Kodesh* [in Hebrew] (Jerusalem: Va'ad Hasidei Piaseczno, 2008) 279–322; Mendel Piekarz, *The Last Hasidic Literary Document Written in Poland: The Teachings of the Piaseczner Rebbe in the Warsaw Ghetto* [in Hebrew] (Jerusalem: Yad Vashem, 1979). For biographical details focusing on the period of the Holocaust derived from testimonial and archival material, see Esther Farbstein, *Hidden in Thunder*, trans. Deborah Stern (Jerusalem: Mossad Harav Kook, 2007), 479–88; Isaac Hershkowitz, "Rabbi Kalonymus Kalmish Shapira, The Piasechner Rebbe His Holocaust and Pre-Holocaust Thought, Continuity or Discontinuity?" [in Hebrew] (master's thesis, Bar-Ilan University, 2005), 17–18; Zvi Leshem, "Between Messianism and Prophecy: Hasidism According to the Piaseczner Rebbe" [in Hebrew] (PhD dissertation, Bar-Ilan University, 2007), 1–5; Ron Wacks, *The Flame of the Holy Fire: Perspectives on the Teachings of Rabbi Kalonymous Kalmish Shapira of*

Piaczena [in Hebrew] (Alon Shvut: Tevunot, 2010), 21–33; Kalonymus Kalman Shapira, *Sermons from the Years of Rage* [in Hebrew], ed. Daniel Reiser, 2 vols. (Jerusalem: Herzog Academic College, 2017), 1:13–24; Nehemia Polen, *The Holy Fire: The Teachings of Rabbi Kalonymus Kalman Shapira, the Rebbe of the Warsaw Ghetto* (Northvale, NJ: Jason Aronson, 1994), 1–14; David Biale et al., *Hasidism: A New History* (Princeton: Princeton University Press, 2018), 614–16, 660–62. Also, see the recent extensive work in Polish, Marta Dudzik-Rudkowska, *Pisma Rabina Kalonimusa Szapiro* (Warszawa: Żydowski Instytut Historyczny, 2017), ix–xxx.

2. Prominent works include Yissakhar Shlomo Teichtal, *Eim Habanim Semeichah: On Eretz Yisrael, Redemption, and Unity*, trans. Moshe Lichtman (Israel: Kol Mevaser Publishers, 2000), originally published in Budapest, 1943; Ephraim Oshry, *Responsa from the Holocaust*, trans. Y. Leiman, rev. ed. (New York: Judaica Press, 2001). For other Orthodox writings from the Holocaust, see Esther Farbstein, *Hidden in Thunder*; Farbstein, ed., *Leaves of Bitterness: Diaries, Responsa, and Theology in the Holocaust: The Writings of Rabbi Yehoshua Moshe Aronson* [in Hebrew] (Jerusalem: Mossad Harav Kook, 2014); Steven T. Katz, Shlomo Biderman, and Gershon Greenberg, eds., *Wrestling with God: Jewish Theological Responses during and after the Holocaust* (Oxford: Oxford University Press, 2007). While the value of these works should not be minimized, it should be noted that *Em ha-Banim Semehah* was largely written in Hungary prior to the Nazi invasion of that country, while *Responsa from the Holocaust* was edited following the Holocaust and is primarily concerned with issues of halakhah rather than philosophy. Because it was written in the midst of the terrible suffering, *Sermons from the Years of Rage* is a unique work entirely devoted to the subject of suffering and tribulations.

3. The process of orally delivering the sermons on the Sabbath and reconstructing and transcribing them afterward from memory is indicated by the text of the sermons themselves. See, for example, *Sermons from the Years of Rage*, 1:226: "We said on the holy Sabbath at the kiddush," and "Now, as I write this down, I can add that other people told me so as well"; ibid., *parashat mishpatim-shekalim* 5702 (1942), 1:271: "As we said last week"; and ibid., *parashat bo* 5700 (1940), 2:33: "I do not remember what more we said on this matter." (This last sermon was later stricken out.)

4. Polen, *Holy Fire*, 17–20. Regarding the forced cutting of beards, see: Shapira, *Sermons from the Years of Rage*, *parashat toledot* 5700 (1939), 1:92: "They also cut off the beards of the elders of Israel, such that they are no longer externally recognizable." Regarding the closure of Jewish workplaces, see ibid., *parashat be-shalah* 5700 (1940), 1:103: "And similarly, when the workers are idle, God forbid, they are in a very embittered mood, for your nation Israel needs sustenance." Regarding aid organizations, see ibid., *parashat vayyikra* 5700 (1940), 1:112: "When they give alms to one other and receive help from each other." Regarding hunger and the persecution or humiliation of Jews in the streets, see

ibid., 1:113: "For has an angel tasted the suffering of a Jew at the moment he is beaten, the shame he feels as they pursue and debase him . . . or his hardship when he lacks for food?" Regarding the Nazi justifications for killing Jews and plundering their property, see ibid., *parashat zakhor* 5700 (1940), 1:115: "Now they contrive rationales and explanations for why theft, burglary, murder, and all other foulness are good"; and ibid., *shabbat ha-gadol* 5700 (1940), 1:118–20. Regarding the killing of Jews, see ibid., *pesah* 5700 (1940), 1:125–26; on the prohibition of public prayer, see ibid., *parashat nitsavim* 5700 (1940), 1:153–54; on the plundering of Jewish property, see ibid., *rosh ha-shanah* 5701 (1940), 1:155–58. Regarding the murder of Jews, see ibid., *sukkot* 5702 (1941), 1:226–30; ibid., *parashat zakhor* 5702 (1942), 1:275–82; and on the murder of children, ibid., *hukkat* 5702 (1942), 1:288–306. Regarding the spread of typhus in the Ghetto, see ibid., *parashat toledot* 5702 (1941), 1:233–36. See also Esther-Judith Thidor-Baumel, "*Esh Kodesh*: The Book of the Piaseczner Rebbe and Its Place in Understanding Religious Life in the Warsaw Ghetto" [in Hebrew], *Yalkut Moreshet* 29 (1980): 173–87. For an extensive study of the sermons in light of their historical background, see Henry Abramson, *Torah from the Years of Wrath 1939-1943: The Historical Context of the Aish Kodesh* (CreateSpace Independent Publishing Platform, 2017).

5. Polen, *Holy Fire*, 16. Regarding humiliation and threats to human dignity from the beginning of the war, see *Sermons from the Years of Rage*, *parashat toledot* 5700 (1939), 1:92–93: "Now he is trampled and tread upon until he can no longer sense whether he is a Jew, a human being, or an animal that has no sense of self." R. Shapira next offers words of consolation and support.

6. For example, see *Sermons from the Years of Rage*, *parashat shoftim* 5701 (1941), 1:214: "For amid all of our suffering, we see that if everyone were to be suddenly informed that they were to be saved the next day, a great share of the hopeless would still find strength. Regrettably, however, they perceive no end to the darkness, and many have no means of fortifying themselves and are filled with despair as their spirits collapse, God forbid." It is worth mentioning that rather than hiding this fact from his Hasidim, R. Shapira discusses their dire circumstances in his sermons and may have thus allowed them to process the experience together within the dignified, spiritual framework of the Hasidic gathering.

7. *Sermons from the Years of Rage*, *parashat ekev* 5701 (1941), 1:209–10. See his note from the end of ibid., 5702 (1942), 1:212 on the destruction of Polish Jewry: "For the holy community is nearly in a state of complete destruction."

8. Polen, *Holy Fire*, 23–24.

9. See *Sermons from the Years of Rage*, 1:55–56.

10. Ibid., *shabbat hazon* 5702 (1942), 1:313–14.

11. See below, for example, on his feelings of guilt over the very act of writing these sermons.

12. *Sermons from the Years of Rage*, *parashat vayyeshev* 5700 (1939), 1:97. Although he paraphrases biblical verses, it is clear that R. Shapira's remarks

allude to both his personal circumstances and his task, as a Hasidic tsaddik, to arouse divine mercy. See ibid.: "The blessed Holy One said, 'It is not enough for the righteous, that which is prepared for them in the world to come.' It truly is not enough for it be good in the future—mercy must be aroused now [by the tsaddikim]." Regarding the theurgical quality of these sermons, see Don Seeman, "Ritual Efficacy, Hasidic Mysticism and 'Useless Suffering' in the Warsaw Ghetto," *Harvard Theological Review* 101, no. 3–4 (2008): 480–502; James A. Diamond, "The Warsaw Ghetto Rebbe: Diverting God's Gaze from a Utopian End to an Anguished Now," *Modern Judaism* 30, no. 3 (2010): 299–331.

13. *Sermons from the Years of Rage, parashat ki tavo* 5700 (1940), 1:152.

14. Ibid., *shabbat zakhor* 5702 (1942), 1:277.

15. ŻIH (Żydowski Instytut Historyczny) Archives, manuscript no. ARG II 15 (Ring. II/370).

16. See Daniel Reiser, "*Esh Kodesh*: A New Evaluation in Light of a Philological Examination of the Manuscript," *Yad Vashem Studies* 44, no. 1 (2016): 65–97.

17. *Sermons from the Years of Rage, parshat ha-hodesh* 5702 (1942), 1:293. See also Seeman, "Ritual Efficacy, Hasidic Mysticism, and 'Useless Suffering' in the Warsaw Ghetto," 488–89.

18. Ernest Becker, *The Denial of Death* (New York: Free Press, 1973).

19. The need to write as a type of promise for eternal life is already expressed by R. Shapira in 1928: "It is best for a person to write down all his thoughts. Not to earn fame by writing a book, but rather to engrave his soul on paper. By that he will sustain his soul's worries, its successes and failures . . . and grant it an eternal life within the lives of his readers" (*Tsav ve-zeruz*, 1).

20. See Plato's dialogues "Apology," "Crido," and "Phaedo" in *Plato: Complete Works*, ed. John M. Cooper (Indianapolis: Hackett, 1997).

21. Ibid., 28.

22. Ibid., 30.

23. See Yehuda Liebes, "The Consolation of Philosophy: An Introduction to a Translation of the Opening Fragments of Boethius' *Consolation of Philosophy*" [in Hebrew], *Alpayim* 21 (2001): 215–23.

24. Ibid.

25. Viktor Frankl, *Man's Search for Meaning* (New York: Washington Square Press, 1984).

26. Ibid., 126–27. For more on art and creative activity as a means of contending with pain and suffering in Jewish culture, see B. Kahana, C. Deutsch, and Redman, eds., *The Enigma of Suffering* [in Hebrew] (Tel Aviv: Yedioth Ahronoth Books, 2012), 319–48.

27. The irony of discussing Heidegger together with R. Shapira is not lost on this author. Heidegger is a controversial figure, largely for his affiliation with Nazism, for which he neither apologized nor publicly expressed regret.

28. Martin Heidegger, *Being and Time*, trans. J. Macquarrie and E. Robinson (San Francisco: Harper, 1962), 285–311. See also William Large, *Heidegger's Being and Time* (Edinburgh: Edinburgh University Press, 2008), 73–79.

29. Rosenzweig, *The Star of Redemption*, 9.

30. Ibid., 9–31.

31. Eccl 1:2 (NJPS).

32. Such a philosophical approach had already been developed by Arthur Schopenhauer, Søren Kierkegaard, and in numerous works of Russian literature, but Shestov brought it to a climax. See Adir Cohen, "Thinking Your Life: The Personal Story Meets the Philosophical Story" [in Hebrew], *Iyun u-Nehkar be-Hakhsharat Morim* 10 (2006): 191–219; Nikolai Alexandrovich Berdyaev, "Lev Shestov i Kirkegaard," *Sovremennye Zapiski* 62 (1936), 376–82 [English trans. by Fr. S. Janos, http://www.berdyaev.com/berdiaev/berd_lib/1936_419.html]. See also Elliot Wolfson, *Alef, Mem, Tau: Kabbalistic Musings on Time, Truth, and Death* (Berkeley: University of California Press, 2006), 156–74.

33. Ps 130:1.

34. Ps 22:2.

35. Ps 42:10.

36. Lev Shestov, *Athens and Jerusalem*, trans. B. Martin (Athens: Ohio University Press, 1966), 489. *Besinnen* in German means to think about something.

37. Shestov did not reject scientific truth or technological advancement, but he did not think that science could endow man's life with meaning.

38. Cohen, "Thinking Your Life," 201.

39. Ibid., 202. A similar perception, without the element of faith, appears in the philosophy of Heidegger. For him, death must by necessity lead to life, to the powerful longing to live life to the fullest and actualize the potential latent within us. Death "attracts" us in order that we might thrust it aside, in order that we put an end to that routine that transforms us into creations engaged in evading being rather than being itself. Our escape from death is the escape from life into the "safe" hands of "them," who endow us with false meaning and security and take away from us our most precious possession—our selfhood. See the summary in Heidegger, *Being and Time*, 311.

40. Hillel Zeitlin, "Rebbe: Craftsman and Pedagogue" [in Hebrew], in Zeitlin, *Sifran shel Yehidim* (Jerusalem: Mossad Harav Kook, 1979), 241–44.

41. Hillel Zeitlin, "From the Depths of Doubt and Despair (On the Tremendous Striving of Lev Shestov)" [in Hebrew], *Ha-Tekufah* 20 (1923): 425–44 and 21 (1924): 369–79. I am grateful to Sam Glauber for drawing my attention to important differences between Hillel Zeitlin's original words, which were published in his lifetime, and his edited books, which were published after his death.

42. Ibid., 427.

43. Ibid., 428–29. See further ibid., 442–43.

44. Hillel Zeitlin, "L. Shestov" [in Hebrew], *Ha-Me'orer* 2, no. 5 (1907): 177.

45. B. Bava Batra 10b. See Zeitlin, "L. Shestov," who observes that the discussion pertains to martyrdom: "Martyrs—no other creation can stand in their company." See also *Midrash Zuta Kohelet* 9:10 [Buber]; *Kohelet Rabba* 9:1 [Vilna].

46. Kalonymus Kalman Shapira, *Derekh ha-Melekh parashat vayyeshev* 5690 (1929), 51. The word *roshem* in Hebrew has two meanings: "impression" and "to write." R. Shapira makes clever use of the word, implying both meanings.

47. Ibid., 53. See also ibid., 433: "I am writing notes (*reshimot*) on *Sefer ha-Zohar*, that these notes will, with God's help, inscribe the holy *Zohar* within me (*ve-yirashem be-Zohar ha-kadosh*).

48. M. Avot 4:16.

49. However, see an attempt to indicate a gradated doctrine: Polen, *Holy Fire*; Hershkowitz, "Rabbi Kalonymus Kalmish Shapira."

50. See Don Seeman, "Sacred Fire (Review)," *Common Knowledge* 9, no. 3 (2003): 547; Seeman, "Otherwise Than Meaning: On the Generosity of Ritual," *Social Analysis* 48, no. 2 (2004): 55–71; Seeman, "Ritual Efficacy," 465–505.

51. Seeman, "Ritual Efficacy," 505.

52. Seeman, "Otherwise Than Meaning," 57–59.

53. Ibid., 67.

54. Seeman, "Ritual Efficacy," 480.

55. Ibid., 501.

56. See Elliot Wolfson, "The Mystical Significance of Torah Study in German Pietism," *JQR* 84 (1993): 43–78; Moshe Idel, "Torah: Between Presence and Representation of the Divine in Jewish Mysticism," in Idel, *Representing God* (Boston: Brill, 2014), 31–70. Regarding Talmud study as a devotional practice and a search for mystical self-expression in the teachings of R. Shapira, see Ariel Evan Mayse's article in this volume.

57. Seeman, "Otherwise Than Meaning," 66.

58. Seeman, "Ritual Efficacy," 498.

59. See Norman Lamm, "Pukhovitzer's concept of Torah lishmah," *Jewish Social Studies* 30, no. 3 (1968): 149–56; Lamm, *Torah Lishmah: Torah for Torah's Sake in the Works of Rabbi Hayyim of Volozhin and His Contemporaries* (New York: Yeshiva University Press, 1989); Roland Goetschel, "Torah Lishmah as a Central Concept in the 'Degel mahane Efrayim' of Moses Hayyim Ephraim of Sudylkow," in *Hasidism Reappraised*, ed. Ada Rapoport-Albert (London: Vallentine Mitchell, 1996), 258–67.

60. M. Peah 1:1: "The study of Torah exceeds them all."

61. I want to emphasize that R. Shapira's depiction of writing as a natural obligation was already expressed in his prewar *Tsav ve-zeruz*, 42: "When will I pay my debts to *my soul*, after I promised her [my soul] to deliver from within her books and other writings . . . with which she is pregnant." Emphasis added. I would like to thank Shalom Matan Shalom for bringing this passage to my attention.

62. See Ariel Evan Mayse, this volume.

63. *Sermons from the Years of Rage*, 1:52, 70–72.

64. Seeman, "Ritual Efficacy," 467.

65. In contrast to that of R. Shapira, R. Teikhtal's writing during the Holocaust (the work *Eim Ha-Banim Semehah*) is a clear example of writing that is done declaredly as an active mystical ritual. Teikhtal writes his book as an act of mystical activity in order to attract the merit (*zekhut*) of the Land of Israel to the Diaspora and thereby be saved. See Eliezer Schweid, *From Ruin to Salvation* [in Hebrew] (Tel Aviv: Hakibbutz Hameuchad, 1994), 100–104.

9

Miriam, Moses, and the Divinity of Children

Human Individuation at the
Cusp of Persistence and Perishability

Nehemia Polen

Rabbi Kalonymus Kalmish Shapira's teachings in occupied Warsaw and the Warsaw Ghetto, 1939–1942, have been examined for their views on theodicy, suffering, the destiny of the Jewish people, and the challenge of spiritual leadership in a time of acute collective and personal crisis. This volume is testament to those efforts. Furthermore, thanks to the publication of Daniel Reiser's new edition of Shapira's *Sermons from the Years of Rage* (previously published under the title *Esh kodesh*), we now have a fully accurate presentation of these wartime sermons (*derashot*) that faithfully reflects the author's intentions. Reiser's new edition, arguably the best critical edition of any Hasidic text from any period, allows us to focus on the *derashot* as carefully crafted compositions and to see how they were written, revised, augmented, and updated by the author. I have written about these homilies in the past on the basis of the first edition (1960), but Reiser's new publication provides the opportunity to examine more closely the crystallization of Shapira's thinking and writing. Reiser's meticulous editing affords us nearly unprecedented access to Shapira's carefully laid-out structure, revealing luminous creativity from impenetrable darkness. We now see the original manuscript in its rich layering, and on facing pages we have an eminently readable transcription that preserves the strata while bringing clarity to the homilies in their entirety. Of special interest is the paragraphing that indicates the major sections of the pieces. As Reiser notes, the first edition did not always accurately reflect Shapira's own paragraphing. This is particularly significant in light of the fact that Shapira himself took great care to graphically indicate and preserve his divisional schema.

I take this opportunity to focus on one sermon, *parashat hukkat* 5702 (June 27, 1942).[1] By any measure, this sermon is a large and substantial composition, which is notable and rather surprising in light of the historical circumstances in which it was composed. In spite of the chaos and utter collapse of the Ghetto at the precipice of annihilation after three crushing years, we have before us not fragmentary notes or haphazard jottings but a complex, cohesive effort, reflecting sustained and penetrating deliberation about ultimate theological matters. The sermon was written in the summer of 1942, at a time when the violence directed against the defenseless and starving Ghetto residents had reached a shocking level of intensity and most of the remaining Jews were soon to be deported to their deaths. Just at this moment, when the total scope of the catastrophe must have been coming into clear view for R. Shapira, we find several sermons that are the most complex, deeply reflective, movingly written, and tightly constructed in his entire Ghetto corpus.[2] Evidently tapping new resources of insight and creativity, Shapira deploys familiar texts and sacred themes in boldly provocative and penetrating ways.[3] This *derashah* is worthy of fine-grained analysis not only because it is one of the last homilies he wrote but also because it is an extraordinary example of the author's power in adversity, his astonishing originality, his emotional and intellectual range, and his depth of penetration into the human condition. My analysis aims to show that these extended *derashot* bear an inner coherence not immediately evident in a piece that ranges widely over different ideas, motifs, moods, and images. The architectural integrity of the piece reveals Shapira's compositional control, and this recognition of structural coherence—how the parts and the whole fit together—will enable us to grasp his message more securely, with firmer comprehensiveness.

Unlike the earlier printed edition, Reiser's edition faithfully preserves Shapira's paragraphing, revealing six individual sections. Most paragraphs are indicated by blank spaces in the manuscript, either at the beginning of a new line or at the end of a line. These sectional divisions were quite important to Shapira, as evidenced by the fact that the open spaces were preserved throughout the stages of revision and markup. That is, the manuscript reveals successive stages of correction, amplification, augmentation, and updating, all meticulously presented in the Reiser edition. In order to find room for additional words, Shapira wrote on the margins of his paper and devised a system of letter-keys, enabling him to add sizeable new blocks of material at the top or bottom of the sheets (see Reiser, this volume). Paper was at a premium, and it often took ingenuity to find an appropriate area of sufficient amplitude on the page to hold the added words. With all that, Shapira never compromised the paragraphing schema by utilizing the readily available blank lines in his layout. (In one case, he indicated the end of a section with a markup sign equivalent to our letter "Z," reproduced faithfully by Reiser.) All this indicates that Shapira considered the design of his *derashah,* its divisions and overall structure, to be essential to his message and crafted them with care and attention to the finest detail. We would do well, therefore, to follow his lead by paying attention to this structure, holding the parts and their relationship with one another in our consciousness as we attempt to grasp it in its entirety.

What follows is a presentation of each of the six sections, including key passages in translation, as well as a summary of each section.

Introduction and Section One

The *derashah* for *parashat hukkat* 1942 focuses on a text in Numbers 20, so it will be helpful to briefly review the main points of this biblical chapter. Near the end of their long wilderness trek, the Israelites are camped at Kadesh, about to begin the final stage of their journey to the promised land (v. 1). Miriam dies and is buried there (v. 2). Immediately thereafter, water runs out, causing the people to angrily confront their leaders, Moses and Aaron (v. 3). It is worth noting that rabbinic tradition suggests that the proximity of the water crisis with Miriam's death indicates that her merit prevented this crisis while she lived. In response to the people's complaint, God instructs Moses to take his special rod and speak to a certain rock, which will bring forth water for the people (v. 8). Moses follows God's instructions, but instead of speaking to the rock, he strikes it with his rod (v. 11). Water does flow abundantly, but Moses's deviation from the divine command is considered a sin, and Moses loses the opportunity to lead the people into the promised land (v. 12).[4]

According to early rabbinic chronology, these events took place in the final year of the forty-year wilderness trek following the exodus. As early as the biblical period, the prophet Micah proclaimed that God had sent the Israelites three great leaders: Moses, Aaron, and Miriam (Mic 6:4). Building on this theme, a talmudic passage states that "three great leaders arose for the Israelites: Moses, Aaron and Miriam; and three good gifts were bestowed upon the people in their virtue: the well, the clouds of glory, and the manna. The well was provided in the merit of Miriam, the cloud in the merit of Aaron, and the manna in the merit of Moses."[5]

This rabbinic reading highlights three miraculous phenomena that provided the Israelites with their most basic needs during their forty-year wilderness trek: the well, a constant source of water that miraculously accompanied the people wherever they encamped; the divine cloud that directed their travels and gave visible evidence of God's presence; and the "food from heaven," or manna. The association of the cloud with Aaron makes perfect sense, since Aaron presided over the tabernacle, where the cloud was located (Exod 40:34–38; Lev 16:2; Num 10:11). Moses is central to the manna narrative in Exod 16, and, as the one figure who actually went all the way to the top of Sinai to be with God, it is natural that he should be the one associated with the "food from heaven." But what about Miriam? What is her connection to the well in particular? It is true that the juxtaposition of the water crisis and Miriam's death (Num 20:2–3) suggests that as long as Miriam was alive, the well's water was provided in her merit.[6] But, Shapira asks, what is the *inner* significance of this juxtaposition? What was it about Miriam that made her the most appropriate conduit for a miraculous water supply? He quickly adds that he is not attempting to comprehend Miriam's spiritual level, which is, he says, entirely beyond our ability to assess. This is a hermeneutic of ethical, epistemological, and spiritual humility, an acknowledgment of incommensurate horizons. Rather, Shapira writes, his intention is to probe what lesson we might derive from the linkage of Miriam and the well. As he puts it, "What does this suggest to us [for our own spiritual lives]"?

His answer invokes another talmudic teaching about the three great leaders of the wilderness period. Based on a literal reading of the phrase *al pi Adonai* (Num 33:38; Deut 34:5), the deaths of Moses and Aaron are said to have been brought about by "God's mouth," by a divine kiss. The Talmud adds Miriam to this most rare group of individuals whose lives came to an end in blissful mouth-to-mouth intimacy with their divine creator.[7] But, the Talmud asks, why does Scripture not say this explicitly? The account of Miriam's death does not mention the key phrase *al pi Adonai*. The Talmud answers, as conveyed by Rashi, that it would not have been respectful to portray God kissing a woman. Yet the Talmud does not hesitate to fill in this key detail: Miriam *did* die, like her brothers, by divine kiss, although Scripture was reticent to say so explicitly.

Shapira asks the obvious question: Since God does not have a body, the "kiss" must be understood figuratively, so what is disrespectful about saying that God kissed Miriam?[8]

Shapira's response invokes a cornerstone of Hasidic theology: that a life of religious aspiration and virtuous action is attributable to divine grace. What impels some people and not others to strive for virtue and holiness? Where does the yearning come from, if not from God?

Shapira suggests that this logic applies most directly to men, rather than to women.

As he puts it:

> When a woman becomes a *tsaddeket* [feminine form of *tsaddik*], studies Torah, and fulfills the commandments, that is her own accomplishment, since she is not under any obligation to do so; heaven has not really aroused her to do what she did.
>
> Miriam did indeed die by a divine kiss. But Scripture does not apply the key phrase *al pi Adonai*, "by God's mouth," to Miriam, because her level of spiritual attainment was even higher [than that of Moses and Aaron], since her achievements were not attributable to divine elicitation but rather to her own self-generated effort. She was not responding to the command of "God's mouth." The source of her service was within her; it flowed [internally] from her. That is why the well, the flowing source of holy living water, appeared by virtue of her merit.

Here is the connection between the well and Miriam: The water that miraculously accompanied the Israelites was a flowing artesian well, gushing on its own, not needing to be primed or pumped. Similarly, Miriam's spirituality was self-generated. Drawing upon her own inner resources and flowing from the depth of her being, it depended upon no other—not even, as it were, the divine Other.

This exegesis is daring in the context of traditional Jewish thought, which typically sees heteronomous submission to a divine command as superior to autonomous, voluntary performance of a good deed. In the classic formulation of the Talmud, "One who is commanded and fulfils the command is greater than one who fulfils it without being commanded."

Indeed, a major determinant of women's lesser standing in certain areas of Jewish law is their status as persons "not commanded." Shapira actually uses the talmudic language here: *einah metsuvah ve-osah* (one who acts without being commanded), but instead of a barrier to full religious standing, he turns it into an asset.

Section Two: Eternity Realized through Children

The sermon's next section raises the question of why Moses hit the rock in an effort to supply water even though God had commanded him to speak to it. This question is an old crux that has been discussed over several centuries, but Shapira's concern here is not so much to add yet another layer to a vast body of scriptural interpretation as it is to explore the question from the perspective of *be-remez la-avodah* (textual hints for sacred service). Much like the hermeneutic modesty we saw above with regard to comprehending the distinction granted to Miriam, the rabbi reminds us that we cannot comprehend the inner life of Moses, which is utterly beyond our own religious horizons. Rather, we are looking for useful guidance in our own lives. The assumption is that if the Torah tells us the story of what appears to be a sin on Moses's part, there must be some lesson for readers throughout the ages and especially for the rabbi's own time and place (Warsaw Ghetto, June 1942); there must be an accessible hint for sacred service.

Shapira begins the development of this section by introducing a *Zohar* teaching that blessing a person's children is equivalent to blessing that person him- or herself.[9] This in turn launches an exploration of why humans identify so strongly with the fate of their children. Drawing on traditional sources, he asserts that before Adam's sin, humans would have lived forever, but now the survival of the individual is only through his or her descendants. The urge to live and survive is primal, at the constitutive core of what it means to be human, and in the post-Edenic world, that urge is only realizable through the ongoing survival of one's children and subsequent generations. This is a reflection of being "children of God" (Deut 14:1); as God's children, we have a tacit intuition of eternity that can only be realized by having children and seeing them survive and flourish. The intensity of one's identification with one's children therefore emerges from a deep sense of our divine nature. We are bearers of eternity and feel impelled to realize and instantiate that capacity. Sin makes us mortal, but our godly nature is still intact, reflected in the urge to have children.

Section Three: Time and Individuation

The homily has thus far been grounded in issues suggested by biblical narratives and themes: Miriam's death and water, Eden and sin, mortality and survival, children and eternity. This next section turns to more overtly mystical ideas, introducing the principle of generativity (*holadot*) as the core of the kabbalistic process of creation. The *sefirot*—the ten manifestations of the unnamed infinite—are conceived here as dynamic foci of incessant propagation. Popular introductions to the Kabbalah typically display the *sefirot* as circular foci arrayed in stable triadic groups. This can be misleading, since it suggests that the *sefirot* are static characterizations of divinity with fixed positions. It is better to think of them as dynamic constellations interacting with and shaping each other in an ever-fluid cosmic divine dance. The *sefirot* reveal the Absolute turning toward Being in a great chain, and this concatenation is ever-unfolding in relational exchange, an inter-sefirotic cascade that is supple, vital, endlessly fertile. As Shapira puts it, "[T]he main activity of the [parallel, superimposed] worlds [described in Lurianic Kabbalah] and the *sefirot* is generativity and incessant novelty."[10]

Next, Shapira cites a famous comment by the medieval commentator Rashi on Gen 1:1: "Initially, God intended to create the world to be governed under the rule of strict justice (*middat ha-din*), but God realized that the world could not thus endure and therefore gave precedence to divine mercy and affiliated it with divine justice (*middat ha-rahamim*)." This dictum is conventionally understood to mean that God had originally wanted the world (and in particular, humanity) to be governed by a strict principle of reward and punishment. Sins would trigger swift and inescapable retribution. But God saw that the world could not survive under such a regime, and God tempered *din* with *rahamim* (mercy). *Din* is justice, judgment, and rigor. When carefully measured and titrated, it is important for the smooth running of the world; it is the basis of all legal systems and standards of assessment. When it is allowed to swell excessively, however, it may morph into undue severity and even malevolence. As Gershom Scholem pointed out, one kabbalistic explanation for evil is that it represents the "hypertrophy of *din*."[11] *Rahamim* is the principle of compassion that sweetens *din,* keeping the principle of rigor in check and saving it from its own temptation to immoderation.

In a creative rereading of this dictum, Shapira frames the terms rather differently. Instead of opposing dispensations held in balance, polar modes of adjudicating the world pulling in contrary directions that must temper each other, they become two possibilities of the temporal unfolding of being. As we saw in the previous section, God is revealed in generativity. But the principle of *din* is now understood to mean continual creation. Here, Shapira invites us to imagine a counter-world, a kabbalistic thought experiment. In this world, everything is in ceaseless, constant flux. There is no permanence, for absolutely everything is subject to continual and immediate change. Every state of being instantaneously collapses into another state. A close analogy to what Shapira has in mind is the world of quantum mechanics, where many elementary particles are fundamentally unstable, decaying into other particles that in turn may be annihilated, only detectable by the traces they leave in a cloud chamber. These resonances come into being—if "being" is the right term—for an instant and immediately change to some other state or resonance. They are virtual particles whose fate is to vanish in a flash into another particle or particles. This is the way Shapira wants us to imagine a world governed solely by *middat ha-din*: it would be a web of ceaseless flux and impermanence.

As he puts it, "Divine self-disclosure is through acts of creation: continual creation in an ongoing, endlessly cascading sequence." But creation is one thing, and endurance is another. Human existence requires a measure of duration. Durative time is necessary for a unique personality to develop, for acts of agency, for the ability to innovate and the freedom to make mistakes; in a word: for individuation.

A world governed by pure *din* could not endure in any meaningful human sense. It would have no permanence, no possibility of stability consistent with identity formation. In such a world, human beings would not be possible, for to be human means to have the opportunity to develop a personality that is fluid yet ripens toward a coherent sense of self. Therefore, God combined the principle of *din* with *middat ha-rahamim,* the principle of compassion. This principle is now understood as the durative temporality to develop, to grow, to err, to recover, to pick up where one has left off and carry forward. *Rahamim* slows the pace of change just enough so that human personality, with all its imperfections, false starts, stumbles, and linked recoveries, has room to grow and be nurtured. To be human requires a delicate balance of permanence and change. In a world of pure *middat ha-din,* all existents would be no more than vectors of generativity, ceaselessly collapsing into other states or resonances in an endless sequence. *Middat ha-rahamim* allows for growth out of the ground of imperfection, a modified stability that affords an ample yet limited lifespan. The yearning for permanent survival, for the image of God embedded in humans, is still evident, expressed in the urge to have children. In the parlance of classic rabbinic theology, to be human is to have *behirah,* freedom of choice, including freedom to sin. This entails that each individual life will come to closure, yet human beings still leave tracks pointing to eternity, through their progeny.

And "progeny" here does not only mean one's biological children. Shapira adduces the talmudic teaching that "when a person teaches Torah to someone else's child, Scripture accounts it as if they had given birth to that child." He explains that teaching Torah "is like inter-sefirotic generation: to teach someone Torah is to cultivate and reveal their inner luminosity and holiness." Having a hand in the spiritual growth of another person, especially a child, is as significant as giving birth to biological progeny—in a kabbalistic sense, perhaps even more significant.

Section Four: Schoolchildren as the Face of the Shekhinah

The fourth section of the sermon continues the theme of teaching Torah, now evoking the motif that "schoolchildren are the face of the Shekhinah." Teaching—the elicitation of new insight and realization in another person, especially a young person—is the very essence of what it means to create; it is a this-worldly parallel to inter-sefirotic generativity. Nothing partakes of divinity more than assisting in the moral, intellectual, and spiritual formation of another person, especially a young person whose physical and spiritual growth are unfolding in tandem. Schoolchildren, in their openness, energetic vitality, and eagerness to learn, are the embodied personification of divinity's cutting edge. In the faces of children, one can discern the leading surface of godly generativity. Furthermore, as noted above, one's progeny are emissaries to the future, voyagers of the self sent ahead in time to stake out a claim that gestures to eternity. A tragic consequence of the sacredness and vulnerability of children is that they are often the first targets of attack by malevolent actors who wish to harm not just Jews but God's very self. Furthermore, to murder children (as R.

Shapira had now witnessed in the Ghetto) is to reach into the afterlife (the "Garden of Eden," in his words, where individual souls retain their identities and enjoy beatific awareness) and harm their departed parents, since the prospects of the dead for survival in the earthly plane are bound up with the fate of their descendants. To murder the children of those already slain is thus to slay the dead a second time. The rabbi writes, "Even now [June 1942], to our great distress, we see that, beyond all the astonishingly sadistic, murderous actions directed against us, the house of Israel, the sadism and murderous actions directed against little boys and girls exceeds everything. Woe! What has befallen us?!"

Section Five: The Omnipresence of God, the Preciousness of Individuals, the Suffering of Children

Section five is by far the longest of all the sections (for specifics, see footnote).[12] It exceeds the other sections not just in lines of text but also in its wide range of mood and register. R. Shapira writes:

> Every Israelite person[13] believes that "there is none else beside him" (Deut 4:35). Our mystical literature interprets this verse to mean not only that there is no other deity beside him but that there is no existence at all in the universe other than him; the entire universe and all that is within it is the luminous aura of divinity. For that reason, nothing in the world should be taken as an isolated entity, an existent unto itself, but rather as God's aura. So it is with progeny, Israelite children: one must not take them to be an isolated class. One should not think of them as "our children" [in a proprietary sense]. Rather, think of children as living exemplars of the cosmic processes of creation and innovation. Children reveal divinity in this world. They also represent Israel's linkage to eternity. So it is with Torah study: the Torah that we learn with little children, or collegial Torah study with friends, or moments when we give ethical instruction and spiritual direction. One should not think of these activities as isolated endeavors [set apart from a broader, more expansive horizon of meaning]. Rather, they are supernal processes, enactments of divine revelation. They are manifestations of cosmic renewal and generativity.

Think this way: at first your interlocutor was not a scholar of Torah, not a person of cultivated ethical sensibility, and now [in part as a result of your instruction], he has been given new life, transformed into a Torah scholar, an exemplar of moral stature and noble disposition. To cite the talmudic dictum again, teaching someone else is like giving birth to that person. Indeed, all acts of regeneration and creation are revelations of divinity, since there is nothing other than God, no other entity in existence. It follows that everything an Israelite person does and says is really, in their heart of hearts, directed to God. The person's soul knows that there is nothing other than God, that everything is divinity; the soul is already directing all action and speech toward God. But human corporeality hides this, just as it hides the soul's holiness and yearning for God. It only appears to the person that he is engaged in activities and saying words relevant to physical needs, [while in actuality these are mundane projections of higher-order spiritual aspirations]. And when we ask another Israelite for a favor, the soul knows that only God can grant the favor, and the human to whom we are making the request is just God's messenger. [On the conscious level,] we may think that we're asking a specific person for the favor, but our soul within is beseeching God, who has the power to grant all things, who as compassionate parent will have compassion and deliver us. When we hear victims crying in agony, *ratevet, ratevet* [Help! Help!], we must know that this is their soul's cry—indeed, the cry of us all to God the compassionate parent, *rateve, rateve*, while there is still a spark of life within us. It is indeed astonishing that the world still stands after so many such cries. . . . Innocent children, pure angels, are being killed and slaughtered just because they are Israelites. . . . They fill the entire space of the cosmos with their cries—and yet the world does not revert to primordial liquidity. It remains standing, as if God were unmoved, heaven forfend! . . . It is incomprehensible [why the cries do not burst through all barriers, reach God's ears, and provoke immediate intervention to save them]. Surely, we are not alone in our prayers. Surely our ancestors—our patriarchs and matriarchs, all the male and female prophets [*nevi'im u-nevi'ot*], all the saintly men and women [*tsaddikim ve-tsadkaniyot*] are not resting, not silent in the face of our distress. Surely, they are raising an uproar, shaking up the Edenic afterworld and all the heavenly chambers with the magnitude of our calamity. Surely, they are not taking comfort in the complacent suggestion that "in any event the people of Israel will survive." [This is entirely inadequate, since] one must suspend the sanctity of Sabbath in order to save even one Israelite in danger. Tsaddikim in this world prayed not only for the community but for each individual Israelite person. Surely now [in the afterworld] they are raising a furor on behalf of each Israelite.

This section begins with a reference to the classic Hasidic teaching of acosmism, the doctrine that denies ultimate reality to the cosmos. Perhaps the most famous and forceful articulation of this teaching is that of Rabbi Shneur Zalman of Liadi, the founder of Chabad Hasidism, in his *Gate of Unity and Faith*. He writes,

If the eye was permitted to see and perceive the living force and the spiritual essence of each created being, bestowed upon it from the source of God's mouth and the breath of His mouth, the physicality of the created being and its materiality and reality would not appear at all to our eyes. For its existence is really negated in relation to the living force and spirituality that is within it. . . . Accordingly "there is nothing else beside Him," in truth.[14]

Yet Shapira immediately reframes this classic Hasidic doctrine in a manner that encourages the development of an individual spiritual self (see Maayan, this volume), countering the temptation to understand the dictum that "there is nothing other than God" as a negation of the world, or at least a negation of the value of particulars. If everything is God, as early Hasidic sources emphasize, then one may be prone to see all existence as homogeneous and undifferentiated, without meaningful texture and granularity. In particular, erasure of difference might seem to leave little room for the flourishing of individual human beings. So, consistent with the rest of his corpus and indeed with his entire life's work, Shapira endeavors to show how the omnipresence of God can foster awareness of the uniqueness and inestimable significance of individuals (see Seeman, this volume). The mysticism here is not one of negation of the world and absorption into the Absolute but of the centrality and sacredness of unique individuals, especially children. It follows that there is momentous significance to participating in the creation of other persons, whether by biological generativity (procreation) or in the formation of mind and spirit by teaching Torah. Divinity is everywhere, but the traces of the divine are to be found in the nodal points where one human being interacts with another in positive ways, fostering the development of the divine face that is the living, growing human being.

Section five also contains a passage of extreme emotion, an intense and unsuppressed cry of pain, no doubt provoked by an atrocity he had witnessed, still raw in his mind. "When we hear victims crying in agony, *ratevet, ratevet* [Help! Help!] we must know that this is their soul's cry—indeed the cry of us all to God, the compassionate parent, *ratevet, rateve,* while there is still a spark of life within us." This kind of outburst is quite unusual for the rabbi, who generally keeps his emotions in check and writes with a sobriety and judicious balance that is quite astonishing given the circumstances.[15] Yet here he allows his agony to burst forth onto the page. Evidently, children under fearful torture were crying desperately for help,[16] with parents and onlookers unable to save them. Perhaps even more troubling, it seemed that God himself was indifferent to those cries, cries that should have shaken the world to its foundations. Eschewing the lame consolation that while individuals may die, the Jewish people as a whole will survive, he conjures a vivid image of departed saints mounting a loud protest in the afterworld, demanding divine intervention.

Section Six: Miriam as Model for Bold Religious Initiative; Moses as Model of Leadership through Imperfection

The last section of the sermon for *parashat hukkat* 1942 recaps the main themes of the homily and returns to the framing questions posed in section one: What is the relationship between Miriam's death and the lack of water in the desert? How is it possible to understand the "sin" of Moses in this context? Articulating and distilling the core message, it lifts up the individual strands and weaves them into a thickly textured tapestry, providing a powerful thematic resolution.

In conclusion: There is nothing other than God. Everything is divinity's aura. All modalities of generativity and origination—

including the act of teaching another person—are not isolated activities but revelatory moments of divine illumination. Even our freely chosen good deeds are ultimately attributable to God—since there is nothing other, no other than God. [But if so, what room is there for human initiative?] What is left for the person to do? We can ask that God inspire us with the desire to choose the good, with awareness of what "good" is. . . . [There is a virtuous circle here. Understanding what holiness is, its value and transformative power, leads to deeper and more intense desire to approach God.] A yearning person will work to prepare himself, to make himself worthy to receive holy light, supernal desire, and awareness. Returning now to Miriam: She was the leader whose good deeds were self-generated, not a response to prior divine command. This indicates that the spiritual elevation she achieved, the commanding heights of her virtue, were the result of an abundance of intense yearning that came from within her. So as long as Miriam was alive, she was able to transmit her mode of service to the rest of Israel, sparking them to feel yearning for God and enabling them to be worthy of receiving the supernal lights channeled by Moses. But when she passed away, their yearning dissipated, and they were no longer able to receive Moses's supernal light. Moses needed to find a way to restore their internal yearning, to rouse them and elevate them, but in a manner that would be appropriate for them, not for him. How to do this? He was compelled to meet them at their level by doing something that would be considered a sin for him, a sin related to theirs. The people bickered about water, and Moses—in bringing forth water—disobeyed an aspect of God's command, hitting the rock rather than speaking to it. He inclined himself to the people's level by contravening the precise terms of God's command, generating the need for his own repentance. By placing himself in the role of sinner, he was able to bond with the people. If you are attempting to lift up others in need, you must share their predicament. Moses yearned to return to a fully right relationship with God, and that yearning was transmitted to the people. Thus, Moses found a way to substitute for Miriam's self-generated yearning. He did indeed lift up the people and effected the return of the overflowing wellspring. And along with the return of the water, there came a rush of spiritual bounty and great deliverance.

Summary and Discussion

We now survey this *derashah* as a whole, reviewing the individual sections, tracing common threads, and discerning unifying themes.

Section one launches with a midrash-inflected reading of Num 20:1–3, deployed to assert the unique significance of women's spirituality. Such an emphasis is unusual even today in the tradition-bound society of Hasidism and was still more so in Shapira's day.[17] Miriam serves as a biblical exemplar for autonomous spiritual yearning, establishing a domain that in some measure avoids the ineluctable attribution of virtue to God. Miriam's spirituality is self-generated, drawing upon her own inner resources. In this approach, men's religious practice is always commanded by God and therefore not truly innovative. The religious acts of men are always in response to a prior heavenly call and therefore can never be considered the result of their own initiative. Women, however, are not obligated to fulfill temporally linked commandments, so when they take the initiative to do so, they achieve autonomous, self-generated stature.

Section two also focuses on biblical texts read through a rabbinic lens, beginning with Num 20:11, in which Moses strikes the rock to bring forth water for his people. For reasons that only become clear much later in the homily, the rabbi then moves to the topic of parents and children, beginning with Gen 48:15, Jacob's blessing to Joseph, which turns out to be Jacob's blessing to Joseph's *children*. Then the focus turns to death and the limits on the human lifespan, understood as a consequence of the sin in the Garden of Eden (Gen 3:19). Conversely, Deut 14:1 suggests that as "children of God," we have an impulse for permanence, a yearning for eternity expressed in the desire for progeny. Shapira's reading of these sources is supported by contemporary scholars who note that the biblical cultural milieu "understands the self in familial, transgenerational terms" and that in the biblical period death did not have the finality that it has in our own culture, "with a more individualistic, atomistic understanding of the self."[18]

Section three moves on to a kabbalistic development of the themes of limited lifespan and survival through children. Divine compassion (*rahamim*) enables individuals to survive and develop into robust yet fragile personalities. In a bold interpretive move, the rabbi frames the old Talmudic-midrashic phrase *middat ha-rahamim* as describing the moderation of a primal rate of change, a disposition that allows for the emergence of human personhood, flawed and shadowed by death yet buoyed by constant opportunity for improvement and self-correction and impelled by an internal divine spark to seek eternity through progeny. The rabbi's thinking here may be helpfully illuminated by the words of a recent expositor of Bible and Kabbalah who does not mention the work of Shapira but whose writing is very congenial to it. I refer to the late Charles Mopsik, who, in an important article called "The Body of Engenderment," writes:

> A single notion qualifies cosmogonic becoming and human genealogy: in both cases the text employs the term *toledot*, which can be translated as either "engenderments," "begettings" or "generation." . . . The process of creation and the process of procreation, though different, are designated by the same vocable, which implies that the concept of human generation and filiation is rightfully inscribed within the divine creative movement, that procreation merely continues cosmogenesis, that it is a later stage of cosmogenesis.[19] . . . By reproducing, religious man imitates the divine work of the original organization of the cosmos and his procreative act is perhaps considered as the ritual reenactment of cosmogony.[20]

Section four amplifies these themes further, focusing on schoolchildren, exemplars of growth on the cusp of bodily, emotional, intellectual, and spiritual development. The "face of the Shekhinah" is a human being in dynamic process, the leading edge of emergent personhood. To assist in the healthy growth of such a being is akin to participating in sefirotic propagation. Teaching Torah is truly a divine activity.

Section five begins with the classic Hasidic formulation of acosmism, but the point is not the dissolution of the self or the negation of one's being. Personality is not transcended but developed and refined, without ego-attachment or self-absorption. In a very powerful passage within this section, Shapira reminds his readers that parents should not view their children in a proprietary manner. Parents ought not be thinking of "our children," as he puts it. Similarly, teachers cannot claim ownership—

intellectual or otherwise—of their disciples. The relationship is recast as a metaphysical one: the parent or the teacher is participating in a divine process of birthing new personality, of character formation. This surely has the result of setting one's children and students free to find their own path, but in this context, it functions as sober and painful pastoral advice to soften the blow of death. Losing a child—as Shapira did—is the worst fate a parent could imagine, yet the rabbi is reminding himself and others that children never belong to parents as possessions. They are not property or assets to be grasped, held onto, or, God forbid, lost to death but are the face of divinity that one has been privileged to engender and mentor. Hasidic acosmism is marshaled in the service of individuation, dialogical relationship, and some measure of pastoral easing of pain.

The sixth and final section draws together all the themes of the sermon. Since "everything is an aura of divinity," the real religious question is: What room is there for personhood, for freedom of choice, for the action of the individual in a world where all is divine? The response returns us to Miriam and her wellspring and later to Moses hitting the rock. Miriam is the model of self-generated yearning, and Moses is the exemplar of the near-perfect leader adopting the burden of imperfection in order to identify with his flawed people to channel yearning, clearing space for return and growth. Moses's "sin" was a replacement for the loss of Miriam's self-generated religious initiative, her wellspring of yearning. The personalities of Miriam and Moses shine precisely at the moment they display autonomy and initiative, when they seemingly defy the mystical narrative of "all-is-God." While the formula *ein od milvado* (there is nothing other than God) is evoked, the formula is deployed differently from the way it was typically understood in early Hasidism. Rather than the dissolution of particulars into the monistic One, it conveys the emergence and embodiment of particulars from the One, especially in human individuation and development. All-embracing divinity does not absorb everything back into itself so much as it propagates by transmission from node to node in an ever-expanding relational lattice that we call birthing, teaching, and mentoring. To quote Mopsik again:

> By mating and procreating man furthers the theophanic lineage—each new generation is thus a stage . . . of the manifestation of God in time. God does not fulfill [God's] being in one individual at one unique moment. In order to

move toward [God's] fulfillment, in order to be personified [God] must pass into time's texture woven by the threads of engenderment.[21]

Coda: Miriam Shows the Way of Leadership to Moses

We now see the six sections—the biblical interpretations, the kabbalistic expositions, the cries of pain and protest, the theology of personalism, the references to his own situation—coalescing. Because the human condition is biologically and temporally bounded, the importance of what we leave for others is heightened. We savor the sanctity of the particular the more we grasp the pervading immanence of the absolute. The mystic maxim of acosmism, "There is nothing other than divinity," points to the irreducible granularity of existence and to the sacredness of human life, with its shout of joys and, tragically, its desperate calls for help. Divinity emergent in the world is embedded in an ever-propagating distributed network, and divinity's leading edge—the face of the Shekhinah—is the face of the child: vulnerable, open, vitally keen to grow and learn.

The focus on Miriam and women's spiritual autonomy, the motivation for Moses's puzzling disobedience in striking the rock, the framing of human existence on the cusp of persistence versus perishability, and the fragile holiness of children: these are all ways of reserving a space for human initiative, enabling agency and creative movement, unencumbered by the overwhelming weight of omnipresent divinity, despite this being the undisputed cornerstone of Hasidic theology, including R. Shapira's own. We might also suggest that by focusing on Miriam and Moses, the rabbi is alluding to his own situation, bereft of his own wife, Miriam, grieving the death of his son, and fearful for the fate of his daughter, struggling to lead his flock with some measure of hope and comfort, perhaps "hitting the rock"—imploring God with uncharacteristically sharp cries of pain and protest—seeing everything through the eyes of a chastened yet deeper faith.[22]

What the rabbi offers us here is not so much a philosophical or theological system but rather a devotional stance. It will be recalled that he emphasizes again and again that his goal is not some graspable ultimate Truth (which, he avers, remains unreachable) but rather *remez le-inyan avodah*—pointers, hints for sacred service and devotional practice. He is offering a way to think about the human condition, about birth, growth, death, and the way one person may beneficently influence another by inspiration, mentoring, and teaching.

The horrors of the moment are not divorced from this perspective. They are gazed at directly from within it. That gaze does not diminish their pain, does not make them more palatable or understandable. But it does give the believer a language to give meaningful voice to that pain, to protest, to remain present and engaged, to retain hope, to participate in the pain of others, including the pain of God.

I hope to have demonstrated the benefit of seeing a *derashah* as a whole rather than as merely a resource for mining, piecemeal. This sermon is cohesive in all its parts and its meaning emerges most powerfully when we keep all the parts in our awareness simultaneously (see also Wiskind, this volume). This approach highlights the importance of Daniel Reiser's edition, which provides unprecedented access to the original work, its layers, unfolding, and structure. In addition, I hope to have indicated the great importance of this particular teaching, *parashat hukkat* 5702. Rather than attempting to offer an explanation for what was transpiring, the sermon shuttles between theological polarities, each of which is inadequate in isolation: immanence and transcendence; autonomy and heteronomy; the infinite preciousness and holiness of humans, especially children, versus the reality of horrific attacks aimed specifically at the most vulnerable. Only by shuttling between opposites, only by traversing the places in between, could Shapira authentically respond to both the extremity of the evil on the one hand and the windows of blessed possibility that he still perceived on the other. Not a position paper, not a theodicy (compare Magid and Seeman, this volume), it may well be the single most profound Hasidic teaching delivered and written at the very precipice of destruction.

This is quite an agenda for any single discourse. Coming shortly before the so-called Great Deportation—the nearly total annihilation of the Warsaw Ghetto and the brutal removal of its inhabitants to their destruction—I see it as a self-aware reflection on Shapira's own role and the legacy he wished to leave, a kind of spiritual will for posterity. The biblical exegesis, kabbalistic and Hasidic motifs, and descriptions of heartrending contemporary events are all aspects of a coherent composition, traversing the widest emotional and theological range imaginable. Together, they stand as a testament to a truly great spirit, who described himself in early 1943, just as he was consigning his manuscript to the hidden Ringelblum archive, as "one who is broken and crushed from my sorrows and the sorrows of Israel, sorrows as profound as the Great Deep and reaching as high as the highest heaven; one who waits for God's salvation, which comes in the blink of an eye."

Notes

1. Kalonymus Kalman Shapira, *Sermons from the Years of Rage* [in Hebrew], ed. Daniel Reiser, 2 vols. (Jerusalem: Herzog Academic College, 2017), 1:224–32; 2:232–39.

2. I am drawing upon my observations in *Holy Fire: The Teachings of Rabbi Kalonymus Shapira, the Rebbe of the Warsaw Ghetto* (Northvale, NJ: Jason Aronson, 1994), 33–34.

3. Ibid., 146.

4. I am simplifying a very large body of interpretive opinions on how to understand the nature of Moses's misstep, but for our purposes it is sufficient to mention the view of Rashi that forms the basis of Shapira's exposition.

5. B. Ta'anit 9a, in the name of R. Yose b. Yehudah.

6. Rashi, based on b. Ta'anit 9a.

7. B. Mo'ed Katan 28a.

8. Maimonides draws upon the notion of death by divine kiss in his *Guide of the Perplexed* (3.51). For him, it exemplifies "spiritual death in rapture," as discussed by Michael Fishbane, *The Kiss of God: Spiritual and Mystical Death in Judaism* (Seattle: University of Washington Press, 1994), esp. 24–27. For Maimonides, the kiss signifies union with the divine intellect. But this interpretation does not address why the Torah did not tell us directly that Miriam as well as her brothers died by the divine kiss. This is particularly enigmatic in light of the common assertion that the Hebrew God is really above gender. As Peter Eli Gordon observes, "There is something quite odd in Maimonides' reluctance to speak of God's kissing Miriam." See Peter Eli Gordon, "The Erotics of Negative Theology: Maimonides on Apprehension," *Jewish Studies Quarterly* 2 (1995): 1–38. This comment is on 34n71.

9. Zohar 1:211b.

10. Reiser, volume I: 301.

11. See Gershom Scholem, *Major Trends in Jewish Mysticism* (New York: Schocken, 1995), 405n108 and 411n54.

12. Shapira's writing spans ninety-two manuscript lines (see volume two). Reiser carefully preserves the rabbi's original line arrangement, it being understood that in many cases—especially when the original manuscript line is augmented by a marginal amplification—it was necessary to transcribe a single original line onto two or three printed lines, indicated by a hanging indent. The typographical convention of hanging indent signals that, allowing for the page layout constraints

of the printed book, we are tracking a single line of the original manuscript, together with any associated marginal notes.

Assigning numbers to each line of the derashah, the first section runs from line one through line eleven, for a total of eleven lines. The second section goes from line twelve through line twenty-three, for twelve lines. The third section covers lines twenty-four through forty-one, eighteen lines. The fourth section spans lines forty-two to fifty-three, for twelve lines. The fifth section spans lines fifty-four through eighty-one, for twenty-eight lines. The sixth and final section runs from line eighty-two through ninety-two, eleven lines. In tabular format:

Section one—11 lines
Section two—12 lines
Section three—18 lines
Section four—12 lines
Section five—28 lines
Section six—11 lines

13. Translation note: When referring to members of his community, the rabbi generally uses "person of Israel" or "Israelite" rather than the more familiar "Jewish person" or "Jew." This is clearly a deliberate choice, and my English rendition tracks these terms.

14. Translation by Mark Verman, from his essay "Panentheism and Acosmism in the Kabbalah," *Studia Mystica* 10, no. 2 (1987): 24–37 (with minor modifications).

15. For discussion of this feature of the text, see Don Seeman, "Ritual Efficacy, Hasidic Mysticism and 'Useless Suffering' in the Warsaw Ghetto," *Harvard Theological Review* 101 (2008): 465–505.

16. According to Adolf Berman, "The Fate of the Children in the Warsaw Ghetto," in *The Catastrophe of European Jewry: Antecedents-History-Reflections*, ed. Yisrael Gutman and Livia Rothkirchen (Jerusalem: Yad Vashem, 1976), 400–421, the first Aktion aimed against children took place on July 22, 1942. This teaching was delivered on June 27; evidently, brutal outrages took place before the Aktion began in earnest. Berman writes that "the children sensed the danger threatening them and resisted the police, struggled with them, and tried to escape. The streets echoed with the heart-rending screams and crying of children" (ibid., 421).

17. We might add here that the association of Miriam with water is already noticeable in earlier biblical narratives that are not explicitly mentioned but hover in the background, such as Exod 2:4–10 and 15:20–21.

18. These formulations are drawn from Kevin J. Madigan and Jon D. Levenson, *Resurrection and the Restoration of Israel: The Ultimate Victory of the God of Life* (New Haven: Yale University Press, 2008), 107.

19. Charles Mopsik, "The Body of Engenderment in the Hebrew Bible, the Rabbinic Tradition and the Kabbalah," in *Fragments for a History of the Human Body*, ed. Michel Feher with Ramona Nadaff and Nadia Tazi (Cambridge: MIT Press, 1989), 1:51.

20. Ibid., 53.

21. Ibid., 61.

22. The self-referential aspect is underscored when we note that his wife's name was Miriam (Rahel Hayyah Miriam) and that she died on Shabbat parashat hukkat, 10 Tammuz 5697 (1937). This teaching is in part a eulogy for his wife and a reflection on the rabbi's own situation, bereft of his life partner but still charged with leading his community in an unprecedented crisis. It also bears remembering that the passages on losing children were directly and painfully relevant for Shapira, whose beloved son Elimelekh Ben-Zion was severely wounded during the initial bombing of Warsaw in September 1939 and who died days later after agonizing attempts to save his life. His daughter Rekhell Yehudis was still alive at this time, but she was deported a few months later, before the burial of the manuscript.

10

Raging against Reason

Overcoming Sekhel in R. Shapira's Thought

JAMES A. DIAMOND

Kalonymus Kalman Shapira, the Piaseczner Rebbe, spent his last years theologizing, sermonizing, and writing in the Warsaw Ghetto. Like Franz Rosenzweig before him, who wrote much of the *Star of Redemption*, his philosophical magnum opus, under the extreme conditions of a war-ravaged landscape during World War I, R. Shapira produced his own theologically tormented masterpiece within an environment designed for the sole purpose of generating suffering—a death space. This chapter addresses Shapira's paradoxical adaptation of Maimonidean rationalism in service of his own mystical-Hasidic attempt to overcome rationalism in the context of extreme suffering.

My aim here is to further advance an argument that I have presented elsewhere: that the full force of R. Shapira's exegetical strategy can be appreciated only in light of the long history of engagement with Maimonidean thought from the Middle Ages to the modern period.[1] I will also elaborate on how this striking transformation of a bedrock of Maimonides's Aristotelian epistemology into a Hasidic mystical theology of suffering serves as the logical culmination of R. Shapira's own prewar engagement with Maimonides. This revamped theology was made necessary by heightened fear and awareness of the "rage" (za'am) that R. Shapira understood as the defining characteristic of the escalating devastation unfolding around him from the beginning of the war until his death in 1943. Thus, it is crucial to probe what R. Shapira meant by the term *za'am*, which he used in the title of his Holocaust-era sermons.

Setting the Stage for Dealing with *Za'am*

Daniel Reiser's new edition of R. Shapira's collection wisely preserves his original title, "Sermons from the Years of Rage," rather than the more commonly known "Holy Fire" (*Esh kodesh*), chosen by the Piaseczner Hasidim who edited the original edition.[2] While their choice of a title containing an allusion to R. Shapira's own name as well as to the martyrs (*kedoshim*) who went up in flames was well intentioned, it undermines the author's original design and risks essentializing his work. The Hebrew term *za'am*, which Shapira chose to describe the period in which he delivered his sermons, will be shown to be central to his conception of the events befalling his community and to the context of the spiritual response he mounts to this challenge. We should therefore follow his lead and choose terms with great care.

In a sermon from July 1940, Shapira cites a talmudic source describing an infinitesimal moment (*rega*) that occurs daily, when God is said to be gripped by "rage" (*za'am*) toward his people. Balaam, the Israelites' biblical nemesis, is described as having a unique talent for pinpointing and exploiting these moments to release a force of divine rage and annihilation upon Israel. The Talmud then extols God's beneficence for never having succumbed to this *za'am*, for had he done so, "there would have been not a single remnant in Israel." The prooftext for this divine suppression of *za'am* is Balaam's assertion of the futility of any initiative that runs counter to divine will: *How can I rage against whom the Lord has not raged?* (Num 23:8).[3] Though R. Shapira expresses the conviction that Israel will withstand its suffering and ultimately prevail over its enemies, there is nevertheless a revealing "instant" in this sermon at which he contemplates the possibility of total national obliteration. In horror, he imagines that "should the suffering last any longer, heaven forbid (*has ve-shalom*), it will consist of an assault on the 'essential dimension of Israel' that affords it everlastingness."[4]

It is inconceivable that a man as intimately absorbed in the language of his tradition as R. Shapira would have chosen the term *rage* (*za'am*) arbitrarily. His choice of a title for his book as he prepared to consign it for burial with the rest of the Ringelblum archives in 1943 must have resonated with that 1940 sermon and with other uses of the term *zaʿam* that were familiar to him from biblical and rabbinic literature.[5] The term appears in his Ghetto sermons as well as in some of the prewar sermons that he continued to edit throughout the Ghetto period.[6]

Another rabbinic source that R. Shapira would certainly have known identifies "wisdom," *hokhmah,* as an instrument of protection against the rage (*zaʿam*) posed by a powerful human king.[7] I would suggest that R. Shapira's portrayal of the situation in the Warsaw Ghetto is in conversation with this text, since the Jews were exposed to chaotic, destructive forces of *zaʿam* against which "wisdom" in its colloquial sense had lost any of the potency it may once have held. This is where Shapira enlists Maimonides in a surprising reversal of this rabbinic source, whereby *zaʿam* becomes, as it were, the positive catalyst for overcoming reason, here portrayed as an *obstacle* to spiritual salvation. This claim requires some unpacking.

Many passages in the Ghetto sermons (see Polen, Magid, Leib Smokler, this volume) reveal the depths of deprivation with which inhabitants of the Ghetto were confronted. R. Shapira's own experience of suffering defied all reason, historical, political, or theological. So it is ironic that he resorts to Maimonides, the most celebrated exponent of Jewish rationalism, to find a way to persist in that realm beyond reason. Maimonides, who not only holds reason supreme in his philosophical works but grounds his entire code of Jewish law in "knowing" (*daʿat*), is the last thinker one would imagine being able to offer theological solace when reason was no longer equipped to respond to the madness that engulfed R. Shapira and his community.[8] I believe that this counterintuitive reliance on Maimonides is best understood as an expression of a longstanding endeavor by Jewish thinkers of many kinds to hold onto Maimonides at any cost.[9] Medieval rationalists, including Maimonides, responded to the problem of evil by negating its positive reality, which they attributed solely to the "privation of good." Faced with the experience of "radical" evil in the Warsaw Ghetto, however, Shapira creatively and desperately invokes Maimonides himself in an effort to overcome the inadequacy of that position. The view that evil is merely the absence of good and therefore not attributable to any positive act of a Creator God stands impotent in the face of the palpable suffering in the Ghetto and the soon-to-be-discovered horror of a million children systematically gassed and burned.[10] Zoharic and Lurianic Kabbalah had already opted for a view of evil as a substantive force in the world even to the point of locating its source in the Godhead itself.[11]

If the philosophical dismissal of evil as an illusion fell short in the Middle Ages, it was certainly untenable in the context of the horrors of the Shoah. As Gershom Scholem wrote, "It is cold comfort to those who are genuinely plagued by fear and sorrow to be told that their troubles are but the workings of their own imagination."[12]

To gain a sense of how theologically destitute R. Shapira was rendered by a few years of life in the Ghetto, it is important to consider a note of retraction that he famously appended, at the end of 1942, to a sermon he had delivered earlier during Hanukkah of December 1941. In that original sermon, Shapira decried those who believed that Ghetto suffering outstripped other examples of suffering throughout Jewish history, rendering them superfluous. At the time, R. Shapira had urged his readers to remain steadfast in the knowledge that their own plight was no different, intrinsically, from those their ancestors had survived since ancient times. As Magid (this volume) describes at length, however, by late 1942, R. Shapira had changed his mind. In a remarkable gesture of intellectual and theological courage, he appended a note to his earlier sermon admitting that events had proven him wrong. In this note, he frankly admits that as far as "the monstrous torments, the terrible and freakish deaths which the malevolent murderers invented against us, the House of Israel, from that point on [the middle of 1942]—according to my *knowledge of rabbinic literature and Jewish history* in general, there has never been anything like them"[13] (emphasis added).

In Shapira's thought, then, the Holocaust confronts us with a historical *novum*, a manifestation of evil so heinously novel as to constitute a "rupture" that literally shatters the causal historical continuum.[14] Shapira's careful articulation of the Shoah's uniqueness measures it against both history and what he would have considered the very essence of Jewish thought: rabbinic literature. The historical precedents he refers to—the destruction of the temple and Betar—are constituents of a kind of *Heilsgeschichte*, in which they signify far more than mere past events. They are rabbinically constructed as the quintessential Jewish tragedies, to which the classical rabbis responded legally and theologically in order to maintain and perpetuate their faith. These events thus form living theological, as well as historical, archetypes to which all Jews are meant to turn in times of pain and distress for their own spiritual sustenance. Yet by the end of 1942, this was no longer adequate.[15] Thus, the Hasidic rebbe, whose life and thought are filtered through the lens of the vast midrashic corpus of his rabbinic predecessors, remains completely vulnerable to the theological challenges of the radical evil of his own day. The momentous nature of this shift can be seen when his sermons from the "years of rage" are compared with his earlier sermons.

Like Maimonides in his *Guide of the Perplexed*, Shapira contemplates readers of different kinds engaging with his work. However, while Maimonides crafted his writing to accommodate wide disparities in the intellectual capacity of his readers, Shapira directs himself to two ontologically distinct audiences. Along what we might call the horizontal plane, his work is addressed to his own disintegrating community, offering hope, consolation, and motivation to persevere in the face of its increasingly diminishing prospects for survival. The relationship between Shapira and his Hasidim already points to a path beyond reason, moored as it is in an I-Thou encounter, "impossible to attain," as he writes elsewhere, "by things related to the intellect."[16] On the vertical plane, meanwhile, these writings assume a metaphysical tenor analogous to supplicatory or petitionary prayer (see Seeman, this volume). In that sense, they are also desperate appeals to rouse a seemingly oblivious God to live up to both his specific biblical characterization as a guardian of Israel and his universal role as Creator and architect of historical events.

Persecution, deprivation, and suffering were entrenched conditions of eastern European Jewry long before the advent of World War II. R. Shapira's Ghetto sermons were written in the same Hasidic tradition that motivated earlier Hasidic masters such as Dov Baer of Mezritsh, one of the pioneers of the Hasidic movement (see Idel, this volume). In the preface to his own classic work, Dov Baer testified that the force driving him to set pen to paper was "to inform the entire nation of God that our God has not abandoned us even during this bitter exile, sustained in this impure land, and that he has sent us great and insightful tsaddikim to sustain us."[17] Likewise, R. Shapira's sermons were not simply abstruse rabbinic homilies or detached ruminations on the meaning of suffering. Though the sermons were evoked by a life lived in painful extremis, Shapira never lost sight of the relationships that had always consumed him both with God and with his community. We can track the suffering in the Ghetto and its rapid deterioration historically to an exact time and place.[18] However, in a sense, suffering was also an opportunity for R. Shapira, since it is precisely suffering that jolts the righteous person, or the Hasidic master, to become conscious of his calling, for "God desires the prayers of the righteous."[19]

A 1929 sermon preserved in *Derekh ha-melekh* (see Wiskind, this volume) indicates the urgency and intensity this role must have assumed for Shapira later in the Ghetto. The sermon posits that God desires prayer and that suffering naturally evokes prayer from the righteous sufferer. The supplicant acknowledges the divine need for prayer, and since suffering evokes his prayer, the experience of suffering can also be conceived as being for God's benefit. R. Shapira then characterizes his suffering as a form of self-sacrifice for God's sake: "If I am fulfilling your will with this, and if I suffer for you because you desire my prayer, then I endure it all because of you." God responds with an empathic consolation, a quid pro quo of mutually advantageous suffering: "You suffer for me, and I will suffer for you."[20] Every sermon in the Ghetto can be appreciated within this paradigm of reciprocal suffering between R. Shapira and God. Like prayer, R. Shapira's sermons address God from the depths of unbearable agony. Each one, then, is in a sense a sufferer's prayer to God. The sermons are reenactments of the tortured relationship of reciprocal suffering between God and man intended to elicit a divine response that might alleviate that very suffering.

A Hasidic Rebbe Reads Maimonides

R. Shapira's process of engaging and reinventing Maimonides did not begin during his captivity in the Warsaw Ghetto. At this point, I mention just one of those prewar Maimonidean encounters, which lays the theological groundwork for R. Shapira's later adaptation of Maimonides in his Ghetto sermons. I choose this example because it strikes at the very heart of the Maimonidean project, which locates the core of Jewish life and practice in the mind rather than the deed. In this passage, Shapira essentially reinvents one of Maimonides's thirteen principles of faith as filtered through the popular *Ani ma'amin* version, an anonymously authored Hebrew adaptation that has become a standard part of Jewish daily prayer books since the middle of the sixteenth century.[21] The third of these principles posits God's incorporeality, asserting that "God is not a body, and that nothing material can attach to him, and that he is free of any form." In a classic midrashic mold, Shapira re-parses the principle to read "and *the nothing*, it apprehends [God] in corporeal terms" (emphasis added). Rather than exclude entirely any possibility of conceiving God anthropomorphically, Shapira reads the principle as actually *allowing* for such popular conceptions. He rereads it as a dispensation for an inferior "nothing" mode of knowing God indulged in by those "who only apprehend corporeal things and whose hearts and minds are filled with corporeal matters."[22] This kind of knowledge partially succeeds in approaching God because

God undergoes a process of self-limitation (*tsimtsum*), which allows his divinity to inhere in the material world, rendering it accessible through the world.[23] Thus, even the ignoramus can find his way toward God through the medium of the lowest rungs of existence.

What is important for our purposes is that R. Shapira here reads Maimonides against the grain of a philosophically abstruse conception of a purely immaterial God. He thus turns the principle that privileges abstraction, and theoretical reasoning as the only means of grasping that abstraction, on its head. Arthur Hyman goes so far as to consider Maimonides's third principle the only one that is wholly conceptual and asserts that it therefore serves as grounding for several others. As he puts it, "Of the five principles concerning God, that of Divine corporeality is the only one which guarantees *conceptual* knowledge of Him for all. . . . Once God is to be known as incorporeal, this knowledge can only be conceptual."[24] In R. Shapira's hands (and in line with much Hasidic immanentism), Maimonides's third principle demands precisely the opposite. It actually calls for concretizing God in the material world and dismisses the notion that philosophy and conceptualization are the exclusive means of apprehending God (see Maayan, this volume).

This radical overhauling of an intellectualized principle of belief chips away at Maimonides's advocacy of reason as the exclusive route toward God. In addition, by bridging what appears to be an unbridgeable impasse between the corporeal world and an incorporeal Being that shares nothing in common with that world, R. Shapira opens the door to invoking Maimonides again when he is confronted with the theological impasse posed by the inordinate suffering of the Warsaw Ghetto. He essentially reconfigures Maimonides into a Hasidic pantheist.[25] He transforms Maimonides's third principle, which is actually grounded in the absolute separation between God and the world—"There is, in truth, no relation in any respect between him and any of his creatures"—into an actual bridge between the two.[26] Shapira was not the first, as scholars of medieval Jewish mysticism have noted, to convert Maimonides and his philosophy into a "principal positive catalyzer of Jewish mysticism."[27]

Maimonides in the Warsaw Ghetto

In a passage from the third and final annual cycle of sermons in the Warsaw Ghetto (culminating in the summer of 1942), R. Shapira attempts to salvage some positive theological value from his pessimistic expectation of the implosion of the world to its originating chaos. He does so by returning to his rabbinic ideational homeland and his own prewar theology, searching beyond reason for the true plane of convergence between the human and the transcendent. We are now in a position to understand how that desperate reach beyond reason crucially hinges on a particular characteristic reading of Maimonides. The pertinent sermon was delivered on February 7, 1942 (*parashat yitro*), five months before the mass deportations from the Ghetto to the death camps began.[28] R. Shapira seizes on a verse in which "knowledge" (*da'at*) is central as an opportune starting point for his adaptation of Maimonides's theory of knowledge. God commands Moses to relate to the Israelites the importance and sanctity of Sabbath observance: "Go and inform them, to know that I, the Lord, have consecrated you" (Exod 31:13). R. Shapira then midrashically rereads the verse, broadening this "knowledge" that Moses conveys into an overarching principle underlying observance and piety. Maimonides's interpretation of "to know" in this verse is that Israel's Sabbath observance becomes an inspiring model of religious performance for members of other religions: "in order that the religious communities should know."[29] However, R. Shapira elides this natural understanding of "to know" as referring to informing others, opting instead for a mystical/Hasidic understanding of the term as referring to knowledge of God's knowledge. God is now depicted as informing the people of Israel about the nature of their self-knowledge when performing God's commandments: "[T]hat even the very knowledge by which one experiences that one is righteous (*hasid*) is itself an integral part of divine knowledge (*da'at elohim*), and through it, one knows." In other words, the source of awareness of one's own piety is God's knowledge of that piety. The question remains as to how anyone can hope to enter the mind of God.

R. Shapira proceeds to anchor this interpretation in Maimonides's theory of the acquisition of knowledge by God and, in a somewhat analogous way, by human beings: "It is well known, according to the Rambam [Maimonides], cited by the mystics (*mekubbalim*), that God's knowledge is acquired by knowing himself, which we have discussed previously. Consequently, God's cognizance of one's worship and righteousness is also contained in the knowledge of himself. For a man's worship and righteousness belongs to God, since he grants him the will, the strength, the intellect, and the emotions to worship. And when God grants a part of his knowledge to the man and through it he knows of his own worship, then he realizes that it is not his but that everything belongs to

God." R. Shapira bases his interpretation on kabbalistic conceptions of the human being as a mirror of the divine *anthropos*.[30] Shapira asserts that the usual means of acquiring knowledge, by reason or experience, must be surrendered, since they are actually obstacles to the ultimate truths of divine knowledge. In support, he draws paradoxically on what has been considered a supremely rationalist view, namely, Maimonides's Aristotelian conception of God as "thought thinking itself."[31] For divine knowledge to enter and suffuse the world, he writes, human thought must abandon its own sense of self-attainment. The self is a barrier to God's knowledge, and so, any claim to the acquisition of knowledge as one's own rather than God's obstructs the identity between the human and the divine knowers.[32] The result is Maimonides channeled through the kabbalistic tradition—as R. Shapira puts it, "according to the Rambam [Maimonides], cited by the mystics (*mekubbalim*)."

Once he grounds the authority for this theory of knowledge in Maimonides, Shapira proceeds to the crux of his sermon and the positive role suffering plays within it: "Now it is known that in Egypt," he writes, "knowledge [*da'at*] was in exile. . . . Worship consists of extricating knowledge from exile. That is why it states, 'And God knew' (Exod 2:25). When they left Egypt, it states that 'I, the Lord, have consecrated you' (31:13), and when the messiah arrives, "the world will be filled with the knowledge of God' (Isa 11:9)." R. Shapira traces a historical trajectory along a plane of divine knowledge that becomes increasingly reflected in the world through the ongoing collapse of the barrier between human knowledge and God's knowledge. Ideal knowledge begins in an alienated state (exile) and is progressively repatriated to its ultimate messianic return, when all human beings will acknowledge that their knowledge is really God's knowledge. God's "knowing" in Egypt is thus an interim stage between total exile and the time of the messiah, when knowledge gone astray begins to peek into the world because of suffering. God's "knowing," noted in Exod 2:25, evolves from a chain of sensory and mental awareness consisting of hearing (*God heard their mourning*), remembering (*God remembered his covenant*), feeling (*their cry for help from bondage rose up to God*—that is, God was touched by an embodied form of Israel's anguish), and seeing (*God looked upon the Israelites*) (Exod 2:24–25). It was human suffering experienced below that evoked all these divine sensations. Suffering propels human knowledge to merge incrementally with divine knowledge.

"All the sufferings then in Egypt and now, though they defy knowledge, are in any event for this purpose—to crush and override human cognition, with which man thinks he cognizes and on which he relies in the sense of 'increasing knowledge increases pain' (Eccl 1:18)—to crush it and override it so that the divine mind can reveal itself in each and every individual internally and through the entire world." R. Shapira reverses the causal order of the common sense of Eccl 1:18 by considering the second clause of the verse, "increasing pain," as the catalyst for the first clause, "increasing knowledge." In other words, suffering precipitates the acquisition of ideal knowledge through its crushing effects on the human mind. In philosophical terms, suffering provokes an epistemological rupture, which vacates the human mind of its usual modes of knowing, leading to a noetic paradigm shift in which they are replaced by a divine episteme. The human intellect, and humanity's confidence in its own ability to make sense of the world, must be abandoned to gain access to the divine mind. Only then can one make sense of what is an insurmountably senseless world.

This notion of displacing the *sekhel*, or transcending it, to gain true knowledge, or knowledge from a divine perspective, has deep roots in Hasidic thinking. Like other Hasidic masters who preceded him, R. Shapira is emblematic of how central Maimonides was to a movement that largely eschewed rationalism as its path toward God and ultimate metaphysical truth.[33] One can trace the idea that suffering plays a positive role in weakening the body and thereby strengthening the soul as far back as the Middle Ages, to the *Zohar*, the canonical scripture of all subsequent Jewish mysticism. God inflicts "sufferings of love" (see Leib Smokler, this volume) when he "crushes the body to empower the soul; then the person is drawn to him in love fittingly, the soul dominant, the body weakened."[34] Although Maimonides does consider there to be an inverse relationship in strength between the body and the intellect, he rejects the notion of sufferings of love out of hand as inconsistent with divine justice.[35]

It therefore is all the more ironic to see this idea surface in a Maimonidean guise in the nascent Hasidic movement of the eighteenth century. R. Schneur Zalman of Liadi (1745–1812), one of Hasidism's pioneers and the founding father of the Chabad Hasidic dynasty, whose kabbalistic theosophy exercised a seminal influence on R. Shapira, promotes a pantheistic Maimonidean incarnation of the very idea Maimonides rejects.[36] Regardless of the extent to which a human being perfects the intellect, Maimonides insists on a strict separation between God and the world, and advances a theology that maintains an "unbridgeable chasm separating the divine essence and the human essence."[37] R. Schneur Zalman also repeatedly cites Maimonides's Aristotelian-influenced identification of the knower, knowing, and known as a kind of mystical axiom to which many of the "sages of kabbalah admit."[38] The fact that God is one with what he knows implies that he knows everything, because he knows himself. In other words, according to R. Schneur Zalman there is nothing that exists outside God. In short, Maimonides's medieval rational epistemological theory, which is borrowed from Aristotle, the founding father of the Western rational philosophical tradition, forms the underpinning for Chabad's eighteenth-century kabbalistic acosmism. Maimonidean deism becomes a support for the radically theistic view that all of reality is a facet of God.

Maimonides's own formulation of divine knowledge, regarded in isolation from his overall philosophical theology, lends itself to this mystical appropriation, which absorbs all being into the divine Being. It appears in both of his most seminal works: his legal halakhic code, the *Mishneh Torah*, and his philosophical treatise, the *Guide of the Perplexed*.[39] The *Mishneh Torah* "codifies" the way God knows as follows: "All existences external to the Creator, from the first form to the smallest insect there could be in the heart of the earth, exist because of the power of his truth; *and because he knows his own being and perceives his greatness, glory, and truth, he knows everything*, and nothing is hidden from him" (emphasis mine).[40] After presenting an Aristotelian epistemological theory of the unification of the knower with the knowing and the known (Greek *nous, noesis, noeton* = Hebrew *sekhel, maskil, muskal*) that is constantly the state of God's knowledge, Maimonides then explicitly draws the logical conclusion that "because he knows himself, he knows everything, because everything is contingent on his being."[41] Similarly, the *Guide* endorses the unity of cognition, where God "is the intellect, as well as the intellectually cognizing subject and the intellectually cognized object," which also identifies anything known with the knower.[42] Thus, though there are serious inconsistencies between the two works that have endlessly exercised scholars, on this score, Maimonides's jurisprudence and philosophy harmoniously and radically intersect.[43] Indeed, some contemporary scholars might view the Hasidic version of Maimonides's theory of divine knowledge as a logical consequence of a Maimonidean "post-rational" philosophical mysticism.[44] Even some who disagree conclude that Maimonides can in fact be read as a "pantheist of sorts," because "if, in cognition, subject and object are identical, then mysticism follows when man knows God, or ultimate reality, and pantheism of some sort follows when God apprehends the world. In either case the opposition between subject and object collapses."[45]

Although I cannot do justice to this discussion here, it is sufficient for our purposes to note that other Hasidic readers before R. Shapira underlined the potentially panentheistic consequence of this identity of the knower with the known, which collapses all being into a divine oneness.[46] For kabbalists, that unity is only manifest by way of the composite emanation of the *sefirot*, whose unity with the divine essence is not, in the words of R. Schneur Zalman, "within the bounds of human comprehension." "It is an esoteric principle of faith," he writes, "which "lies beyond the intellect."[47] If this is a mode of intellection that surpasses the limits of human comprehension, then perhaps the only way of entering that mode is to abandon the normal modes of human reason. The pioneers of Hasidic theology already postulated this idea of overcoming the self (*bittul*), including one's intellect, to achieve the true self, to an extreme degree. One must undergo a "complete extinction of reflective consciousness" as the necessary precondition for acquiring "a 'new intellect,' a form of pure spiritual thought which is beyond time."[48]

To understand the extent of this nonrational wisdom in R. Shapira's ambit, we need to go back nearly two decades, to a sermon he delivered on the Jewish New Year of 1925, which also recalibrates Maimonides's Aristotelian epistemology in a kabbalistic register. Shapira draws on the notion of a "concealed wisdom" (*hokhmah stima'a*) that exists on a plane far beyond rational wisdom, an idea that traces its roots back to the *Zohar*.[49] The wisdom inherent in the extant Torah as well as empirical reality are merely pale reflections of this concealed wisdom, which "is the beginning of the emanations when it is still without clothing." It is located in the unified "wisdom" (*hokhmah*) at the very highest level of the kabbalistically constructed Godhead, consisting of various dimensions known as *sefirot*. This "wisdom" undergoes a transformation from its pristine state in the uppermost sefirotic triad of God's being, whereby it becomes "clothed" in the *sefirah* of "understanding" (*binah*)[50] on the way to our world of differentiation or fragmentation (*pirud*).[51] The total unity contemplated by Maimonides's epistemological formulation of the unity of the knower, the known, and the knowing is operative only in that realm. Once knowledge is acquired in the lower world of fragmentation and the supernal unified wisdom has been packaged, so to speak, to be comprehensible to human minds, that packaging, or "clothing" (*levush*), separates the knower from that which is known.[52] In the realm of mundane wisdom, "there is differentiation, the knower and that which is known [are distinct], the knower apprehends the known, because wisdom (*hokhmah*) has already been clothed with a cover . . ." Shapira then continues to distinguish the other wisdom, which inhabits a higher plane of existence. Since "concealed wisdom" is not packaged, it does not inhere in the world of separation or fragmentation but rather is absolutely unified. Thus, there is nothing to separate the knower from that which is known. R. Shapira then asserts that one realizes true apprehension "only by way of unification, that is, apprehension takes place only in a unified form, by way of man who first uncovers the concealed wisdom in it and then unites the two of them."[53]

This bifurcation of an earthly wisdom and a supernal, concealed one and its sharp swerve away from Maimonides's own conception of "wisdom" are also essential to appreciating R. Shapira's use of Maimonidean epistemology in the Ghetto. Maimonides's definition of the different senses of the term *hokhmah* (wisdom) are all confined to its mundane usages and are all within the scope of the human intellect's range, or what R. Shapira would consider an embodied wisdom that is "clothed." In fact, the highest form of wisdom for Maimonides is precisely that which is independently acquired by rational demonstration.[54] At the very core of R. Shapira's Maimonidean edifice is an irreconcilable difference that renders his conclusion of overcoming reason in order to achieve true wisdom or to somehow unite with the Godhead all the more startling.

It is precisely in the sharpness of this difference, particularly on the nature of Torah wisdom, that Shapira's theology can be best appreciated. Both agree that Torah wisdom exists on two different planes and must be acquired by two methods. Maimonides classifies wisdom learned from the Bible and the ancient rabbis by way of transmission, or simply by accepting what has been passed down from ancestors, as one distinct kind. The other is wisdom by which "the rational matter we receive from the Law through tradition is demonstrated."[55] For R. Shapira, the Torah that is received, the Torah in its external form, is (drawing on a midrash) a "withered" form of the supernal wisdom, the product of a process beginning in the upper *sefirot* that progressively waters down that wisdom which transcends the intellect for the sake of human comprehension.[56]

Indeed, R. Shapira cites this very midrash nearly two decades later in the Ghetto as a preface to the passage engaging Maimonides that has been the focus of my examination.[57] That midrash presents the theology that anchors that passage and establishes the principle that "investigation by normal modes of reason ruins transcendence."[58] In order to acquire a text's concealed wisdom, one needs to pierce through the text to its supernal underpinnings. Overcoming the text is accomplished by overcoming the normal modes of thought and reason. This seemingly strange idea that ideal understanding is only achieved by suppressing the commonly accepted means of cognition emerges from a long-standing struggle with the role reason plays in spiritual ascendance. Thus, R. Shapira turns Maimonides's distinction between Torah wisdom acquired by tradition and that acquired by rational demonstration on its head. While Maimonides requires the exertion of reasoned demonstration to mine the true concealed wisdom of Torah, Shapira calls for reason's surrender as the key to the Torah's true, supra-rational wisdom.

The Evil of Philosophical Wisdom

What is particularly noteworthy about this radical epistemology is the historical context of suffering from which it emerged. During the first year of his wartime sermons, R. Shapira's sermon for Shabbat *Zakhor*, when the evil committed by the biblical nation Amalek is traditionally commemorated, features an exposition of how Amalek's evil seeped into the fabric of Israelite society. Rarely, if ever, does R. Shapira refer to the Nazis or Germans by name, so it is reasonable to assume in this case that Amalek stands in for the Nazis.[59] As is his wont, R. Shapira applies some exegetical ingenuity to biblical verse and rabbinic midrash, leading him to the conclusion that the "external wisdom," or science and philosophy, by which Amalek gained world renown appealed to some Israelites and served to dampen (literally, "cool down") their faith in "Torah wisdom."[60] The same collection of sermons that reinvents Maimonides for a world gone mad, with which reason cannot cope and regarding which it must concede it cannot fathom, also renounces reason—which is, in Maimonides's view, the only characteristic that human beings share with God.[61] For R. Shapira, a reason-based faith is a watered-down faith, identified with the nation considered by Jewish theology to be evil incarnate.

R. Shapira envisages the Germans as the intellectual successors to the biblical nation of Amalek and to medieval Spain. The enemy of the Jews in Shapira's day was in fact the embodiment of the very summit of Western culture and rationality. It was represented at its most rational peak by the Nazi philosopher Martin Heidegger, arguably one of the greatest intellects of the twentieth century. In his prewar writing, R. Shapira explicitly describes Germany as reaching the highest level of science and rationalism while at the same time sinking to the abysmal depths of immorality, to the point of becoming "the very worst of the civilized world."[62] But in his sermons during the war, he can no longer bring himself to even utter the name of Germany, simply identifying it with Amalek. R. Shapira clearly parts ways with Maimonides's classification of "rational virtues" as the "ultimate end" of "true human perfection" and of "moral virtues" as merely preparatory to this end.[63]

Historically, according to R. Shapira, the very phenomenon of Jewish attraction to philosophical wisdom accounts for the great catastrophe of the Spanish expulsion in the fifteenth century. Morality grounded in autonomous reason is fickle, since "those same sciences and rationales that previously led autonomously to a beautiful ethics are now being used to justify theft, robbery, and murder, and all the other disgusting characteristics as good."[64] The only absolute ground of human behavior that allows for no relativism is God's word. Whereas rabbinic tradition classified commandments as either *mishpatim,* rational commandments, or *hukkim,* nonrational commandments, R. Shapira asserts that obedience to all commandments must be motivated by submission to the divine will rather than conformity to reason, for "all commandments are divine *hukkim,* whether one understands them with one's reason or not."[65]

This position is consistent with R. Shapira's prewar theology. In one of his prewar sermons, Shapira asserts that "anyone who performs a *mitsvah* solely because he understands it, that *mitsvah* remains incomplete, since he fulfils the *mitsvah* only as a result of his intellect and his own will but not because of the divine will."[66] For R. Shapira, rational understanding is only useful in providing the practical knowledge necessary for the performance of a *mitsvah.* It is absolutely useless for discovering the rationales for commandments, the *ta'amei ha-mtisvot,* a classic enterprise, the chief exponent of which was Maimonides. He goes so far as to assert that "even the *mishpatim* of the Torah, that is to say, something that appears reasonable, are also *hukkim.* God wishes the commandment to transcend intellect."[67] The "red heifer" (*parah adumah*), a classic rabbinic example of a law that defies rational understanding, becomes emblematic of the entire Torah.[68]

This notion also pervades a trilogy of works concerning R. Shapira's educational philosophy, typified by the following pedagogical advice to young students who might be attracted to reason (*sekhel*) as the measure of their approach to studying Torah. After distinguishing the *sekhel* of Torah from all other natural forms of reason and stating that in relation to Torah wisdom, all non-Torah wisdom simply pales as "useless nothingness,"

Shapira insists on resorting to reason. Paradoxically, however, he instructs his students to reason their way to the pointlessness of that very reason, "so that also through your knowledge (da'at) you will comprehend that you must negate your knowledge so that only simple faith (emunah peshutah) will govern your entire being."[69]

The Maimonidean Path to *Emunah Peshutah*

In a sermon delivered on Purim of 1925, R. Shapira engages Maimonides's assertion that God "cannot be apprehended in corporeal terms" to reinforce the idea that the way to God is not through theoretical abstraction (see Seeman, this volume) but through *emunah peshutah*, "simple faith." For R. Shapira, "remembering" the God who cannot be pictured because "he cannot be apprehended by corporeal apprehensions" requires contemplation that is so deep as to become integrated into one's essence. Thus, in good Maimonidean terms, faith cannot be accomplished through acceptance of ancestral tradition or via obedience to commandments. Rather, it is "necessary to realize the belief also independently through investigation (*hakirah*) and reason (*sekhel*)."[70] Maimonides also disqualifies mere belief based on tradition, or *mesorah*, from being true knowledge. However, R. Shapira understands autonomous reasoning as a preliminary stage only on the way to achieving a bond between God and one's soul (essence). From that stage, one breaks away from the intellect to inculcate *emunah peshutah*, which forges an existential intimacy with God to which reason alone cannot aspire. As in his advice to young students urging them to "know" that they must nullify "knowing," he advocates the use of reason to move beyond reason.[71]

R. Shapira further resorts to Maimonidean philosophy to posit a decidedly anti-Maimonidean notion of a kind of merging with God in which knowledge and memory of God is so ingrained as to become etched in God's very own memory. He draws on Maimonides's theory of attributes, which limits our knowledge of the Divine to attributes of action, but adds the inference that "the force of the actor inheres in that which is acted upon."[72] Thus, as humans are creations of God, and God acts and affects human beings, God as actor inheres in human beings who are acted upon. Thus, once divinity is integrated into the human being, any human thinking *about* God becomes integral to God's own thought, further attracting divine knowledge of the one thinking of him. In R.

Shapira's hands, the theory of attributes of action, originally intended to divert human knowing from God's unknowable being toward what is knowable in the world, reorients human thought back toward God and ultimately toward assimilation into the divine mind.

This understanding of "simple faith" further elucidates Shapira's characterization of his time in the Ghetto as "years of rage (za'am)." In a lengthy meditation on the virtues of contemplating one's day of death, he offers graphic descriptions of a terminally ill person caught in the throes of intense pain. The pain becomes so unbearable that the person feels as if his entire body were disintegrating, to the point of feeling swallowed by the grave. At that point, the person realizes that "the instruments of rage (za'am) have been sent from heaven to dismantle his body and consume him, ending in the grave."[73] As the vitality of every limb drains away, the "*shekhinah* stands over him," presenting the opportunity to "cleave to the divine presence."[74] This "rage" of imminent death may very well approximate the rage of the Ghetto, where the only way to make sense of the incomprehensible wasting of the body is to surrender to its incomprehensibility. At that point, the intellect joins the body in an act of self-negation that opens itself up to divine immanence.

Conclusion

Maimonides understands the divine unified mode of knowing, whose unity is unlike that of any knowing with which human beings are familiar, as being beyond the bounds of human comprehension.[75] His excursus on this epistemology in the *Guide of the Perplexed* clarifies the distinction between human and divine cognition. When human beings exercise their intellects, they effect a transition from potential knowledge to actualized knowledge. It is only in the state of potentiality that knower, knowing, and known are separate. However, when "the intellect is realized *in actu,* the three notions become one." When it comes to God, that state of unified knowledge is constant and always actualized.[76]

In a sermon from the end of Yom Kippur of 1930, R. Shapira revisits Maimonides's epistemological union of the knower, the known, and the knowing in a way that contributes significantly to our understanding of his engagement with Ghetto life. In this sermon, he blurs the rigid distinction that Maimonides posits between the limits of the human intellect and divine knowing. Grounding himself in Maimonides's epistemology, he concludes that "only when one enters the source of holiness, when one ascends in thought beyond differentiation and sees the source of knowledge in which God resides, does one see from the perspective of this supernal seeing that everything is one."[77] Whereas Maimonides maintains a strict bifurcation between the human domain and the divine one, Shapira, adopting Maimonides's terminology, identifies divine knowing as an achievable end of human efforts and as a key to entering the divine realm, where all is one.

Within the setting of the Ghetto's intolerable suffering, however, we can now understand the horrifying "advantage" this theology provides in making it possible to jolt God himself into a heightened consciousness. The very last sermon calls on God not merely to know but to "see" the suffering experienced in the Ghetto and includes a desperate final plea to "open your eyes and see!"[78] This suffering is so extreme as to eviscerate the normal modes of intellect and allow human thought, along with its torments, to ascend to the divine "source of knowledge." If all is one on that plane, once the human being elevates his tortured thought to that point, God's knowledge also transforms itself in the reverse direction, and God can feel and "see" the human suffering below. Human knowledge, which transcends intellect and unites with divine knowledge, causes God's perception to shift downward from an ideal realm where all is good back to the world of differentiation where all is not good, where suffering is experienced. Prior to the Ghetto, Maimonidean rationalism provided a model for human beings to overcome reason and reach the heights of divine existence. In the Ghetto, it became a model for God to overcome his own ideal knowledge so that he could experience the depths of human suffering.

Notes

1. James A. Diamond, "Maimonides and R. Kalonymous Kalman Shapira: Abandoning Reason in the Warsaw Ghetto," in Menachem Kellner and James A. Diamond, *Reinventing Maimonides in Contemporary Jewish Thought* (London: Littman Library of Jewish Civilization, 2019), 87–105. For a book-length treatment of seminal Jewish thinkers reading and rereading Maimonides, see my *Maimonides and the Shaping the Jewish Canon* (Cambridge: Cambridge University Press, 2014).

2. Kalonymus Kalman Shapira, *Sermons from the Years of Rage* [in Hebrew], ed. Daniel Reiser, 2 vols. (Jerusalem: Herzog Academic College, 2017).

3. B. Berakhot 7a and b. Sanhedrin 105b, where that instant is said to be the precise equivalent of 1/58,888 of an hour.

4. *Sermons from the Years of Rage, parashat balak* 5700 (1940), 1:145–46.

5. For the term's use in the context of Balaam, see Num 23:7–8; See also, for example, Ps 78:49; Nah 2:6; Isa 26:20, among others. For but one of the other rabbinic sources, see b. Zevahim 41b.

6. See Reiser's introduction to *Sermons from the Years of Rage*, 1:50–53.

7. Y. Berakhot 7:2: Shimon ben Shetah addresses the king, who is angry with him: "I heard that my master was angry at me and I wanted to fulfill this verse: 'Hide yourselves for a little while until the wrath (*za'am*) is past' [Isa 26:20]. And it was said concerning me, 'And the advantage of knowledge is that wisdom preserves the life of him who has it' [Ecc 7:12]."

8. The first sentence of the *Mishneh torah* (henceforth, *MT*) begins: "The foundation of all foundations and the pillar of sciences is *to know*" (see *MT, Hilkhot yesodei ha-torah* 1:1). Its final paragraph is the climax of his vision of the messianic era, when "the entire world will be filled with the *knowledge* of God" (*MT, Hilkhot melakhim* 12:5). Maimonides's entire legal project, then, is bracketed by knowledge. His philosophical project in the *Guide of the Perplexed*, trans. Shlomo Pines (Chicago: University of Chicago Press, 1963) (henceforth, *GP*), is anchored in the human faculty that enables knowing: the image (*tselem*) of God (*GP* 1:1).

9. On this phenomenon, see James A. Diamond, *Maimonides and the Shaping of the Jewish Canon* (Cambridge: Cambridge University Press, 2014).

10. *GP* 3:12. For a good exposition of Maimonides's position on this issue, see Oliver Leaman, *Evil and Suffering in Jewish Philosophy* (Cambridge: Cambridge University Press, 1995), ch. 4.

11. See Gershom Scholem's discussion in *Major Trends in Jewish Mysticism* (New York: Schocken, 1995), 35–36; and Isaiah Tishby, *The Doctrine of Evil in Lurianic Kabbalah*, trans. David Solomon (London: Kegan Paul Library of Jewish Studies, 2008).

12. Scholem, *Major Trends*, 35. For a defense of the philosophical position in the context of the Shoah, see Warren Zev Harvey's lucid discussion in "Two Jewish Approaches to Evil in History," in *Wrestling with God: Jewish Theological Responses during and after the Holocaust*, ed. Steven T. Katz, Shlomo Biderman, and Gershon Greenberg (New York: Oxford University Press, 2007), 326–31.

13. Quoting from Nehemia Polen's translation in his *The Holy Fire: The Teachings of Rabbi Kalonymus Kalman Shapira* (Lanham, MD: Rowman and Littlefield, 2004), 35. The original appears in *Sermons from the Years of Rage, hanukkah* 5702 (1941), 1:242.

14. Emil Fackenheim famously advanced this philosophical conception of the Holocaust. A succinct statement of Fackenheim's *novum* in the history of evil intended to challenge professional philosophers was made by Fackenheim at an

American Philosophical Association symposium in 1985. See his "The Holocaust and Philosophy," in *The Journal of Philosophy* 82, no. 10 (1985): 505–14. In fact, this retraction is precisely what Fackenheim zeroed in on. Shapira's courageously honest amendment is one of only two passages that Fackenheim cites in his entire corpus.

15. For a comprehensive review of scholars grappling with the theological adequacy of analogies between the ancient temple destruction and the Holocaust, see Jonathan Klawans, "Josephus, the Rabbis, and Responses to Catastrophes Ancient and Modern," *Jewish Quarterly Review* 100, no. 2 (2010): 278–309.

16. Kalonymus Kalman Shapira, *Mevo ha-she'arim* (Jerusalem, 1962), 242.

17. See introduction to *Maggid devarav le-Ya'akov*, ed. Rivka Schatz-Uffenheimer (Jerusalem: Magnes, 1990), 3.

18. The dates of each sermon are known, and the physical conditions Shapira addressed can be correlated to other dated accounts, such Chaim Kaplan's diary, *Megilat Yissurin—Yoman Getto Varsha* ["Scroll of Agony—Warsaw Ghetto Diary"], *September 1, 1939–August 4, 1942* (Tel Aviv: 1966). However, as Daniel Reiser astutely points out, a clear-cut historical progression in his thought is complicated by Shapira's continuous revisions to the sermons. See *Sermons from the Years of Rage*, 1:70–72.

19. B. Yevamot 64a.

20. Kalonymus Kalman Shapira, *Derekh ha-melekh* (Jerusalem: Feldheim, 2011), *parashat vayyishlah* 5690 (1929), 75.

21. See Marc Shapiro, "Ani Maamin," *Encyclopedia Judaica*, 2nd ed. (Macmillan Reference USA, 2007), 165.

22. *Derekh ha-melekh, vayyiggash* 5689 (1928), 105.

23. Gershom Scholem, *Major Trends*, 260, considered this idea "one of the most amazing and far-reaching conceptions ever put forward in the history of kabbalism." *Tsimtsum's* implication of distancing of God from the world was placed in tension with its Hasidic incarnations, which tended toward God's immanence in the world. On this, see Rachel Elior, *The Paradoxical Ascent to God: The Kabbalistic Theosophy of Habad Hasidism* (Albany: State University of New York Press, 1993), 79–91.

24. "Maimonides's Thirteen Principles," in *Jewish Medieval and Renaissance Studies,* ed. Alexander Altmann (Cambridge: Harvard University Press, 1967), 119–44.

25. See James A. Diamond, *Reinventing Maimonides*, 92–93, where I discuss this passage. Here, I reach a more radical conclusion regarding the extent of R. Shapira's pantheistic transformation of Maimonides's ontology.

26. See *GP* 1:52. See also *GP* 1:56. For another example of a radical rereading of *MT, yesodei ha-torah*, which configures Maimonides as a proponent of Chabad acosmism, see Jacob Gotleib, *Rationalism in Hasidic Attire: Habad's Harmonistic*

Approach to Maimonides [in Hebrew] (Ramat Gan, Israel: Bar-Ilan University Press, 2009), 56–59.

27. See Moshe Idel, "Maimonides and Kabbalah," in *Studies in Maimonides*, ed. Isadore Twersky (Cambridge: Harvard University Press, 1981), 67. See also Elliot Wolfson, "Via Negativa in Maimonides and Its Impact on Thirteenth Century Kabbalah," *Maimonidean Studies* 5 (2008): 393–442, which argues for a "genuine intellectual and spiritual kinship" between Maimonides and kabbalists.

28. *Sermons from the Years of Rage, parashat yitro* 5702 (1942), 1:267–68.

29. *GP* 3:24, 498. Prior to Maimonides, Rashi adopted this reading as well. See my extensive treatment of the Sabbath's role, where I conclude that Sabbath in fact signifies God stepping back from the world and allowing nature to run its course in James A. Diamond, *Converts, Heretics, and Lepers: Maimonides and the Outsider* (Notre Dame: University of Notre Dame Press, 2007), 191–226.

30. See Gershom Scholem, "On the Mystical Shape of the Godhead," in *On the Mystical Shape of the Godhead*, trans. Joachim Neugroschel (New York: Schocken, 1991), 15–55.

31. For but one excellent treatment of Aristotle's conception of how God knows, see Thomas De Koninck, "Aristotle on God as Thought Thinking Itself," *The Review of Metaphysics* 47, no. 3 (1994): 471–515.

32. This is a corollary of the Hasidic theological principle *bittul ha-yesh.* Chabad is a leading exponent of this. As Elliot Wolfson defines it, "to apprehend reality one must strip it of its materiality, a reversal of the process of creation of something from nothing." Elliot Wolfson, *Open Secret: Postmessianic Messianism and the Mystical Revision of Menahem Mendel Schneerson* (New York: Columbia University Press, 2009), 80.

33. See, for example, Rachel Elior's "Faith that Transcends Intellect and Contemplation," in *The Paradoxical Ascent to God: The Kabbalistic Theosophy of Habad Hasidism* (Albany: State University of New York Press, 1993), 179–83.

34. *Zohar* 1:180b, and *The Zohar: Pritzker Edition*, trans. Daniel Matt (Stanford: Stanford University Press, 2006), 3:93–94.

35. See *GP* 3:24. For talmudic notions of "sufferings of love," see, for example, b. Berakhot 5a; b. Kiddushin 40b.

36. Daniel Reiser pointed out to me that whenever R. Shapira cites another rabbi or rebbe, he always does so by name, with the exception of R. Schneur Zalman, whom he refers to as *ha-rav*, "the rabbi." This is further evidence of the importance of Schneur Zalman's influence on Shapira's thought.

37. See Howard Kreisel, "Imitatio Dei in Maimonides's *Guide of the Perplexed*," *AJS Review* 19, no. 2 (1994): 169–211, at 191.

38. *Likkutei amarim—Tanya* (Brooklyn: Kehot Publication Society, 2000), ch. 2. For the near-obsessive focus of Chabad Hasidism on Maimonides and its transformation of him into an exponent of its brand of mysticism, see Naftali

Lowenthal, "The Image of Maimonides in Habad Hasidism," in *Traditions of Maimonideanism*, ed. Carlos Fraenkel (Leiden: Brill, 2009), 277–312.

39. See also Moses Maimonides's commentary on the Mishnah, *Mishnah im perush Rabenu Moshe ben Maimon*, trans. Joseph David Kafih (Jerusalem: Mossad HaRav Kook, 1965), 2:285, m. Avot 3:20; m. Sanhedrin, introduction to ch. 10, 138. Although there are statements in this work that indicate the capacity of the human mind to abstract God's form, which seem to assume the logic of the identity of the knower and the known, this would directly contradict other statements that deny the human intellect's ability to know God's essence. On this issue, see Herbert Davidson, *Maimonides the Rationalist* (Portland, OR: The Littman Library of Jewish Civilization, 2011), 64–69; 201–206.

40. *MT, hilkhot yesodei ha-torah* 2:9.

41. Ibid., 2:10, which concludes that God knows creation by knowing himself.

42. *GP* 1:68, 163.

43. For just one good example of a study on the differences between Maimonides qua philosopher and Maimonides qua halakhist, see Yaakov Levinger, *Maimonides as Philosopher and Codifier* [in Hebrew] (Jerusalem: Mossad Bialik, 1990).

44. See, for example, David Blumenthal, "Maimonides' Philosophical Mysticism," in *Maimonides and Mysticism*, ed. A. Elqayam and D. Schwartz, *Daat* 64–66 (Ramat Gan: Bar-Ilan University Press, 2009) v–xxv, and the comprehensive bibliography compiled at xxii–xxv.

45. See Gad Freudenthal, "The Philosophical Mysticism of Maimonides and Maimon," in *Maimonides and His Heritage,* ed. Idit Dobbs-Weinstein, Lenn Goodman, and James Grady (Albany: State University of New York Press, 2009), 113–52, at 122.

46. It is important to note that this mystified version of a Maimonidean epistemological formulation also finds its way into the non-Hasidic rabbinic world of the twentieth century in the figure of Joseph Dov Soloveitchik, who joins the Hasidic enterprise of adapting the Maimonidean epistemological unity between the knowing, knower, and known in quasi-mystical terms, resulting in intellectualist mysticism. See Joseph Dov Soloveitchik, *On Repentance: From the Discourses of Rabbi Joseph B. Soloveitchik*, ed. Pinchas Peli (Jerusalem: World Zionist Federation, 1974), 196–97, and Dov Schwartz, "R. Soloveitchik as a Maimonidean: The Unity of Cognization" [in Hebrew], in *Maimonides and Mysticism: Presented to Moshe Hallamish on the Occasion of his Retirement*, ed. A. Elqayam, D. Schwartz, *Daat* 64–66 (2009) 301–21, at 321.

47. *Likkutei amarim—Tanya, shaʾar ha-yihud ve-ha-emunah*, ch. 9.

48. See Rivka Schatz Uffenheimer, *Hasidism as Mysticism: Quietistic Elements in Eighteenth-Century Hasidic Thought* (Princeton: Princeton University Press, 1993), 176.

49. For early Hasidic formulations of this trans-intellectual intellect in Dov Ber of Mezeritsch and his disciple R. Schneur Zalman of Liadi, see Gershom

Scholem, "The Unconscious and the Concept of the Primordial Intellect in Hasidic Literature," in *Explications and Implications: Writings on Jewish Heritage and Renaissance* [in Hebrew] (Tel Aviv: Am Oved, 1975), 351–60.

50. The *sefirot* are the staple of kabbalistic literature in all their various manifestations and are essentially ten emanations that bridge an abstract unknowable God with the world. For a good introduction, see Arthur Green, *A Guide to the Zohar* (Stanford: Stanford University Press, 2004).

51. *Derekh ha-melekh, rosh ha-shanah* 5686 (1925), 305. The origins of this term can be traced back to the *Zohar*. For the purposes of this analysis, it connotes the emergence out of absolute divine unity at the very highest level of the supernal Godhead into a divine manifestation of more variegated dimensions (the *sefirot*) and thus a transition from the "world of unity" (*yihuda*) to the "world of separation" (*peruda*).

52. This is the kabbalistic parallel to Maimonides's far more pragmatic reason for the present form of the Torah, which employs anthropomorphic language regarding God because it is geared to the average human mind, which finds philosophical abstraction too difficult. It "speaks in the language of men" (*dibberah torah bilshon benei adam*). See GP 1:26, pp. 56–57.

53. GP 1:26, 306. Although there are some subtle differences, Moses Cordovero already restricts the Maimonidean notion of the unity of knower, knowing, and known to the upper sefirotic triad in his *Pardes rimmonim*, 8:13.

54. See GP 3:54, 635, where the highest human perfection is acquiring "wisdom" in the sense of "rational virtues."

55. GP 3:54, 633.

56. *Derekh ha-melekh, rosh ha-shanah* 5686 (1925), 305, based on Bereshit Rabbah 17:5, which uses the term *novel,* a term borrowed from the natural world normally related to shriveled or withered fruit or leaves on a vine (e.g., Isa 34:4). This idea can be traced back to the *Zohar*. See, for example, *Zohar* 3:152a, when the Torah "came down into the world, the world could not have tolerated it if it had not clothed itself in the garments of this world." See also Gershom Scholem, "The Meaning of the Torah in Jewish Mysticism," *Diogenes* (1956) 4(14): 36–47.

57. *Sermons from the Years of Rage, parashat yitro* 5702 (1942), 1:265.

58. Ibid., 1:266.

59. According to Alana Vincent, R. Shapira's sermon on Amalek both enabled his followers "to interpret their experiences within the narrative framework provided by the cultural memory transmitted through the regular recital of scripture" and "buttressed the viability of the Amalek narrative as a cultural memory, a part of their own living (and lived) experience." Alana Vincent, *Making Memory: Jewish and Christian Explorations in Monument, Narrative, and Liturgy* (Cambridge: James Clarke, 2014), 30.

60. This distinction between Torah wisdom and "external" wisdom traces its roots all the way back to classical rabbinic literature. For a good overview of one extensive engagement with the notion of some wisdom among gentiles in

the Hasidic/Lurianic tradition, see Yaakov Elman, "The History of Gentile Wisdom According to R. Zadok ha-Kohen of Lublin," *Journal of Jewish Thought and Philosophy* 3 (1993): 153–87.

61. *GP* 1:1.

62. *Derekh ha-melekh, shabbat teshuvah* 2 (1937), 604. In that same prewar sermon, R. Shapira also laments the crisis that the Jews were experiencing in Germany a few years after Hitler's rise to power, which had rapidly deteriorated in the previous "five years," before which German Jews enjoyed freedom and success and "nearly all the great intellectuals, the professors who glorified Germany's reputation throughout the world, the majority were Jews."

63. See *GP* 3:54.

64. *Sermons from the Years of Rage, shabbat zakhor* 1940, 1:114–15. See also *Derekh ha-melekh, shabbat parah* 5696 (1938), 170, where he similarly laments the fact that "some nations have deteriorated to such an extent . . . that the more evil something is, the more admirable it is, and they pride themselves with every perversion."

65. *Sermons from the Years of Rage, shabbat zakhor* 1940, 1:115.

66. See *Derekh ha-melekh, shabbat teshuvah*, 11.

67. Ibid., *shabbat parah* 1930, 169.

68. Ibid., *shabbat parah* 1925, 175.

69. Shapira, *Mevo ha-she'arim* (Jerusalem: Feldheim, 2000), 197. For another theological response to the Holocaust also grounded in *emunah peshutah* that involves an annulment of the ego, see Gershon Greenberg, "Areleh Roth's 'Pristine Faith,'" *Journal of Modern Jewish Studies* 14, no. 1 (2015): 77, which cites Roth saying that "Israel's sole means of endurance through and means of responding to the eruption of Amalek's *tumah* was *emunah peshutah*."

70. *Derekh ha-melekh, purim* 5685 (1925), 477.

71. The phrase *emunah peshutah* is often used in contrast to faith that is grounded in reasoned research and investigation in Hasidic and kabbalistic literature. For but two examples, see R. Abraham Isaac Kook, *Shemonah kevatsim* (Jerusalem, 2004), 3:333, and R. Nahman of Bratslav, *Likkutei moharan* (New York: 1976), 2:5.

72. *Derekh ha-melekh, purim* 5685 (1925), 478.

73. *Hakhsharat ha-avreikhim*, 92.

74. Ibid., 98.

75. *MT, yesodei ha-torah*, 2:10–12.

76. *GP* 1:68.

77. *Derekh ha-melekh, motsa'ei yom ha-kippurim* 5691 (1930), 395–96.

78. *Sermons from the Years of Rage, shabbat hazon* 5702 (1942), 1:314.

11

At the Edge of Explanation

Rethinking "Afflictions of Love" in *Sermons from the Years of Rage*

ERIN LEIB SMOKLER

Introduction

R. Kalonymous Kalman Shapira's *Sermons from the Years of Rage* (more popularly known as *Esh kodesh* or *Holy Fire*) draws on ancient tropes of the Jewish canon in its efforts to reckon with the suffering of its era. R. Shapira deployed, interpreted, and reinterpreted inherited models of theodicy throughout his work, tweaking his understanding and shifting his exegetical-existential vision over time. Examples of such biblical and rabbinic explanatory paradigms include, but are not limited to, the trope of sin and punishment, the binding of Isaac, the hiding of God's face, and the destruction of the temple in Jerusalem. Each of these offered Shapira a lens through which to view the increasingly dire circumstances that he and his community faced in Warsaw from September 1939 to July 1942. I wish to argue that *Esh kodesh* is in many respects an exercise in the elasticity of paradigmatic thinking (see Idel, this volume), an example of how a supple theologian may stretch and reinterpret earlier models of suffering in order to provide a framework for contemporary suffering. But Shapira's sermons also explore the limits of such thinking, as the ever-increasing intensity of life—and death—in the Warsaw Ghetto forced him to confront the very limit of theological explanation.

One particularly poignant model of theodicy taken up by Shapira—and one that exemplifies this elasticity—is that of *yissurim shel ahavah,* "afflictions of love." In the earlier biblical rendering of this notion, God's parent-like commitment to God's people generates singular expectations of them.[1] God loves the children of Israel so profoundly that God offers them more than other nations and also demands more of them. The byproduct of this unique divine concern is a heightened level of human accountability and thus a greater susceptibility to chastisement. In the words of David Kraemer, "That God cares to punish through afflictions is a sign of God's love. If God did not care, God would not punish; thus [those] who are punished must be, by that very evidence, God's select nation."[2] This theodicy overlaps with that of sin and punishment, but it accents the divine affection that undergirds suffering in place of more punitive motivations.

An extensive talmudic treatment of the matter in b. Berakhot, however, steers the paradigm in a different direction, casting divine love as that which helps to free or refine human beings through their pain.[3] This talmudic source suggests that "afflictions of love" are loving insofar as they promote these desirable ends even in the absence of punishment for sin. Suffering yields freedom or purification, and so afflictions ought to be treated as divine gifts, bestowing goods in this world and also, potentially, in the world to come.[4] The classical discussion of *yissurim shel ahavah* portrays them as wounding pains that are in truth an offering of a loving God, for they can bring benefits just over the horizon of the current experience.

Yet if afflictions of love constitute a kind of alternate theodicy to the one of sin and punishment, the talmudic discussion itself demonstrates that the rabbis who used this term were actually struggling with the limits of explanation. Indeed, *yissurim shel ahavah* are proposed in response to failed attempts at justification through appeal to sin; they are said to be applied only with the loving consent (*kiblam me-ahavah*) of those who receive them and within certain parameters (i.e., they cannot be too extreme). Such suffering, furthermore, promotes ends that might be considered desirable but which also come at a very high price—one that some of the talmudic rabbis in question would prefer not to pay. In the course of the extended talmudic discussion in b. Berakhot 5a-b, several rabbis who participated in the theoretical discussion of the meaning of suffering fall ill. When each of them is asked by his colleagues whether his afflictions are beloved to him (as afflictions of love ought to be), they exclaim in turn, "Neither they nor their rewards!"[5] *Yissurim shel ahavah* is thus a paradigm that seems to fall apart as it confronts the irreducible quality of individuals' real pain. The very rabbis who espouse it buckle under its weight. Rather than a theory of suffering, then, this rabbinic construct seems to serve as a placeholder for the terrifying awareness that one has actually run out of theories. It is in this sense an anti-theodicy, a theodic model that reckons with the potential breakdown of theodicy as a religious project.[6]

It is this complicated view that Shapira contends with most explicitly. My aim in this chapter is to trace Shapira's use of *yissurim shel ahavah* in his wartime sermons, interrogating his sustained development of this liminal category. I will argue that without explicitly saying so, without conceding the end of explanation, he made use of this theodic paradigm in *Esh kodesh* to acknowledge those moments that seemed to be beyond explanation. In the face of swelling suffering, *yissurim shel ahavah* offered him a language with which to wrestle publicly with pain that flouted language altogether.

October 5, 1940: Forcing God's Hand

The theme of *yissurim shel ahavah* is first referenced in the Ghetto sermons on October 5, 1940, on the occasion of *Shabbat Teshuvah*, the "Sabbath of Repentance" between Rosh Hashanah and Yom Kippur. The sermon opens, however, with a highly condensed reference to a different talmudic tale from b. Shabbat 89a.The full story follows, with Shapira's small selection italicized.

> R. Joshua b. Levi also said: When Moses ascended on high, he found the Holy One, blessed be He, tying crowns on the letters [of the Torah]. Said God to him, "Moses, is there no [greeting of] peace in your town?" "Shall a servant extend [a greeting of] peace to his master?!" replied Moses. "*Yet you should have assisted Me*," said God. *Immediately Moses cried out to Him (Numbers 14:17), "And now, I pray, let the power of the Lord be great, just as You have said."*[7]

In this rather surprising episode, Moses encounters God on high and is chastised for not offering a greeting. Explaining that he thought it unbecoming of a lowly slave like himself to address God directly, God dismisses this silencing humility and asserts that Moses ought to help him with his words. Moses does so through praise: "Let the power of the Lord be great." Human language somehow aids God, empowering the divine, though it is unclear whether this assistance pertains to the specific task mentioned (writing a Torah) or to God's broader engagement in the world.

Shapira introduces this story as a way of grounding and explaining a similar verse found in the Torah portion of the week: "When I proclaim God's name, give greatness to the name of God."[8] The interpretation of this verse attributed to the classical commentator Rashi (R. Shlomo Yitzhaki) is that when a person pronounces God's name, *then* God is rendered great. God relies on human speech to establish and reify divine power in the world. Shapira makes this claim very briefly and without argument, so one must pause to take note of its subversive quality, which cuts against the plain meaning of the verses he cites. Both Deut 32:3 and Num 14:17 (cited in the Talmud) explicitly extol the greatness of God's name and the power of the Lord, respectively. They highlight God's wondrous strength, presumably over and above that of human strength. It is therefore noteworthy that these very verses become the basis of a teaching about God's reliance on humanity, such that God's power actually depends on human willingness to proclaim it.

Shapira's selective quotation of the talmudic story—omitting its location (on high) and God's first exchange with Moses—elevates human agency over divine power. It also strips the story of a context that points toward another famous talmudic tale, one with very different implications: "When Moses ascended on high, he found the Holy One, blessed be he, tying crowns on the letters [of the Torah]," says R. Joshua b. Levi in b. Shabbat 89a, the story referenced by Shapira. A parallel text from b. Menahot 29b—in a story cited by Shapira several times in *Esh kodesh*[9]—opens with the exact same image: "R. Judah said in the name of Rav: When Moses ascended on high, he found the Holy One, blessed be he, tying crowns on the letters [of the Torah] . . ." This tale then continues with a harrowing dialogue between God and Moses, centered on the fate of R. Akiva, the martyred rabbi of the Mishnah:

> Said Moses, "Lord of the Universe, Who stays Thy hand?" He answered, "There will arise a man, at the end of many generations, Akiva b. Joseph by name, who will expound upon each

tittle heaps and heaps of laws." "Lord of the Universe," said
Moses, "permit me to see him." He replied, "Turn thee round."
Moses went and sat down behind eight rows [and listened to
the discourses upon the law]. . . . Then said Moses, "Lord of the
Universe, Thou hast shown me his Torah, show me his reward."
"Turn thee round," said He; and Moses turned round and saw
them weighing out his [R. Akiva's] flesh at the market-stalls.
"Lord of the Universe," cried Moses, "such Torah, and such a
reward?!" He replied, "Be silent, for such is My decree."

Shapira has much to say about this passage elsewhere, but I have cited
it here—where he elides it—to demonstrate the associations that Shapira
avoids by not quoting the full context of b. Shabbat 89a. The tale of b.
Menahot 29b highlights human impotency—R. Akiva's powerlessness in
the face of an enemy that sought his flesh and Moses's powerlessness in
his inability to make sense of divine justice. God offers no explanation to
Moses, merely declaring by fiat, "Be silent, for such is My decree." Human
beings certainly do not enable or augment God's power here. They are
victims of it. This is not the message that Shapira wishes to invoke in
October 1940. His selective hermeneutic reflects his emphasis on human
power, language, and agency at this early point in his Ghetto writing.

Having just placed human speech at the center of a theology of
human-God partnership, Shapira turns to another human activity that
similarly bolsters God: sacrifice. He writes:

It is only through a person's worship in this world—when he
gives all his strength and soul in his worship of God, in his
study of Torah, and in his prayers to God—that he sacrifices
part of his soul to Him, blessed be He. . . . Nowadays, when
there are no animal sacrifices, the study of Torah, prayer, and
intense worship has become the essential sacrifice, determined
by the extent of the soul invested in them.

This is what our teacher Moses meant when he said, "Give
greatness to the name of God." Help God, as it were, through
blessing His name, and by offering up your soul in your blessing
as a sacrifice to God. These sacrifices then become "the bread of
God" (cf. Leviticus 21–22). (Sacrifices are referred to as "bread
of God" because just as bread gives a person strength, so our
sacrifices give, as it were, strength to God.)[10]

In line with earlier rabbinic thinking that sought to internalize sacrifice, Shapira transforms the notion from a physical act to an act of language.[11] Though he nods approvingly toward the days of animal sacrifice of the past, he privileges sacrificing one's soul, something that entails devotional acts, study, and prayer. Words—chanted words, analyzed words, spoken words—are the primary conduit for connecting to God.[12]

The effect of this transference is dramatic. Shapira not only transforms a bodily act performed on another (an animal) into an internal one but significantly redirects the very purpose of sacrifice. A sacrifice is not a gift that a human being might give to God in recognition of God's power and in deference to it, as it is frequently construed to be. It is, rather, what establishes and enables God's power.[13] The human being is the driver of the process, not a meek participant in it. One has the unique capacity to "feed" God on high through an offering of utterances, unleashing God's strength using "the gifts of [one's] mouth" alone.[14]

With this empowering message regarding the human voice, some implicit questions arise for Shapira: Do all vocalizations function as nourishment for God? How much specificity and how much intention are needed to spur God to powerful action? What is needed for sacrifice to take place? To these he responds: "When a Jew shouts out to God from pain, even though it is only pain and not his desire to worship God that causes him to shout, nevertheless, since suffering washes away sins and he is crying out to God, this is also counted as a sacrifice."[15]

Despite the insinuations of the grounding verse of this essay—"When I proclaim God's name, give greatness to the name of God"[16]—that one must use specific words (God's name) or praising language to elicit God's power, Shapira argues otherwise. Cries of agony, inarticulate though they may be, can function in the same way. By virtue of the fact that the suffering Jew directs his cries to God, he names God as the one powerful enough to respond to his pain. And in so doing, he reifies that power. He crowns God as king, so to speak, when he identifies God as the proper address for his woeful screams.[17] Thus, the Jew in pain who himself feels so very impotent in the face of his oppressor is hereby recast by Shapira as an agent of immense potency, capable of unleashing divine force.

There is one more aspect of suffering that renders it spiritually efficacious. "Suffering washes away sins," Shapira claims. It is in this context that the text of *yissurim shel ahavah* is introduced: "The Talmud (b. Berakhot 5a) explains the verse (Ps 94:12) 'Happy is the man whom You, O Lord, chasten, teaching him [*telamdeno*] out of Your law': Teach us this from Your Law *a fortiori* from [the laws of] the tooth and the eye."[18] The remainder of the talmudic passage—not included in the Hebrew original—elevates suffering qua suffering into a redemptive force. It suggests that Jews ought to welcome it, to enjoy it as an expression of their fortune, to revel in it as a kind of liberation.

But that is not at all Shapira's emphasis. In focusing exclusively on a fortiori logic learned from the laws of slave damages (and leaving out all framing references to the grandeur of pain), he points toward a different message: that suffering can be empowering in its ability to force God's hand. Suffering renders one not a victim but a more commanding agent. In the analogy cited, a master who harms his slave likely does so as a reminder of his absolute power over him. But the result of the abuse is that the slave actually wields greater power over the master. According to biblical law, the slave sets himself free the moment that he announces his master's ill treatment. So too with human suffering vis-à-vis God, suggests Shapira. It might look like Jews are being weakened on account of their abuse (by Nazis or by a punitive or abandoning God), but actually, their abuse foments their burgeoning strength. Through their voices alone, they will force God's hand. Through their cries, which are a kind of sacrifice, God's redemptive power will have to be unleashed. Like Moses in b. Shabbat 89a, they will assist God in writing the next chapter of Jewish history.

Shapira concludes this section by restating the verse from Psalms referenced in b. Berakhot 5a: "Happy is the man whom You, O Lord, chasten, teaching him out of Your Law."[19] He adds, "This we learn from the Law: that pain cleanses and atones for sins."[20] By now it should be clear that Shapira is not suggesting that pain itself exonerates one from sin or automatically purifies one's soul. Rather, torment generates wrenching cries, and it is those voices, those vocal sacrifices, that in turn stir God to forgiving, redemptive action. Thus, the grounding text of the notion of *yissurim shel ahavah* here gets stripped down and reinterpreted entirely. Rather than justifying unjustified pain as an expression of God's potent love for humanity, Shapira has repurposed b. Berakhot 5a as an expression of humanity's power over God, or, at the very least, necessary partnership with God.

Lest one think that Shapira presents too rosy a picture of suffering's potential here, he ends this essay with a subtle note of protest against a God who asks for this kind of assistance.

> In the prophetic reading (*Haftorah*) for this week (Hosea 14) we say, "Return, Israel, to God your Lord for you are ensnared in your iniquity. Take with you words and return to God, saying to Him, 'Forgive all our sins and take the good, we will pay You oxen with our lips.' "[21] . . . Why must we bring sacrifices of pain and suffering, God forbid, offering "oxen with our lips" by crying in pain? God might rather "take the good," and then the offerings we make—"the oxen we pay with our lips"—would come from the good, and salvation from our singing and praising of God.[22]

In other words, the elevation of tears to the height of sacrifice comes at a grave price, for this form of human empowerment demands a tremendous amount of pain. Shapira is using the concept of *yissurim shel ahavah,* here reifying language as a mode of empowerment and seeming to reinforce the vision of mutuality, devotion, and sacrifice he found in the talmudic materials. But Shapira, quietly echoing the outrage of Moses in b. Menahot 29b, poignantly asks: Could the God who invites human partnership not find that assistance through human joy as opposed to human suffering? Must the "gifts of one's mouth" always be cries? Shapira fares no better than Moses did in the face of Rabbi Akiva's martyrdom: God replied simply, "Be silent." For Shapira in October of 1940, these questions ominously dangle in silence.

January 31, 1942: On Suffering, Song, and Silence

The paradigm of *yissurim shel ahavah* and its attendant themes does not resurface again in the wartime sermons until January 31, 1942. The primary question that animates this essay for the Torah portion of *Beshalah* (Exod 13:17–17:16) is: Can one sing in the midst of suffering?[23] Homiletically, this question arises out of the central episode of the Torah portion, the exuberant singing of the Israelites upon witnessing the miracle of the splitting of the Red Sea.[24] Conceptually, Shapira reckons here with the despair that seems to have overtaken his community. How might anyone find a way toward song or toward hope during dark times?

Introducing the song at the Red Sea, Exod 15:1 states: "Then Moses and the children of Israel sang this song to the Lord, and they spoke, saying, I will sing to the Lord, for very exalted is He; a horse and its rider He cast into the sea." The unusual use of the future tense in the words "I will sing" captured the attention of many biblical commentators throughout the ages, and they similarly interest Rabbi Shapira. He cites two related explanations at the start of his essay. First, Rashi states that at the moment of the splitting of the sea, the Israelites felt moved to sing. Shapira then refers to Rabbi Levi Yitzhak of Berditchev (1740–1809), who suggests a different timeline. According to R. Levi Yitzhak, the Israelites had to envision singing before they actually sang, and the two acts were rather far apart. On this reading, the "Song of the Red Sea" was in fact composed while the Israelites were still enslaved in Egypt. In the midst of their oppression, they were able to imagine a time of liberation, and so they sang in the future tense, projecting themselves into a reality that would come but had not yet arrived. The Song of the Red Sea was thus a rendition of a song written long ago when dreaming of a possibility that was now coming to pass. "I will sing" were the words of a slave, certain that one day she would indeed sing again. Though deeply mired in the pain of servitude, a better future was imagined. But how reasonable is it to demand this kind of future-oriented consciousness from suffering people?

Shapira recognizes the uniqueness of the ancient Israelite who could sing in the midst of her suffering, just as he identifies the peculiarity of King David, who composed a song describing the rebellion against him of his own son Absalom.[25] He writes:

> It is possible to accept suffering and endure it with love [*yekholin lekabel yissurim b'ahavah*], and to have faith that everything is from God, but to actually sing while enduring it is difficult. In order for a person to sing, his essential self—his soul and his heart—must burst into song. One of the conditions of prophecy was the necessity for the prophet to be in a state of *simcha*—blissful joy—at all times, even while in pain, as we learn in the book *Sha'ar Ha-Kedusha,* by R. Hayyim Vital, of blessed memory. . . . [W]hen a level of *simcha* has been reached, [then] a person can sing to God even about pain.[26]

Shapira here invokes the theme of *yissurim shel ahavah* not as an explanation for suffering but as a framework for reckoning with it. Using language lifted directly from b. Berakhot 5a, the notion of "accepting [pain] with love" is cited as a reasonable expectation. One can conceivably choose to interpret one's lot as an expression of God's loving involvement in one's life. As the Talmud states, one can endure suffering "with consent," appropriating it as part of one's spiritual identity and tying it to a divine origin so that it is constitutive of a larger divine aim. But this interpretive process has limits, Shapira insists. "To actually sing while enduring [pain] is difficult." Acceptance is one thing; celebration is another. Or, rendered differently, we might say that cognitive assimilation of suffering into one's self-understanding might be possible and even praiseworthy, while affective, enthusiastic celebration of such suffering seems inhumane and beyond reasonable expectation.

The Talmud, cited by Shapira, addresses this issue regarding King David. How could he have sung in celebration of his son's uprising against him? Instead of "A song of David," the Psalm regarding Absalom should have read "a lamentation of David," it argues.[27] The Talmud resolves:

> When the Holy Blessed One said to David (2 Sam 12:11), "Behold I will raise up evil against you out of your own house," David began to worry. He thought, "It may be a slave or bastard who will have no pity on me." When he saw that it was Absalom, his son, he said, "Any normal son has a care for his father," and so he rejoiced. Hence, "A song of David."[28]

Shapira interprets this passage thus: "How was David able to sing? The Talmud answers that in suffering, he saw a miracle from heaven, because things could have been so much worse, God forbid. King David rejoiced over this miracle until he could sing about his pain."[29] David's song was not one of unadulterated, exuberant joy. It was a humble acknowledgment that, deeply injured though he was, he had not been afflicted with the worst of all possible wounds.[30] He could imagine a fate more damning than the treachery of his own son, and for this modest reprieve, he was grateful. He trusted that his son would show a modicum of mercy. From this place of relief, he found the strength to sing.

In a move uncharacteristic of Hasidic homilies—but not entirely uncommon in *Sermons from the Years of Rage*—Shapira extrapolates from the biblical character's experience to the experience of his own community: "This is an important rule for us," he writes. "In all suffering, when there is nothing with which to encourage ourselves, we must strengthen ourselves and rejoice in the reflection that it could have been, God forbid, so much worse."[31] Five months before the mass deportations from the Warsaw Ghetto to Treblinka would begin, Shapira pauses to note with gratitude that the dire circumstances of the moment are still not the worst of all possible worlds. Concentration camps had already been established and mass deportations had already begun elsewhere (from Lodz, for example) at the end of January 1942. But for Warsaw's Jews, the worst was indeed yet to come: between July 22 and September 12, 1942, 265,000 Jews would be deported from the Warsaw Ghetto to Treblinka.[32]

Though perhaps buoyed temporarily by this perspective, Shapira has no illusions about the long-term effectiveness of this coping strategy. He writes:

> But when, God forbid, the suffering is so great that one is completely crushed and the mind has crumbled, when there is insufficient personality left intact for it to be able to be strengthened, then it is difficult to rejoice in reflections like those of David. This is the reason why the Israelites [in Exod 6:9] "did not listen to Moses" [in Egypt].[33]

Though the Israelites in Egypt began, in this homily, as exemplars of hope in the midst of despair, Shapira returns to them here to speak of their encounter with numbing despondency. Exodus reports that when Moses first introduced himself as a redeemer to the enslaved population, "they did not listen to Moses because of their shortness of breath and the hard work."[34] There were no songs sung, no dreams of the future confirmed. On the contrary, the people were so mired in their years of crushing oppression, so stuck in their self-understanding as trapped victims, that they could not hear Moses's promise of freedom. The possibility of an alternate reality was simply incomprehensible to them, and so they rejected the bearer of that unimaginable message.

There are two stages of despair, suggests Shapira, and two concomitant pathways for tempering it. The first is exemplified by King David and by the earlier generations of enslaved Jews in Egypt (as interpreted by Levi Yitzhak of Berditchev). This is a despair that can still see beyond itself, either toward a better future or in comparison with what could have been worse. This form of despair can still sing about its suffering. It can vocalize its pain. It can imagine the possibility of release from pain and find a way to move toward it over time. The second stage of despair, however, is silent, hollowed out, without energy or perspective. It paralyzes and renders mute. It darkens worlds and robs people of the ability to even contemplate a way out. This was the horrific condition of the Jews in Egypt in advanced stages of their oppression, and he strongly implies that it threatens to overtake the Jews of his own time as well.[35]

The classification of different forms of silence recurs several times in the Ghetto sermons (see Seeman, this volume). The 1940 sermon we have been discussing echoes an earlier treatment of "muteness" (*ilmut*) in the sermon of December 2, 1939. After accounting for a kind of "silence" born of suppressed speech (*harishah*), he describes the following condition:

> When a Jew is, God forbid, crushed and broken to the point where he has nothing to speak, he doesn't comprehend or feel, he even has no mind or heart left with which to comprehend or emote, at which point it is no longer *harishah* but *ilmut*, like a mute that has no ability to speak.[36]

As pain increases, the depth of one's silence grows even more severe, resulting in what James A. Diamond calls "total communicatory paralysis."[37] Drawing upon André Neher, Diamond describes this bleak condition: "A more appropriate term for this kind of silence . . . is André Neher's nocturnal metasilence or 'nonsilence' (*lo dumiyah*) of Psalms 22:3, which he defines as 'more silent than silence. It is the fall of silence into a deeper stratum of nothingness; it is a shaft hollowed out beneath silence, which leads to its most vertiginous depths.'"[38] This is the painful, paralyzing silence that Shapira refers to in this January 1942 sermon as "more silent than silence" while his community hovers on the edge of its final catastrophe.

To address this kind of debilitating despair, self-generated and future-oriented hope are unavailable. When Moses expresses frustration to God about his contemporaries' inability to hear his message, the Bible recounts: "God spoke to Moses and Aaron and commanded them concerning the Israelites and concerning Pharaoh, the king of Egypt, to let the children of Israel out of the land of Egypt."[39] The content of the commandment to Moses and Aaron regarding the Israelite people is ambiguous here. Just what were they told to do? Shapira cites Rashi's explanation: "God commanded them to lead the Jewish people with gentleness and to have patience with them."[40]

God's strategy to enable people who have been deafened by the enormity of their own suffering to begin to hear once more is to treat them with extraordinary compassion. Perhaps over time, through the experience of being heard, they might learn to hear again, to trust in the voice of one who promises a future beyond pain. Yet Shapira interprets this gloss by Rashi in an entirely unexpected way:

> The meaning of this is that it was the duty of the shepherds of the Jewish people to bring about a change in Heaven's policy regarding the Jews, forcing it to administer the world with gentleness and patience, instead of inflicting pain, God forbid. This would allow the people to sing and to listen.[41]

Moses and Aaron were not commanded to turn to the people with gentleness and patience. They were commanded by God to turn *to God* to demand gentleness and patience on their behalf. They were to demand of heaven—to *force* God—to change the fate of the Jewish people.[42] The way out of numbing suffering was not to comfort the sufferers but to undo their suffering by confronting the one responsible. Shapira takes great interpretive license here. First, nowhere does Rashi or the biblical text itself indicate that the object of the biblical dictate is God. The chain of command is entirely straightforward and thoroughly hierarchical: God tells Moses and Aaron to communicate something to the people. Second, Shapira has redirected the content of the command to God, calling for a change in heavenly direction. The theology that undergirds this reimagined command is ultimately anthropocentric. As in b. Shabbat 89a, previously invoked by Shapira, God here demands that Moses assist him in changing the fate of the Jewish people. God once again needs human beings, specifically leaders or "shepherds," to help God be a better God.[43]

The partnership envisioned dramatically augments the power of human leaders (and we can reasonably assume that Shapira understood himself to be one such leader). In so doing, it also undermines God's omnipotence, which is otherwise assumed by the biblical text. Israel's suffering cannot be lifted until the right person makes the right kind of demand of God. Shapira quotes the Talmud to support this claim: "The tsaddik, the pious person, decrees, and the Holy Blessed One fulfills."[44] It seems that God on high does not, or cannot, dispense kindness without prompting from below. According to Shapira, God *commands* that he be moved to mercy by people so that he might act toward them with compassion. This leaves human beings with power over God.

But, again, not just any human being. Behind the veil of the exodus story, Shapira implies that only a tsaddik—perhaps one like himself—can bring hopeful song back into the lives of his followers now. As he says regarding Moses:

> [God] commanded that, by decree, a change must be wrought in the Divine administration of the world, decreeing that the

Jewish people be led mercifully. This would bring an end to their slavery, and enable them, even while they were still in Egypt, to sing and praise God and to prepare themselves for the singing and praising they would do upon redemption.[45]

Moses succeeded in doing this. By storming the heavens, so to speak, he enabled his people to cultivate receptivity to redemption even before redemption came. Shapira clearly hopes that he can do the same. He too implicitly demands "that a change . . . be wrought in the Divine administration of the world" to bolster the spirits of his people, to open them to the possibility of future song, even as they remain stuck in the mire of Nazi oppression. Perhaps they could, after all, with his help "accept suffering and endure it with love," *yekholin le-kabbel yissurim be-ahavah*.[46] This is consistent with his earlier depictions of love's affliction, though by 1942 he apparently came to emphasize the prayers of the tsaddikim over the songs of the Jewish masses. Shapira implicitly puts himself forward as one who might prevail on God to "let [his] people go."[47] But note that he quietly modifies his redemptive aspiration, now no longer foregrounding a miraculous redemption so much as the mere ability to imagine the possibility of life beyond affliction.

July 11, 1942: At the Edge of Explanation

The last time that Shapira mentions *yissurim shel ahavah* is on July 11, 1942, in the penultimate sermon of his wartime collection. It is here, I believe, that Shapira finally concedes the inadequacy of this trope as an explanatory frame for the experiences of the Jews of his time. This sermon on the Torah portion of *mattot* continues the theme of joy as a necessary prerequisite for the perception of God and concomitant hope in the world. Tying his claims to a variety of classical biblical, talmudic, and mystical traditions,[48] Shapira declares not only that prophecy is unattainable in a state of despondency and sadness but also that such a condition precludes even lower-level spiritual engagement.

> [Sadness] also affects one's ability to take some homiletic teaching from the painful experience, for even this is impossible when a person is grief-stricken and spirit-crushed. There are even times when it is impossible for a person to force himself

to say anything or to interpret events at all because of the immensity of the breakdown and decline, may the Merciful One protect us.[49]

Having guided his students thus far, offering them sermons that reflect the crushing experience of the Warsaw Ghetto, Shapira is clearly entering here into a paradigm of absolute crisis. He never fully leaves behind his veil of impersonality as an author, but it does grow thin over time. The mass deportations from Warsaw to Treblinka would soon begin (on July 22, 1942), but the Ghetto had already seen its share of misery, and Shapira's tone indicates that he is shaken. Just a few months before, he had put himself forward as a leader and pleader before God on behalf of his diminished and weakened community. Now, he too lacks the strength, and certainly the joy, to storm the heavens and force God's hand. And so he asks: "With what can [a crushed soul] strengthen itself, at least a little, so long as salvation has not appeared? And with what can the spirit be elevated, even the tiniest bit, while crushed and broken like this?"[50] Note that the questions here are personal and anthropocentric. He does not ask how to bring about salvation from on high as he did before but rather how to cope with the now evident failure of such deliverance to arrive.

To this challenge, he offers several preliminary answers. First, holding onto slipping hope, he suggests prayer and faith that God will not entirely abandon his children to annihilation. He encourages trust in the mercy of God and in the idea of redemption itself, even as it tarries. Though Shapira will never explicitly give up on the possibility of divine intervention, his focus here shifts subtly. This response, cloaked in theological language, seems less an assertion of God's salvific power and more a claim about the salubrious effects of belief in that power. "With what can [one] strengthen [one]self?" he asks. "With prayer and with faith," he answers.[51] These religious tools are spiritually strengthening, whether or not they engender physical rescue. The belief in ultimate endurance—of one's people, if not of oneself—itself elevates the spirit, he suggests, even if it will not save the body. This is a strategy for psychic survival.

Yet Shapira painfully acknowledges that as the numbers of the dead increase, this belief becomes less plausible and thus less effective. He asks:

With what shall we gather strength over those, the holy ones, who have already, God protect us, been murdered, relatives and loved ones, and other unrelated Jews, many of whom touch us like our very own souls? And how will we encourage ourselves, at least somewhat, in face of the terrifying reports, old and new, that we hear, shattering our bones and dissolving our hearts?[52]

To this, he offers another approach. When trust in communal endurance fails, when it looks like God just might allow for the end of the Jewish people, trust in shared misery should prevail. Jews ought to take comfort in knowing that they do not suffer alone, but rather that God suffers alongside them. Ps 91:15 states, "I am with him in distress," and this, for Shapira, grounds a doctrine of solidarity. He again foregoes a strong affirmation of divine salvation in favor of a soft declaration of divine consolation. God will not necessarily save all of his people from pain, but out of his particular love for them, he will join them in their pain. God bears the burdens thrust upon his people together with them, dispersing and thereby lightening their heavy load.

This theme of divine solidarity is one that he returns to often throughout *Sermons from the Years of Rage*.[53] What distinguishes this particular reference—his last—is the way in which it is set so clearly in contrast to divine deliverance. It is invoked precisely to account for the growing awareness of God's noninterference. Solidarity is offered as spiritual compensation for the lack of physical salvation.

Yet even the notion of divine solidarity cannot satisfy those with "shatter[ed] . . . bones and dissolve[ed] . . . hearts." The suffering has grown intolerable, and a God who merely joins in it but does not remove it fails to offer the solace that is much needed. So Shapira adds a third approach:

> There is suffering we endure individually for our sins, or pangs of love [*yissurim shel ahavah*] that soften [or polish] and purify us. In all of this, God merely suffers with us. But then there is suffering in which we merely suffer with Him, so to speak—suffering for the sanctification of God's name. . . . The chief suffering is really for God's sake, and because of Him we are ennobled and exalted by this sort of pain. With this, we may encourage ourselves, at least a little.[54]

In this final stage of his Ghetto sermons, Shapira explicitly abandons the notion of *yissurim shel ahavah* and reiterates the inapplicability of divine retribution for Israel's sin or iniquity. The conceptual tool of "afflictions of love," which itself struggles with the end of explanation, must be dismissed as insufficiently explanatory on account of the growing sense of desperation. Instead, a new category is introduced: *yissurim shel kiddush Hashem*, sufferings for the sanctification of God's name.[55]

In the Talmud, *kiddush Hashem* refers to martyrdom, to Jews giving their lives to God as a symbol of devotion.[56] Yet Shapira uses it now to describe dying on behalf of God or as God's proxy. In a direct reversal of his earlier doctrine of divine solidarity with humanity, Shapira here advances the doctrine of human solidarity with God. The Jewish people, as representatives of God in the world, suffer with God, on account of God, and on behalf of God. Sometimes God is the real target of anti-Jewish action and Jews the byproducts of that assault. They bear God's burdens.[57] They are with him in his pain. Shapira writes:

> The liturgy [for the holiday of Sukkot] reads: "Hosanna, save those who learn Your fear, Hosanna. Hosanna, save those who are slapped upon the cheek, Hosanna. Hosanna, save those who are given to beatings, Hosanna. Hosanna, save those who bear Your burden, Hosanna." By "those who learn Your fear," we mean those who learn the whole of Torah. . . . How is it possible to learn when we are being "slapped upon the face" and "given over to beatings?" Because Israel knows that she "bears Your burden," and from this she is able to take some little encouragement.[58]

It is rare for Shapira to ground an argument in Jewish liturgy rather than biblical or talmudic texts, but here he must be more innovative than usual if he is to construct a new paradigm of theodicy. The holiday of Sukkot is still a few months away for him, yet the refrain of "Hosanna" in one of its central prayers—an elision of the Hebrew words for "save us please"—is timely. In simply referencing this repetitive prayer, Shapira subtly gives voice to the desperation of his people, who are in search of a savior, while simultaneously offering justification for the failure of the savior to come. God, as it were, is under attack by the Nazis (though Nazis are never explicitly named), and the Jews, slapped and beaten, are bearing his burden together with him. Not quite as empowered as they were in previous essays, God's children are hurting terribly along with God, but this time they cannot assist him. They can only share in his pain and presence.

Awareness of this phenomenon ought to bring a modicum of relief. The mirroring of God's fate is a privilege, according to these late sermons, a reflection of deep intimacy, connection, and inextricable identification. Jews become God's image in the world, echoing below the reality on high. Suffering is a mere manifestation of this singular human-God relationship, and thus, the Jews "are ennobled and exalted by this sort of pain."[59]

Still, Shapira is not naive enough to believe that this recontextualization can fully relieve Israel of its sorrows. His language is consistently modest. At best, he writes, "we may encourage ourselves, at least a little" or "from this [Israel] is able to take some little encouragement."[60] As a third attempt to identify a strategy to maintain psychic cohesion in the face of near-breakdown, this attempt falls short, even for Shapira himself. Indeed, he caps his investigation into this matter with a plea that is a protest: " 'Return O God, until when?' (Ps 90:13). Jews are giving their lives for the sanctification of God's name. 'Please, O God!' He will have mercy on His people and on His children who are killed and tortured for His blessed sake."[61] Sufferings for the sanctification of God's name, exalted as they may be in theory, hurt as much physically, and almost as much spiritually, as any suffering, and so Shapira begs God to release his beloved people from this unbearable burden.

Concluding Remarks

The concept of *yissurim shel ahavah* is explicitly and finally relinquished in the sermon of July 11, 1942. It is inadequate to the task of finding a frame in which to process Jewish suffering. And yet, in replacing it with a parallel concept, Shapira may be said to retain the structure of the paradigm that he rejects. *Yissurim shel kiddush Hashem* is patterned linguistically, as well as conceptually, on *yissurim shel ahavah*. Both are essentially rooted in love. Both make Jewish suffering the outgrowth of the unique relationship between God and Israel. Both make the claim that pain recontextualized is pain diminished. Both place the psalmist's declaration "I am with him in his distress" at the core of their message.[62] The difference between them lies in the direction of empathy. *Yissurim shel ahavah* bear witness to divine love for human beings. *Yissurim shel kiddush Hashem* bear witness to human love for and presence with God.

And so, as this penultimate sermon ends, afflictions of love are decidedly renounced, but their imprint continues to reverberate in Shapira's new, if unsatisfying, model: afflictions of sanctification. What is gained in this process of substitution is subtle. In shifting the onus of suffering entirely onto God, Shapira effectively removes any and all vestiges of blame from the Jews. Not only are they not culpable for their own suffering, they are not even its true subjects. Implicated though they are by God's travails, those travails are fundamentally not their own—either as sinners, or as martyrs, or as purified lovers.

On the cusp of his final sermon, on the verge of the Great Deportation, Shapira stands at the edge of his own capacity for explanation. The theory of *yissurim shel ahavah* has failed to justify suffering and has failed to console the remnants of a community undone by pain. Though it began as a model of human empowerment in October 1940 and reverberated through sermons as late as January 1942, the paradigm could not ultimately be sustained in the face of relentless devastation. It did, however, offer a rich framework within which to grapple with the potential loss of redemptive frameworks altogether. Like the ailing rabbis of b. Berakhot 5b, who, faced with their own illnesses, came to reject their abstract notions about beloved suffering, Shapira ultimately, if implicitly, declares in July 1942, *Lo hem ve-lo sekharam*,[63] "We do not welcome our sufferings, nor do we welcome their reward."

Notes

1. See, for example, Deut 8:5; Prov 3:12; 13:24; Ps 94:12.

2. David Kraemer, *Responses to Suffering in Classical Rabbinic Literature* (New York: Oxford University Press, 1995), 23.

3. The rabbinic understanding of the relationship between love and suffering centers on one rather lengthy discussion, in b. Berakhot 5a-b, the longest treatment of suffering in all of classical rabbinic literature.

4. See Rashi on b. Berakhot 5a, s.v. "afflictions of love."

5. B. Berakhot 5b.

6. For a review of Jewish anti-theodicy, see Zachary Braiterman, *(God) After Auschwitz* (Princeton: Princeton University Press, 1998).

7. Translation from Kalonymus Kalman Shapira, *Sacred Fire: Torah from the Years of Fury 1939–1942*, trans. J. Hershy Worch (New York: Rowman and Littlefield, 2002), 165. Also see Kalonymus Kalman Shapira, *Sermons from the Years of Rage* [in Hebrew], ed. Daniel Reiser, 2 vols. (Jerusalem: Herzog Academic College, 2017), 1:158–59. Unless otherwise noted, translations in this chapter are from Worch, with additional citation from Reiser's Hebrew edition. Please

note that in this case, only the Hebrew original cites the condensed version of the talmudic story. Worch added in the surrounding context—a move that I will argue undermines Shapira's intent.

8. Deut 32:3.

9. See *Sacred Fire*, 248, 252, 263; *Sermons from the Years of Rage*, *rosh ha-shanah* 5702 (1941), 1:218; ibid., *parashat vayyishlah* 5702 (1941), 1:239; ibid., *hanukkah* 5702 (1941), 1:243; and ibid., *parashat va'era* 5702 (1942), 1:250–51.

10. *Sacred Fire*, 136; *Sermons from the Years of Rage*, *shabbat shuvah* 5701 (1940), 1:159. See note 11 for a discussion of the controversial status of the parentheses.

11. For rabbinic precedents, see, for example, b. Menahot 110a and b. Ta'anit 2a.

12. See Ariel Evan Mayse, *Speaking Infinites: God and Language in the Teachings of Rabbi Dov Ber of Mezritsh* (Philadelphia: University of Pennsylvania Press, 2020).

13. See Jonathan Garb, *Manifestations of Power in Jewish Mysticism* (Jerusalem: Magnes, 2005); and Hartley Lachter, *Kabbalistic Revolution: Reimagining Judaism in Medieval Spain* (New Brunswick: Rutgers University Press, 2014).

14. Ps 94:12.

15. On laughter, song, and tears as a mode of overcoming tragedy and absurdity, see also Ariel Evan Mayse, "Stories Untold: Theology, Language and the Hasidic Spirit in Elie Wiesel's *The Gates of the Forest*," in *The Struggle for Understanding: Elie Wiesel's Literary Works*, ed. Victoria Nesfield and Philip Smith (Albany: State University of New York Press, 2019), 137–67.

16. Deut 32:3.

17. See also Arthur Green, *Keter: The Crown of God in Early Jewish Mysticism* (Princeton: Princeton University Press, 1997).

18. *Sacred Fire*, 118; *Sermons from the Years of Rage*, *shabbat shuvah* 5701 (1940), 1:159.

19. Ps 94:12.

20. *Sacred Fire*,137; *Sermons from the Years of Rage*, *shabbat shuvah* 5701 (1940), 1:160.

21. Hos 14:2–3.

22. *Sacred Fire*, 137; *Sermons from the Years of Rage*, *shabbat shuvah* 5701 (1940), 1:160.

23. See Nehemia Polen, "*Niggun* as Spiritual Practice, with Special Focus on the Writings of Rabbi Kalonymus Shapiro, the Rebbe of Piaseczna" (forthcoming).

24. See Exod 15:1–21.

25. Psalm 3 begins: "A song of David, when he fled from Absalom his son . . ." See also 2 Sam 15–18.

26. *Sacred Fire*, 276; *Sermons from the Years of Rage*, *parashat be-shalah* 5702 (1942), 1:261.

27. b. Berakhot 7b.

28. Ibid.

29. *Sacred Fire*, 276; *Sermons from the Years of Rage, parashat be-shalah* 5702 (1942), 1:261.

30. Betrayal by one's own flesh and blood surely could be seen by some as the most painful affront possible. Yet the Talmud imagines David to find comfort in this instead, hopeful that his son will show him mercies that others would not. In light of the activities of the *Judenrat* (Jewish councils directed by the Nazis) already active in the Warsaw Ghetto at this time, Shapira's use of this image gains poignancy. Perhaps he too thought that the fate of the Jews would be less severe if their persecution was mediated through fellow Jews.

31. *Sacred Fire*, 276–77; *Sermons from the Years of Rage, parashat be-shalah* 5702 (1942), 1:261.

32. See Yisrael Gutman, *The Jews of Warsaw* (Bloomington: Indiana University Press, 1989), 197.

33. *Sacred Fire*, 277; *Sermons from the Years of Rage, parashat be-shalah* 5702 (1942), 1:261.

34. Exod 6:9.

35. According to Exod 12:40, the Israelites were enslaved in Egypt for 430 years. Shapira proposes that there were two phases of oppression during this time. During the first, the Israelites, though persecuted, were still able to accomplish their work and, thus, their spirits remained intact. During the second, conditions worsened as Pharaoh denied them the materials needed to execute their work orders (see Exod 5:7). This added oppression to oppression and sent the Israelites into deep despair.

36. *Sacred Fire*, 22; *Sermons from the Years of Rage, parashat vayyeshev* 5700 (1939), 1:97.

37. James A. Diamond, "The Warsaw Ghetto Rebbe: Diverting God's Gaze from a Utopian End to an Anguished Now," *Modern Judaism* 30, no. 3 (2010): 299–331, at 302.

38. Ibid.

39. Exod 6:13.

40. Rashi on Exod 6:13.

41. *Sacred Fire*, 277; *Sermons from the Years of Rage, parashat be-shalah* 5702 (1942), 1:262.

42. See Dov Weiss, *Pious Irreverence: Confronting God in Rabbinic Judaism* (Philadelphia: University of Pennsylvania Press, 2017).

43. See Don Seeman, "Ritual Efficacy, Hasidic Mysticism and 'Useless Suffering' in the Warsaw Ghetto," *Harvard Theological Review* 101, no. 3–4 (2008): 465–505.

44. B. Sotah 12a. This text, and the parallel in b. Mo'ed Katan 16b, are frequently cited in Hasidic sources extolling the power of the tsaddik. See Arthur

Green, "Typologies of Leadership and the Hasidic Zaddiq," *Jewish Spirituality II: From the Sixteenth-Century Revival to the Present*, ed. Arthur Green (New York: Continuum, 1987), 127–56; Green, "The *Zaddiq* as *Axis Mundi* in Later Judaism," *Journal of the American Academy of Religion* 45, no. 3 (1977): 327–47.

45. *Sacred Fire*, 278; *Sermons from the Years of Rage, be-shalah* 5702 (1942), 1:262.

46. B. Berakhot 5a, cited in *Sacred Fire*, 276; *Sermons from the Years of Rage, be-shalah* 5702 (1942), 1:261.

47. Exod 9:1.

48. See 2 Kgs 3:15; b. Shabbat 30b; and Hayyim Vital, *Sha'arei ha-kedushah*, 17–22.

49. *Sacred Fire*, 333; *Sermons from the Years of Rage, parashat mattot* 5702 (1942), 1:310.

50. Ibid.

51. Ibid.

52. Ibid., 334; *Sermons from the Years of Rage*, 1:310.

53. See, for example, *Sacred Fire*, 54, 154, 158, 211, 315; *Sermons from the Years of Rage, parashat vayyikra* 5700 (1940), 1:113; ibid., *parashat toledot* 5701 (1940), 1:171; ibid., *parashat vayyishlah* 5701 (1940), 1:173; ibid., *parashat re'eh* 5701 (1941), 1:213; ibid., *parashat mishpatim-shekalim* 5702 (1942), 1:272; and ibid., *parashat ha-hodesh* 5702 (1942), 1:292.

54. *Sermons from the Years of Rage, parashat ha-hodesh* 5702 (1942), 1:287–294; *Sermons from the Years of Rage, mattot* 5702 (1942), 1:311.

55. See the classic study of Shimon Huberband, *Kiddush Hashem: Jewish Religious and Cultural Life in Poland During the Holocaust*, trans. David E. Fishman (Hoboken: Ktav, 1987).

56. See, for example, b. Bava Kama 113a and b. Sanhedrin 74a.

57. For a discussion of *yissurim shel kiddush Hashem*, see Nehemia Polen, *The Holy Fire: The Teachings of Rabbi Kalonymus Kalman Shapira, the Rebbe of the Warsaw Ghetto* (Northvale: Jason Aronson, 1994), 120–21.

58. *Sacred Fire*, 334; *Sermons from the Years of Rage, parashat mattot* 5702 (1942), 1:311.

59. Ibid.

60. Ibid.

61. Ibid.

62. Ps 91:15.

63. B. Berakhot 5b.

12

"Living with the Times"

Historical Context in the Wartime Writings of Rabbi Kalonymus Kalman Shapira

Henry Abramson

Rabbi Shapira's wartime sermons seem completely disconnected from the quotidian reality of the Ghetto, citing and explaining sources from the Jewish literary tradition as if the world were not collapsing around both its author and his immediate audience. The mood of the sermons is dark—Shapira's writings constitute perhaps the most sustained theological meditation on theodicy and human suffering since Nahmanides, or perhaps even the biblical book of Job—but the almost total lack of explicit historical references in this work is striking. If we understand history solely in terms of Leopold von Ranke's nineteenth-century definition, *wie es eigentlich gewesen war* (what actually happened), then Rabbi Shapira's works represent a distinct challenge, because he seems to have been virtually impervious to the temptation to make explicit reference to any political or social occurrence in his Shabbat sermons. He preferred to situate his weekly message in the ahistorical world that simultaneously included biblical Egypt, talmudic commentators from Babylon, medieval exegetes from pre-expulsion Spain, and Hasidic masters from eastern Europe (see Wodziński, Wiskind, this volume). Given this literary-religious style, how can anyone glean actual historical data from *Sermons from the Years of Rage*?

It is true that the written record of R. Shapira's handwritten manuscript preserved in the Ringelblum archives contains only a distillation of
the actual discourses he taught. Common Hasidic practice suggests that
he delivered his messages in Yiddish rather than Rabbinic Hebrew and
probably spoke at much greater length than the brief entries, recorded
from memory on Saturday nights, suggest.[1] Perhaps he prefaced his oral
remarks with explicit discussion of the historical moment; we simply
don't know. The written record, however, preserves what can be nothing
but a conscious attempt to avoid, with only a few exceptions, almost any
reference to historical context.[2]

There are multiple reasons why explicit references to contemporary
historical events might be ignored in a rabbinic sermon, as Marc Saperstein
has amply demonstrated. "Addressed to a familiar audience at a specific
moment," he writes, "the sermon is by its nature an allusive genre. The
preacher can refer to 'the dramatic events of the past few days,' to an
incident that had become the topic of widespread discussion . . . confident
that the listeners would follow."[3] Moreover, converting that oral presentation to a written document might lead the author to eliminate details
that would cause the material to seem (literally) dated.[4] Nevertheless, the
almost complete absence of historical references, especially during the
terrifying years of the Holocaust, calls for better explanation.

Reading History in *Sermons from the Years of Rage*

Judith Thidor-Baumel proposed as early as 1980 that a careful comparison of R. Shapira's dated sermons with what is known of the day-to-day
microhistory of the Ghetto might shed light on the internal life of the
Hasidic community and how it came to understand the unfolding events
of the Holocaust.[5] The challenge to the historian, she argued, would be to
read these Sabbath sermons as commentaries on *history* as much as they
were commentaries on *Torah*. On a fundamental level, I am arguing that
this is precisely what Shapira was hoping to achieve with his sermons.
Confronted with confused, bewildered, and beleaguered Hasidim who
sought comfort and consolation, the rebbe would mine his extensive
knowledge of the Jewish literary tradition to place the horrendous events
of the Ghetto into the metahistorical context of Torah. The explicit words
of the sermon might be describing the tribulations of the Jews in Egypt,
on this reading, but the crucial subterranean meaning would directly

address the suffering of the Jews in contemporary Warsaw and later in the Warsaw Ghetto.

The artistry of R. Shapira's approach is remarkable. The underlying meaning—literally the "subtext"—remains opaque to unprepared twenty-first-century readers, but it would have been transparent to his audience. Through allusive language and references to biblical models, his style would ipso facto reinforce the notion that the contemporary suffering of Jews under German occupation was part of the larger pattern of Jewish history, a traditional concept encapsulated in the phrase *ma'aseh avot siman le-vanim*, "the experiences of the ancestors are a sign for their descendants."[6] This literary device also served to reinforce the promise of ultimate redemption: just as the ancestors were ultimately saved from the Egyptian crucible, so too would their descendants emerge from the Nazi inferno.

The data to be gleaned from reading the wartime sermons in this way is unlikely to yield much that is new in the way of modernist historiographic data. We are not about to learn many new details about how the *Judenrat* operated, or about the structure and function of the Jewish resistance, or even about the size and complexion of the Hasidic community. Rather, I would argue that the historical data we may derive from R. Shapira's wartime writings are more *postmodern* in nature, to adapt a distinction articulated by Rabbi Shimon Gershon Rosenberg (Rav Shagar). *Sermons from the Years of Rage* can help us appreciate the *specific truths* of Warsaw Jewry, even though they remain largely silent on the *general truths* frequently sought by historians.[7]

Consider the following exception, which may help to prove the rule. In one of his early Ghetto sermons, R. Shapira comments briefly (in just five Hebrew words!) on a contemporary trial faced by pious Jews in Warsaw: the forced and public shaving of their beards (see Seeman, this volume). Rabbi Shimon Huberband, a relative and member of Shapira's yeshiva in Warsaw, provides personal testimony to this widespread practice in the initial weeks of the German occupation beginning in October, 1939:

> Two other Jews were seized along with us; one with a black beard, the other with a long yellowish beard. A moment later, they grabbed an elegantly dressed young lady and forced her to shear off my beard and Shtayer's. The girl wept as she cut our hair, for the honor of the Jewish people which was being disgraced in public by the evil ones . . .

These barbarities were done not only to grown men but also to children with earlocks. In Praga, a group of German officers chanced upon the ten-year-old Avrom Igelnik, at the gate of 32 Brukowa Street. They took him away to their headquarters, where they set fire to his earlocks. The young boy was lucky to have been left alive.[8]

R. Shapira makes mention of this cruelty in his sermon for *parashat tole-dot,* November 11, 1939, through reflection on a verse in Isaiah (27:13):

And then they will come, those who are lost in the land of Assyria, and those who are dispersed in the land of Egypt. There are two distinct categories: the lost and the dispersed. The dispersed refers to one who is displaced to a distant locale yet remains distinct and recognizable. This is in contradistinction to the lost—this person is lost and is neither distinct nor recognizable. For when the hardships are presently so compounded that they even cut off the beards of Jews, which makes them outwardly unrecognizable—and due to unimaginable persecution and unbearable afflictions, they are no longer recognizable internally—such a person loses himself, he ceases to recognize himself. How did he feel a year ago, on the Sabbath, or on a weekday prior to prayers, or during prayers, etc.? Now he is trampled and crushed, such that he no longer senses if he is a Jew or not, or a human being or not, or an animal that has no capacity to feel. This is the nature of one who is lost, yet they will come, those who are lost.[9]

One may imagine the impact of these words on his audience, which likely included individuals whose beards and earlocks had already been shorn by the Nazis. Marshaling his keen psychological insight, Shapira empathizes with the victims and affirms the deep connection between the external markers of identity and a person's internal state: "he ceases to recognize himself." Shapira concludes with a message of encouragement to his listeners and readers:

The Talmud states that the one who lost something seeks after his lost object.[10] When he lost it, it was no longer perceptible nor recognizable, and thus the owner seeks to find it, to pick it up and bring it home. And is it not God who is the master of we who are lost? Are we not the lost possessions of God? . . . May the Owner of the lost return to find us . . . [11]

The element of historical context, that is, the clear reference to the shearing of the beards of Orthodox Jewish men, is the slight deviation from the pattern established for the vast majority of the entries in *Sermons from the Years of Rage*. Shapira's goal throughout was to provide consolation and guidance to his audience, and to accomplish this pastoral objective, he adopted the following basic pattern:

1. Locate the sermon within the context of the Jewish calendar, typically with a reference to the text of the week's Torah reading or a practice in a proximate holiday.

2. Refer in an allusive, oblique manner to experiences of contemporary Warsaw Jews. Demonstrate his awareness of their suffering and validate it.

3. Return to the scriptural reference and conclude with a message of consolation and hope for both physical and spiritual redemption (see Maayan, this volume).

Viewed in this light, *Sermons from the Years of Rage* represents a sustained, heroic effort by R. Shapira to provide spiritual leadership to his followers in extremis for the duration of the war. He clearly refused to see his wartime sermons simply as intellectual discourses on esoteric subjects: he was invested in the suffering of his community and took on the awesome, exhausting mantle of responsibility to care for their spiritual and mental well-being under incomprehensible circumstances.

Detailed reading of the wartime sermons will yield a small number of references that have value in terms of historical context, but they tend to be of very local, specific importance, revealing more about the personal well-being of the author and the conditions under which he spoke and wrote than what Warsaw Jews endured as a whole. We learn, for example, that he went into hiding when the Nazis were arresting Jewish communal leaders in retaliation for the assassination of a soldier by the Jewish resistance, and that he survived a bout of typhus.[12] We also see explicit references to historical events such as *yortsayts,* or death-anniversaries: two for his son Bentsion Elimelekh, killed in the initial Luftwaffe bombing of Warsaw in October 1939, and once for R. Shapira's father.[13] From a historical point of view, these *derashot* (sermons) do not add much to our knowledge of the condition of the Warsaw Jewish community.

More common in R. Shapira's wartime writing are allusive references, often quite central to the sermon in question, that directly address the concerns of the community. Consider, for example, his remarks on *parashat metsora* 5700 (April 13, 1940). Earlier that month, Warsaw Jews were distressed to witness the initial construction of walls in several parts of the city. Up until the building of these walls, the concentration of Jews in certain parts of Warsaw had been effected only by administrative decree, with few permanent structures demarcating the boundaries of the ghetto.

R. Shapira's sermon begins with a citation from the medieval commentator Rashi regarding the treatment of a house that had been placed under quarantine after it showed signs of the plague known in Scripture as *tsara'at* (Lev 14). Biblical law mandates that such a home be quarantined as impure for seven days and then examined to see whether the plague remains before destroying it. Rashi cites an ancient midrash according to which the owners of a particular home began to dismantle their home as the law requires, only to find a treasure hidden within the walls by previous inhabitants, long ago:

> Let us understand: if such is the case, why is one required to seal the house for seven days at the outset and only afterward remove the stones [i.e., dismantle the structure]? Once the plague is visible, one knows that treasures are to be found there! This is especially true according to the understanding of Nahmanides, cited in the works of my holy father, that plagues on houses and clothing are supernatural occurrences and are only for the benefit of the Jewish people in order to reveal the hidden treasures.[14] Why, then, does the Torah command us to render the house impure at the onset of the seven days?[15]

To restate Shapira's question: If the *tsara'at* is to be understood as a supernatural signal to the Jews that there are treasures hidden within their walls, then what is the point of the quarantine? Shouldn't the Jews simply destroy the walls immediately once the first indications of *tsara'at* are evident? One can only imagine how his question must have electrified his Hasidim, who were seeking guidance on the meaning of the walls being constructed around them in Warsaw. Shapira's reference to long-lost treasure may have alluded to a hidden benefit in the walls, but did these words also contain a hint of rebellion or advocacy of sabotage? He continues:

> In truth, the intent of the Torah and its commandments is beyond our grasp. We can, however, perceive allusions, for we know and believe that all that God does for us—even, Heaven forbid, when God strikes us—is all for our benefit. At the present time we see, however, we are not solely smitten with physical afflictions but also, Heaven forbid, with those [afflictions] that distance us from the Blessed One. There is neither primary Torah school nor a yeshiva; neither study hall in which to pray as a congregation nor mikveh, and so on. Consequently, a glimmer of doubt, Heaven forbid, arises within us: is it possible that even now God's intent is for our benefit? If it is for our benefit, God should have chastised us with those things which would have drawn us closer, not with the cessation of Torah study and prayer or, Heaven forbid, the fulfillment of the entire Torah![16]

Before answering his own question, Shapira probes even further by specifically referring to the present condition of Warsaw Jewry. The punishments of the spring of 1940 seemed to serve only to distance Jews from their spiritual occupation, he avers. How could the new Ghetto walls possibly hold good tidings for the suffering Jews of Warsaw? What did they mean, and how should Hasidim relate to their construction? Shapira returns to this question by digging deeper into the talmudic teaching that only a member of the priestly caste (*kohanim*) has the authority to place a home under quarantine. A non-priest, even an expert, may only render an opinion:

> A person must only say *it resembles a plague to me,*[17] and even a Torah scholar who knows that it is in fact a plague must nonetheless say "it resembles a plague," because a person is incapable of saying if it is in truth a plague or affliction. It is a matter of perception, such that one must say, "it resembles a plague," whereas in truth it is an act of benevolence for the Jewish people by means of which God does good for us.[18]

Shapira's concluding words contained several distinct messages. First, he validates the suffering of the Jews and its deleterious impact on their spiritual growth. Second, he remains steadfast in his faith that developments in the Ghetto were somehow beneficial in the larger plan of the Almighty. Finally, like the expert who is not a member of the priestly caste, he can only state that "it resembles a plague": he cannot definitively pronounce that it is in fact a plague, thereby initiating the quarantine and subsequent discovery of the treasure. By analogy, he can only speculate on the meaning of the Ghetto walls—"it resembles a plague"—yet he believes with perfect faith that there is an ultimate divine purpose that will ultimately be revealed as a valuable treasure. His response to his Hasidim, troubled by the meaning of the walls, validates their fears but urges them to strengthen their faith in divine providence. Viewed *without* the historical context of the microhistory of the Ghetto (the initial construction of the Ghetto walls in early April 1940), the sermon remains intelligible, but it loses its original, and primary, purpose. The sermon becomes more pointed still when we realize that Ghetto walls were first proposed by German public health officials to protect occupying forces from contagion by infectious disease that ran rampant among the malnourished population.[19]

Another relatively accessible example of Shapira's style may be seen in his comments on *parashat shelah*, delivered shortly after the news of the fall of Paris in June 1940. The Nazi victory ruined the immediate post-Shavuot atmosphere by casting an additional layer of gloom over the city. Shimon Huberband records an example of the black humor typical of the Ghetto circulating at that time:

> Jews are now very pious. They observe all the ritual laws: they are stabbed and punched with holes like *matsot*, and have as much bread as on Passover; they are beaten like *hoshanot*, rattled like Haman; they are green as *etrogim* and thin as *lulavim*; they fast as if it were Yom Kippur; they are burnt as if it were Hanukah, and their moods are as if it were the Ninth of Av.[20]

With the fall of France, the Third Reich neared its high-water mark, stretching from the English Channel to the Soviet Union, and the rumor-ridden Ghetto population sank even more deeply into despair. R. Shapira responded with a remarkably powerful, undiluted message of courage. The starting point is, as usual, a biblical text. After the spies return from the land of Canaan with a baleful report of the impossibility of the Israelite cause (Num 13), Caleb rejects their pessimism with a call to action. Rabbi Shapira writes:

Let us go up and take it over, for we certainly can.[21] Let us understand: the spies certainly spoke meaningfully and reasonably [when they said], *but the nation is powerful . . . and the cities are fortified.*[22] Why did Caleb not argue with them to rebut their rationale and their arguments? Instead, he simply said, *let us ascend.*

Such must be the faith of the Jew. Not only when he sees an opening and path to his salvation, which is to say that he reasonably believes, according to the course of natural events, that God will save him, and thereby he is strengthened; but also at the time when he does not see, heaven forbid, any reasonable opening through the course of natural events for his salvation, he must still believe that God will save him, and he is thereby strengthened in his faith and trust. On the contrary, at such a time it is better that he not engage in intellectual convolutions to find some rationale and opening through natural means, since it is clear that he will not find one—consequently it is possible that his faith will be diminished. This diminution in his faith and trust in God might serve to prevent his salvation, heaven forbid. Rather, he must declare that it is all true, that the nation that lives there [in the land] is in fact powerful, that its cities are really fortified. Nonetheless, I proclaim my faith in God, that God is beyond limitation and nature, and that God will save us. *Let us go up and take it over*, beyond reason and beyond logic. Such faith and trust in God draws our salvation closer.[23]

Shapira's message here is clear: despite the terrible news from the western front, Jews were not to give credence to the doomsayers. Like Caleb's report to Moses on the enemy forces in Canaan, the Jews need not focus on the power of the German army. They need only proclaim, *Let us go up and take it over, for we certainly can.* The Third Reich, no matter how powerful, is no match for the Almighty.[24]

Annotations as Historical Markers in R. Shapira's Oeuvre

Given his general preference for only indirect reference to contemporary events unfolding around him, it is characteristic and worth nothing that

R. Shapira sometimes historicizes an otherwise apparently ahistorical sermon or teaching through the striking use of brief annotations or apparently incidental mention of historical contexts. This begins in his prewar writings and continues into *Sermons from the Years of Rage*. There is a powerful example of this in the only one of R. Shapira's works that was published and widely circulated before the war, *Hovot ha-talmidim* (*The Obligation of Students*), the 1932 classic that catapulted him to fame as a master educator.

Like his wartime sermons, *Hovot ha-talmidim* mostly eschews explicit historical references. Though he situates his book historically in an introduction written "to parents and educators," the body of the text is composed as timeless spiritual advice for young people who wish to take responsibility for their own religious development. In a chapter dedicated to discouraging laziness, Shapira describes the complicated parable of a pious but impoverished shoemaker who falls on hard times. Weak with starvation and unable to face the hunger of his wife and children, this shoemaker goes off into the fields to pour out his heart in prayer, and collapses from sheer exhaustion. Later, he is revived by the scent of an unusual flower, which he resolves to bring home for his family to enjoy. On his way home, however, he is approached by a nobleman who offers him a large sum for the special flower; blinded by hunger and poverty, the shoemaker sells it for a paltry two loaves of bread to feed his family. That night, his father comes to him in a dream and castigates him for selling the miraculous flower so cheaply. His prayers had so moved the heavens, his father told him, that Satan the deceiver was sent to trick him into giving up his precious gift for a single meal:

> My son, you have harmed not only yourself but all of Israel and even the Holy One of Israel. It was all in your hands: the forefathers, prophets, tsaddikim, even the messiah—and you lost it all for a loaf of bread.[25]

The surface meaning of the parable is clear: that a student must resist the temptation to give up the disciplines of prayer and study for merely material gain. It is framed as a *ma'aseh*, a story that once happened in an imaginary setting. "There once was a poor shoemaker in the land of Israel, who lived near a crossroads."[26] Just two paragraphs later, however, Shapira inserts a jarring note of historical context (emphasis added): "*At the beginning of the Great War*, all traveling in that area ceased, and what little sustenance the shoemaker had earned was reduced to nothing."

Why did R. Shapira feel it necessary to place his otherwise timeless parable so precisely in relation to the recent outbreak of the Great War in 1914? I believe he used this technique specifically *because* the story of the shoemaker is otherwise so timeless that it risks being treated as merely a story. The sudden mention of the Great War, which many of his readers would have known about in a very personal way (see Wodziński, this volume), shocks the reader's system and forces the audience to understand the relevance of the parable to their own life and circumstances. This technique of inserting an element of historical context is deliberate, and in fact, we see Shapira utilizing it on a number of occasions in his wartime writings as well, most notably in his address on *parashat zakhor* 5702 (February 28, 1942), when the first Great War was again specifically mentioned.

More significant for our purposes here are the several annotations that Shapira appended to his sermons toward the end of *Sermons from the Years of Rage*. As Daniel Reiser has amply demonstrated in his critical two-volume edition of wartime sermons, Shapira engaged in heavy editing of each address—even a casual glance at the facsimile of the manuscript (reproduced as the second volume of Reiser's critical edition) reveals hundreds of strikeouts, emendations, and additions to the text. The vast majority of these changes are literary or religious in nature, illustrating R. Shapira's attempt to find the most effective phrase to express a theological concept, and might more be more valuable as such to scholars in other disciplines than to historians. Three of these additions, however, are dated—uncharacteristically for Shapira—lending support to the idea that their historical setting was important to him.[27] Let us examine each of these in turn.

Annotation to *Ekev* 5701 (August/September 1942)

In early 1942, a young Jewish man escaped from Chelmno, one of the notorious Nazi death camps, and made his way to Warsaw, where he connected with the Warsaw Jewish underground.[28] His chilling description of how the Germans had deported the Jews of his village to a remote location and murdered them with gas was one of the first indications of the so-called "Final Solution" in practice. The refugee only survived immediate destruction because he had been selected as one of the *Sonderkommando*, prisoners given the awful duty of transporting the bodies of the dead for mass burial, and was able to somehow slip away from his captors. The Jewish resistance transcribed his testimony and smuggled it out to the West, but even before the Grojanowski report was released, its contents were broadly known to the residents of the Warsaw Ghetto.[29]

R. Shapira's sermons from this period, beginning with *parashat mishpatim* 5702 (February 14, 1942), are markedly different in tone and intensity from earlier sermons. This intensity continues until *parashat hazon* (July 18, 1942), when the great deportations of Warsaw Jews to Treblinka began. R. Shapira was not sent to the death camp but was rather selected to serve in Schultz's "shop," one of the various industries that the Nazis maintained with slave labor after the depopulation of the majority of Jews had been accomplished. Between July 1942 and January 1943, Shapira reviewed his writings with a view to eventual publication. A note reproduced in the 2007 printing of *Esh kodesh* records Shapira's wishes that the manuscript version of one of his books include his recent updates.[30] The date on the note, August 3, 1942, suggests that Shapira diverted his attention to the review of his manuscripts after the deportations. The annotations to the sermons were likely written after August 1942 but no later than January 1943, when Shapira handed them to Oneg Shabbat. The milk container that held his work, along with many other documents written by the clandestine group of Ghetto scholars, was buried at 68 Nowolipkie Street in February and would remain there until its accidental discovery in December 1950.[31]

It is impossible to determine with certainty when each of the hundreds of textual emendations was noted on the original manuscript, but most are very brief in nature, two or three words at most. The three dated annotations, by contrast, are much longer and speak directly to the reader. They were composed with the explicit intent that future editors not integrate them into the message itself. Rather, their distinctive voice was to be preserved separately, as a note printed below the sermon. In other words, the sermons read, almost without exception, like transcripts of oral addresses, which is basically what they are. The dated annotations, on the other hand, read as if Shapira were speaking directly to a single reader.

The original sermon for *parashat ekev* 5701 (August 16, 1941) included the following passage:

Certainly, it is true that at a time when every mind is depressed and every heart is ill, it is difficult to study and pray as one ought. There are some people, however, who become overly preoccupied with their suffering and idly waste their time speaking of foolish matters all day. Even if it is impossible for such a person to study in depth in these times, let him at least recite Psalms.[32]

R. Shapira's comment represents a fairly conventional exhortation intended to encourage Jews to engage in religious activity. Recognizing the huge psychic burden carried by the suffering Jews of Warsaw, Shapira urged them not to succumb to despair but rather to assuage their woes with more productive use of their depleted spiritual energies, either through study of Torah or, failing that more intellectually demanding task, at least the pious recital of Psalms. A year later, and with a view to posterity, he felt the need to qualify his words.

I said and recorded these words in 5701. At that time, even though there was much bitter suffering, some of which is apparent in my words, nonetheless, at this time it was still possible to lament them and relate a small portion of them in words, to experience anguish over the survivors, to cry regarding the future—how will the schools and yeshivot be built once again and so on, even to strengthen the survivors and encourage them to study and fulfill Torah. This is no longer the case at the end of 5702, because the holy communities have all but been irrevocably destroyed. Even the few who survive are overcome with this Egyptian servitude, crushed and living in mortal fear. They no longer have the ability to express lament over their troubles, and there is no one left to encourage, no heart to awaken to divine service and Torah study. Prayers are only recited under difficult conditions, and the observance of the Sabbath, even for those who truly wish to observe it, is exceptionally onerous, and how much more so is it difficult to cry regarding the future, and regarding the establishments that have been devastated, at a time when (may God have mercy and save us) no spirit or heart remains. It is up to God alone to have compassion and save us in the blink of an eye and reestablish the devastated. Only with the final redemption and the resurrection of the dead will the Blessed One be able to rebuild and heal. I beseech you, God, have mercy and do not delay our salvation.[33]

This comment is rich in significance. The continuity of his message, encouraging Jews to remain steadfast in their faith despite persecution, was broken by the severity of suffering after the great deportation. Theologically, the implications are dramatic: "No spirit or heart remains. It is up to God alone to have compassion and save us." The Jews can no longer contribute to their own redemption, as they did in Egypt by at least crying out for salvation. This "arousal from below" (hit'aruta de-letata), to use Hasidic terminology, provoked God to respond with overwhelming "signs and wonders" (i.e., "arousal from above"), leading the Jews to freedom. This pattern was simply no longer relevant after the great deportation. Suffering had so depleted the spiritual reserves of Warsaw's Jews that they simply could not summon the energy to pray for redemption. Thus, Shapira argued, "it is up to God alone."[34]

Annotation to *Hanukkah* 5702 (November 27, 1942)

Evidence that Shapira viewed the great deportation as a major rift in the cosmos, altering the millennia-long relationship between the Jews and their God, is also present in his annotation on his sermon for Hanukkah 5702. The eight-day holiday was celebrated between the fourteenth and the twenty-first of December 1941. He spoke then about the need to place the current suffering in historical perspective.

And in truth, what place is there for our questions, heaven forbid, and supplications, even though it is true that trials such as we are enduring now come only once every few centuries? But in any case, how can they help us understand these acts of God? And they can damage, heaven forbid, if we do not understand them. If we do not even understand a single blade of grass made by God, how much more will we not understand a soul, and how much more an angel, and how much more the mind of the Blessed One? And how can this help our minds to understand that which the Blessed and Exalted One knows and understands and why a person like this is hurt with these trials nowadays, more than the trials the Jews have ever endured? Why, when one learns a verse, Talmud, or midrash, and hears of the suffering of Jews from then until now, is his faith not damaged? But now it is damaged? For those people who say that trials such as these never existed in Jewish history are in error. What of the destruction of the temple, Betar, and so on? May God have mercy and say "enough" to our suffering and redeem us immediately and forthwith, from now and forever.[35]

Once again, Shapira's original message was fairly conventional in nature. He sought to provide some comfort to his congregation by moderating their suffering, fitting their contemporary experience within a larger philosophy of history. The model of cyclical, periodic persecution is a well-known feature of Jewish culture: "In every generation," reads the text of the Passover liturgy, "someone rises up to destroy us, but the Holy One who is Blessed rescues us from their hands." Prior generations witnessed horrible persecution, and it would be overly optimistic to argue that Jews need no longer fear persecution in the future. Shapira's thought, resonant with references to the destruction of the temple in Jerusalem and the fall of Betar, essentially asks, "Why should our generation be any different?" (For more on this passage, see Diamond, Magid, this volume.)

As in the previous cases, R. Shapira answers his own question with a dramatic annotation to this sermon:

> Note: Only the suffering up to the end of 5702 had previously existed. The unusual suffering, the evil and grotesque murders that the wicked, twisted murderers innovated for us, the House of Israel, from the end of 5702, in my opinion, from the words of the sages of blessed memory and the chronicles of the Jewish people in general, there never was anything like them, and God should have mercy upon us and rescue us from their hands in the blink of an eye. The eve of the holy Sabbath, 18 Kislev 5703. The author.

The eighteenth of Kislev 5703, to which this annotation is dated, was Friday, November 27, 1942.[36] Taken together with his previous note on *parashat ekev* 5701, it is clear that Shapira now believed that a fundamental change had occurred in the universe. The events later known by the name *Holocaust* represented an occurrence sui generis, a degree of persecution so awful that the term *inhuman* cannot capture its cruelty. Not only was the quality of the Holocaust a complete *novum* in world history (Diamond, this volume, also invokes this term) but its impact was such that it affected the very nature of the relationship between the Jews and their God. On Hanukkah 1941, Shapira had argued that though the Nazi persecution was bitter, it was in the final analysis comparable to previous historical episodes. By November 1942, he regretted these words: The Holocaust, he now suggested, could not be compared to any prior tribulation the Jews had ever endured in their long history.

One can only imagine the traumatic impact this recognition had on R. Shapira's internal spiritual outlook. His entire raison d'être, expressed in so many ways throughout the corpus of his literary oeuvre, had been to inspire Jewish youth to engage and develop their spiritual capacities and prophetic selves.[37] What must he have thought of himself as a rebbe and teacher, now that his Hasidim were destroyed in the gas chambers of Treblinka? Dr. Daniel Reiser, while examining R. Shapira's original manuscripts in Warsaw, was arrested by the way in which Shapira recorded his name on the cover page of the prewar pedagogic manuscript entitled *Mevo ha-she'arim*.[38] As was customary, he typically wrote his full Hebrew name on title pages: "Kalonymus Kalmish, son of the holy rabbi, my teacher, Elimelekh of Grodzisk." Underneath his signature are two words, struck out with violent, heavy strokes. Reiser was barely able to decipher the underlying script, which read "Head of the Jewish Court (*av beit din*), Piaseczno." Reiser suggests that this unusually aggressive obliteration of R. Shapira's prewar title took place after the great deportations, an expression of utter anguish over the destruction of his prior home in the village of Piaseczno (on the significance of this town, see Wodziński's chapter in this volume). Recall that at this moment in the autumn of 1942, Shapira was among the few remaining survivors of the entire Jewish community of Piaseczno. The erasure of his own title, which mirrored the utter destruction of his Hasidic court, seems to point to a more profound erasure of identity: How could he continue to be a Rebbe without his Hasidim?

A similar phenomenon may be evident in the title page to the wartime sermons themselves.[39] It is apparent that paper was not easily acquired in the Ghetto, because the title page was clearly adapted from an earlier use. A small strikeout appears at the very top: the Hebrew letters forming the year 5700. This title page was likely the original, dating from the beginning of the war. It is written in Shapira's own hand, not that of the scribe who recorded the earliest sermons, so it was probably created some time after the spring of 1940, a reflection of Shapira's decision to publish these sermons in a special collection after the war's conclusion. The page carries a simple working title: "Words of Torah that I spoke on the Sabbath and Holidays of the years 5700, 5701, and 5702." Below this title is a mysterious paper patch, glued to the cover page, replacing an original text. Underneath it, Shapira simply and humbly signs his name, "Kalonymus."

What was originally written below the patch? In personal correspondence, Reiser has said that it is impossible to determine what this text may have contained. It is possible that the original document bore the author's name and title, his lineage, and perhaps a few honorifics like "author of *Hovat ha-talmidim*," as is common in Hasidic works. Perhaps R. Shapira sought to obliterate all of these secondary markers of identity, in a manner comparable to his dramatic strikeout on the title page of his *Mevo ha-she'arim* manuscript. After the great deportation, perhaps he no longer wished to be reminded of his murdered Hasidim and remained simply "Kalonymus."

Did the Holocaust cause R. Shapira to lose his faith, as some scholars (see Magid, this volume) claim? Even a cursory reading of his wartime writings demonstrates the absurdity of the question. At no point does R. Shapira ever despair of God's existence and omnipotence, even up to his final will and testament, bequeathing his manuscripts to his brother in Israel. He maintains an active, passionate relationship with God throughout his wartime sermons, sometimes raising his voice in anguish and fear but always confident in God's ability to save the Jewish people "in the blink of an eye." Why, then, did God not intervene to save the Jews of Europe? This tortured question is implicitly or explicitly present in every sermon Shapira delivered since the outbreak of the war. I do not believe he presumed to provide a definitive, absolute answer: even Moses's request to "know God's ways" was denied. Shapira nevertheless responded to his congregation's need for an answer by providing several approaches to the question, some of them conventional, some highly innovative. Three interrelated lines of argument have been identified by theologians researching Shapira's thought. Early in the war, he portrayed suffering as retribution for Jewish abandonment of religious values and practices, confident that a mass return to tradition would right the balance and end their tribulations. By the summer of 1941, this position had not been fundamentally altered, but Shapira had come to place greater emphasis on the sympathetic suffering of God with his people. Then, with Jacob Grojanowski's escape from Chelmno and report on the conduct of the "final solution" in January 1942, something shifted once again, and he turned in his final sermons to contemplating God's own unfathomable suffering. God withdraws, as it were, to a hidden chamber, there to weep terrible, calamitous tears.[40]

Yet I think it is important to emphasize that Shapira's faith in God was unshaken—what broke was his faith in *history*. Jacob Grojanowski's report from Chelmno put the lie to misplaced hopes: the Nazis fully intended to murder every last Jew in Europe and seemed well on their way to succeeding through their terrible bureaucratic apparatus of death. Shapira could no longer fit the suffering of Warsaw Jewry into any previous paradigm of history, least of all suffering as a redemptive response to sin, bringing with it the hope of repentance. His post-deportation note on *parashat ekev* 5701 laments that the persecution has gone too far: the Jews simply have no energy left with which to repent.

For Shapira, the world had changed beyond recognition. The Holocaust was a seam in time—what lay beyond the abyss was a *novum* in the history of the cosmos, altering the theological laws of gravity forever. Shapira did not theorize abstractly what this new reality meant for the Jews, other than to throw himself and the entire Jewish people on the unmitigated mercy of God, beyond reason (see Diamond, this volume). His apprehension of suffering had breached all limits, yet he would not relinquish his firm grip on faith in his Creator. Like the biblical Job, Shapira came to personify the verse "though God may slay me, yet I will trust in God" (13:15). Unlike Job, however, he would not uphold the latter, more rebellious second half of the verse: "but I will maintain mine own ways before him." He could not comprehend, even theoretically, what possible purpose the Holocaust might have in the divine plan, yet he retained, perhaps even fortified, his unshakeable faith in the Almighty.

Last Will and Testament, January 3, 1943[41]

Like many contributors to Emmanuel Ringelblum's secret *Oneg Shabbat* archival project, Shapira penned his last will and testament before submitting his precious manuscripts to the society for burial. He wrote a cover letter in Yiddish, well known to all students of Piaseczno Hasidism, headed by a single, dramatically underlined word followed by three exclamation points:

ATTENTION!!!

Blessed is God. I have the honor of requesting the esteemed individual or institution that finds my enclosed writings *Hakhsharat ha-avreichim, Mevo ha-she'arim* (from *Hovat ha-avreikhim*), *Tsav ve-zeruz,* and *Torah Insights on the Weekly Readings for the Years 5700, 5701 and 5702,* to please exert themselves to send them to the Land of Israel to the following address: Rabbi Yeshaya Shapira, Tel Aviv, Palestine. Please also send the enclosed letter. When the Blessed One shows mercy and I and the remaining Jews survive the war, please return all materials to me or to the Warsaw rabbinate for Kalonymus, and may God have mercy upon us, the remnant of Israel in every place, and rescue us, and sustain us, and save us in the blink of an eye.

With deep, heartfelt gratitude, Kalonymus[42]

Switching to eloquent Rabbinic Hebrew, Rabbi Shapira then pens a message to his brother Yeshaya Shapira (the so-called Pioneer Rebbe, living on an agricultural settlement in Mandatory Palestine), describing the nature of the manuscripts and asking that they be prepared for publication. This letter, Rabbi Shapira's final will and testament, also contains an exhortation to future readers of his work. "Please also print in every work," he wrote, "that I urge every single Jew to study my books, and that the merit of my holy ancestors will stand by every student and his family, now and forever." This letter is dated 27 Tevet 5703 (January 3, 1943) and concludes with the words "May God have mercy upon us."

In this note—certainly his most direct and perhaps his most personal—R. Shapira expresses the precise state of his belief in the face of imminent destruction. On the surface, for public consumption, he projected confidence within a sacred humility: the Jews required divine mercy, but he expected that he, or at least the Warsaw rabbinate, would survive the war. In his private note to his brother, however, he left instructions for posthumous publication of his writings.

Conclusion: "Living with the Times"

Tradition claims that Rabbi Shneur Zalman of Liadi, the eighteenth-century founder of Chabad Hasidim, who is frequently quoted in Shapira's work, once said that "Hasidim must live with the times." Lest one think that this statement referred to a modernizing impulse, requiring Hasidim to somehow adapt their thought and practice to contemporary mores, the author of the *Tanya* continues, "meaning, one must live with the weekly *parashah* (Torah portion)."[43] Time is not defined by the calendar for Hasidim. It is contextualized and made comprehensible by the weekly cycle of Torah readings.

This is precisely the literary-theological method by which Shapira fulfilled his sacred leadership task. By firmly, and exclusively, planting the locus of historical context in the sacred text rather than quotidian events, he reaffirmed this message week after week, utterly devoting himself to strengthening the resolve of his Hasidim. Making explicit reference to historical context would only have served to cheapen his message, surrendering the centrality of the Torah to the daily profanity of the Warsaw Ghetto and ultimately the Nazis themselves. The Torah, not the German oppressors, would dictate his message. With the exception of a few passages, R. Shapira placed his writings within a larger, timeless context, guaranteeing their relevance for as long as Jews followed the weekly cycle of Torah readings. The few exceptions discussed here only serve to clarify this pattern.

I opened this chapter with the proposition that in addition to their primary religious significance, Shapira's writings also held value for historical research. Determining this value requires a profound realignment of focus. If we were to restrict our understanding of history to von Ranke's *wie es eigentlich gewesen war* (what actually happened), we would be limited to noting certain biographical details mentioned in the text: that R. Shapira survived a bout of typhus, that he went into hiding, and so on. This is more biographical than historical. I believe we need to shift our focus from understanding external events to understanding the internal life of Warsaw Jewry, including the hundreds of thousands who were murdered with no record of their inner lives. What can we know about these silent, martyred Jews?

The hallmark of postmodernism (whether of the "hard" or "soft" variety) is the fundamental inaccessibility of what we once called "objective truth": we come to understand the importance of vantage point and perception (of the participant as well as the historian) to any account of the past or its meaning. By first immersing ourselves in the detailed history of the Ghetto and then reading corresponding entries from *Sermons from the Years of Rage*, it is my hope that we may be able—from a great distance and with the inevitable distortion of our comfortable postwar conditions—to enter R. Shapira's *beit midrash*, to hear his Torah for ourselves, and to replicate, on at least some level, the experience of his Hasidim. Is this history? It is the most important kind.

Notes

1. See Kalonymus Kalman Shapira, *Sermons from the Years of Rage* [in Hebrew], ed. Daniel Reiser, 2 vols. (Jerusalem: Herzog Academic College, 2017), 1:66n5. See also Ariel Evan Mayse and Daniel Reiser, "Territories and Textures: The Hasidic Sermon as the Crossroads of Language and Culture," *Jewish Social Studies* 24, no. 1 (2018): 127–60. Internal literary evidence indicates that the derashot were recorded after they were delivered, including the entry of January 3, 1940, which includes Shapira's concluding comment, "more than this I cannot recall."

2. This point is made effectively in Ariel Evan Mayse's review article "Words of Flames and Madness," *Studies in Judaism, Humanities and the Social Sciences* 3, no. 1 (2019): 124–30.

3. Marc Saperstein, ed., *Jewish Preaching in Times of War 1800–2001* (Oxford: Littman Library of Jewish Civilization, 2008), xvi.

4. I am grateful to Dean Stanley Boylan for this observation.

5. Ester Yehudit Thidor-Baumel, " 'Esh kodesh,' sifro shel ha-admo"r mi-Piaseczno, u-mekomo be-havanat ha-hayyim ha-dati'im be-gito Varshah," *Yalkut Moreshet* 29 (1980): 173–87.

6. The literary roots of this notion extend to the midrash Bereshit Rabbah, and it finds its clearest expression in the thirteenth-century commentary of Nahmanides (for example, on Gen 12:6: "everything that happened to the ancestors is a sign for their descendants").

7. See Rabbi Shimon Gershon Rosenberg, *Faith Shattered and Restored: Judaism in the Postmodern Age* (New York: Maggid Books, 2017), especially the chapters entitled "My Faith: Faith in a Postmodern World" and "Justice and Ethics in a Postmodern World."

8. Shimon Huberband, *Kiddush Hashem: Jewish Religious and Cultural Life during the Holocaust* (New York: Yeshiva University Press, 1987), 190–91.

9. *Sermons from the Years of Rage, parashat toledot* 5700 [1939], 1:92–93. See also Don Seeman, "Ritual Efficacy, Hasidic Mysticism and 'Useless Suffering' in the Warsaw Ghetto," *Harvard Theological Review* 101 (2008): 481.

10. See b. Kiddushin 2b, which is in turn an allusion to Adam seeking Eve, his "lost" rib.

11. *Sermons from the Years of Rage, parashat toledot* 5700, 1:93.

12. See *Sermons from the Years of Rage, parashat yitro* 5700 (1940), 1:103–5; and ibid., *parashat toledot* 5702 (1941), 1:233–36.

13. See *Sermons from the Years of Rage, sukkot* 2 5701 (1940), 1:160–63; ibid., *sukkot* 5702, 1:226–30; and ibid., *rosh hodesh nisan* 5702, 1:295–98.

14. Nahmanides on Leviticus 13:47, cited in *Imrei Elimelekh*, 111b–112a and *Divrei Elimelekh*, 138b.

15. *Sermons from the Years of Rage, parashat metsora* 5700 (1940), 1:128–29. It is worth mentioning that for reasons that are unclear, this entry appears out of sequence in R. Shapira's original handwritten manuscript (see *Sermons from the Years of Rage*, 2:88–91).

16. *Sermons from the Years of Rage, parashat emor* 5700, 1:129.

17. Lev 14:35.

18. *Sermons from the Years of Rage, parashat emor* 5700, 1:129.

19. See Christopher Browning, "Genocide and Public Health: German Doctors and Polish Jews 1939–1941," *Holocaust and Genocide Studies* 3 (1988): 21–36; Don Seeman, "Ritual Efficacy, Hasidic Mysticism and 'Useless Suffering' ": 481.

20. Huberband, *Kiddush Hashem*, 113.

21. Num 13:30.

22. See Zohar 3:193a.

23. *Sermons from the Years of Rage, parashat shelah* 5700, 1:144–45.

24. This is in contradistinction to the explicit reference to contemporary events in writings by some other rabbinic writers during the same period. See, for example, Gershon Greenberg, "The Suffering of the Righteous according to Shlomo Zalman Unsdorfer of Bratislava, 1939–1944," in *Remembering for the Future: The Holocaust in an Age of Genocide*, ed. John K. Roth et al. (New York: Palgrave Macmillan, 2001), 422–38; Gershon Greenberg and Asaf Yedidya, eds., *Mishpateha tehom rabah: Tagovot hegotiyot ortodiksiyot la-sho'ah* (Jerusalem: Mosad Ha-Rav Kook, 2016); and Saperstein, *Jewish Preaching in Times of War*.

25. Rabbi Kalonymus Kalman Shapira, *A Student's Obligation: Advice from Shapira of the Warsaw Ghetto*, trans. Micah Odenheimer (New York: Jason Aronson, 1991), 44.

26. Ibid., 42.

27. The weekly parashah, of course, generates an equivalent calendar date as well. The point here is that by explicitly indicating the calendar date in these annotations, Shapira clearly wished to convey his desire that these references be understood as later additions. This is also evident from the style guide he left for future editors, discussed in *Sermons from the Years of Rage*, 2:9–14.

28. I have discussed this period in greater depth in the fourth chapter of *Torah from the Years of Wrath, 1939–1943: The Historical Context of the Aish Kodesh* (New York: Sam Sapozhnik, 2017).

29. See Samuel Kassow, *Who Will Write Our History? Emanuel Ringelblum, the Warsaw Ghetto, and the Oyneg Shabes Archive* (Bloomington: Indiana University Press), 285–95.

30. *Aish Kodesh*, unpaginated section prior to sermons that begin at Sermons from the Years of Rage, 1:7.

31. At present, a detailed study of annotations to Shapira's other works buried in the Oneg Shabbat archive remains unwritten. Reading the printed versions of the three works in question (*Hakhsharat ha-avreikhim*, *Mevo ha-she'arim*, and *Tsav ve-zeruz*), it seems unlikely that the manuscripts contain any annotations of historical value for the war years themselves, with the exception of some passages in *Tsav ve-zeruz* surrounding the death of his son in 1939.

32. *Sermons from the Years of Rage, parashat re'eh* 5701, 1:212.

33. Ibid.

34. On this theme, see Isaac Hershkowitz, "Rabbi Kalonymus Kalmish Shapira, the Piaseczner Rebbe His Holocaust and Pre-Holocaust Thought, Continuity or Discontinuity?" [in Hebrew] (master's thesis, Bar-Ilan University, 2005), 17–18.

35. *Sermons from the Years of Rage, hanukkah* 5702, 1:242.

36. Hanukkah was to be commemorated the following week, reinforcing the possibility that Shapira was reviewing the sermons roughly according to their chronological dating at least up to January 1942–43.

37. See Seeman, "Ritual Efficacy."

38. *Sermons from the Years of Rage*, 1:52.

39. Ibid., 2:16–17.

40. See the works of Polen and Seeman on this subject.

41. *Sermons from the Years of Rage*, 1:328.

42. Shapira's cover letter is reproduced in *Sermons from the Years of Rage*, 1:328.

43. Cited in *Hayom yom* for 1 Heshvan.

13

Covenantal Rupture and
Broken Faith in *Esh Kodesh*

SHAUL MAGID

"Is he willing to prevent evil, but not able? Then he is impotent. Is he able but not willing? Then he is malevolent. Is he both willing and able? Whence then is evil?"

—Epicurus cited by Lucretius, *De Rerum natura*

Introduction

Commenting on the verse in Gen 7:23 "And he remained Noah," the Hasidic master R. Ya'akov Yitzhak Horowitz, known the Seer of Lublin (1745–1814), adapting the standard reading of the verse "And Noah remained," asked, "'And he remained Noah?' After Noah witnessed the destruction of the world, can it be he remained as he was?" In a similar vein, Elie Wiesel was alleged to have said, "I understand people who lived through the Shoah who didn't believe in God before the Shoah and believed in God afterward. And I understand people who did believe in God before the Shoah and didn't believe in God afterward. What I don't understand is someone whose belief was not altered by living through the Shoah. How can it have remained the same?"[1] Both of these comments gesture to the relationship between belief (or nonbelief) and experience, more pointedly between belief (or nonbelief) and an experience that renders that belief (or nonbelief) untenable. Events certainly stretch, test, and challenge beliefs about the world, in some cases causing us to revise our beliefs, in some cases to defend then, and in some cases events simply justify what we already believe. For many Jews, the Holocaust was an event that betrayed any attempt at justification according to common traditional belief in divine providence. One way to articulate this view would be to say that believing God was present in the Holocaust is blasphemy, yet to believe God was absent is heresy.[2]

There was, of course, much more reflection on these matters after the final bodies were laid to rest, after survivors began to rebuild their lives, after the fear of extinction proved false but near annihilation proved true. There were some cases of individuals, scholars, rabbis, and laypeople, who did write about the implications of the events as they were happening. One case of note was the Hasidic rabbi Kalonymus Kalman Shapira of Piaseczno (1889–1943), whose Holocaust testimony in the form of sermons from the Warsaw Ghetto were collected and hidden before the destruction of the Ghetto. They were subsequently found after the war and published in 1960.[3] The oddity of these sermons as a testimony of the Holocaust, as opposed to, say, the work of Primo Levi and many others, is that Shapira never mentions the Nazis, almost never mentions current events, never even overtly mentions the deaths of his family.[4] The sermons are therefore somewhat of a unique testimony of the Holocaust purely through the lens of Torah from the years 1939–1942, embedded in sermons preached in Shapira's synagogue in the Ghetto.[5] Noteworthy is that the sermons were dated and thus ostensibly enable us to read them in light of the events that unfolded as they were being written and delivered. I say "ostensibly" because the very recent work by Daniel Reiser, a two-volume reworking of the texts of these sermons from manuscript with an important intro-duction, show us that what we thought was a linear progression in these sermons is a far more complex exercise of editorial review and revision, what he calls a "layered approach," which undermines the linearity of the material. What Reiser proves through a close examination of the manu-script written in Shapira's own hand is that he continually returned to his work, adding, deleting, and including marginalia, errata, and notes until he gave over his materials to the *Oyneg Shabbos* archives in the winter of 1943. Some of these markings prove significant in regard to viewing the dates the sermons were initially written as definitive of Shapira's reaction to any particular event.[6]

Below I explore the question asked by both the Seer of Lublin and Elie Wiesel: whether and how a believer can sustain their previous belief in light of a world-historical disaster. Or, asked in a somewhat different vein by Israeli scholar Eliezer Schweid, "How is it possible to withstand [a test of faith] when the suffering is so intense as to destroy the sole means capable of reinforcing faith in God and the Torah in the present age?"[7] Schweid argues with others who have written on these sermons that Shapira, given the caveat of his theological protest and the erosion of the congruity of his belief, expresses in these sermons a sustained belief in God and covenant to the very end. Schweid writes that the goal "of all the sermons was to find ways in which the faithful could maintain their faith."[8] In general, this is correct. However, I will argue that there is a distinction between Shapira's public persona as it comes through in his sermons and his own struggles with faith after the Great Deportation in late summer 1942 expressed in the last words we have from his pen, and the future audience he was writing for in these final entries.[9]

Shapira's career as a Hasidic master was, for better or worse, over-shadowed by the survival and publication of these wartime sermons. He called his collection of Ghetto sermons simply *Hiddushei Torah auf sedros*, *Torah Novella from the Weekly Parsha*, or *Derashot Mi-Shenot Ha-Za'am* (*Sermons from the Years of Rage*). They were later published under the title *Esh kodesh* (*Holy Fire*). Before the war, Shapira was widely known as an innovative Hasidic rebbe. During that time, he wrote a trilogy on Jewish education, including educating young men for prophecy, only one volume of which was published in his lifetime.[10] Two of those volumes, *A Student's Obligation: Advice from the Rebbe of the Warsaw Ghetto* (*Hovot ha-talmidim*) for young children, and very recently, *Jewish-Spiritual Growth: A Step-by-Step Guide by a Hasidic Master* (*Hakhsharat ha-avreikhim*) for adolescents, have appeared in English. Another slim volume on building community, *Benei mahshavah tovah* (*Conscious Community*), appeared in translation in 1996 and has become popular in Jewish Renewal circles.[11] A collection of earlier sermons called *Derkeh ha-melekh* (*The Way of the King*) is widely viewed as a Hasidic classic of the period.[12] But it is his Warsaw Ghetto sermons, published as *Esh kodesh* (appearing in English in 2000 as *Sacred Fire: Torah from the Years of Fury 1939–1942*) that has become the most popular.

The fact that these heart-wrenching sermons were dated to the years of the Ghetto gives us a startling view into one man's struggle with faith, as the world—and, ultimately, I will argue, his faith—collapsed around, and within, him. Nechemia Polen, in his *The Holy Fire* (1999), calls this book "a testament of fidelity to Torah and tradition, in the face of the enemy's efforts to destroy both."[13] Polen, whose work initiates English-language scholarship on Shapira, adeptly traces the trajectory of his struggle with the incongruence between tradition and destruction as life in the Ghetto became unbearable and, ultimately, unlivable. Following him, James Diamond views the sermons through a dialectical lens, showing the ways Shapira reaches the precipice of hopelessness, and faithlessness, only to retreat back into faith, only to approach the precipice once again.[14] While each scholar who has written on Shapira has offered novel contributions to this emotionally charged tribute to the struggle of one man against human evil and a God whose behavior appears increasingly incomprehensible, all maintain that Shapira died in the embrace of a belief he never abandoned. For example, while he acknowledges that Shapira's last sermons in the spring and summer of 1942 indicate a shift in his theological orientation, Polen claims that to the end Shapira remained committed to faith in a God that could not, or would not, save him. Henry Abrahamson does so as well, when he writes, "Did the Rebbe lose his faith in the Holocaust? Even a cursory reading of his wartime writings demonstrates the absurdity of that question. At no point does he ever despair of God's existence and omnipotence, even up to his final will and testament."[15] Daniel Reiser makes a similar but by no means identical observation.

> Now, as his sermons are about to end, and as "the woes continue," he tells his public that he no longer has the ability to strengthen and comfort either himself or others. Furthermore, the Rebbe admits that his exhortations no longer affect him, and he is aware that they do not have any effect on his listeners either. Lest this be misunderstood, what we observe here is not a loss of faith—the continuation of this sermon [referring to a sermon delivered on *Shabbat Zakhor*, February 28, 1942] and the ensuing sermons rule that possibility out—but extraordinary candor and a sharing of his profound agony and personal vacillations with the reader.[16]

Below I suggest that Abramson's description of what loss of faith might mean—"despair of God's existence and omnipotence"—does not negate what I call Shapira's broken faith that resulted from Shapira's realization that God will not save the Jews from the fires of Nazi evil and that nothing the Jews might have done deserved that fate. And while Reiser's "loss of faith" is never quite explained—i.e., what was the faith that was not lost?—I want to suggest that indeed there was a loss of faith but not its total erasure, especially in the transition between the final sermon in the summer of 1942 and the addendum added in November of that year. It is worth pointing out that Shapira does end that infamous note with a classical liturgical flourish: "May God have mercy upon us, and save us from their hands, in the blink of an eye (*ke-heref ayin*)." Is that not a prayer? Perhaps. But I would suggest we see it otherwise for the very fact that it undermines the note that precedes it. Rather, I see this as a classic kind of liturgical conclusion (*hatimah*), a formulaic finale to one who has, in effect, stopped praying, or at least stopped believing in the efficacy of his prayer, because he knows those prayers will not be answered, not unlike the fictitious Yosl Rackover (see my discussion of him below), who continues to pray to God despite his acknowledging that God has abandoned him. We cannot know why Shapira decided to end this very radical note, really his final comment to us, with such a formulaic liturgical conclusion. But I certainly do not think we can conclude from this that the note that precedes it does not undermine the very covenantal frame in which such liturgical formulas are operative.

My assessment of what Shapira comes to in the end respectfully moves in another direction from Polen, Abramson, Reiser, Schweid, and others.[17] My reasoning is that these scholars never quite define what they mean by faith (faith in what?) and thus the claim that faith remained is not adequate. Most of those mentioned above do acknowledge that something changed, but what it was is not clear. Abrahamson suggests what was lost was not faith in God but "faith in history." "The Rebbe could no longer fit the suffering of Warsaw Jewry into his paradigm of history, which operated with the notion that persecution promoted repentance, which brought about redemption."[18] Here, I side with Jacob Neusner, Yosef Yerushalmi, and Amos Funkenstein (discussed below) that in a covenantal model, there cannot be a loss of faith in history without also a loss of faith in God. The disunion between history and God in a covenantal and providential model is, to my mind, not tenable.[19] From a classical Jewish standpoint, to distinguish between God and history, which is what Abrahamson suggests, it to leave the orbit of covenantal theology. This notion is shared by many others as well. For example, biblical historian

Ernst Wright writes, "Biblical history is the confessional recital of the redemptive acts of God in a particular history, *because history is the chief medium of revelation*" [italics added].[20]

I would like to revisit these sermons in order to suggest that something *seismic* indeed shifts in Shapira's belief, in the very *possibility* of belief, as it may have existed before, even as late as 1942. I am specifically interested in his final sermon in the summer of 1942 and a brief addendum he added in November 1942 to a previous sermon, which to my mind breaks through something Shapira never quite acknowledged before: that what he and his community are experiencing, what the Jews are experiencing, has never been experienced before. This admission, apparently a final edit to his writings after he had put his pen to rest, likely a rereading of an earlier sermon after the Great Deportation, is more than a mere depressing flourish, although certainly that too; I think it breaks faith in a covenantal God and sets the stage for what would become post-Holocaust theology a few decades later. The observation that Shapira's Ghetto sermons set the stage for post-Holocaust theology is not new; it was already made by Erin Leib in her 2014 dissertation "God in the Years of Fury."[21]

Leib frames Shapira's sermons around the question of theodicy and anti-theodicy in Zachary Braiterman's study of post-Holocaust theology *(God) After Auschwitz*.[22] Braiterman claims that the engine that generates post-Holocaust theology in thinkers such as Richard Rubenstein, Eliezer Berkovits, Irving (Yitz) Greenberg, and others largely rests on the notion of anti-theodicy, that the question of evil can no longer be an integral part of God and God's relationship to the Jewish people or the world. Braiterman defines anti-theodicy this way: "By anti-theodicy we mean any religious response to the problem of evil whose proponents refuse to justify, explain, accept as something meaningful the relationship between God and suffering."[23] For post-Holocaust theologians, the Holocaust made classical theodicy impossible. Belief in God can continue to exist, but it can no longer be wed to the problem of evil. If it is believing at all, it is believing "otherwise." Amos Funkenstein puts it this way. "Jewish theologians . . . such as Emil Fackenheim or E. Berkovits admit that they see no rationale to the Holocaust. The Holocaust is incomprehensible, they say, *and defies all theodicies*. . . . Even these diluted versions of theodicy are offensive" [italics added].[24] On Braiterman's reading, post-Holocaust theologians from the more traditional Berkovits to the more progressive Rubenstein all work along the anti-theodic spectrum founded on the notion that the Holocaust was unprecedented and, as such, drove a stake into classic notions of covenantal belief. Braiterman contends that this notion "gains a larger currency in specifically religious circles only after the Holocaust."[25] Leib suggests that "*Esh Kodesh* demonstrates that, in fact, the 20th century turn toward anti-theodicy actually began during the war itself."[26] She notes, "In this final sermon, we find a turn toward anti-theodicy, a quiet but final abandonment of the project of theodicy altogether. Either God will soon respond to Jewish suffering with salvation or he will not, but either way, the attempt to rationalize, reframe, or justify it is over."[27] I agree with her view here and would like to move the discussion from the metaphysical or even theological frame of theodicy to the realm of faith—what kind of God can one believe in when theodicy ceases to function? And can we label such belief as identical, or even categorically similar to, a theodic one?

The consequences of anti-theodicy are varied. As Braiterman notes, "Although it borders on blasphemy, anti-theodicy does not constitute atheism; it might even express love that human persons have for God."[28] In the final section of this essay I will explore this insight through a reading of Zvi Kolitz's *Yosl Rakover Speaks to God* and Shlomo Carlebach's story of the "Holy Hunchback" about a student of Shapira Carlebach allegedly met in Tel Aviv.[29] For now, the border where blasphemy can coexist with love for God is where I would like to place Shapira's broken faith. As opposed to Abrahamson, this is not a loss of faith in history; it is a loss of faith of *God* in history.[30] The God that remains, the God that can be believed in, or loved, after theodicy, after history is de-theologized, is not the same God as before theodicy crumbled with the Ghetto walls or the Great Deportation. Before getting there, however, some preliminary remarks are in order.

Holocaust Theology and Post-Holocaust Theology

Few traditionalists wrote about the Holocaust in any systematic way. And those who did record reflections of the war raging around them, did not tend to view it as an event that shattered the covenantal foundation upon which Judaism is constructed. The traditional, and ultra-traditional, mindset, it has been argued, lives in what Jacob Neusner called "paradigmatic thinking"—a belief that all events correspond to a predetermined notion of covenant, even if that correspondence, or God's providence, may be veiled from view, for example, in a state of *hester panim* or *deus obsconditus*.

Neusner believed that "paradigmatic thinking," and thus the traditional model of the covenant, became impossible with the introduction of historicism.[31] His view of "paradigmatic thinking" is that history conforms to a special model of theological cause and effect, even if not always evident, that cannot bear the weight of a historicist critique. That is, for Neusner, once history becomes the lens through which Judaism or the covenant is viewed, classical theodicy can only function as a historically contingent phenomenon and no longer an operative theological principle. Barbara Krawcowicz put it nicely when she wrote, "[For Neusner] it is the paradigm that defines and shapes reality and not the other way round. Paradigmatic thinking identifies, 'a happening not by its consequence . . . but by its conformity to the appropriate paradigm.' "[32] Yosef Hayim Yerushalmi sums up "paradigmatic thinking" quite nicely in his seminal book *Zakhor*: "What has occurred now is similar to the persecutions of old, and all that happened to the forefathers has happened to their descendants. Upon the former already the earlier generations composed selihot and narrated the events. It is all one."[33] Paradigmatic thinking offers a cyclical view of history determined by a promise made that lies beyond historical contingency. This is, of course, a play on a popular rabbinic dictum, "the acts of the fathers are signs for their children."[34] We live in a world of reward and punishment not totally of our own making but not arbitrary either. "It is all one."

For post-Holocaust theologians, the Holocaust could not fit into this paradigm. More strongly, the belief that it could, for some, might itself be blasphemous (for an anti-theodician theodicy is heresy). Jewish historian Amos Funkenstein notes in his essay about the Holocaust, "To the most courageous among recent theologians, the very meaninglessness of the Holocaust is itself, they say, a matter of faith, a positive religious act."[35] Believing in a covenantal God after the Holocaust was, for many, an act of "bad faith." Braiterman puts it this way: "With Auschwitz in mind, many contemporary readers are repelled by theodicies found in traditional Jewish sources."[36] Acknowledging this rupture was not solely the product of Richard Rubenstein's groundbreaking *After Auschwitz*. Rubenstein's teacher Mordecai Kaplan, who really never wrote directly about the Holocaust, wrote obliquely in his 1970 book *The Religion of Ethical Nationhood*, "[The Holocaust] rendered the traditional idea of God untenable."[37]

All post-Holocaust theologians were deeply influenced by modernity, even though some, such as Berkovits and Greenberg, were Orthodox.

Shapira, as the proto-post-Holocaust theologian, one who understood the depth of the covenantal rupture and its implications as it was happening, is in one way an exception and in another a sign that the impossibility of faith after such a rupture is not dependent on modernity per se but can be gleaned through a stark and honest confrontation with the limitations of tradition. Braiterman notes that classical Jewish texts do indeed contain anti-theodic elements even as they are mostly overwhelmed by a theodicy response. Modernity may be a tool that makes post-Holocaust theology permissible but it is not a theological *novum* as much as turning up the volume of a whisper that, in my view, already appears in the tension between Shapira's final sermon in the summer of 1942 and his addendum in November 1942.

If Shapira is an exception, what of most other ultra-Orthodox Jews? Some, such as rabbis Yoel Teitelbaum of Satmar (saved from almost certain death in Bergen-Belsen by the Katzner transports),[38] Yosef Yizhak of Lubavitch, and Elhanan Wasserman (who was murdered by Lithuanian collaborators of the Nazis in the summer of 1941 after he returned to Europe from America to be with his students), maintained a belief in the traditional covenant and viewed the Holocaust as punishment for Jewish secularism, including Zionism.[39] Others, such as rabbis Zvi Yehudah Kook and Yaakov Moshe Charlap, viewed the Holocaust as a punishment for not leaving Europe after the Balfour Declaration. That is, for rejecting Zionism.[40] Zvi Yehuda even called the Holocaust an act of "divine surgery." Each case, however different, is an exercise in "paradigmatic thinking," and as different as these views are from one another, they actually share more with each other than they do with any post-Holocaust theologian or, I would argue, with Shapira. Shapira might have agreed with these views in one form or another at the outset of the war, but by the summer of 1942 and certainly after the Great Deportation, I hope to show that he did not.

If the frame of anti-theodicy requires rupture of theodicy, on what foundations does classical theodicy rest? Here I am indebted to my graduate student Barbara Krawcowicz, whose 2013 dissertation, "Covenantal Theodicy among Haredi and Modern Jewish Thinkers During and After the Holocaust," deftly explores ultra-Orthodox responses to the Holocaust during the war.[41] Krawcowicz is the first to deploy Neusner's notion of "paradigmatic thinking" in reference to the Holocaust by treating some of the major ultra-Orthodox rabbis who reflected on the events during and immediately after the war. Krawcowicz argued that many of these figures who wrote about the Holocaust during the war, such as Rabbis Shlomo

Zalman Ehrenreich (1862–1944), Shlomo Zalman Unsdorfer (1888–1944), and Yissakhar Teichthal (1885–1945), all of whom perished, while they did not conclude, as did many post-Holocaust theologians did afterward, that the covenant was irreparably broken, nevertheless also did not offer reasons for the Holocaust that fit neatly into the paradigmatic thinking that, as Hayyim Yerushalmi stated, "It is all one." For them, the Holocaust posed a theological dilemma but not a theological crisis. Teichthal is an interesting case here because the Holocaust did evoke in him a radical shift from being a staunch anti-Zionist to one who believed that establishment of a Jewish homeland in Erets Yisrael was indeed a priority.[42]

Krawcowicz chose not to include Shapira in her dissertation, but here I would suggest that Shapira stands somewhere between her ultra-Ortho-dox subjects and the modern post-Holocaust theologians. More strongly, I think Shapira presages post-Holocaust theology from the very depths of its destructive fire. He chose a path none of the others dared to tread. Shapira, of course, never lived to further articulate some of his more radical notions articulated in his final sermons. At the end of the Ghetto revolt in May 1943, Shapira, with many other Jews who remained in the Ghetto, was deported to the Trawniki labor camp. Although we do not know for certain, it is thought that he was murdered November 3 in what was known as "the Harvest Festival" (Aktion Erntefest) in response to violent uprisings in other camps.[43]

Considering their historical import, it is surprising that the collection of Shapira's sermons in the Ghetto was not published until 1960. Even after its publication, *Esh kodesh* remained very much within Hasidic circles until Shlomo Carlebach and a few others discovered the work and began conveying its teachings in non-Hasidic communities. Carlebach captured this work in his story "The Holy Hunchback," the story of a broken, elderly street cleaner Carlebach encountered in Tel Aviv who, as a child, was one of Shapira's students in his yeshiva in Warsaw.

Esh Kodesh as Holocaust Testimony

Daniel Reiser's two-volume work *Sermons from the Years of Rage* is more than another significant contribution to the study of R. Kalonymus Kal-man Shapira. It is a piece of scholarship that potentially changes how the wartime sermons are studied and understood, in part because Reiser shows mistakes, errors, and misreadings in some of the transcriptions that became the 1960 printing of *Esh kodesh*. As I mentioned above, one of the distinctive characteristics of *Sermons from the Years of Rage* is that we know when each sermon was delivered and thus can link that week with events in the Ghetto, suggesting the ways in which the unfolding horror of the Ghetto, including the travails of Shapira's own family, may be embedded in the sermon. Given that Shapira does not mention events in the sermons themselves, the dating is the primary way for us to view this work as a Holocaust testimony, that is, to view it as an account of the tragedy of the Warsaw Ghetto. Reiser's reexamination of the original manuscript using new technology to make it more easily discernible enabled him to make many corrections in the only printed edition until now (1960) and produce a corrected text that includes many significant changes. More relevant to our purposes, Reiser reproduces the manuscript, which exhibits detailed editing, deletions, redistribution of paragraphs, and addenda in the margins of many of the sermons. Analyzing the different markings, he concludes that Shapira seemed to continue to rework and edit the sermons throughout his time in the Ghetto.[44] Thus, he concludes, "It seems to me that, although different phases in the Rebbe's theology of suffering are discernible and have been clearly distinguished, this differentiation is not clear cut and each phrase does not constitute a paradigm in itself. One may detect, for example, a 'late' concept of suffering in the Rebbe's early sermons and an 'early' one in later sermons. Nevertheless, this does not refute the thesis that his theory was of an evolutionary nature; it merely refines it."[45] Toward the end of his English essay on *Esh kodesh*, largely a translation from a section of his Hebrew introduction to *Sermons from the Years of Rage*, Reiser makes a slightly more definitive claim: "Given the layered nature of the entire manuscript, it is virtually impossible to attempt to date each and every sermon. . . . Accordingly, I prefer to avoid any discourse about 'meaning' and to propose a different research approach. Instead of seeking development and meaning this views *Esh Kodesh* as a work that re-expresses the question of suffering in phenomenological terms and takes its readers on a jarring spiritual journey."[46]

In the next section, I look at two texts from *Esh kodesh*: first, Shapira's final sermon delivered on the Shabbat before Tisha be-Av (*Shabbat Hazon*) 1942 and second, a well-known addendum to an earlier sermon delivered on Hanukkah 1941 that serves as the last written testimony we have from his hand.[47] This addendum was written in November 1942. I want to offer a "phenomenological" reading of the space between the Shabbat Hazon sermon and the later addendum, paying attention to how the addendum appeared in the manuscript, and offer a reading that suggests how the subtle shift from the Shabbat Hazon sermon to the addendum marks a break in Shapira's faith as he reconciled the impending doom that was about to unfold. This gestures back to Schweid's question that I noted at the outset: "How is it possible to withstand [a test of faith] when the suffering is so intense as to destroy the sole means capable of reinforcing faith in God and the Torah in the present age?" Unlike Schweid, I suggested that it wasn't.

The Final Sermon: Marginalia, Addendum, and Revision

Shapira's final sermon focused on the first verse of the *haftarah*, Isa 1:1, "A vision, shown to Isaiah son of Amoz." This first chapter in Isaiah is one of the darkest in the prophets, as it describes the destruction of Israel in vivid and horrific terms. The final verse of the chapter, "The mighty will become tinder and his work a spark, both will burn together and no one to quench the fire," could not but catch the attention of Shapira living in circumstances surrounded by fire and the righteous being relegated to hapless victims of the power of evil. The sermon revolves around the distinction between "seeing," "hearing," and "knowing." His midrashic text is from Song of Songs Rabba 3:2, "There are ten expressions of prophecy, but which one is the most difficult? R. Eliezer said, 'A vision is the hardest,' as it says, *A cruel vision was told to me* (Isa 21:1)." Asking about the seeming incongruity between "seeing" and "knowing" in the verse "I have truly **seen** the suffering of my people . . . for I **know** their pain" (Exod 3:7), Shapira likens this to a father who knows the necessity of a son's operation yet cannot bear to watch it because seeing it makes him unable to truly know that the operation is for the son's own good. That is, the experience of the pain of a loved one makes knowledge of its benefits impossible. So therefore, God says, "Now go, I am sending you to Pharaoh, take My people out of Egypt," (Exod 3:10) as if to say, "I cannot watch, just go . . ." The "vision" is the hardest level of prophecy because it disables any recognition of a future; it is stuck in the present moment of seeing. This is one example where Diamond's dialectical approach is operative. Shapira comes to the precipice; the pain of seeing the fire of the Ghetto, the degradation of the righteous, the vision that makes "knowing" impossible, makes a future impossible, makes the covenant impossible. And at that very moment Shapira digs back into Torah to grasp onto

Dan 9:18, "Open your eyes and see." This is part of Daniel's prayer for Israel. Verses 18 and 19 read, "O my God, incline Your ear and hear; open Your eyes and see our desolations, and the city which is called by Your name; for we do not present our supplications before You because of our righteous deeds, but because of Your great mercies. O Lord, hear! O Lord, forgive! O Lord, listen and act! Do not delay for Your own sake, my God, for Your city and Your people are called by Your name." Even in the moment where vision blinds knowledge of the good end, perhaps the *belief* in any good end, there is Daniel, who beseeches God for salvation. And so, Daniel's call here is answered by the final verse in the *haftarah* (the sages knew better, I think, to end here and not read to the end of the chapter), "Zion will be redeemed with justice, and her captives with charity" (Is 1:27). With that, Shapira put down his pen. Almost. As Reiser shows, while he did not write any more sermons, he apparently continued to revise the ones already written.

In a sermon delivered on Hanukkah, December 1941, Shapira reflected on the liturgical insert for Hanukkah known as *al ha-nissim*, one of the earliest extant liturgies in the Jewish tradition. In general, though, the sermon is about faith (*emunah*), one of the more sustained sermons about faith in *Esh kodesh*. Shapira comments that Israel's faith and Abraham's faith are categorically different because Abraham's faith "was an act of righteousness" (since he was not reared in faith), while Israel's faith is intrinsic to who Israel is, as an inheritor of Abrahamic faith ("faith is the light and holiness of God inside the Jew"). Following this he turns to his present situation. "To our chagrin, we see that even among those who have faith, there are now certain individuals whose faith has been damaged [*nifgamah ha-emunah etslam*]. They question God, saying, 'Why have you forsaken us? . . . Why is the Torah and everything sacred being destroyed?'" Responding to this sentiment, while not denying its emotional impact, he launches into what can be viewed as a classical theodic claim preached from a moment of high anxiety and utter turmoil.

> Faith must be with one's whole being (*bi-mesirat nefesh*, "self-sacrifice") because all *mesirat nefesh* comes from faith. If faith is not exercised with *mesirat nefesh*, how can *mesirat nefesh* exist at all! The notion of *mesirat nefesh* in faith must be operative, and even when God is concealed (*ha-hester*), one must believe that everything is from God and is for the good and the just and all suffering is filled with God's love for

Israel. . . . In truth, there is no room for questioning [heaven forbid]. Truthfully, the sufferings we are experiencing are like those we've suffered every few hundred years. . . . What excuse does one have to question God and have his faith damaged by this suffering more than the Jews who suffered in the past? Why should one's faith be damaged now when it wasn't when he reads descriptions of Jewish suffering from the past? Why is it that when one reads a line from the Talmud or Midrash and hears of past sufferings in Israel his faith is not damaged but now [confronting the experience on the Ghetto] it is? Those who say that the suffering now has never happened before to Israel are mistaken. The destruction of the temple and the massacre at Betar were like what we are suffering now. May God have mercy and call an end to our suffering; may God save us now, immediately, and forever.[48]

This is an impassioned and quintessential expression of classical Jewish theodicy, almost angry, quite atypical of Shapira's wartime sermons. So many of Shapira's sermons stress suffering and express empathy and understanding, and yet here he turns into a fire and brimstone orator chiding his listeners, warning them not to be deluded that they are living in some unprecedented reality. While we do not know for sure, it appears that this change in attitude may have been instigated by "those who say that the suffering now has never happened before." To whom this refers we do not know. In any case, I think Shapira deeply understood the theological implications of such an assertion, likely more than his listeners, and perhaps that is why he was pushing back so hard against it. The very foundations of faith that he speaks about in the beginning of the passage, the faith driven by *mesirat nefesh*, the faith in God's saving power, is dependent on the covenantal principle of "paradigmatic thinking," that what we are experiencing not is not a *novum*, that providence remains in operation, that salvation is still possible. That nothing here is new, that this is our covenant, that this is the test we must pass ("every few hundred years") to maintain our place in God's love is what underlies the passion of these comments.[49] As Neusner puts it, "A paradigm predetermines and selects happenings in accord with a pattern possessed of its own logic and meaning, unresponsive to the illogic of happenings, whether chaotic or orderly, from the human perspective. . . . Paradigms admit to time—the spell that intervenes between this and that, the this and the that beyond *defined within the paradigm*" (italics added).[50]

As Reiser has shown us, Shapira continually revisited and revised these sermons throughout his time in the Ghetto. He writes, "The Rebbe's renunciation of certain perceptions that he had presented and his decision to delete them are crucial for our understanding of his thinking vacillations, and change of heart during the Holocaust years."[51] Sometimes he crossed out a word leaving the word legible, sometimes he drew a line through an entire section of a sermon, sometimes he blackened a word beyond recognition and replaced it with another; in many cases he added marginalia, clarifying a point. In some cases, the meaning of the original comment is altered, sometimes it is nuanced, but rarely is it rejected entirely.[52] In one case, in the sermon he delivered on Hanukkah 1941, he did something quite unusual: he added an addendum (in Hebrew, *haga'ah*) on the bottom of the page (not in the margins). The addendum relates back to the passage quoted regarding faith.

> It is only the suffering (*tsarot*) that were experienced until the middle of 1942 that were precedented (*hayu kevar*). But the bizarre suffering (*tsarot meshunot*) and the evil bizarre deaths (*u-mitot ra'ot u-meshunot*) that were invented by these evil bizarre murderers on Israel in the middle of 1942, according my opinion and the teachings of the sages of the chronicles of the Jewish people more generally, there were none like these before. And God should have mercy on us and save us from their hands in the blink of an eye. Erev Shabbat Kodesh, 18 Kislev 1943. The author.[53]

The suggestion that the tragedy unfolding was both unprecedented and unparalleled ("there were none like these before") may seem ordinary, even obvious, to many contemporary readers. However, much of the thinking about the Holocaust, both by scholars and laypeople, and much of the way the Holocaust has been ceremonialized (e.g., establishing a national Holocaust Memorial Day), is founded on this very principle. Much of the *haredi* protest against Holocaust Memorial Day is precisely that the Holocaust is *not* unprecedented and should thus be folded into Tisha b'Av.[54] Zvi Yehuda Kook included his reflections on the Holocaust as an extension of his sermons of the tenth of Tevet, a fast day commemorating the beginning of the siege of Jerusalem.[55] But for a Hasidic Jew in 1942 or 1943 who lived deep within the orbit of the covenantal theology and "paradigmatic thinking" of Judaism, such a comment, even if thought, was almost never stated outright; it gestured to what would become a few decades later a radical reassessment of the Holocaust as a full-blown theological crisis and a serious challenge to the Jewish tradition. A full-blown theological crisis, in this case, emerges only when two conditions are met simultaneously: first, the belief that the Holocaust was an unprecedented event in Jewish history; and second, that this unprecedented event must irrevocably rupture the covenantal framework established in the Hebrew Bible. Shapira's comment certainly adopts the first condition and, I would argue, also gestures toward the second.

The way this addendum appears in the original manuscript, thanks to Resier's publication of it, I think strengthens my point. Shapira could have simply crossed out the theodicy paragraph in the original Hanukkah sermon. We see in the manuscript that he often does that. Or he could have softened its harshness with marginalia, which he does quite often as well. He did neither. He left this statement of covenantal theology intact and, in a note (*haga'ah*) on the bottom of the page, he qualified it out of existence. The foundational notion of exercising faith through self-sacrifice (*mesirat nefesh*) by arguing that faith serves as the bedrock of all acts of *mesirat nefesh*, the belief in God's salvific promise and potential, in his mind did not survive the Great Deportation that occurred between July and September 1942. The Shabbat Hazon sermon delivered on July 18, 1942 was a final testament to an entire theological structure that would collapse for Shapira in the coming months. As that was his last sermon that has survived, almost nothing remains extant from him after July 1942 aside from this addendum, which he added in November of that year.

One can only shudder to imagine Shapira sitting in his home during those dark months, hungry and weak, reading through these sermons one more time only to come across his Hanukkah sermon of 1941, read his exhortation about faith and the fact that "this (suffering) happens every few hundred years" and how dare we think otherwise, and then pick up his pen, one more time, to add a few final sentences. I assume he wanted his reader to know that something changed between the autumn of 1941 and November 1942. He did not blot out his call to faith. Rather, he contextualized it by saying that it was no longer relevant. His comment in the Hanukkah sermon, that "those who say that the suffering now has never happened before to Israel are mistaken," is undermined. His comment that "there are now certain individuals whose faith has been damaged" is justified. And now he counts himself among them. This is an example of a courageous admission of error in the time of crisis; and he apparently *wanted* his reader to know he was mistaken as he left his words from Hanukkah 1941 and November 1942 to posterity. That mistake, I suggest, was not simply an empirical admission of miscalculation but a deep theological rupture, as I read the claim of the Holocaust as an "unprecedented" event that makes "paradigmatic thinking" impossible, as Rubenstein and other post-Holocaust theologians argue as well. If we return once more to Diamond's dialectical hypothesis, I would argue that there is no stepping back from that final note in November 1942; in other words, the dialectic is broken. This is a step off the cliff of theodicy into the abyss of anti-theodicy and, more relevant to my concerns here, a move from theodic faith to broken faith. To reiterate, I am not saying that Shapira lost faith in God entirely; I think he did not. But the faith he had after November 1942, based on the only words we have, is not the faith he had previously. It structurally cannot be for the simple reason that he removed the very theological, and theodic, structure that made that faith possible.

What is noticeably different in Shapira's Hanukkah addendum is that his unprecedented claim does not come from historicism or secularism, or even from theology, but from a deep existential realization of the utter inability of the tradition, which was for him until those months of darkness ironclad and indestructible, to withstand this level of radical evil. He brings no anti-theodic text, in fact no text at all, just an empirical observation with what seemed to him an obvious conclusion. Theodicy collapses and nothing exists to take its place. Disbelief was untenable. But belief as previously defined was no longer possible. God remained, but the covenant, at least as it existed previously, did not.

Taking Reiser's "layered approach" into account, I suggest that *Esh kodesh* can be divided into three distinct but overlapping parts, not linearly defined, that loosely correspond to the period when he began his sermons in the Ghetto in September 1939 until the final recorded sermon on the Shabbat before Tisha B'Av in the summer of 1942. These three periods can be marked by three aspects of his vocation: In the first phase, Shapira functioned largely as a pastor, offering his community words of strength in times of peril. Here, he thought very much within the paradigmatic model that what Jews are facing is not categorically different from previous times of Jewish suffering. Perhaps the sermon on Hanukkah 1941 is the quintessence of that.

In the second phase, Shapira had the ominous job of teaching his people how to die. This is illustrated in his many sermons about martyrdom and suffering that were deftly discussed by Polen, Schweid, Diamond, Seeman, Hershkovitz, Abrahamson, and Leib, among others. These sermons about martyrdom are nothing less than learning how to die with dignity; how to understand that, although beyond comprehension, they are part of some divine drama and serve as its cadre of heroes. One gets a sense in these sermons that Shapira knew he was speaking to individuals who would likely not be alive the following year. To read these sermons with that in mind is heartbreaking. In the final period, ending abruptly in July 1942, with the crucial addendum in November 1942, Shapira emerges as a radical theologian, implicitly rejecting, or certainly contesting, some of his earlier sermons by suggesting that this moment does not fit into any paradigm, that what he and his constituents were experiencing was "unprecedented and unparalleled." These two words separate Shapira from his ultra-Orthodox colleagues and, as Leib notes, plant the seeds of what would become post-Holocaust theology a few decades later. Paradigmatic thinking cannot absorb a true novum.

The paradigm that enabled Jews to withstand disbelief throughout Jewish history simply would no longer carry the burden of this historical moment even as it was not historicism that broke the back of "paradigmatic thinking" but rather witnessing the pure and bizarre evil that erased a covenantal God. By this time, more than the previous two, one gets the sense that Shapira is preaching largely to himself or, perhaps with that final note, writing for posterity, to those who might read these sermons if any Jews survived at all. Shapira seems left alone to process the brokenness of his inner world as the world around him collapsed.

As to the theological, or historical, question "Is the Holocaust a novum?" I think that question was utterly irrelevant for Shapira because that question is an act of historical, or historicist, explanation one way or the other. It is significant that Shapira is not advocating silence in the moment where the paradigm, and faith, reaches its limit, where God seems to absent Godself from history such as we see in other ultra-Orthodox thinkers writing during the war, examined in Barbara Krawcowicz's work.[56] Shapira realizes that he will die with a God who has abandoned his people, a faith shattered, a belief in a God who is broken, a God who cannot save or will not save. To believe in God becomes as absurd and as blasphemous as not to believe in God. Braiterman uses the term "anti-theodicy" to describe post-Holocaust theology as that which refuses to view catastrophe as instrumental in the divine covenant. Sharpira was not anti-theodic in that sense; and here I disagree slightly with Leib and suggest that Shapira's view might more accurately be described as a "broken theodicy." His final flourish, "God have mercy on us and save us like the blink of an eye," was not only rhetorical. Yet it was no longer coming from the faith that had existed before. Perhaps that breach, between pure rhetoric and uttering something that he no longer believed but also could not put to rest, opened the door for the anti-theodicy that was to come a few decades later.

In the final section I want to explore a little more deeply what may have been the nature of Shapira's "broken faith." I do so by comparing my reading of Shapira with two fictitious careers from the Warsaw Ghetto: those of Yosl Rakover, the creation of Zvi Kolitz, and the Holy Hunchback, the creation of Shlomo Carlebach.

Rabbi Shipira, Yosl Rakover, and the Holy Hunchback

When the story "Yosl Rakover Speaks to God" first appeared in a Yiddish newspaper in Buenos Aires in 1946, it was thought to be an authentic document of one of the last Jews in the Warsaw Ghetto in April 1943 discovered in the rubble of the Ghetto. It was then edited by the great poet Abraham Sutzkver for the Yiddish press in Israel and appeared in French in 1955. It soon came to be known that it was a fictitious story written by Zvi Kolitz, a Jew from Lithuania living in Israel who was visiting Argentina on an assignment for the Zionist Revisonist Movement. The fictitious nature of the story did not diminish its power, or its influence, and this story quickly became iconic and inspired commentaries by the likes of Emmanuel Levinas, among others.[57]

Briefly, the story is about a Jew, a Hasid from the Hasidic court of Ger, trapped in a building as the Ghetto collapses, preparing for one last assault on the Germans below (he has a few jerry cans of gasoline he will use to drop on the Nazis and gleefully watch them burn) before he succumbs to inevitable death.[58] The story is often cited as one Jew's defiant belief in God, even despite God. "You may torture me to death—I will always believe in You. I will love you always and forever—*even despite You*" (italics added). He remains a "believer but not a supplicant, a lover of

God but not His blind Amen-sayer."[59] He says that "I cannot say after all I lived through, that my relation to God is unchanged. But with absolute certainly I can say that my faith in Him has not altered a hair's-breath."[60] This takes us back to Wiesel's comment at the outset: Can it really be that someone experiences what Yosl experienced and his faith has not changed one bit? That is precisely what Wiesel fails to comprehend. And yet this appears to be what Yosl is saying. I think not.

In his short rendering of the French version of the essay published in the Zionist Parisian paper *La terre retrouvee*, Emmanuel Levinas offers an indirect response to Wiesel's question. Levinas writes, "On the road that leads to the one and only God, there must be a way station without God. True monotheism must frame answers to the legitimate demands of atheism. An adult's God reveals Himself precisely in the emptiness of the child's heaven."[61] For Levinas, the lynchpin in Kolitz's essay is the rabbinic citation, "I love God, but I love God's Torah even more . . . and even if I have been deceived by Him and, as it were, disenchanted, I would nonetheless observe the precepts of God's Torah." This was one of Levinas's early essays on Judaism, and Tamra Wright argues that the idea that for Judaism love of Torah precedes love of God, certainly of a God who reveals Godself to humans, becomes a fundamental principle for Levinas's later work.[62] For Levinas, teaching, as opposed to experience, becomes the very contribution Judaism has to answer the legitimate question of the atheist. For our purposes, Levinas suggests that Yosl frames his final "belief" on a protest that becomes the transition from the "emptiness of the child's heaven" to the one who stands ready to die, not necessarily for God, but for Torah. And so Levinas ends his brief commentary, "To love the Torah more than God—this means precisely to find a personal God against whom it is possible to revolt, that is to say, one for whom one can die."

Levinas does not mention that Yosl was a Hasid, but perhaps it is relevant to his rendering. The God Yosl believes in at the end, at least according to Levinas, is no longer the Hasidic God. It is not a God with whom one can experience *devekut*. It is a God who has abandoned Israel but left the Torah behind. "The emptiness of the child's heaven" is the great and legitimate question of the atheist, especially after the Holocaust, a question Levinas claims monotheism must answer. For the believer without Torah, Levinas implies, citing Simone Weil, there is no real answer to atheism, surely not after the Holocaust, which is why Levinas says to Weil, "you do not understand anything about the Torah!"[63] What does Yosl love? An absent God? An "empty heaven"? No, Yosl loves a God who gave Torah because that is the only thing from God that remains, even though, or precisely that, God may not.[64]

As not to be misunderstood, I do not think there is an exact symmetry between Yosl and Shapira. But there is a resemblance worth noting. Shapira's final note to us, one he never shared with his congregants, stated the following: "The God of the covenant, the God who saves, the God to whom prayer is efficacious, that God is no longer. That God cannot survive the death of theodicy, the 'unparalleled and unprecedented.' But there is still the God who created the world, even as that very God is now destroying it." And Shapira can still believe in and love that God. But in relation to what existed before, that faith is not whole; that faith is broken.[65] Yosl professes love for God, but in that rabbinic quote there is a protest. "I love you despite the fact that you have abandoned me. Why? Because you left us Torah. That's all. It's not what I had hoped, but I guess it will have to be enough." Levinas calls it "mature" faith. I call it broken faith, a faith without theodicy, in some way, a faith without covenant. Whether Levinas would agree with that formulation, we will never know. The difference between theodic faith and anti- or post-theodic faith is that anti- or post-theodic faith can never claim superiority over nonfaith. It can never fully answer the atheist because it is faith in a God who is not there. It is faith in a God who has torn the covenant.

"The greatest thing in the world," said the Holy Hunchback, quoting his rebbe, Kalonymus Kalman Shapira of Piaseczno, to Shlomo Carlebach on the Yarkon in Tel Aviv, "is to do someone else a favor." In the story of the Holy Hunchback, Shlomo meets an elderly Jew, a street cleaner in Tel Aviv who reveals himself as one of Shapira's students in his yeshiva for children. The story served as one of the ways Shapira's work *Esh kodesh* became popular among non-Hasidic Jews worldwide. When asked to repeat any Torah he learned from Shapira, the Holy Hunchback can only remember what the rebbe used to repeat at the Shabbat table. "My children, listen, the greatest thing in the world is to do someone else a favor." It is with these words, and with the story of the Holy Hunchback, that Shapira became known to the non-Hasidic world.

Here, the Holy Hunchback enters through the portal of Shlomo Carlebach. "Can you tell me please," asks Carlebach, "tell me something you learned from him [Shapira]?" The Holy Hunchback puts down his broom. He washes his hands, puts on his jacket and hat, straightens his tie. "From my years in Auschwitz, I have long forgotten his Torah," he says in a heavy Polish Yiddish, "but I remember that during the Friday night Shabbos meal, between every course, between the soup and the fish and the fish and the chicken, he used to say to us, 'Children, take heed, the greatest thing in the world is to do someone else a favor.'" And then Carlebach added, "Do you know how many favors you can do in Auschwitz?"

The Holy Hunchback's recollection—if it happened at all—happened before the Ghetto, when Shapira had a yeshiva, Da'at Moshe, for children in Warsaw. But perhaps there is some foresight here as to what would happen some years later, a response to Shapira's own realization that the covenant is fractured beyond repair, that we are left to take care of ourselves. In that world where God will not save, where history will not conform to the confines of tradition, where we are left alone in the thralls of radical evil; in that place of utter despair, "unprecedented and unparalleled," there is nothing better than doing someone else a favor. That becomes the covenant. Perhaps Shapira's message is that after the Holocaust, the only thing left is the ethical. And a new Torah, if it will be constructed at all, will be constructed on that foundation. And any new Torah without that foundation is not worth having. What is a belief in God without a covenant? Doing someone else a favor.

Some months later, Carlebach returned to the Yarkon in Tel Aviv to find the Holy Hunchback. He looked everywhere, to no avail. He asked a passerby, "Have you seen the Holy Hunchback?" only to realize that he had left the world. But he had passed on his torah of broken faith.

Tragically, Shapira did not live long enough to offer any resolution to what I take to be his crisis of faith. He never had the opportunity to explain to us what he meant in that last addendum from November 1942. But in any case, he also did not fool those who would read his words after the war into believing that the covenant could carry the burden or could survive what transpired in the summer of 1942. It could not. The pastoral vocation in the first period of his work had become, for him, obsolete. He taught his congregation how to die; many of them had already died. And now he was left to his own devices, quite different and yet also oddly similar to Yosl Rakover. It is better to die facing the truth of the moment, even if it tears the fabric of tradition, than to defend a paradigm that has already become obsolete. Shapira famously said in numerous places in *Esh kodesh*, "Since God does this, that is the way it is supposed to be." But from the perspective of paradigmatic thinking, or covenantal theology, if something is unparalleled, that is precisely not the way it is supposed to be. Shlomo Zalman Unsdorfer and Shlomo Zalman Ehrenreich could respond to the Holocaust only with silence. But Shapira was not silent. He added that note in November 1942 to say something to his future reader. In my view, that note was not written by a man of faith; it was written by a man of broken faith. Faith may have remained, but it was not like before. It could not be. And so what we are left with is a Hasidic master who was not able to finish his theological work, a Hasidic master who in the privacy of his dilapidated home, in the months before he too would succumb to the Nazi evil, wrote the ostensibly blasphemous final words that this catastrophe was not like all the others. That it was unprecedented. It was a tear in, or rupture of, the covenant. All (of Jewish history) is not one. With that stroke of his pen, post-Holocaust theology truly begins.

Notes

I would like to offer my thanks to James A. Diamond, David Maayan, Daniel Reiser, and Don Seeman for their invaluable comments and suggestions. חברותא או מיתותא.

1. I heard this orally from someone who heard it from Wiesel, but I have not found a source for this.

2. Of course, there are post-Holocaust theologies such as Eliezer Berkovits's *Faith after the Holocaust* that present theories of *hester panim,* or God concealing God's face, as a traditional theological posture that could explain God and also justify God's inactivity in the Holocaust. For more examples, see David Wolpe, "Hester Panim in Modern Jewish Thought," *Modern Judaism* 17, no. 1 (1997): 25–56. I would suggest that for many Jews, rabbis, theologians, and laypeople alike, such a rabbinic category does not adequately explain the Holocaust. In some way, post-Holocaust theology exists between the poles of Berkovits's *hester paim* theory and Richard Rubenstein's covenantal rupture theory.

3. I will not rehearse the many stories about the how these sermons were concealed and how they were found. This has been expertly done by Daniel Reiser in his "*Esh Kodesh*: A New Evaluation in Light of a Philological Examination of the Manuscript," *Yad Vashem Studies* 44 (2016): 66–69.

4. See Kalonymus Kalman Shapira, *Sermons from the Years of Rage* [in Hebrew], ed. Daniel Reiser, 2 vols. (Jerusalem: Herzog Academic College, 2017), 1:55.

5. We don't actually know whether the written sermons, even in manuscript form, were exactly those that were preached. Shapira could have easily excised things he felt were redundant or added things he thought about later. Thanks to David Maayan for this insight.

6. Reiser, ed., *Sermons from the Years of Rage*.

7. Eliezer Schweid, "The Bush Is Aflame—But the Bush Is not Consumed," in *From Ruin to Salvation* [in Hebrew] (Tel Aviv, 1994), 105 and James A. Diamond, "The Warsaw Ghetto Rebbe: Diverting God's Gaze from a Utopian End to an Anguished Now," *Modern Judaism* 30, no. 1 (2010): 299. Shapira was not the only one who lived through the Holocaust who seriously confronted the question of faith in light of it. Aside from the many works of Wiesel, it is worth mentioning David Halinvi's *The Book and the Sword* (New York: Farrar, Strauss, and Giroux, 1996). More recently see Yishai Mevorach, *Theology of Absence: On Faith after Chaos* [in Hebrew] (Tel Aviv: Reisling, 2016). Mevorach, a student of Rav Shagar, works through the writings of Rav Shapira and also discusses Shapira, Nahman of Bratslav, and others on the question of faith and absence in the contemporary religious life.

8. Schweid, *From Ruin to Salvation*, 138.

9. This is not exactly true. We do have a note that he wrote on January 3, 1943 (17 Tevet), that offers instructions to the one who finds his writings to mail them to his brother Isaiah in Tel Aviv. In it, he writes about his other works as well and, like the final note in November 1942, he ends with a liturgical flourish, using the same locution that "God should save us in the blink of an eye (*ke-heref ayin*)." See below where I offer a reading of this end to his note in November 1942. I suggest the same would apply here. While this note certainly postdates his final insertion in *Esh kodesh*, it does not relate to the events and their significance but rather is more practical. Thus, I claimed above that the final note in November 1942 is really the last significant thing we have from him. I want to thank Daniel Reiser for pointing out this final note from January 1943.

10. This is discussed at length in Don Seeman, "Ritual Efficacy, Hasidic Mysticism, and Useless Suffering in the Warsaw Ghetto," *Harvard Theological Review* 101, no. 3–4 (2008): 465–505. Cf. Zvi Leshem, "Between Mysticism and Prophecy: Hasidism According to the Piaseczner Rebbe" [in Hebrew] (PhD diss., Bar Ilan University, 2008); and David Maayan, "The Call of the Self: Devotional Individuation in the Teachings of Rabbi Kalonymous Kalman Shapira of Piaseczno" (master's thesis, Hebrew College, 2017).

11. See Kalonymous Kalman Shapira, *A Student's Obligation: Advice from the Rebbe of the Warsaw Ghetto (Hovot Ha-Talmidim)*, trans. M. Odenheimer (Northvale, NJ: Jason Aronson, 1995); Shapira, *Jewish Spiritual Growth: A Step-by-Step Guide of a Hasidic Master*, trans. Yaacov David Shulman (CreateSpace Independent Publishing, 2016); and Shapira, *Conscious Community*, trans. Andrea Cohen-Kiener (Northvale, NJ: Jason Aronson, 1997).

12. In 1917, Shapira moved from Piaseczno to Warsaw, where he founded the yeshiva Da'at Moshe. In the ensuing years, he traveled back and forth from Piaseczno to Warsaw, residing mainly in Warsaw. See *Sermons from the Years of Rage*, 1:14.

13. Nehemia Polen, *The Holy Fire: The Teachings of Rabbi Kalonymus Kalman Shapira, the Rebbe of the Warsaw Ghetto* (Northvale, NJ: Jason Aronson, 1994), 19. Others who have written about *Esh kodesh* include Mendel Piekarz in his *Polish Hasidism: Between the Wars* (1978); Pesach Schindler in *Hasidic Responses to the Holocaust in Light of Hasidic Thought* (Hoboken, NJ: KTAV, 1990); Henry Abramson, *Torah from the Years of Wrath 1939–1943: The Historical Context of the Aish Kodesh* (CreateSpace Independent Publishing Platform, 2017); Itzhak Hershkowitz, "Rabbi Kalomymus Kalman Shapira, the Piasechner Rebbe: His Holocaust and Pre-Holocaust Thought" [in Hebrew] (master's thesis, Bar-Ilan University, 2005); Don Seeman, "Ritual Efficacy, Hasidic Mysticism and 'Useless Suffering' in the Warsaw Ghetto," *Harvard Theological Review* 101, no. 3/4 (2008): 465–505; Diamond, "The Warsaw Rebbe," 299–331; Ron Wacks, *The Flame of the Holy Fire* [in Hebrew] (Alon Shevut: Tevunot, 2010); Erin Leib, "God in the Years of Fury: Theodicy and Anti-Theodicy in the Holocaust Writings of Rabbi Kalonymous Kalman Shapira" (PhD diss., University of Chicago, 2014); and most recently Daniel Reiser's new two-volume Hebrew work on the manuscript edition of *Sermons from the Years of Rage* (2017).

14. See Diamond, "The Warsaw Rebbe," 299–331.

15. Abramson, *Torah from the Years of Wrath*, 249.

16. Reiser, "*Esh kodesh*: A New Evaluation," 70. A more apologetic reading by Esther Farber in *Hidden in Thunder: Perspectives on Faith, Halacha, and Leadership during the Holocaust,* 2 vols. (New York: Feldheim, 2007), 579–612 pushes back even harder against any notion that Shapira's faith diminished at all.

17. In his essay "Ritual Efficacy," Don Seeman does indeed address the notion of broken faith in the final sermons of Shapira. Like few others—James A. Diamond would be another example—Seeman entertains the real possibility that by 1942 Shapira loses something he had before, although he does not go as far as I do in suggesting that for Shapira faith in the covenant itself collapses. See Seeman, "Ritual Efficacy," 503–504. On Seeman's reading of the final added footnote, see ibid., 494. Seeman does not read into that note as much as I do, though he does recognize its significance.

18. Abramson, *Torah from the Years of Wrath*, 251.

19. See, for example, in Jacob Neusner's *The Idea of History in Rabbinical Literature* (London: Brill, 2004); and Neusner, "Paradigmatic Versus Historical Thinking: The Case of Rabbinic Judaism," *History and Theory* 36, no. 3 (1977): 353–77.

20. Wright, *God Who Acts: Biblical Theology and Recital* (London: LSCM, 1954), 13 and Barbara Krawcowicz, "Covenantal Theodicy among Haredi and Modern Jewish Thinkers During and After the Holocaust" (PhD diss., Indiana University, 2013), 19 (in typescript).

21. Leib, "God in the Years of Fury."

22. *Theodicy* is a term coined by Gottfried Wilhelm Leibnitz in 1709. See his *Theodicy: Essays on the Goodness of God, the Freedom of Man, and the Origin*

of Evil (La Salle, IL: Open Court, 1996). It was a term that was criticized often by people from Voltaire to William James.

23. Zachary Braiterman, *(God) After Auschwitz: Tradition and Change in Post-Holocaust Jewish Thought* (Princeton: Princeton University Press, 1998), 31.

24. Amos Funkenstein, *Perceptions of Jewish History* (Los Angeles: University of California Press, 1993), 310, 311.

25. Zachary Braiterman, *(God) After Auschwitz*, 14.

26. Leib, "Theodicy and Anti-Theodicy," 12.

27. Ibid., 178.

28. Braiterman, *(God) After Auschwitz*, 4.

29. Zvi Kolitz, *Yossel Rackover Speaks to God* (New Jersey: Ktav, 1995).

30. For a theological reflection of God in relation to history on the question of the Holocaust, see Emil Fackenheim, *God's Presence in History* (New York: Harper Torchbooks, 1972), who rarely mentions the *Sermons from the Years of Rage*. He does discuss this work in *What Is Judaism: An Interpretation for the Present Age* (New York: Syracuse University Press, 1999) 290ff., where he thanks Nehemia Polen for introducing him to Shapira. It remains somewhat curious that the *Sermons* were printed in 1960 as *Esh kodesh*, yet Fackenheim did not know of Shapira's work until the 1980s when he read about him in Polen.

31. See Jacob Neusner, "Paradigmatic versus Historical Thinking."

32. Barbara Krawcowicz, "Covenantal Theodicy among Haredi and Modern Jewish Thinkers During and After the Holocaust" (PhD diss., Indiana University, 2013), 24 (in typescript). I want to thank Barbara Krawcowicz for sharing the revisions of her dissertation.

33. Yosef Hayim Yerushalmi, *Zakhor: Jewish History and Jewish Memory* (Seattle: University of Washington Press, 1996), 50.

34. Midrash Tanhuma 9.

35. Funkenstein, *Perceptions of Jewish History*, 329.

36. Braiterman, *(God) After Auschwitz*, 30.

37. Mordecai M. Kaplan, *The Religion of Ethical Nationhood: Judaism Contribution to World Peace* (New York: Macmillan, 1970), 202.

38. See Teitelbaum, *Vayoel Moshe* (Jerusalem, 1961), 7–9. See also Menachem Keren-Krantz, "R. Joel Teitelbaum: A Biography" (PhD diss., Tel Aviv University, 2013). He stated this in other places in very explicit terms. See, for example, in the journal *Ha-Me'or*, Tammuz 1958, 3–9, cited in Keren-Krantz, 291, where he adds a political reason for Zionism's culpability. "Today it is known that Zionism caused the death of six million Jews. This is not only because they positioned the hearts of many in Israel with their heresy . . . for it is known that heresy is the cause of evil, but their very political behavior and irresponsibility was responsible for the death of millions of Jews because they believed that the establishment of a sovereign state can only come about with Jewish blood. In the Nazi tragedy there were many opportunities to save thousands of Jews . . . we see now from

the Katzner trials that reveal only a small part of the Zionists' culpability in saving the lives of Jews."

39. An indispensable collection of translated material from these and other traditional thinkers on the Holocaust can be found in Gershon Greenberg and Steven T. Katz, *Wrestling with God: Jewish Theological Responses during and after the Holocaust* (New York: Oxford University Press, 2007). In addition, see the many essays written on a variety of ultra-Orthodox thinkers on the Holocaust by Gershon Greenberg and Elizer Schweid, *Wrestling until Daybreak: Searching for Meaning in Thinking on the Holocaust* (Lanham, MD: University Press of America, 1994).

40. See, for example, R. Zvi Yehuda Kook, "Ha-shoah," in *Sihot R. Zvi Yehuda Kook: Moadim—Rosh ha-Shana-Purim*, ed. Shlomo Aviner (Jerusalem: Hava, 2013), 264–86. For a more extensive rendering of Kookian views on the Holocaust, see Shlomo Aviner, *Me'orot me-ofel: Al ha-shoah* (Jerusalem: Hava, 2010).

41. Barbara Krawcowicz, "Covenantal Theodicy."

42. See in Teichtal's *Em habanim semeichah*, now in English as Yissakhar Shlomo Teichtal, *Em Habanim Semeichah: Erez Yisrael, Redemption, and Unity* (Jerusalem: Urim, 2002).

43. See *Sermons from the Years of Rage*, 1:24, where Reiser gives November 2 as the date of his death.

44. See ibid., 1:59, 60.

45. Ibid., 72.

46. Ibid., 97. Cf. Seeman, "Ritual Efficacy," esp. 488–93.

47. For the Hanukkah sermon, see *Sermons from the Years of Rage*, hanukkah 5702 (1942), 2:240. The addendum appears there as well.

48. Ibid., 2:173–75.

49. Diamond seems to recognize this change, even noting that after the summer of 1942 the "traditional rationale for suffering as a necessary stage in the unfolding of the divine plan [was] . . . no longer viable"—that is, after the Great Deportation—but he does not extend this to its natural conclusion of the end of theodicy for Shapira and its, to my mind, necessary and radical consequences. See Diamond, "The Warsaw Ghetto Rebbe," 4; and Seeman, "Ritual Efficacy." Cf. idem, "Otherwise than Meaning: On the Generosity of Ritual," *Social Analysis* 48, no. 2 (Summer 2004), 62–67.

50. Jacob Neusner, "Paradigmatic versus Historical Thinking: The Case of Rabbinic Judaism," *History and Theory* 36, no. 3 (1997): 359.

51. Reiser, "*Esh kodesh*," 91.

52. This is all laid out in detail in Reiser's introduction to the wartime *derashot*. In English, see Reiser, "*Esh kodesh*," 83–97. See especially 90–91. On crossing out an entire sermon, see *Sermons from the Years of Rage*, *parashat kedoshim* 5700 (1940), 2:62–63. Reiser notes that this sermon was printed in the 1960 edition without any indication that it had been crossed out.

53. This translation comes from Reiser's manuscript edition in *Sermons from the Years of Rage*, 2:175. There are some differences between previous translations, e.g., *Sacred Fire: Torah from the Years of Fury 1939–1942*, trans. J. Hershy Worch (New York: Rowman and Littlefield, 2002), 251. I tried to offer a more literal, if also perhaps more clumsy, translation in order to render a reading as close as possible to the original. For example, Worch uses the terms "unprecedented and unparalleled" for "there were none like them before" (*lo hayu ke-motam*). I agree with Worch's reading, which in some sense makes my point even more strongly, but I wanted to keep it as close to a literal rendering as possible.

54. See 2 Kgs 25:1–25.

55. See Zvi Yehuda Kook, *Sihot Ha-Rav Zvi Yehuda: Festivals*, 264–86.

56. Barbara Krawcowicz, "Covenantal Theodicy."

57. See, for example, Franz Josef Van Beeck, *Loving the Torah More than God: Towards a Catholic Appreciation of Judaism* (Chicago: Loyola, 1989). Cf. Leon Wieseltier's Introduction to *Yosl Rakover Talks to God* (New York: Vintage, 2000); and Marvin Fox, "Yossel Rakover," in *Yossel Rakover Speaks to God* (New Jersey: Ktav, 1995).

58. The only place where I have seen the Hasidic identity of Yosl playing a central role in the story is in Marvin Fox's "Holocaust Challenges to Religious Faith: The Case of Yossele Rakover, Hersh Rasseyner, and Chaim Vilner," in Zvi Kolitz, *Yossel Rakover Speaks to God: Holocaust Challenges to Religious Faith* (New Jersey: Ktav, 1995), 73–100.

59. All citations are from Zvi Kolitz, *Yosl Rakover Talks to God*, trans. Carol Brown Janeway (New York: Vintage, 2000), 9.

60. Ibid., 3.

61. Levinas, "To Love the Torah More than God," reprinted in Zvi Kolitz, *Yossel Rakover Speaks to God: Holocaust Challenges to Religious Faith*, 29.

62. See Tamra Wright, *The Twilight of Jewish Philosophy: Levinas' Ethical Hermeneutics* (London and New York: Routledge, 213), 99, 100.

63. Op. cit., 30.

64. In some way this can be seen as following the rabbinic teaching in *Pesikta de Rav Kahane* 15:5, "R. Huna, R. Jeremiah said in the name of R. Hiyya bar Abba, *Me they have abandoned*? (Jeremiah 16:11). Is it possible that they have kept My Torah? Would that they would have abandoned me and kept My Torah!"

65. Here, Seeman seems to concur although he maintains that even the covenant remains whereas I do not. See his "Ritual Efficacy."

14

Pain and Words

On Suffering, Hasidic Modernism,
and the Phenomenological Turn

Don Seeman

The decade and more that have passed since the publication of my essay "Ritual Efficacy, Hasidic Mysticism and 'Useless Suffering' in the Warsaw Ghetto" have witnessed an explosion in published scholarship on the life and work of R. Kalonymus Kalman Shapira.[1] In addition to the classic studies on R. Shapira's Holocaust-era writings by Mendel Piekarz, Nehemia Polen, Eliezer Schweid, and others, we now have a variety of challenging and important studies on his educational theories, his prophetic/contemplative teachings, and his exegetical practices, as well as Daniel Reiser's new critical edition of his *Sermons from the Years of Rage*. R. Shapira's popularity among the general public has also grown apace: he has been invoked in debates over post-Holocaust theology (see Magid, Reiser, and Abramson this volume) and emerged as a hero of Neo-Hasidism (Idel, this volume). Yet despite this upwelling of truly admirable work of all kinds, I confess to a continuing sense of unease with some of the ways in which R. Shapira and his legacy have been represented. Sometimes, the author of the Warsaw Ghetto sermons seems to serve as little more than a place holder for contemporary writers' commitment to their own paradigmatic narratives of meaning in suffering and unbroken faith—or of faith's inevitable demise. This is less than R. Shapira deserves.

In my previous work, I invoked the theme of ritual efficacy—the "complex, differentially constructed, even contested" ways in which ritual can be said to convey pragmatic effects such as healing, cosmic renewal, or distinctive forms of moral experience—as an alternative to the intellectualizing fascination with "Hasidic doctrine" and cultural "meaning-making" in Jewish studies and Geertzian anthropology, respectively.[2] Focusing on the contingencies of ritual efficacy (particularly those described or conveyed through Hasidic textual practice) has allowed me to trace literary and thematic connections among a variety of different dimensions of R. Shapira's wartime and prewar writings. These include his pursuit of prophetic subjectivity and his later desperate attempts to avoid emotional collapse in the Warsaw Ghetto by bracketing the force of that subjectivity, his desire to channel divine salvation to his people, and the devastating moral cost he clearly associated with his own survival in the face of so much suffering.[3] None of these pressing and sometimes paradoxical dilemmas map neatly onto the projects pursued by scholars far removed from the events R. Shapira suffered.

The question that so vexed early scholars such as Piekarz and Polen, who debated whether R. Shapira's wartime writings followed *any* discernible pattern of thematic development, looks quite different when viewed from the perspective of ritual efficacy. The unfolding of the text, on my reading, serves not just to convey a set of doctrines but also to convey vitality for healing and defense of human subjectivity or to mediate intimacy with unspeakable divine grief.[4] I do not mean to suggest, with Pierkarz, that the Holocaust-era sermons contain little more than "ideas and fragments of ideas" or "paraphrases of Hasidic writers from the generation between the wars" haphazardly set down in sermons lacking any underlying coherence.[5] Rather, I mean to insist that we seek evidence of that coherence in R. Shapira's own terms, in what seems to be at stake for him in the writings he shared, and in his own frequent acknowledgment that ritual and moral failure were always real—and all-too-frequently realized—possibilities.[6]

I am glad that my previous work has helped to stimulate interest in the undeniable relationship between R. Shapira's Holocaust-era sermons and his impressive prewar corpus of sermons and contemplative manuals.[7] Indeed, the thematic connections between his early and later writings have yet to be fully plumbed (see Diamond, Wiskind, this volume). Yet I also have come to feel that my earlier emphasis on the sheer immediacy of suffering depicted in these Holocaust-era sermons ought to be qualified by greater attention to the self-conscious literary strategies that R. Shapira employed in depicting the catastrophe he witnessed. We now know, thanks to Daniel Reiser's critical edition, that R. Shapira continually edited and made stylistic changes to his wartime writings before finally consigning them to the secret Ringelblum archives some time after the completion of his final sermon of mid-July, 1942.[8] His searing and unprecedented evocation of suffering and moral injury in the Warsaw Ghetto was built in part on literary strategies he developed long before the war in pursuit of new imaginational techniques and prophetic revitalization.[9] If what I contend is true, then ritual efficacy and literary efficacy, activity in the religo-moral and aesthetic spheres, respectively, were so intertwined in R. Shapira's phenomenology of suffering that they demand a fully integrated sort of analysis.[10] I will argue that his experimentation with new literary and contemplative techniques, his phenomenological turn, and his interest in reaching new audiences for Hasidism amount to a distinctive kind of "Hasidic modernism" through which all of his efforts should be understood. This is a project that must attend, among other things, to the emergent and often ritually mediated relationship between words and bodies in R. Shapira's literary production: the capacity of bodies to both bear and transcend discursive meaning; the capacity of words to both bear and be broken by infinite longing and pain.

Hasidic Modernism and the Phenomenological Turn

R. Shapira focused more intensely and insistently than other Hasidic writers on the description of everyday religious experience and the experience of suffering. Moshe Idel (this volume) argues perceptively that although R. Shapira had much closer genealogical connections to the so-called "magical" school of early Polish Hasidism—a Hasidism focused heavily on wonder-working and the power of the tsaddik—his own prewar teaching seems far more attentive to the spiritual training and contemplative discipline required of ordinary and aspiring Hasidim.[11] For Idel, this puts R. Shapira into the typologically "spiritual" school that he associates with figures such as the Maggid of Mezritsh, R. Nachman of Bratslav, R. Schneur Zalman of Liady, or even R. Menachem Mendl of Kotsk and R. Mordecai Leiner of Izhbits.[12] Even if Idel's thesis warrants some qualification (the tsaddik is not nearly as marginal to R. Shapira's prewar sermons as Idel implies), he is right that this feature of his writing contributes to R. Shapira's later popularity in Neo-Hasidic circles that emphasize spirituality and contemplative technique over the magical power of tsaddikim. Be that as it may, my argument is that R. Shapira's career exemplified a broader "Hasidic modernism" that was socially, genealogically, and in some ways ideologically continuous with the great prewar Hasidic communities of eastern Europe.[13]

While scholarship has begun to explore the contours of Neo-Hasidism among Jews influenced by figures like Zeitlin, Buber, and Heschel, who either "rediscovered" or repackaged Hasidism for a Western audience, it is important to remember that some forms of Hasidism were themselves evolving toward new audiences and changing circumstances on their own terms.[14] My understanding of Hasidic modernism is derived in part from parallels with studies of "Buddhist modernism," which developed as Buddhist traditions migrated from Asia to the West or confronted Western scientific, religious, and colonial claims in Asia.[15] Exploring new forms of congruence between Hasidism and contemporary science or medicine (especially professional psychology), experimenting with new literary and educational techniques for a diverse audience, and emphasizing the validity of individual subjectivity and contemplative technique while downplaying "magic" are all elements of Hasidic modernism that have close parallels in the Buddhist modernism context. Idel (this volume) notes provocatively that the development of modern Neo-Hasidism might have been influenced directly by modernizing forms of Buddhism and Hinduism to which European Jews were exposed during the early twentieth century. We should not, however, overlook the possibility of convergent adaptation to similar modernizing conditions.[16] The analytic frame of Hasidic modernism is broad enough to encompass both Neo-Hasidism as Idel defines it and other diverse, modernizing facets of traditional Hasidic communities.

Daniel Reiser, for example, has argued that R. Shapira was the first Hasidic leader to develop extended, almost "cinematic" programs for lengthy contemplative visualization—a suggestive development that depended in part on psychological sensibilities informed by the rise of hypnosis, mesmerism, and the widespread concept of "creative imagination" as well as the growing popularity of cinematic entertainment.[17] Though clearly drawing, as Idel has shown, on medieval "ecstatic" kabbalah and earlier Hasidic sources, R. Shapira also contributed to a broad interest in the renewal of prophecy among twentieth-century Jews.[18] All of his prewar tracts are devoted to this "prophetic" project, which he identifies with classical Hasidism but to which he attends with unprecedented detail, pedagogic systematicity, and concern for literary accessibility.[19] His shift in emphasis from the mystical powers of the tsaddikim to the religious experience of students and everyday Hasidim also resonates with Marcin Wodziński's suggestion (this volume) that R. Shapira catered specifically to a new community of displaced, urbanized, and "à la carte Hasidim" who did not offer their allegiance to any single rebbe in Poland between the wars.[20]

Support for this view can be gleaned from R. Shapira's famous introduction to his prewar *Hovat ha-talmidim* (the only work published during his lifetime), which was explicitly directed to a broad and, in many cases, secularizing public.[21] But there is also more direct evidence. After encouraging students to undertake individualized spiritual training in one prewar sermon, R. Shapira acknowledges that some students may find the well-trodden paths of earlier generations easier to follow but denies that they must pick any one tsaddik to emulate:

> If it is difficult for you to make [spiritual] progress, then follow the trail that has already been blazed. Take into your thoughts the path of a particular tsaddik, such as R. Elimelekh [of Lizhensk]. . . . Not just to have knowledge of this path but to contemplate it. Even though I have no apprehension of the tsaddik's greatness and sanctity, nevertheless, whatever I have apprehended from his book or the stories I have heard about him, I should visualize this path and sanctity in my mind. . . . Nor should this necessarily be limited to just one tsaddik! Rather, you might visualize, according to your apprehension, this path of R. Elimelekh and that path of the Maggid of Kozhnits, in order to see the whole chariot and higher sanctity even in this world and to serve God with joy and enthusiasm from what you have seen before you.[22]

This passage clearly envisions readers who would know the great Hasidic masters primarily through their books and stories rather than presuming any close attachment to a particular Hasidic court. I believe that this was also the context in which R. Shapira worked to innovate new literary and pedagogic styles that would appeal to this growing audience, provide them with tools for spiritual self-edification, and establish his own distinctive voice in the crowded field of Polish Hasidism.[23]

From his illustrious forbears, R. Shapira inherited a broadly panentheistic tendency and an emphasis on *avodah be-gashmiyut* (divine service in and through corporeality). He was not the first Hasidic writer to describe the "nerves" as bodily conduits of divine vitality (a similar formulation is also found in the *ma'amorim* of R. Dov Ber Schneuri [1773–1827] of Chabad).[24] He does, however, seem to have been the first to articulate a coherent theory of prophetic experience grounded in a contemporary medical idiom of nervous disorder.[25] Thus, the supposed susceptibility of Jews to neurasthenic complaints, which was part of a familiar anti-Semitic trope, becomes in R. Shapira's hands a sign of special Jewish receptivity to the prophetic impulse, which courses through Jewish religious experience but can lead to nervous illness when it is not properly developed.[26]

This is not the place to review what I have described at length elsewhere, but I recall it here in order to emphasize that this psycho-physiological theory of prophecy encapsulates key elements of R. Shapira's phenomenological turn, as well as its embeddedness in concerns about ritual and therapeutic efficacy. It locates both prophecy and the pathological failure of prophecy in a bodily network associated by the psychology of his day with emotional, "nervous" experience and its potential for excess, all described in a contemporary medical idiom.[27] Although he never returns explicitly to this nervous-energy theory in his Holocaust-era sermons, it can be understood as a backdrop to themes of ritual efficacy, emotional overload, and loss of the human that are central to those later writings. I will return to this observation in the context of the debate over R. Shapira's disputed "crisis of faith" toward the end of his wartime sermons (see Abramson and Magid, this volume), because it may suggest an alternative to the intellectualist or theological reading that focuses on problems of belief rather than more pragmatic concerns such as loss of vitality and nervous collapse.

R. Shapira's appeal to lived experience and embodied subjectivity is thorough and unwavering (see Maayan, this volume) and even conditions his account of Hasidic metaphysics. There is no valid academic or merely cognitive knowledge of Kabbalah's complex cosmologies, he writes, because these cosmologies represent guides to the attainment of distinctive subjective states rather than esoteric knowledge to be mastered.[28] "You believe, and yet do not believe," he writes to his close disciples, "that it will be possible for you to ascend to a state in which you will see spirituality and sanctity in the whole world; not just that you will understand this with your intellect but that you will truly *see* sanctity, souls, and [divine] names." A person who studies Kabbalah with this goal in mind may well come to know the conditions and permutations of the spiritual potencies that underlie phenomenal reality, he adds, but this only applies to a kabbalist who is *also* a Hasid. "A person who is not a Hasid, a *dried up* person who comes to study Kabbalah with dried out senses [*hushim*], will perceive nothing but confusion and contradictions within himself," unable to escape the false dualism of natural attitudes that perceive only physical sustenance (rather than divine vitality) in a loaf of bread.[29] Study of Hasidism and Kabbalah implies a whole panoply of personal disciplines focused heavily on the cultivation of new affective possibilities. Even studies of law and Talmud, as Ariel Evan Mayse has effectively shown in this volume, are pressed into the service of this revitalizing project.

R. Shapira sees himself as standing squarely within the Hasidic tradition, even when he subtly expands upon it. "From my flesh, I will see God" (*mi-besari ehezeh eloha*) is a standard motif of Hasidic sermons, often conveying that the best way to conceive divinity is by analogy to embodied human experience. Scholem observed that this analogizing goes both ways. "With every one of the endless stages of the theosophical world corresponding to a given state of the soul," Scholem writes, "Kabbalism becomes an instrument of psychological analysis and self-knowledge . . . the precision of which is not infrequently rather astounding."[30] R. Shapira, too, insists on "the correspondence between the various levels of the soul as it emanates from the lofty divine realm down into the body and the stages of contraction represented by the various worlds."[31] Yet rather than insisting on a uniform cosmology that must choose between or harmonize the different approaches of classical masters such as R. Cordovero, R. Luria, or the Baal Shem Tov, R. Shapira nods to the historicizing sensibilities of modern readers by frankly acknowledging the apparent incompatibility of different teachings. He argues that each sage's perception of the heavenly order was conditioned by the distinctive structure of his own personality and is therefore independently *valid as such*. There is precedent for interpretive pluralism in kabbalistic literature—R. Hayyim Vital is said to have encouraged his students to develop different interpretations of his work—but here it is surprisingly central and explicit even in teachings for young children.[32] The grounding of this pluralism in an explicit theory of unique, individual subjectivity is also worthy of note.

Earlier in the same work, R. Shapira emphasizes to his young students that their own apperception of the upper worlds of Kabbalah is limited to "your own portion of these worlds and of your own *nefesh, ruah, neshamah, haya, and yehidah* [attributes of the human soul]."[33] There is a sense in which a person can only know *their own* Torah, corresponding to their own distinctive psychospiritual attributes and to their current level of self-understanding. On a more prosaic level, R. Shapira's well-known introduction to his prewar educational tract *Hovat ha-talmidim* emphasizes the desperate need of contemporary Jewish educators to perceive, and tailor their educational efforts to, the unique needs and capacities of each individual child.[34]

Young children who would once have happily followed in their parents' footsteps now see themselves prematurely as adults, he writes, and need to be approached with this new individualism in mind. The rhetorical effect is to justify his own educational innovations by calling attention to the crisis of changing times (see Wodziński, this volume), but it also constitutes an unusually self-conscious pedagogical bridge between ancestral and modernizing forms of Hasidism. The cultivation of an individual's ramified subjective distinctiveness emerges as one of the central emphases of ritual or devotional labor (*avodah*) in R. Shapira's corpus.[35]

Everywhere, R. Shapira is energized by the need to spiritualize distinctively modern dilemmas of individual subjectivity. In one 1929 sermon, he suggests that the experience of diffuse anxiety with no discernible cause can be understood as a reminder that a person needs to reorient their lives or return to God (*teshuvah*).[36] The solution is characteristically pietistic, but R. Shapira is well aware that there is no more distinctively modern problem than the profusion of rootless and inexplicable anxiety described in literature, philosophy, and medicine of the time.[37]

Perhaps even more telling is R. Shapira's comment in his spiritual handbook *Tsav ve-zeruz* that students who "groan to themselves, 'Where is my free will?'" ought to respond by developing their individual thoughts and innovations (*hiddushim*) in Torah study.[38] This is not just a response to the student's struggle with religious apathy and worldly desire, which threaten to eclipse freedom, but is also an act of self-conscious resistance to the deterministic theories of the age.[39] He speaks of the need to "distinguish oneself [as an individual] from the rest of the [human] species" and from "the laws and tendencies that encompass the species, without individuality or [freely] choosing personalities."[40] In order to bear free will, a person must first strengthen their subjective sense of uniqueness to become a choosing subject.

This goes well beyond the traditional language of Torah study as an antidote to illicit desire. Just as any alert reader can immediately distinguish between the distinctive style and ethico-spiritual stance of a text by Maimonides and one by Nahmanides, for example, so R. Shapira insists that the antidote to the deterministic fallacy is to sharpen one's own sense of individuality and literary style. Each student is "called upon to reveal their own distinctive spiritual form and image" through innovative scholarship. "This is *his* [individual] path in Torah, and this is *his* [individual] path in devotion."[41]

This is a key passage for me because it shows how an ostensibly scholarly/textual practice focused on intellectual or even literary/aesthetic goals (the development of a distinctive literary voice and persona) may be deployed to further the habitudes of moral subjectivity. R. Shapira responds to the crisis in free will not by arguing for the reality of free will on discursive intellectual grounds, but by encouraging the revitalization of each student's unique personality, so that the problem is itself raised to an entirely different experiential register. Freedom is not an intellectual but an existential concern, which can only be addressed by shifting the existential ground on which the sufferer stands. The recommended way for an aspiring scholar to accomplish this is through innovative scholarship (*hiddushim*) and writing.

Bodies, Letters, and Texts

Text, experience, and divine vitality are clearly linked in R. Shapira's exposition of a classical Hasidic teaching attributed to the Baal Shem Tov, which holds that all of creation is at every moment continuously enlivened by the vitality (or "light") contained within the letters of divine speech that continuously bring them into being.[42] "Man does not live by bread alone but by all that goes forth from the mouth of the Lord" (Deut 8:3) is explained to mean that corporeal bread can only sustain life because of the divine vitality contained by the divine (Hebrew) letters through which it is constituted.[43] This isn't yet about the lexical or literary meaning of texts but about something far more atomistic and therefore boundless— the sheer facticity of the letters (not yet words) of Torah that are read or pronounced.

This is the theme of a powerful sermon from January 1930.[44] R. Shapira notes that the appellation *Hasid* applies to a person who conducts himself *lifnim mishurat ha-din* (one who goes beyond the requirements of Jewish law) not simply because he wants to be strict in his performance of the commandments but because his inner life is connected to the *letters* of the Torah he studies (see Wiskind, this volume). "For it is known from the Holy ARI that the letters are rooted in a very high place that cannot be contracted to human intellect."[45] The letters are essentially unbounded in a way that words and sentences—the units of semantic meaning—cannot be, and this is the place beyond reason (or prior to reason) where Hasidism locates the origin of subjectivity. It is significant that R. Shapira's version of this teaching focuses here on the consciousness of the Hasid rather than that of the tsaddik. Characteristically, he also uses this as an opportunity to discuss the pedagogic implications of this idea. Perhaps, he suggests, the infinitude of the letters can help to explain the fact that many traditional Jews "begin [in teaching their children to read] with the study of letters rather than whole words as they now seek to do in the 'improved' [i.e., more modern] schools."[46] Even the simplest of traditional Jewish learning practices—here, the distinctive manner in which children are taught to read by focusing on the sounds made by one Hebrew letter and vowel combination at a time rather than jumping to the larger semantic unit—serves to promote the distinctive intensity of Hasidic devotion. The manner of learning how to read, the cultivated awareness of divine infinitude, and the characteristically strict Hasidic attitude toward Jewish ritual observance are all mutually constitutive and interdependent facets of efficacious practice.

This is not limited to children. With characteristic attention to bodily and perceptual experience, R. Shapira describes how the Hasid, fundamentally unbounded by the limited lexical meaning of the text, also "gazes upon the world in an unbounded way . . . as the Baal Shem teaches that 'when you gaze upon the world you gaze upon [God] and [God] gazes back at you.' "[47] When such a person comes to Torah, says R. Shapira, "he [or she] is not satisfied with the simple contextual meaning [*peshat*] of the Torah or of the Kabbalah but is forced to see in everything an unbounded vision" accompanied by equally limitless longing for God. With due respect to the importance of literary reading of Hasidic sermons, it is unclear to me how any poetics grounded solely in the lexical meaning of texts and committed to the ordinary, commonsense distinction between words and things (or language and corporeality) might accommodate this teaching.

The Hasid whose mind and will are fixed on this *lifnim mishurat ha-din* reality attains the power to exercise influence upon the social and physical environment by serving as a channel for the vital infinitude of the letters that breaks through language. While Hasidic literature sometimes portrays the Hasid as the more or less passive *recipient* of the tsaddik's influence, here it is the attainment of the everyday Hasid that has power to influence his or her own environment.[48] The secondary revelation accessible to people in the Hasid's sphere of influence may not always rise to the level of consciousness, but it can be perceived diffusely, "throughout their body."[49] This is intriguing. One might speculate that there is a kind of resonance for R. Shapira between the individual letter of Torah and the individual body because of the way that bodies and letters each stand apart in a kind of atomistic separateness from other people or letters on a page. Indeed, he reminds us later in this sermon that Jewish law mandates the calligraphic separation of every letter in a Torah scroll and even mandates a border of empty parchment around the text as a whole, because the light that fills the empty space transcends even what the letters themselves can hope to convey.[50] Like individual letters on a page, the body is a repository of holiness transcending language.[51] It is only in the community of Hasidim, teachers and students together, that the diffuse bodily knowledge of Torah can be made manifest. "Someone who has a portion of that Hasid—which is to say that he became a Hasid *through* him—he alone will be able to understand, while another person who may be a greater scholar will think he is speaking of things that go against reason or are simple [i.e., unsophisticated] things."[52] The force of letters that transcend reason may not be conveyed linguistically, but through sheer personal presence, where there is a relation of mentorship or teaching between two fellow Hasidim.

Bodies and letters participate in one another's phenomenological horizon. Gazing upon the face of a tsaddik, R. Shapira writes in a 1925 sermon, conveys its own form of transrational blessing (*segulah*), "because you are gazing now at his soul (*nafsho*) and the combinations of letters of his soul that God made to be externally revealed."[53] That is why gazing upon the face of the tsaddik constitutes a form of devotion. "They [the letter combinations] pass over [through the act of gazing] to our soul and work upon the letters of *our* soul to make a good combination or, God forbid, the reverse."[54] "Eyes of flesh see only flesh," R. Shapira writes, "but the eyes are the path that God has made for the *soul* to perceive the letter combinations of another person's soul," and this is a perceptual skill that can be enhanced through training.[55] The blessing conveyed by the image of the tsaddik, at any rate, derives from the combinations of letters through which the world and its contents have been created and sustained. Thus, likewise, "it is forbidden [and deleterious] to gaze upon the face of a wicked person."[56]

I would like to suggest that R. Shapira never completely resolved the tension between this sort of nonlexical, letter-based spirituality and the signal importance he accorded to holistic literary composition as an expression of individual subjectivity. This is the recurring thread of an extended 1929 sermon in which he emphasizes that "every desire of the heart, understanding, and idea related to sanctity that enters the heart and mind of an Israelite [not necessarily a tsaddik!] is a form of prophecy and revelation from heaven" that must be developed in writing:

> He must reveal his spiritual physiognomy [*shi'ur komah*] limb by limb, one more idea related to sanctity, one more path in divine service, one more word of Torah, one more [good] intention. Each one of these becomes a limb, and from all of them, his *shi'ur komah* is revealed . . . so that through him God reveals his prophecy of holiness, which is above any physical garment whatsoever. . . . Therefore, such a person must speak and write at least a small portion of his ideas . . . [57]

Just as a person has a complex physical body made up of parts that must each be sanctified, so too do they have a spiritual body (*shi'ur komah*) made up of the unique insight and spiritual perceptions they have attained. Particularly in our fallen generation, R. Shapira writes, an author must work to invest the text with his own soul (*nishmato*) by renewing or innovating paths of divine service through written composition.[58] It is the investment of the text with the author's vitality as much as the content that matters.

In this register of literary practice, readers too are encouraged to think comprehensively. The student of an isolated text or sermon may encounter the spiritual "limbs" of its author but is likely to be left with doubt and misunderstanding. Contemplation of an entire book or corpus of writings, by contrast, offers privileged access to their author's *shi'ur komah* (spiritual physiognomy), giving readers the ability to perceive "thoughts and paths of understanding" that transcend any semantic content that the texts themselves are able to convey:

> It thus transpires that the revelation of prophecy (*hitgalut nevi'ut*) is the reading of a book! The book reveals not just atomistic elements [*devarim bodedim*] but also the essence of the possessor of a [particular] *shi'ur komah* through which the prophetic revelation occurs; not a revelation of the future . . . but a revelation of guidance and intimacy and sanctification as an Israelite.

Tellingly, R. Shapira eschews the more traditional word *kri'ah*, which can also refer to chanting or reading aloud (an important focus of letter mysticism) in favor of *histaklut ba-sefer* (looking at a book), which seems to refer to the more modern practice of silent reading. This is not a reference to a specialized visualization technique, in other words, but a potential consequence of ordinary, attentive reading. "Everyone knows and perceives," he writes, "that sometimes when he reads a great deal, a person will suddenly be moved by something and taken aback, and it will burrow into his heart without rest for many years until it has the capacity to transform him into another man and to sanctify him and raise him up." A person may have read many books on similar topics, yet somehow this text, in which the author's essence and individual personality (*ishiyut*) have been revealed, moves him in a correspondingly distinct and individual way.[59] It is inconceivable that R. Shapira did not have the composition and study of his own books and sermons in mind.[60]

This fits nicely with the central theme of all of R. Shapira's prewar educational tracts: that the purpose of Hasidic education is to "reveal the soul" of the student by drawing it out from its corporeal sheath.[61] I am tempted to say that the infinite light of the letters must be channeled or contracted through textual and pedagogic practice into the necessarily more finite but also richer, more densely ramified, and personalistic world of literature, innovation, and unique individual cognitive-emotional apperception of Torah. In this intersubjective frame, the fundamental work of self-revelation by the writer serves to evoke a student's own distinctive prophetic signature in a way that the undifferentiated infinitude of the Hebrew letters alone could not. The tension between the expansiveness of books and the atomism of individual letters expresses an even more fundamental tension in the phenomenology of *tsimtsum* (divine contraction) that both engenders and transcends corporeal language.

A profound ethnographic study of ritual healing among Hasidim in London published some years ago by Roland Littlewood and Simon Dein showed how this interdependence of words, letters, and bodies contributes to everyday forms of ritual efficacy and healing among some contemporary Hasidim.[62] Another way of saying this, which would be perfectly compatible with R. Shapira's teaching, is that the manipulation and organizing powers of sacred language (for example, *tsiruf ha-otiyot*, or letter recombination) can convey power and vitality directly into the phenomenal world. My contribution here, however, is to emphasize both the importance of literary development in its own right and the fact that even these semantic, meaning-producing capacities of language are implicated by R. Shapira in a very broad range of efficacies that include (but also transcend) meaning making.[63] Learning to write in a way that would appeal to students and provoke their strong emotional and aesthetic response was not just a utilitarian necessity for a writer seeking new audiences; it was also part of the ritual-cum-mystical praxis of "revealing souls" and imbuing them with an irreducible prophetic vitality.

Words Fail, Bodies Destroyed

Commenting on the Talmudic articulation of *yissurim shel ahavah* (afflictions of love) in his *Shabbat Teshuvah* sermon for 5690 (1929), R. Shapira cites a passage in which God is said to observe the commandments of the Torah out of love for his people just as his people observe the commandments out of their love for God (see Smokler, this volume). Such reciprocity means that when a Jew sins or undergoes some other kind of moral failure down below, it has the capacity to inflict pain, as it were, upon God on high. A person must pray not just that their love of God finds proper expression in word, deed, and thought but also that they develop the sensitivity to personally identify with at least some spark of the divine pain they may have caused. This feeling, or *hargashah*, can lead them to a "fear of sin" rooted not in the terror of punishment but in the desire to protect one's beloved from affliction.[64] The ability to feel God's pain cannot, however, be taken for granted. "When can an Israelite perceive the supernal anguish? Only when his own mind and heart are untroubled by bodily affliction, for otherwise he cannot know whether the pain he feels is actually from his own affliction or from the pain on high."[65]

Recognition that too much suffering (or the wrong kind of suffering) can forestall prophetic experience or ruin religious subjectivity is thus already well attested in R. Shapira's prewar writings, though it takes on a far more central and terrifying role in his later Ghetto sermons. In his prewar educational tract *Hakhsharat ha-avreikhim*, he laments "the enemies who make our lives exceedingly bitter from without" as well as "the coldness toward Torah and divine service within."[66] In language presaging some of his bleakest comments from the "years of rage," he responds to a rash of suicides brought on by economic collapse between 1926 and 1928, saying, "Do not weep only for the one who kills himself, but weep also for the walking dead, whose very self and essence have grown cold!"[67] This is a stark portrayal of suffering, but it is also a pathological counterimage of the vivified prophetic self at the heart of R. Shapira's literary-educational program.

Consider the early wartime sermon from *parashat toledot* 5700 (1939), in which R. Shapira describes the collapse of basic human subjectivity that results from the torture and humiliation to which Jews in the Ghetto are subject, including the brutal public shaving of men's beards. It is worth citing part of that sermon here at length:

> It is possible . . . that the verse "those who are lost in the land of Assyria and those who are cast off in the land Egypt shall return" [Isa 27:13] means that there is a quality of being lost and a quality of being cast off. "Cast off" means just cast off from one's place to a distant locale, but [such a person] is still visible and recognizable. Not so a "lost person," who is missing, not seen or recognized. For when troubles multiply now to such an extent that the beards of Jews are simply shaved off, by means of which they become unrecognizable in their exteriority, so too the increase in persecution and afflictions is difficult to bear and impossible to estimate, so that their interiority [also] becomes unrecognizable. He is lost to himself [*er farlirt zich*] and does not recognize himself, how he used to feel [*margish*] a year ago on the Sabbath or even on a weekday before and during prayer and so forth. Now he is trampled and smashed till he cannot perceive [*margish*] whether he is an Israelite, whether he is a human being or an animal that has no self to feel[68]—this is what it means to be lost, [as in] "the lost shall return."

While clearly specific to the context of German occupation, this depiction invokes an imagery of inner emptiness—the walking death—that R. Shapira had already developed during the interbellum financial crisis. Here, the sermon continues with a desperate hope that the situation might be reversed through divine salvation, since clearly the Jews cannot save themselves:

> The Talmud [Kiddushin 2b] . . . says that the owner of a lost object must search for it, claim it, and bring it back to himself. The Holy One blessed be he is the owner of that which we

have lost, and therefore, Isaac blessed Jacob our father [with the words] "God will give you":[69] not just when the Israelite is visible and recognized but also with respect to the "lost," he will "return and give again." The owner of the lost object will return to find us and to give us all goodness, to return us to him and to redeem us in body and soul with great kindness and good salvations.[70]

Persons who are lost to themselves cannot effectively perform divine service until God, as it were, first performs the *mitsvah* of returning lost objects (*hashevat avedah*) by returning them to some semblance of their former selves. The observance of *mitsvot* by God in reciprocity with Israel, the feared loss of human subjectivity, and the inability to engage in divine service while suffering are central themes in this wartime sermon that were already emphasized in teachings that R. Shapira wrote at least a decade before. This sermon was not as heavily edited as some in Reiser's critical text, but marginal comments, word deletions, and later insertions for the sake of clarity all betray R. Shapira's sustained attention to the expressive form of his sermons, which he explicitly intended for publication.

I am not retreating from my previous claim that passages like these are remarkable for their unprecedentedly frank and honest depiction of human collapse, possibly unrivaled in the phenomenology of faith and despair.[71] Nor am I denying, as I have written elsewhere, a degree of rupture between his prewar and Holocaust-era thinking. I do, however, want to emphasize that these later sermons cannot be treated merely as unmediated reflections of wartime and Ghetto experience. To the contrary, some of these sermons convey careful attention to chosen ritual, literary, and theological tropes that R. Shapira had been long developing as well as impressive thematic continuity with his prewar compositions on religious subjectivity. They paradoxically portray an author of profound descriptive power marshalling his own formidable talent to describe the collapse of religious experience and human self-awareness in himself and other Ghetto inhabitants. Though he tends to avoid the technical language associated in his earlier writings with visualization or visionary experience, it may not be too much to suggest that these extended meditations on suffering and collapse were also meant to evoke and modulate more limited kinds of prophetic agitation or reverie to master despair. Between debilitating grief and utter loss of human feeling lay the text and the vulnerable skein of intersubjective relations it sought to engender and preserve.

Toward a Post-Holocaust Theology?

We are now in a position to confront the "problem of faith" raised by Abramson, Magid, and others in R. Shapira's context. R. Shapira raises this theme quite explicitly in a prewar sermon from 1936:

> All Israel believe [ma'aminim] in the Holy One blessed be he, and through their faith they draw down his holiness, may he be blessed. It is known from sacred books [i.e., Hasidic literature] that "faith" [emunah] signifies "drawing down" [hamshakhah]. [God] believes in the will and service and sanctity of Israel, and since he believes in us, he draws us upward and joins us to his holiness.[72]

What is clear even from this brief passage is that "faith" is not, in this context, primarily a matter of accepting or "believing in" a set of propositional truths. This is not at all to say that R. Shapira would deny such propositional truths if they were put to him but rather to insist that this is not what he is trying to convey. He is concerned with *hamshakhah*, which implies the drawing of one subject toward another, expressed either as the drawing down of divine vitality or the drawing upward of human subjectivity toward God. It is a dynamic better described in ritual-theurgic than in conventional theological language.

As the sermon continues, R. Shapira focuses on how a person may create the reciprocal conditions under which the vital flow of *emunah* may be strengthened: "When we serve [God] actively and with great desire [teshukah], then he believes in us, and his faith, may he be blessed, works to strengthen our faith in him and the other way around."[73] It is therefore "impossible for a person to achieve strong faith unless he actively performs his devotional service [avodah] with strength and with longing." Preparing for this influx requires self-discipline to improve one's character and a willingness to give oneself wholly to the other. Success cannot be taken for granted. A person may find themselves inconstant in their devotion, or they may be unable to shift attention consistently beyond their own temporal need and desire. R. Shapira's account of faithfulness, or *emunah,* is thus very like his account of prophecy: the intersubjective space in which potentially infinite divine vitality meets determinate forms of human practice and lived experience.

In one early wartime sermon whose theme was ostensibly the sin of the biblical spies that Moses sent to reconnoiter the Promised Land,

R. Shapira describes *emunah* in a more traditional vein of trust in divine salvation, but even here, he deploys vitalistic rather than propositional language. A person ought to believe that God will save them even when there seems to be no rational way forward; indeed, to insist too strongly on being able to perceive the path of God's salvation may lead to a *pegam* (blemish), which will block any salvation that might otherwise have flowed.[74] In a 1940 sermon, he observes that "every blemish in the faith, God forbid, of some Israelites (as when Moses said, 'They [the slaves in Egypt] will not believe in me') is because of the extremity of the affliction that they are suffering from exile."[75] This does not contradict his later claim that the very purpose of Israel's exile in Egypt was to "arouse the longing of Israel, for it is natural that when a person is in spiritual and physical trouble it is easier to rouse their longing for God."[76] That is simply how it is with vital flow—it requires modulation. Too much suffering can block the channel through which faith flows reciprocally between God and humans, just as surely as too "dry" an affect, bereft of longing, can cause the well of faith to run dry. There is some evidence here for the "covenantal theology" Shaul Magid (this volume) thinks R. Shapira eventually abandoned as he was forced to witness the extermination of his people. But to portray this as a fundamentally propositional matter—"faith in the God of history"—strikes me as misconstruing the true nature of the terrible crisis R. Shapira faced.

Indeed, as the Holocaust-era sermons progress, I agree with Magid that faith becomes a more insistent and difficult theme. On Hanukkah 5702 (1941), R. Shapira writes that even though the Jewish people inherit their faith (i.e., their channel of vital flow) from the patriarchs, it may only be self-consciously activated through a willingness to act (as they did) in self-sacrifice. "The matter of self-sacrifice in faith," he writes, "is that even at a time of [God's] hiding, a person will trust in him that everything from him is for the good and that all is justice and that all of the afflictions are filled with God's love for Israel."[77] He acknowledges somewhat restrainedly that "to our distress, we see now, even among those who were always completely faithful, some few individuals whose faith has been injured and who ask, 'Why have You abandoned us?'" What is questioned is not God's existence but his redemptive efficacy: "For if it was in order to bring us closer to Torah and divine service that these afflictions have come, then to the contrary, all Torah and sanctity have been destroyed!"[78] Hard questions are perfectly legitimate "when asked in the language of prayer and supplication and pouring out one's heart before God" but become destructive when they harden into the merely cognitive demand for answers.[79]

A few weeks later, in early 1942, R. Shapira insists once again that faith (*emunah*) "is a spirit of sanctity [*ruah kedushah*] that is in a person and allows him to trust [in God], above his level of understanding or his intellect."[80] Yet faith can also be "weighed down" or compromised by an excess of elemental "earth" in an individual's constitution—a humoral theory of *emunah* according to which it can be broken down or interrupted. "Therefore, many afflictions, God forbid, that break a person and cause him to fall can also injure his faith."[81] This is more than the English word *belief*, with its strong cognitivist bias, can typically convey. R. Shapira's emphasis remains where it has always been, on the experience of the sufferer and the ritual-devotional attitudes required for conditions of unimpeded flow. Thus, my response to the debate between Shaul Magid and Henry Abramson as to whether or not R. Shapira suffered a crisis in faith (and to a much broader set of public contests over the disposition of R. Shapira's legacy) is that this question ought to be reframed (just like the question of free will described above) in ritual and phenomenological terms.

Magid argues that by the time his Ghetto sermons were consigned for burial, R. Shapira had already undergone a crisis that left his faith "broken" and that positioned him as a kind of "radical theologian" who might serve as a missing link with later post-Holocaust theologians. Magid is a subtle reader of Hasidic texts, and there is no need for me to rehearse his argument here except to say that it turns heavily on a single, late 1942 emendation to the Hanukkah sermon he had composed a year before. That emendation, which may be the last surviving writing in R. Shapira's own hand, disputes his earlier claim that the Jews of the Ghetto should view their suffering as being on a clear continuum with that of Jews in previous generations. By the end of 1942, he writes, no comparison is tenable. He does not, however, attempt to emend the rest of his sermon in light of this recognition.

For Magid, R. Shapira's change of heart about the commensurability of suffering is sufficient to indicate a near-total break with any recognizable form of traditional Jewish theodicy. Without adherence to the paradigm of sin, punishment, suffering, and redemption, Magid argues, the whole "Jewish God of history" becomes a sort of logical impossibility, which leads inexorably toward the conclusions of radical post-Holocaust theologians such as Richard Rubinstein or Irving (Yitz) Greenberg, who redefine the very idea of a covenant with God in the wake of the Holocaust. Pointing to assertions of faith throughout the sermons, by contrast, Abramson (this volume) insists simply that R. Shapira "remained steadfast in his faith that the developments [of history] were somehow beneficial in the larger plan of the almighty." Outside the academy, such contestations are often less polite. A writer for one popular Jewish magazine takes aim at Magid's "libelous claim" and accuses him of "besmirching" R. Shapira's "pristine legacy."[82] Magid, for his part, complains with some justice that writers who defend R. Shapira's "unsullied faith" rarely define just what they think this term might imply. My own attempt to clarify R. Shapira's use of the term *emunah* in his prewar and Ghetto writings is intended as a response to this challenge.

For clarity's sake, let me be clear that I do not subscribe to the academic conceit that sometimes resists almost any attempt to appropriate a text such as *Sermons from the Years of Rage* for the sake of a "useable past" that can speak to contemporary concerns. Indeed, I think traditional believers and radical post-Holocaust theologians might both find a great deal in these texts to refine, sensitize, and challenge their respective positions. They have certainly edified and challenged my own spiritual and intellectual adventure in ways I can scarcely fathom. Yet it seems to me that contemporary readers ought to be clear-eyed about the differences between the concerns and existential positions from which they approach these texts and those that animated their author. In one of the last Ghetto sermons from the spring of 1942, R. Shapira expounds upon the verse "Israel saw [the miracles] and believed in God and in his servant Moses" (Exod 14:31). He cites the *Zohar*, which asks why, if Israel already "saw" the wonders, the biblical text emphasizes that they also "believed?" Isn't seeing better than merely believing? To this, R. Shapira replies: "The faith in God of an Israelite is not just that he knows and believes but that he knows and *sees* with his soul, that the soul of the Israelite sees a little bit of the shining of his greatness and sanctity. . . . This is like the visions of the prophets, except that for them, these visions were literally revealed to their eyes, while for us it is an inner knowledge."[83] Here, in one of the last surviving Ghetto sermons, R. Shapira returns to some of the central themes of his whole previous career: the phenomenological turn, the fragile contingency of religious subjectivity, and the reading of classical Jewish terms such as *faith* in light of his vitalistic Hasidic cosmology. From my point of view, both Magid and his critics are committing a categorical error in reading these sermons as expressions of the question, "What does R. Shapira believe?" rather than ritual and literary expressions of his desperate ongoing attempt to resist a final collapse. This is by no means an attempt to rob the sermons of their potential theological or philosophical significance, though the register of ritual efficacy has hardly been touched upon by either field.[84]

Consider the following passage from the sermon just cited, with an eye toward ritual efficacy and religious subjectivity rather than doctrine:

> Besides the need to prepare oneself through divine service to increase love, fear, faith, and other forms of divine effluence, one also requires strengthening and joy, so as to increase the effluence. Therefore, in times of trouble, God forbid, they [love, fear, faith, etc.] are weak and failing, but this is not, God forbid, because [Israelites] lack faith, heaven forfend. They are all believers! Yet they cannot *feel* that faith or the certainty that is revealed by it.

Is this an expression of "pristine faith" or of a significant and undeniable crisis? Support could be found here for either reading, but neither accounts for the dynamic ritual and existential context in which faith, love, and fear of God each emerge as fragile expressions of divine influx that *has been blocked* through suffering too terrible to bear. The felt reality to which this sermon responds is absolutely one of crisis, justification before God of those who have already fallen, and desperate strategies to persevere.

The final sermon to mention *emunah* is from June 1942, just three sermons from the end of the collection. It is a long, meandering exposition that begins with the death of the biblical Miriam and makes a rare explicit reference to the horror of the deportation of children that R. Shapira had recently witnessed. I cannot do justice to the totality of that sermon here (see Polen, this volume), but one section bears comment in this context. "All Israel," he writes, "believe that 'there is none but him' (Deut 4:35), which means not just that there is no other divinity but that there is no reality other than [God] in the world at all and that the whole world and its fullness are revelations of the light of divinity."[85] Therefore, he continues, we must perceive everything in the world not as a thing unto itself but as an expression of divine light:

> Nor should the Jewish children be perceived [merely] as independent beings, as "our children," but as a new creation and renewal and revelation of divinity, as well as the eternity of

> Israel. Neither should the Torah that we teach the little school
> children, nor what anyone teaches his neighbor, nor any word
> of ethical teaching or guidance that is spoken be treated as a
> thing unto itself that we teach but rather as . . . a revelation of
> divinity, since it constitutes renewal and generation. . . . Every
> renewal or creation is a revelation of the divine, for there is
> nothing other than [God], alone.[86]

Here, near the very end, I do not perceive R. Shapira as trying to teach
the Hasidic "doctrine of acosmism," which he simply presupposes as a
backdrop for the work that must be done. The teaching itself is an act of
making divinity present, an attempt to keep the world precariously alive
for one more day even as he grieves its terrible, seemingly inevitable
collapse. How, he asks, does the world even persist, despite the cries of
the children calling from the transports, "Save us, save us!"? This is a
question to which he does not really offer an answer.

In exegetical terms, this sermon addresses one of the perennial questions of Jewish commentary: Why did Moses sin (Num 20) by striking the
rock rather than speaking to it when the people cried out for water—a
sin that the biblical text itself identifies with Moses's lapse of faith: "for
you have not believed in me (Deut 1:32)"? R. Shapira's provocative answer
is that the Israelites had been enduring a kind of drought since the time
of Miriam's death—her presence and longing for God had served as a
conduit of divine vitality that dried up when she was gone. Ultimately,
he suggests, Moses acted like a Hasidic tsaddik: he had to descend to the
level of his people (and bring down the divine influx) by committing an
act that, while not technically a sin, would be accounted as one for a man
of his stature. He did this so that the longing and penitence he would
subsequently experience—it is the experience of *teshuvah* (penitence) that
counts—could prime the wellsprings of faith again for others. This is where
the classical doctrine of the tsaddik whose "descent" into the world brings
life and blessing to his followers meets R. Shapira's phenomenological turn.[87]
The effluence that the tsaddik conveys is premised on blessing of a very
specific kind: the continued ability, despite overwhelming suffering, to feel.

I am in basic agreement with Ora Wiskind's claim that we ought to
attend not just to the extremities of Holocaust suffering in the wartime
sermons but to the hermeneutic strategies their author deploys in defense of
more quotidian goals such as "dimensions of self-awareness, introspection,
the need for inner psychic unity, an urgency of communication, a search

for divine presence in everyday life."[88] These are complex tasks, to which I would add the always uncertain efficacies of healing and vitality, the attempt to perceive the divinity that pulses even through suffering, and the literal attempt to sustain life against genocide. If Magid's and Abramson's concern with the "belief content" of R. Shapira's sermons places them on one side of a broad methodological divide in approaching these texts, then the attention that Wiskind and I give to the text as a field of fragile strategic interventions in human subjectivity places us on the other. It is probable that several of the other contributors to this volume can also be located somewhere along this continuum. There is no need for uniformity, and the Rebbe of Piaseczno would be the last to demand it. Words and pain, religious teaching and the collapse of language, the text as a vehicle of shared vitality and threatened loss of humanity, are the terrible knife's edge on which R. Shapira—for a time—stood.

Notes

This essay is dedicated in love and admiration to my son Noam, who is teaching me how to be a father every day.

1. Don Seeman, "Ritual Efficacy, Hasidic Mysticism, and 'Useless Suffering' in the Warsaw Ghetto," *Harvard Theological Review* 101 (2008): 465–505. See also Don Seeman, "Otherwise than Meaning: On the Generosity of Ritual," *Social Analysis* 48 (2004): 55–71. Although the current chapter stands alone, it can be read most profitably in light of these earlier works.

2. Arthur Kleinman, *Writing at the Margin: Discourse between Anthropology and Medicine* (Berkeley: University of California Press, 1995), 10. See Moshe Idel, "On the Theologization of Kabbalah in Modern Scholarship," in *Religious Apologetics—Philosophical Argumentation*, ed. Yossef Schwartz and Volkhard Krech (Tubingen: Mohr Siebeck, 2004), 123–74.

3. This is a central theme of Seeman, "Ritual Efficacy."

4. Ibid., 493–505.

5. Mendel Piekarz, *Hasidut Polin bein shtei ha-milhamot* (Jerusalem: Mossad Bialik, 1990), 378. Perhaps the first to dispute this claim was Nehemia Polen, *The Holy Fire: The Teachings of R. Kalonymus Kalman Shapira* (Northvale, NJ: Jason Aronson, 1994), xviii.

6. Seeman, "Ritual Efficacy," 504–505. The classic methodological work that informs all my thinking in this area is Arthur Kleinman and Joan Kleinman, "Suffering and Its Professional Transformation: Toward an Ethnography of Interpersonal Experience," *Culture, Medicine and Psychiatry* 15 (1991): 275–301.

7. Kleinman and Kleinman, 468–80.

8. R. Kalonymus Shapira, *Sermons from the Years of Rage* [in Hebrew], ed. Daniel Reiser, 2 vols. (Jerusalem: Herzog Academic College, 2017).

9. Daniel Reiser, *Imagery Techniques in Modern Jewish Mysticism*, trans. Eugene D. Matanky with Daniel Reiser (Berlin: De Gruyter, 2018).

10. See Don Seeman, "Apostasy, Grief, and Literary Practice in Chabad Hasidism," *Prooftexts* 29 (2009): 398–432; Don Seeman and Shaul Magid, "Mystical Poetics: The Jewish Mystical Text as Literature," *Prooftexts* 29 (2009): 317–23.

11. See Moshe Idel, *Hasidism between Ecstasy and Magic* (Albany: State University of New York Press, 1995).

12. For my own exposition of R. Leiner's quite different spiritual project and an earlier version of my focus on ritual efficacy in Hasidism, see Don Seeman, "Martyrdom, Emotion, and the Work of Ritual in R. Mordecai Joseph Leiner of Izbica's *Mei Ha-Shiloah*," *AJS Review* (27): 253–80.

13. The term *Hasidic modernism* was coined by Don Seeman and Michael Karlin, "Mindfulness and Hasidic Modernism: Towards a Contemplative Ethnography," *Society and Religion: Advances in Research* 10 (2019): 44–62. See also Michael Karlin, *To Create a Dwelling Place for God: Life Coaching and the Lubavitch-Chabad Hasidic Movement in Contemporary America* (PhD diss., Emory University, 2014); Don Seeman, "On Mystical Sociology and Turning Judaism Outward," in *Jewish Spirituality and Social Transformation: Hasidism and Society*, ed. Philip Wexler (New York: Herder and Herder, 2019), 17–36.

14. For a selection of essays on the theme of Neo-Hasidism, see Arthur Green and Ariel Evan Mayse, eds., *A New Hasidism: Roots* (Philadelphia: Jewish Publication Society of America, 2019) and idem, *A New Hasidism: Branches* (Philadelphia: Jewish Publication Society of America, 2019).

15. See especially D. L. McMahan, *The Making of Buddhist Modernism* (Oxford: Oxford University Press, 2008); idem., "Modernity and the Early Discourse of Scientific Buddhism," *Journal of the American Academy of Religion* 72 (2004): 897–933; D. S. Lopez, *Buddhism and Science: A Guide for the Perplexed* (Chicago: University of Chicago Press, 2010); Lawrence Kirmayer, "Mindfulness in Cultural Context," *Transcultural Psychiatry* 52 (2015): 447–69; Veronique Altglass, *From Yoga to Kabbalah: Religious Exoticism and the Logics of Bricolage* (Oxford: Oxford University Press, 2014).

16. See Seeman and Karlin, "Mindfulness and Hasidic Modernism."

17. Reiser, "Imagery Techniques," v, 10, 110, 195, 406. For an ethnographic consideration of the relationship between cinema and the religious imagination, see Birgit Meyer, *Sensational Movies: Video, Vision, and Christianity in Ghana* (Berkeley: University of California Press, 2015); Don Seeman, "Sensational Movies and the Anthropology of Religion: Towards a Comparative Moral Imaginary," *Religion* (2016): 1096–1115.

18. Eliezer Schweid, "Prophetic Mysticism in Twentieth Century Jewish Thought," *Modern Judaism* 14 (1994): 173–94; Seeman, "Ritual Efficacy," 474–76.

19. Seeman, "Ritual Efficacy," 468–80.

20. Marcin Wodziński coined the term "à la carte Hasidism" in his "War and Religion: Or, How the First World War Changed Hasidism," *The Jewish Quarterly Review* 106, no. 3 (2016): 283–312.

21. Author's introduction to R. Kalonymus Shapira, *Hovat ha-talmidim* (Jerusalem: Oraysa Publications, 2000), 1–28.

22. Kalonymus Shapira, *Derekh ha-melekh* (Jerusalem: Va'ad Hasidei Piaseczno, 1991), *shabbat teshuvah* 5690 (1929), 231. R. Shapira made similar arguments elsewhere. See Reiser, *Imagery Techniques*, 94n123.

23. A detailed comparison of R. Shapira's literary endeavors with those of his older contemporary R. Abraham Isaac Kook, who addressed secular Zionist pioneers, is the subject of a future essay. On Kook's literary trajectory, see Yehudah Mirsky, *Towards the Mystical Experience of Modernity: The Making of Rav Kook 1865–1904* (Boston: Academic Studies Press, 2021).

24. The Hebrew *atsabim* and the transliterated word *nerves* both appear in this context. See Don Seeman "Apostasy, Grief, and Literary Practice in Habad Hasidism," 410.

25. See Seeman, "Ritual Efficacy," 475–80; *Benei mahshavah tovah*, 14; *Hovat ha-talmidim*, 170; *Haksharat ha-avreikhim*, 10b–11a.

26. Seeman, "Ritual Efficacy," 475–80.

27. Ibid.

28. See, for example, R. Kalonymus Shapira, *Benei mahshavah tovah* (Jerusalem, 1989), 30–32; *Hovat ha-talmidim*, 171–72.

29. *Benei mahshavah tovah*, 31–32; emphasis added. See Steven Vaitkus, "The 'Naturality' of Alfred Schutz's Natural Attitude of the Life World," in *Explorations of the Life-World: Continuing Dialogues with Alfred Schutz*, ed. Martin Endress, George Psathas, and Hisashi Nashu (The Netherlands: Springer, 2005), 97–122.

30. Gershom Scholem, *Major Trends in Jewish Mysticism* (New York: Schoken, 1995), 341; See Seeman, "Ritual Efficacy," 470.

31. *Hovat ha-talmidim* ("Torah, Prayer, and Singing to God"), 98–99, 171.

32. Ibid., 217–18. Elliot Wolfson, "Divine Suffering and the Hermeneutics of Reading," in *Suffering Religion*, ed. Robert Gibbs and Elliot R. Wolfson (London: Routledge, 2002).

33. *Hovat ha-talmidim*, 172.

34. Ibid., 7–28 ("A Conversation with Teachers and Parents").

35. Abraham Joshua Heschel, *The Prophets*, 2 vols. (San Francisco: Harper and Row, 1962), 1:11; On Heschel's phenomenology of religious experience, see Edward K. Kaplan, "Abraham Joshua Heschel," in *Interpreters of Judaism in the Late Twentieth Century*, ed. Steven Katz (New York: B'nai B'rith, 1993), 131–50; Lawrence Perlman, *Abraham Joshua Heschel's Idea of Revelation* (Atlanta: Georgia State University Press, 1989); Arthur Green, "Abraham Joshua Heschel: Recasting

Hasidism for Moderns," *Modern Judaism* (2009): 62–79. See also my more detailed comparison of Heschel and Shapira in Seeman, "Ritual Efficacy," 475–77.

36. *Derekh ha-melekh, shabbat teshuvah* 5690 (1929), 229. See also *Derekh ha-melekh, parashat hayyei sarah* 5690 (1929), 14.

37. See Seeman, "Ritual Efficacy," 478–79.

38. *Tsav ve-zeruz*, 9, par. 10.

39. R. Abraham Isaac Kook also prioritizes the importance of human freedom in his early manuscript now published as *Le-nevukhei ha-dor* (Tel Aviv: Yediot Aharanot, 2014), 27–29. See Don Seeman, "Evolutionary Ethics: The Ta'amei Ha-Mitzvot of Rav Kook," *Hakira: Flatbush Journal of Jewish Law and Thought* 26 (2019): 13–55. In a letter dated 15 Tammuz 2724 (1964), R. Yitzhak Hutner argues that the fundamental problem of the current age is the denial of free will. Yitzhak Hunter, *Pahad Yitzhak: Iggerot u-ketavim* (New York: Gur Aryeh Institute, 1991), 70–71.

40. *Tsav ve-zeruz*, 9, par. 10.

41. Ibid.

42. See Moshe Idel, "Modes of Cleaving to the Letters in the Teaching of Israel Baal Shem Tov: A Sample Analysis," *Jewish History* 27 (2013): 299–317.

43. *Benei mahshavah tovah*, 31–32. See Moshe Idel, *Vocal Rites and Broken Theologies: Cleaving to Vocables in R. Israel Ba'al Shem Tov's Mysticism* (New York: Herder and Herder, 2019).

44. *Derekh ha-melekh, parashat vayyehi* 5690 (1930), 71–75.

45. Ibid., 72.

46. Ibid., 74.

47. Ibid., 73.

48. This should be compared with certain emphases in contemporary Chabad which are beyond the scope of this essay.

49. *Derekh ha-melekh*, 73.

50. For more on the history and implications of this idea, see Moshe Idel, "White Letters: From R. Levi Isaac of Berditchev's Views to Postmodern Hermeneutics," *Modern Judaism* 26 (2006): 162–92.

51. For some of the background to this theme in medieval Kabbalah, see Elliot R. Wolfson, "The Body in the Text: A Kabbalistic Theory of Embodiment," *Jewish Quarterly Review* 95 (2005): 479–500.

52. *Derekh ha-melekh*, 73.

53. *Derekh ha-melekh, motsa'ei yom ha-kippurim* 5686 (1925), 242.

54. Ibid. This may shed some light on the ritual efficacy of practices whose sociopolitical effects are well described by Maya Balakirsky Katz, *The Visual Culture of Chabad* (Cambridge: Cambridge University Press, 2010).

55. Ibid., 241.

56. Ibid., 242.

57. *Derekh ha-melekh, parashat shemot* 5689 (1929), 81.

58. Ibid., 83.

59. Ibid., 82.

60. Compare Don Seeman, "Publishing Godliness: The Lubavitcher Rebbe's Other Revolution," *Jewish Review of Books* (July 16, 2014). https://jewishreviewof-books.com/articles/1085/publishing-godliness-the-lubavitcher-rebbes-other-revolu-tion/; accessed February 03, 2020.

61. This is, for example, a central theme in the first chapters of *Hovat ha-talmidim*. See at length Daniel Reiser, "'To Rend the Entire Veil': Prophecy in the Teachings of R. Kalonymous Kalman Shapira of Piazecna and its Renewal in the Twentieth Century," *Modern Judaism* 34, no. 3 (2014): 334–52.

62. Roland Littlewood and Simon Dein, "The Effectiveness of Words: Religion and Healing among the Lubavitch of Stamford Hill," *Culture, Medicine and Psychiatry* 19 (1995): 339–83.

63. See Seeman, "Otherwise than Meaning."

64. *Derekh ha-melekh, shabbat teshuvah* 5690 (1929), 229.

65. Ibid.

66. *Hakhsharat ha-avreikhim*, 62b; Seeman, Ritual Efficacy," 489.

67. *Tsav ve-zeruz*, 16–17; see Seeman, "Ritual Efficacy," 489.

68. *Sermons from the Years of Rage*, 1:92. This is a good example of Reiser's contribution. The standard published edition of *Esh kodesh* (Jerusalem: Va'ad Hasidei Piaseczno, 1960), on which I based a previous translation of this passage, mistakenly transposed a single letter which changes the meaning of this sentence. Compare Seeman, "Ritual Efficacy," 481.

69. Gen 27:28. The reference is to the beginning of the sermon, not translated here, where R. Shapira cites the gloss of Rashi on this verse, to the effect that God will give to his people and then return and give again.

70. *Sermons from the Years of Rage*, 1:92.

71. Seeman, "Ritual Efficacy."

72. *Derekh ha-melekh, shabbat hazon* 5696 (1936), 159.

73. Ibid., 160.

74. *Sermons from the Years of Rage, parashat shelah* 5700 (1940), 145.

75. Ibid., *parashat vayyeshev* 5701 (1940), 175.

76. Ibid., *shabbat haggadol* 5701 (1941), 183.

77. *Sermons from the Years of Rage, hanukkah* 5702 (1941), 241.

78. Ibid., 241.

79. Ibid., 241.

80. Ibid., *parashat va'era* 5702 (1942), 252.

81. Ibid.

82. Elly Kleinman, "Critiquing a Critique," *Ami Magazine*, April 26, 2017, http://ellykleinman.com/critiquing-a-critic. See also Shaul Magid, "The Rebbe of the Warsaw Ghetto," *Tablet*, April 7, 2017, https://www.tabletmag.com/jewish-arts-and-culture/228300/the-rebbe-of-the-warsaw-ghetto; Henry Abramson, "Hasidim

and Academics Debate a Rebbe's Faith (and on Facebook of all places)," *The Lehrhaus*, March 4, 2019, https://www.thelehrhaus.com/scholarship/hasidim-and-academics-debate-a-rebbes-faith-during-the-holocauston-facebook-of-all-places.

83. *Sermons from the Years of Rage, parashat ha-hodesh* 5702 (1942), 288.

84. See Don Seeman, "Divinity Inhabits the Social: Ethnography in a Phenomenological Key," in *Theologically Engaged Anthropology*, ed. Derrick Lemons (Oxford: Oxford University Press, 2017), 336–54; Seeman, "Otherwise than Meaning."

85. *Sermons from the Years of Rage, parashat hukkat* 5702 (1942), 303–304.

86. Ibid.

87. See, for example, Emmanuel Etkes, "From Esoteric Circle to Mass Movement: The Emergence of Early Hasidism," *Polin* 9–10 (1991): 78–79.

88. Ora Wiskind-Elper, "Hasidic Homiletics in Dialogue with Modernity," *R. Kalonymos Shapira: New Directions in Scholarship.* Conference Paper for the GEOP Interdisciplinary Research Workshop that I was privileged to cohost with Daniel Reiser at the Polin Museum in Warsaw, June 26–29, 2017. A slightly different formulation appears in Wiskind's chapter for this volume.

Contributors

Editors

Don Seeman is associate professor in the Department of Religion and the Tam Institute for Jewish Studies at Emory University. He works at the intersection of social theory, the anthropology of religious experience, and Jewish thought. In 2017 he was co-convener of an international research workshop on *R. Kalonymos Shapira: New Directions in Scholarship* at Polin: Musuem of the History of Polish Jewry in Warsaw. Seeman is co-editor of the Contemporary Anthropology of Religion series at Palgrave and of a forthcoming co-edited volume on *Existential Anthropology and the Study of Religion*. He is also the author of *One People, One Blood: Ethiopian-Israelis and the Return to Judaism* (Rutgers 2009). The working title of his current project is *An Ethiopian Jew Goes to Uman: Existential Anthropology of the Jews*.

Daniel Reiser is associate professor and chair of the Department of Jewish Thought at Hertzog College in Jerusalem. He specializes in Kabbalah, Hasidic philosophy, and theology in the Shoah. He produced a critical edition of R. Shapira's writings, *Sermons from the Years of Rage* (2017). His latest books are *Imagery Techniques in Modern Jewish Mysticism* (2018) and (with Ariel Evan Mayse) *Language of Truth in the Mother Tongue: The Yiddish Sermons of Rabbi Yehudah Aryeh Leib Alter* (2020).

Ariel Evan Mayse is assistant professor of religious studies at Stanford University and Rabbi-in-Residence at *Atiq: Jewish Maker Institute* (atiqmakers.org). He was previously the director of Jewish Studies and visiting assistant professor of Modern Jewish Thought at Hebrew College in Newton, Massachusetts. Mayse holds a PhD in Jewish Studies from Harvard University and rabbinic ordination from Beit Midrash Har'el in Israel. He recently published *Speaking Infinities: God and Language in the Teachings of the Maggid of Mezritsh* (University of Pennsylvania Press) and co-edited (with Arthur Green) the two-volume *A New Hasidism: Roots and Branches* (Jewish Publication Society, 2019).

Contributors

Zvi Leshem is Director of the Gershom Scholem Collection for Kabbalah and Hasidism at the National Library of Israel, Jerusalem. He immigrated to Israel from the United States in 1979. He holds rabbinic ordination from the Chief Rabbinate of Israel and a PhD in Jewish Philosophy from Bar-Ilan University. His current areas of research include Hasidism, Jewish education, Gershom Scholem and the thought of Rav Shagar. He has directed the Gershom Scholem Collection since 2011.

David Maayan is a doctoral student in comparative theology at Boston College. His doctorate focuses on Rabbi Kalonymus Kalman Shapira's insistence that the indispensable heart of Hasidic devotional life consists in the lifelong cultivation of a uniquely articulated, deeply feeling, and centered personhood. Shapira's project is deeply rooted in techniques, images, and teachings of early Hasidism and medieval Kabbalah, yet has nuances and elements which are clearly of the twentieth century. The dissertation will compare Shapira's thought with modern Christian mystical theologies of the transformation of the human person through the lens of divinization and the development of the spiritual senses.

Ora Wiskind is professor and chair of the graduate program in Jewish Studies at Michlalah College in Jerusalem. Her interests include Jewish thought and literary studies, Hasidism, and the interface between scriptural exegesis, culture, and religious experience. Her latest book, *Hasidic Commentary on the Torah* (Littman Library of Jewish Civilization-Liverpool University Press, 2018), is a wide-ranging study comprehending two hundred years of Hasidic teachings (1749–1943). It draws creatively on modern thought, literary theory, and cultural history to demonstrate the contribution of Hasidic thought to Jewish life and tradition. A National Jewish Book Award finalist, it draws creatively on modern thought, literary theory, and cultural history to demonstrate the contribution of Hasidic thought to Jewish life and tradition.

Moria Herman is an independent investigator whose research focuses on Hasidism, education, and Hasidism during the interwar period.

James A. Diamond is Joseph&Wolf Lebovic Chair of Jewish Studies at the University of Waterloo. He specializes in Jewish thought, philosophy, and theology. His most recent books are *Jewish Theology Unbound* (Oxford 2018) and (with Menachem Kellner) *Reinventing Maimonides in Contemporary Jewish Thought* (Littman Library, 2019).

Henry Abramson serves as a dean of Touro College in Brooklyn, New York. He is the author of numerous works, including *Torah from the Years of Wrath, 1939–1943: The Historical Context of the Aish Kodesh*.

Shaul Magid is professor of Jewish Studies at Dartmouth College and Kogod Senior Research Fellow at The Shalom Hartman Institute of North America. He works on Kabbalah, Hasidism, and Modern Jewish thought and culture. His last two books were *Piety and Rebellion: Essay in Hasidism* and *The Bible, The Talmud and the New Testament: Elijah Zvi Soloveitchik's Commentary to the Gospel*, both published in 2019.

Erin Leib Smokler is director of spiritual development and dean of students at Yeshivat Maharat rabbinical school, where she teaches Hasidism and Pastoral Theology. She is also a research fellow at the Shalom Hartman Institute of North America, where she sits on the Theology Research Team. She earned both her PhD and MA from the University of Chicago's Committee on Social Thought, and her BA from Harvard University. Dr. Leib Smokler is currently at work on two books, *Torah of the Night: Pastoral Insights from the Weekly Portion* and *Torah in the Time of Plague: Literature, Law, Liturgy, and Legacy*.

Nehemia Polen is professor of Jewish thought at Hebrew College. He is the author of *The Holy Fire: The Teachings of Rabbi Kalonymus Kalman Shapira, the Rebbe of the Warsaw Ghetto* (Jason Aronson Press, 1994), and *The Rebbe's Daughter: Memoir of a Hasidic Chilhood* (Jewish Publication Society of America, 2002), which was a recipient of the National Jewish Book Award.

Moshe Idel is Emeritus Max Cooper Professor in Jewish Thought at the Hebrew University of Jerusalem, senior researcher at the Shalom Hartman Institute, and Matanel Chair of Kabbalah at the Safed Academic College. He holds a PhD in Kabbalah and has served as visiting professor and researcher at many universities and institutions worldwide, including Yale, Harvard, and Princeton Universities in the United States and École des Hautes Études en Sciences Sociales in Paris. His numerous publications include *Kabbalah: New Perspectives* and *Messianic Mystics* (both by Yale University Press), and *Hasidism: Between Ecstasy and Magic* (SUNY Press, Albany). In 1999, Prof. Idel received the prestigious Israel Prize for excellent achievement in the field of Jewish Philosophy.

Marcin Wodziński is professor of Jewish history and literature at the University of Wrocław in Poland, where he heads the Taube Department of Jewish Studies. Wodziński previously worked as the chief historian for the Museum of the History of Polish Jews in Warsaw. Major publications include the *Historical Atlas of Hasidism* (Princeton University Press, 2018), *Hasidism, Key Questions* (Oxford University Press, 2018) and he is a co-author of *Hasidism: A New History* (Princeton University Press, 2018).

Index

Abraham. *See* biblical characters

Abramson, Henry, 14, 308–309, 349, 351–352, 355

Absolute, 219, 224–225, 230

Abulafia, Abraham, 9, 56–60

Aesthetic, 11, 335, 341, 346

Affliction, 186–187, 260–261, 272, 274–277, 284, 287, 346–347, 350–351. *See also* suffering

Aggadah, 85–91, 98–99, 105n78, 204. See also *halakhah*, theology

Akiva, 112, 166, 266

Amalek. *See* biblical characters

Anthropology, 13, 202–203, 334. *See also* ritual

Anthropos, 243

Aristotle/Aristotelian, 129n51, 245, 255n31

Atheism, 145–146, 311, 324–325. *See also* belief

Auschwitz. *See* concentration camps

Authenticity, 97, 156–158, 171n14, 200–201, 231

Author, 137, 149n22, 156, 167–169, 195, 198, 236, 273, 282, 297, 344–345. *See also* reader

Authority, 31–32, 34, 42, 45, 82, 287

Autonomy, 32, 160, 217, 227, 229–231, 249–250

Avodah (worship), 5, 132, 218, 230, 337–338, 340, 349

Baal Shem Tov (Besht), 5–6, 54–55, 81, 93, 96, 115, 132, 138, 158, 160–162, 167, 339, 341–342

Beard, 206n4, 283–285, 347–348

Becker, Ernest, 12, 198

Being, 92, 97, 137–140, 145, 147, 157–160, 200, 209n39, 217, 219–220, 228–229, 241, 245–246, 251

Belief, 11, 15, 64–66, 241, 250, 273, 305–313, 317, 320–326, 338, 351–355. *See also* faith

Benei mahshava tova, 2, 9, 19n3, 40, 44, 57–59, 107–112, 115–124, 135–136, 153, 307

Berkovits, Eliezer, 310, 312, 327n2

Bialik, Hayyim Nahman, 90

Biblical figures: Aaron, 215–217, 270–271; Abraham, 317; Amalek, 248–249, 257n59, 258n69; Balaam, 236–237, 253n5; David, 267–269, 279n30; Haman, 288; Isaac, 259, 348; Jacob, 131–135, 156–159, 173n32, 227, 348; Joseph, 134–135, 227; Miriam, 7, 215–219, 225–227, 229–230, 353–354; Moses, 159, 215–218, 225–230, 242, 261–266,

Biblical figures (*continued*)
269–272, 297, 349–350, 352, 354;
Noah, 305
Biblical prophets: Hosea, 266; Isaiah,
284, 316; Jeremiah, 19, 332n64;
Micah, 216. *See also* Prophecy/
Prophetic Renewal
Binah. See *sefirot*
Blessing, 55–56, 203–204, 218, 227,
263, 343, 354
Body/Embodiment, 10–11, 84, 90–93,
96, 109–110, 131–137, 141–143,
146–147, 149n26, 157, 164–168,
221, 228–229, 240, 244, 247, 251,
338–339, 343–344, 358n51
Boethius, 199, 208n23
Bones, 165–167, 169, 274
Book, 167–169, 174n43, 210n61, 337,
344–345
Brill, Alan, 69n10, 164
Brown, Benjamin, 20n10, 169n4
Buber, Martin, 18, 21n15, 64, 164,
169n2, 174n33, 336. *See also*
Neo-Hasidism
Buddhism, 17, 19, 60, 66, 73n59,
75n82, 150n36, 336

Caleb, 288–289
Carlebach, Shlomo, 16–18, 64, 67,
311, 314, 325–326
Charlap, Yaakov Moshe, 313
Children, 7, 83, 186–187, 213, 221–
228, 325–326, 339–342, 353–354
Christianity, 20n13, 31, 36, 67, 75n83,
147n1
Commandment (*mitsvah*), 60, 88–90,
92–93, 103n37, 110, 133–134,
147, 152n64, 157, 217, 227, 242,
249–250, 341, 346
Communication, 4, 118, 154, 157–
158, 159

Compassion, 133, 140–141, 152n65,
219–220, 223–228, 270–271,
293–294
Concentration camps: Auschwitz, 17,
199, 312, 325–326; Chelmno, 14,
291, 298; Treblinka, 8, 268–269,
273, 292, 296; Trawniki, 2, 123,
130n57, 314
Contemplation: contemplative
practice, 4, 9, 16–17, 65, 80, 91–92,
135–140, 161, 168, 250–251,
333–337; meditation, 17, 66, 83,
107, 112–113, 122; visualization
techniques, 9, 57–60, 336, 337, 345,
348
Consciousness: consciousness of
the Hasid, 342; corporeality
and, 151n47, 343; extinction of
reflective, 246; future-oriented,
167; heightened, 107, 109, 252;
historical, 153, 184; permeation of
one's, 157, 161, 164, 173n25; self-
creation and, 138, 142–145. *See also*
subjectivity
Corporeality/Physicality, 10–11,
57, 83, 85, 91, 96, 111, 113, 118,
129n50, 132–136, 141, 146, 149n26,
151n47, 160–161, 166–168, 192,
198, 199, 221, 223–224, 240–241,
250, 264, 273, 274, 276, 285,
337–339, 341–345, 350
Cosmos, 65, 93, 97, 203–205,
223–224, 228, 298
Cosmogony, 228
Cosmology, 203, 338–339, 352
Covenant, 14–15, 115, 307, 309–314,
316–327, 350–351
Creativity, 61, 63, 79, 80, 88, 89,
94–95, 103n33, 138–140, 152n64,
154, 186, 198, 202, 205, 208v26,
214, 228, 230, 336. *See also* exegesis

Crisis, 14, 18–19, 37, 41, 43–45, 50n52, 87, 119–120, 164, 169n3, 203, 213, 215–216, 234n22, 258n62, 273, 314, 320–321, 326, 338, 340, 341, 347, 350, 351, 353

Critical Edition, 3, 12, 53, 179–189, 194–198, 213, 291, 333–335

Culture, 23n48, 31, 63, 83, 155–156, 175n44, 198, 201, 208n26, 227, 248, 295

Da'at, 85, 140, 143–146, 157, 237, 242–243, 250. See also sefirot

Death, 2, 7, 8, 9, 12, 45, 123, 137, 138, 149n26, 155, 165–166, 185–186, 191, 192, 196, 198–205, 209n39, 214, 215–216, 216, 219, 225, 227–231, 235, 238, 243, 251, 260, 285, 303n31, 306, 319, 323, 330n38, 347, 353, 354

Deportations, 2, 8, 242, 268–269, 273, 353. See also Great Action/ Deportation

Derekh ha-melekh, 2, 91, 103n30, 104n53, 153–156, 188, 239

Despair, 14, 186, 200–201, 207n6, 266, 269–270, 288, 293, 297, 308, 326, 348. See also belief, faith, suffering

Devekut (attachment), 5, 81, 116–119, 131, 148n8, 170n10, 324

Devotion, 5–6, 10, 17, 55, 79–83, 87, 89–98, 132–133, 140, 230, 264, 266, 275, 340–343, 349–351

Diamond, James A., 13, 308

Disease/Illness, 8, 277, 288, 338

Dislocation, 4, 7, 34–35, 41, 61, 75n83, 155

Doctrine, 11–13, 29, 188, 202, 210n49, 224, 274–275, 334, 353–354

Drink, 5, 111, 125n13. See also corporeality

Economy, 30, 35, 41, 43, 47n10, 55, 120–122, 129n50, 169n3, 346

Ecstasy, 5, 9, 54–59, 66, 68n6, 87–88, 122, 128n41, 336

Education/Pedagogy: Hasidism and, 42, 44–45, 82, 89; Shapira's tracts on, 2, 9–10, 15, 44, 54, 112, 153, 201, 296, 307, 340, 345–346; Shapira's orientation towards, 7, 44, 82–83, 93, 109, 121, 154–155, 249–250, 333, 336–337, 340–345

Egalitarianism, 46n1, 110, 113, 116–118

Egypt, 114–115, 243, 267–272, 281–284, 293–294, 350

Elimelekh of Grodzisk. See Shapira/ Shapiro family

Elimelekh of Lizensk, 6, 55, 166, 170n8, 171n12, 337

Elimelekh Shapira (nephew), 180. See also Shapira/Shapiro family

Emotion/Affect: vital flow and, 10, 15, 346, 350; study and, 81–98, 339, 345; knowledge and, 157, 268, 205, 109, 158–165, 225, 231, 334, 338

Engenderment, 171n15, 228–230

Epicurus, 305

Epstein, Kalonymus, 55, 103n41, 108

Esh Kodesh. See Sermons from the Years of Rage

Esoteric, 82, 84–85, 94, 163–164, 246, 338

Ethnographic/Ethnography, 17, 345, 355n6, 356n13, 360n84. See also anthropology

Evil, 117, 154, 219, 231, 236–238, 248, 258n64, 283, 285, 305, 308–310, 319, 321–322, 326, 327

Exegesis, 79–80, 84, 87–91, 94–95, 98–99, 103n33, 204, 214, 217, 231. *See also* creativity, study
Exile, 122, 161–163, 166, 239, 243, 350
Existentialism, 3, 11, 89, 108, 145–146, 149n24, 160, 200–201, 250, 259, 321, 341, 352–353
Experience: affect and, 15; embodied and lived, 93, 131, 147, 151, 257n59, 268–273, 338–339, 346; of faith and doubt, 200–203, 305–301, 316, 324, 335; Hasidism and, 155–160; mystical or religious, 5, 9, 57–59, 109, 122–124; prophetic, 58–59, 122–124, 168, 338, 346; self-creation and, 137; Shapira's personal, 53, 155, 166, 185–188, 237, 272–273, 283–285; study and, 80, 83–90, 98; suffering and, 240, 243, 252, 295, 346, 348, 349, 351, 354
Explanation: the absence of, 204, 231, 260–261, 263, 267, 275–277
Expulsion, 35, 154, 249

Face, 151n47, 161–162, 221, 225, 228–230, 259, 327n2, 343
Facsimile, 181, 291
Faith (*emunah*): acts of, 123; crisis and loss of, 14–15, 19, 154–155, 164, 192, 297, 307–311, 316, 338, 351; defining, 11; faith beyond intellect, reason and, 168, 200–201, 246, 248–250, 289, 351; simple, 250–251; strengthening of 267, 273, 288–289, 294, 298, 333
Feeling (*hargashah*), 10, 86–87, 96, 133, 141–145, 175n43, 204, 243, 346, 348. *See also* Emotion/Affect
Final Solution, 292, 298

Flesh, 110, 139, 263, 339, 343. *See also* corporeality
France, 288
Frankl, Viktor, 199, 208n25
Fraternity (Mystical Fraternity), 2, 9–10, 40, 43–45, 107–124
Free Will, 109, 340–341, 351, 358n39
Friendship (*haverim*), 113, 116–118
Funkenstein, Amos, 309–310, 312

Garb, Jonathan, 68n5
Gassing as murder, 237, 291, 296
Geertz, Clifford, 203–204, 334
Gender, 12, 232n8. *See also* women
Genocide, 3, 8, 12, 14, 61, 302n19, 355
Gentiles/non-Jews, 48n28, 65–67, 121, 188, 257n60
Germans, 8, 191–192, 248–249, 284, 288–289, 291, 300, 323
Germany, 248–249, 258n62, 288–289
Ghetto: Lodz, 269; Warsaw, 8–11, 98, 153, 180, 184, 203–204, 231, 237, 241, 260, 268–269, 279n30, 292, 300, 315, 323, 333–335; Warsaw Ghetto Uprising, 8
Golem, 65, 149n24, 158–159, 171n15
Great Action/Deportation, 204, 231, 277, 292–298, 307–313, 320, 331n49. *See also* deportations
Greenberg, Yitz, 310, 312
Green, Arthur, 64, 174n33, 257n50
Grodzisk (Mazowiecki), 22n27. *See also* Shapira/Shapiro family
Guide of the Perplexed, 232n8, 239, 245, 251, 253n8, 255n37
Guilt, 198, 204

Halakhah, 8, 81–82, 85–90, 91–92, 99, 104n58, 105n78, 203, 206n2, 341, 343. *See also* commandment

Hakhsharat ha-avreihim, 2, 112, 181, 299, 303n31, 307, 346

Handwriting. *See* writing

Hannukah; 1941 sermon for, 317–319, 350; annotation to 1941 sermon for, 238, 294–296, 315, 317–322, 351

Hasid; definition, 160, 172n18, 341, 339; *tsaddik* and, 36, 39, 164, 342–343; Yosl Rakover's identity as, 323–324

Hasidic Modernism, 9, 19, 150n36, 335–336

Hasidism: "à la carte" Hasidism, 4, 9, 36, 41–43, 337; Belz, 15, 62; Bratslav, 7, 16, 55, 62, 117, 120, 124n3, 172n18, 258n71, 328n7, 335; Chabad/Lubavitch (or Habad), 9, 11, 15–16, 62–63, 104n57, 141–142, 173n26, 173n31, 174n39, 224, 244–245, 254n26, 255n32, 255n38, 300, 313; Ger, 15, 33, 38–39, 42–44, 51n58, 61–63, 80, 82, 323; Golden age of, 7, 43; Izbits, 9, 16, 55, 124n3, 149n24, 335; Karlin-Stolin, 108, 114–119; Komarno, 115, 150n30; Kotsk (Kock), 9, 38, 55, 79, 82, 103n37, 149n24, 335; magical and spiritual, 44, 54–56, 58–65, 67, 168, 335–336; Satmar, 15, 62–63, 75n83, 313; Toledot Aharon, 63; Vizhnits, 15, 62

Healing/Medicine, 8, 14, 54, 179, 192, 294, 334, 336, 340, 345, 355

Heaven/Heavens: emptiness of the child's, 324; initiative from, 217, 227; storming, 271–273; *tsaddik* connecting earth and, 55, 167

Hebrew, 53, 64, 113, 153, 191, 195, 245, 265, 282, 296, 299, 341–342, 345

Heidegger, Martin, 200, 208n27, 209n39, 248

Heresy, 186, 306, 312, 330n38

Heschel, Abraham Joshua, 4, 64, 69n6, 73n63, 164, 336, 357n35

Hinduism, 66–67, 336

History: of ideas, 3; God of, 350–351; Jewish, 238, 265, 283, 295, 320–322, 327; social, 3, 108

Holiness/Sanctity, 94–96, 109–110, 120, 132–136, 146–147, 150n35, 157–168, 217, 221–230, 252, 343–349

Holocaust: as novum, 238, 253n14, 296, 298, 313, 318–322; theology and, 14, 310–314, 321–323, 327, 333, 349–352

Holy Hunchback, 16–17, 311, 314, 323, 325–326

Homily/Homiletics, 12–13, 88, 97–99, 153, 155, 175n44, 204, 213–214, 239, 268–269, 272–273

Hope, 160, 186, 192, 200, 205, 207n6, 230–231, 239, 266–273, 285, 298, 308, 325, 347

Hovat ha-talmidim, 2, 79, 103n30, 120, 297, 337, 340, 359n61

Huberband, Shimon (Szymon), 184, 283, 288

Idel, Moshe, 9, 13, 17, 168, 335–336

Image, 161–164, 276

Imagination, 36, 58, 108, 164, 238, 335–336

Imitatio Dei, 133, 255n37

Immanence, 5, 11, 93, 110, 131, 162, 230–231, 241, 251, 254n23

Incarnation, 10–11, 110, 131, 134, 136–137, 147n1

Individuality/Individualism, 4, 10, 36, 80, 108–109, 128n41, 131, 136–139, 142, 145–146, 152n64, 157–160, 200, 222–225, 227–230, 336–341

Individuation, 142, 200, 219–221, 229

Influx, 57, 59–60, 349, 353–354

Intention (*kavvanah*), 5, 109–110, 113, 117, 120–121, 132, 134–136, 264, 344

Intellect: body and, 244, 251; integration of emotion and, 86–92, 141; transcendence of, 88, 239, 244, 246–247, 249–250, 252, 338–342, 351

Interpretation, 79–80, 88–89, 95–98, 135, 138–139, 143–145, 157, 218, 230, 242–243, 339–341. *See also* creativity; exegesis

Israel, land of, 1, 8, 15–16, 62, 85, 87, 112, 120, 180, 181, 211n65, 290, 297, 299, 323

Israelite: Shapira's use of term, 233n13

Jewish Historical Institute, 180

Joy, 5, 111, 113, 141, 230, 266–268, 272–273, 337, 353

Judgment (*din*): 86, 98, 120, hasid and, 160–161, 341–342; attribute of, 219–221, 341–342

Kabbalah: contemporary interest in, 65–67; Cordovero and, 54, 56–57; ecstatic, 9, 56–59, 336; Hasidism and, 10, 54, 67, 76n86, 81, 96; Lurianic, 5, 67, 97, 112, 219, 237; Shapira on, 82, 85–90, 91–97, 111, 135–136, 160, 338–342; Zeitlin and, 119–121. *See also* Zohar

Kavvanah. See intention

Kedushat Levi. See Levi Yitzhak of Bardishev

Kleinman, Arthur and Joan, 355n2, 355n6

Kook, Abraham Isaac, 16–17, 60, 90, 127n33, 258n71, 357n23, 358n39

Kook, Zvi Yehudah, 313, 319, 331n40

Language, 10, 13, 64, 82, 93, 158, 262, 263, 264, 266, 342–346, 346–355

Laitman, Michael, 65

Leadership: crisis and, 213, 285, 300; models of hasidic, 6, 21n20, 34, 39–45, 55–56, 63, 168; Shapira on, 225–230

Leib-Smokler, Erin, 13, 19, 244, 346

Leshem, Zvi, 9–10, 43, 135

Levi, Primo, 306

Levi Yitzhak of Barditshev, 144–145, 267–269

Levinas, Emmanuel, 203, 323–325

Liebes, Yehuda, 112, 199

Light: divine vitality and, 341–345, 353–354; drawing down of, 59–60, 92, 167; receptivity to, 162, 226; revelation of, 93, 132, 163–164; texts and, 103n37, 167–168; tsaddik and, 165–168

Limbs, 84, 110, 167, 251, 344

Literature: exegetical, 12; general, 3, 119, 340, 345; Hasidic, 148n8, 258n71, 342, 349; kabbalistic, 83, 93, 112, 222, 258n71, 339; *merkavah*, 112; rabbinic, 81–82, 85, 90, 93–97, 143, 194, 237–238, 257n60, 277n3; Russian, 209n32

Lithuania, 16, 61, 80–81, 89–92, 313, 323

Lodz, 83

Longing, 84, 96–98, 209n39, 335, 342, 349–350, 354

Love: afflictions/chastenings of love, 13, 244, 260–261, 274–277, 346; for others, 110–113, 117–118, 141–142, 171n11, 276–277; of and for God, 311, 317–318, 323–325, 350; suffering and, 267–268, 272; "Three Loves" of the Besht, 129n50

Luria, Yitzhak and Lurianic Kabbalah, 5, 67, 81, 97, 108, 112–114, 117, 171n15, 174n39
Luzzatto, Moshe Hayyim, 108, 112

Maayan, David, 10–11, 170n10, 175n45
Magid, Shaul, 14–15, 75n85, 349–355
Maggid: of Mezritsh, 6, 9, 55, 115–117, 149n24, 158, 163, 171n15, 172n24, 335; of Kozhnits, 55, 82, 166, 174n36, 337; of Zlotshev, 81
Manuscripts: Shapira's, 1–3, 153, 169, 180–187, 193–202, 204–205, 213– 215, 232n12, 291–292, 296–299, 303n31, 306, 315–316; various, 57, 114
Ma'or va-shemesh, 103n41, 108, 174n36
Martyr/Martyrdom, 108, 119, 123–124, 210n45, 236, 262–266, 275–277, 300, 322
Mayse, Ariel Evan, 10, 17, 20n11, 131, 204, 210n56, 339
Media/Mediation, 10–11, 23n48, 42, 44–45, 164, 171n15, 279n30, 334–335
Meaninglessness, 155, 186, 200–203, 312
Meditation. *See* contemplation
Mercy (*rahamim*), 1, 110, 118, 165, 179, 208n12, 219–221, 227–228, 268, 271, 273, 276, 293–294, 295, 298, 299, 309, 318, 319, 323
Messianism, 122, 129n54
Metaphor, 158, 163
Mevo he-she'arim, 2, 112, 175n45, 181, 296–297, 299, 303n31
Midrash, 19; Shapira on, 84–90, 98–99, 134–135, 204, 238–242, 295, 318; Shapira's use of, 98–99, 134–

135, 143–146, 159, 165, 180, 204, 227–228, 238, 240–242, 247–248. *See also* Talmud; study
Migration, 7, 155
Mindfulness, 11, 17, 150n36, 160
Miracle, 44, 266–268, 352
Mishnah, 86–87, 99, 110. *See also* Talmud; study
Mitsvah. *See* commandment
Modernization, 6, 19, 36, 73n64, 336–340
Morality, 36, 85, 162, 249, 334–335, 341, 346
Moria, Herman, 12
Mourning, 153, 243
Moses. *See* biblical characters
Murder, 1, 14, 33, 119, 123, 184, 187, 53, 61, 207n4, 221–222, 238, 249, 273, 291, 295, 297–298, 319. *See also* Final Solution, Genocide
Music, 13, 36, 67, 112, 125n13
Mussar, 80, 119
Mysticism, 20n10, 64–66, 112, 154, 203–204, 224–225, 241, 244–245, 345

Nahmanides, 136, 281, 286, 301n6, 302n14, 340
Nazi, 4, 14, 61, 191, 206n2, 207n4, 208n27, 248, 265, 272, 275, 283–285
Negation, 201, 224, 228. *See also* self
Neo-Hasidism, 3, 15–19, 45, 54, 63–67, 154, 169n2, 333, 336. *See also* Buber, Martin; Zeitlin, Hillel
Nerves/Nervous Disorder, 4, 9, 338
Neusner, Jacob, 309, 311–312, 318–319
Newspaper, 23n41, 74n76, 122, 181, 323
Nietzsche, Friedrich, 201

Oneg Shabbat archive, 175n47, 184, 292, 298, 303n31

Palestine. *See* Israel
Pain. *See* suffering
Pantheism, 5, 113, 241, 244–245
Paragraphing, 12, 214–215, 315
Parashiyot (Torah Portions): *Ekev*, 292, 295, 298; *Hazon*, 292; *Hukkat*, 186, 214–231; *Metsora*, 286; *Mishpatim*, 188, 206n3, 292; *Naso*, 188; Shelah, 288; Shemot, 167; Toledot, 284, 347; *Vayyeshev*, 131; Yitro, 182–183, 242; Zakhor, 291
Pedagogy. *See* education
Phenomenology, 3, 9, 12–15, 67, 80, 119, 147, 153–154, 192, 202–205, 315, 335–346, 348, 351–354
Philology, 67, 194–198
Philosophy/Philosophical, 12–13, 60, 64, 119–123, 144–145, 186–188, 198–202, 237–258
Piasezcno (town), 2, 7, 30–34, 40, 45, 51n66, 115, 296
Piekarz, Mendel, 191, 333, 334
Piety, 7, 82, 84, 89, 91, 242, 340
Poland, Interbellum, 1–4, 41–43, 80–82, 89, 119, 347–348
Polen, Nehemia, 12–13, 17, 102n30, 123–124, 308–309, 330n30
Postmodernism, 16, 283, 300–301
Prayer, 5, 9, 31, 36–41, 56–57, 61, 66, 81, 94–95, 97, 109, 113, 117, 120–121, 138, 155, 179, 223, 239–240, 253–254, 272–273, 275, 284, 287, 290, 293, 309, 317, 325, 347, 350
Progeny. *See* children
Proofing, 181, 184–185, 194–196, 204–205
Prophecy/Prophetic Renewal, 4–7, 57–59, 68–76, 88–89, 107, 112, 167–170, 296, 333–338, 344–352

Psalms; interpretation of passages from, 265, 268, 270, 276; recitation of, 293
Psychology/Psychological; 9–11, 123, 153–154, 158, 185–186, 198–205, 336–339
Purification/Purity, 99–100, 122, 260, 265, 274, 277

Rackover, Yosl, 309, 311, 323–325, 326
Rage (*za'am*), 235–237, 251
Rashi, 19, 134, 139, 143–145, 166, 216, 219, 262, 267, 270–271, 286
Reader, 87–89, 97, 137, 147, 167–169, 193–195. *See also* author
Reason/Rationality; Hasidim and, 12, 244; Shapira's relation to, 147, 161, 235–248, 249–253; faith beyond, 289, 350; critique of Western, 200, 248–249
Reciprocity, 167, 240, 346–350
Reformation/Counter-Reformation, 19, 42–45, 51n56
Reiser, Daniel, 2–4, 12, 58, 170n9, 179–189, 214–215, 231, 291, 296–297, 306–332, 333–336, 348
Responsa, 206n2
Revelation; divine, 84, 87, 92, 136; interdependence of divine and human, 136–139; Heschel on, 164, 357n34; ongoing, 164, 167, 222–223, 353–354; of the soul/self, 111, 150n36, 157; through text, 93, 344–345
Ringelblum archives, 1, 231, 237, 282, 298, 335. *See also* Oneg Shabbat archive
Ritual: ritual efficacy, 6, 11–15, 203–204, 333–335, 338, 345, 353; ritual in its own right, 203–205
Rosenzweig, Franz, 12, 191, 200, 235
Rosh Hashanah (New Year), 31–32, 97, 119, 140–146, 261

Rupture, 3, 11, 13–14, 19, 198, 238, 244, 312–313, 320–321, 327, 327n2, 348

Russia, 6, 41, 82, 114, 119

Sabbath, 36, 63, 66, 136, 153, 179, 192, 206n3, 242, 255n29, 284

Sabbateanism, 67

Sacrifice, 240, 263–266, 317, 320, 350

Sadness, 98, 272–273

Safed, 56, 85, 108, 114–115, 124

Salvation: advocacy of irrational faith in, 237, 289, 316–317, 350; coping with lack of apparent, 273–274, 289, 293–294; divine initiative and, 294, 347–348; human activity and, 83, 211n65, 266, 334; possible, 232, 311, 318. See also belief, faith

Sartre, Jean-Paul, 145–146

Scholem, Gershom, 10, 15, 59, 102n19, 114, 219, 238, 254n23, 339

Schweid, Eliezer, 307–309, 316, 322, 333

Secret: Torah and, 85, 94, 111, fraternities, 44, 107, sharing of one's, 111, 119

Secularization, 6, 32, 80, 89, 121

Seeman, Don, 9, 13, 15, 105n79, 139, 150n36, 202–204, 329n17

Seer of Lublin, 47n11, 55, 174n36, 305, 307

Sefirot, 171n15, 219–221, 228, 246–247

Self: self-creation, 138–139, 142–146; self-knowledge, 140, 156–157, 242, 339; self-nullification (bittul), 10–11, 57, 131, 136, 149n24, 158, 170n10, 246; self-recognition, 95, 139–141, 145–146, 284, 347–348; self-referential, 168, 230, 234n22; self-sacrifice (mesirat or mesirut nefesh), 240, 317–320, 350

Sermons from the Years of Rage (Esh Kodesh): 8, 12–19, 153, 193–202, 236, 259, 268, 274, 281–291, 301, 307, 330n30; critical edition of, 3–4, 12, 53, 180, 188–189, 194–198, 213, 236, 291, 314–315, 331n52, 333, 359n68

Schachter-Shalomi, Zalman, 16–17, 24n57, 64, 66, 75n82

Shneur Zalman of Liady, 55, 92, 104n57, 141–142, 173n25, 173n31, 244–246, 255n36, 256n49, 300, 335. See also Tanya

Shapira/Shapiro family: Elimelekh of Grodzisk (father), 7, 22n28, 22n29, 33, 56, 170n8, 174n36, 174n43, 286, 296; Elimelekh (son), 8, 230, 234n22, 285, 303n31; Rahel Hayyah Miriam (wife), 7–8, 22n30, 230, 234n22; Rekhell Yehudis (daughter), 230, 234n22; Yeshaya (brother), 8, 15, 297, 299, 328n9

Shekhinah, 113, 221, 228, 230, 251

Shestov, Lev, 200–201, 209n32, 209n37, 209n41

Shi'ur Komah, 167, 344

Shtibl/Shtiblekh, 9, 36–42, 66, 155

Silence, 159, 263–266, 269–270, 322, 327

Sin, 113, 138, 162, 218–219, 221, 225–229, 259–260, 265, 274, 298, 346, 351, 354

Slavery/Slave, 261–262, 265, 267, 269, 272, 279n35, 292

Socrates, 12, 198–199

Sonderkommando, 292

Song, 67, 111, 266–272, 278n15

Sorrow, 194, 196, 231, 238, 276. See also sadness, suffering

Soul: animal, 111; body and, 84, 131, 141–142, 146–147, 165, 192, 244, 339, 343, 348; God and, 223, 250,

Soul *(continued)*
    263–264; levels and states of, 155,
    339; perception and, 162, 223, 342,
    352; revelation of, 94–97, 105n79,
    111, 139–140, 150n36, 173n27, 345;
    soul of tsaddik, 165–167; study
    and, 83, 85–100; writing and, 137,
    208n19, 210n61, 344
Soviet Union, 288
Speech; thought, deeds and, 91,
    109–110, silence and, 159; public,
    129n53, 169n4; letters of divine,
    341
Spies, 288–289, 349
Spirit, Holy, 86–88, 96
Spirituality, 61–67, 84, 90, 146, 155,
    168, 217, 224, 227, 335–338, 343
Study. *See* Torah
Subject: intersubjectivity, 345,
    348–349; subjectivity, 3, 10–11, 14,
    334, 336, 338–349, 352–355
Suffering: afflictions of love (*yissurim
    shel ahavah*), 13, 260–268, 272–277;
    pain and, 121–122, 141, 192,
    198, 204, 225, 229–231, 238, 244,
    251, 260–261, 264–271, 274–277,
    316, 335, 346, 355; for the Other,
    203–205
Suicide, 17, 154, 169n3
Sukkot, 8, 275

Talmud (Gemara): cited by Shapira,
    166, 216–218, 236, 264–265, 268,
    271, 284; devotion and, 79–98;
    Gemara of Tannaim and Amoraim,
    86–87; in curriculum, 16, 82–83,
    110, 339, 347; transformative study
    and, 99–100; Zohar and, 88
Tanya, 92, 120, 173n25, 300. *See also*
    Shneur Zalman of Liady
Temporal or temporality. *See* time

Testimony, 14, 41, 54–55, 107, 113,
    115, 123, 196, 202, 205, 205n1, 283,
    292, 306, 314–315
Textual practice and textuality, 11–14,
    203, 334, 341, 345
Theodicy, 13, 231, 259–261, 275, 281,
    310–313, 318–323, 325, 329n22,
    331n49, 351. *See also* suffering
Theology: anthropocentric, 263, 271;
    consistency of Shapira's theology,
    247–249, 315; covenantal, 309,
    320–326, 350; Hasidic, 83, 217,
    230, 235, 246; incarnational,
    10, 131; Jewish, 3; law and, 89;
    post-Holocaust, 14, 19, 310–314,
    321–327, 349–352; rabbinic, 221;
    theology of Maimonides, 244–245;
    theology of personalism, 230; Torah
    and, 157
Theurgy, 170n9, 208n12, 349
Tiberius, 9–10, 108, 114–119, 124
Time, 13, 99, 204, 220, 227, 230, 349
Torah: Study of, 79–106, 110–122;
    Letters of, 132, 134–136; self-
    revelation and, 136–139, 157; scroll,
    137
Tradition: alienation from, 89; aura
    of, 34, 36; belief and, 250; challenge
    to, 308, 313, 320–321, 326; fidelity
    to, 308; hasidic, 164, 239, 339;
    hasidic tradition and renewal,
    164, 175n46; Jewish literary, 13,
    281–282; kabbalistic, 243; language
    of, 13, 80, 236; philosophical, 245;
    rabbinic, 215, 249; return to, 297;
    tradition of mystical fraternities,
    112, 115, 119, 121; wisdom and,
    247–248
Transcendence, 134–135, 163, 231,
    242, 247
Trauma, 154, 296. *See also* suffering

Truth, 11, 15, 200, 230, 243–245, 283, 287, 300–301, 326, 349–350

Tsimtsum, 160, 241, 254n23, 345

Tsaddik, 6, 9–10, 33–45, 54–56, 64, 66, 116–118, 151n40, 155, 164–168, 217, 223–224, 271–272, 335–337, 342–344, 354

Tsav ve-zeruz, 2, 105n67, 137, 154, 210n61, 299, 303n31, 340

Ukraine, 5, 62

Ultra-Orthodoxy, 2, 16, 313–314, 322

Veil, 162, 271–273, 311

Vessels, 87, 135, 158, 162

Visualization. See contemplation

Vital, Hayyim, 56–60, 81, 113–114, 267, 339

Vitality/Vital Flow, 5–6, 10–11, 15, 60, 91, 105n79, 133, 168, 196, 203, 219, 334, 338–339, 341, 344–346, 349–352, 354–355

War: devastation and, 30, 154, 192; World War I, 4, 7, 33–37, 41–43, 154, 200, 235, 290–291; World War II, 15, 120, 239

Weber, Max, 10, 65, 202

Weeping/Tears, 5, 154, 179, 185, 196, 266, 278n15, 298, 346. See also suffering

Weil, Simone, 324

Wiesel, Elie, 64, 305, 307, 324

Wiskind, Ora, 10–11, 13, 17, 44, 139, 354–355

Wodziński, Marcin, 4, 9, 17, 155, 337

Wolfson, Eliot R., 23n46, 72n49, 147n1, 173n31, 209n32, 210n56, 255n27, 255n32, 357n32, 358n51

Women, 7, 62, 170n5, 217–218, 223–230

Writing: self and, 137–139, 158; Shapira's reflections on, 167–168, 185; death and, 192, 196, 198–199, 203–205; writing as mystical ritual, 211n65; handwriting, 1–3, 180–181, 188–189, 194, 197, 282

Yerushalmi, Yosef Hayyim, 309, 312, 314

Yeshiva: Bet El, 107, 112–115, 117–119, 124; Da'at Moshe, 7, 42, 44–45, 50n50, 82–83, 102n25, 326; Shapira's teachings in the Zionist yeshiva, 16–17

Yiddish, 2, 16, 53, 64, 103n30, 153, 171n15, 191, 282, 299, 323, 325

Yom Kippur, 2, 160–163, 251, 288

Zeitlin, Hillel, 60, 64, 74n76, 104n57, 108, 119–123, 169n2, 201, 336. See also Neo-Hasidism

Zionism, 7, 16, 313, 330n38

Zohar: cited by Shapira, 218, 352; ideas rooted in, 244, 246, 257n51; mystical fraternities and, 108–109, 112, 115, 117; revelation and, 167; Shapira's commentary on, 85, 210n47; Shapira on exegesis in, 88–89; study of, 88–89, 97, 117, 119–121; view of evil in, 237; Tikkunei Zohar, 161–163

CPSIA information can be obtained
at www.ICGtesting.com
Printed in the USA
LVHW021444261221
707138LV00008B/577